Nixon's First Cover-up

NIXON'S FIRST COVER-UP

The Religious Life
of a
Quaker President

H. LARRY INGLE

For Bruce: — Good reading & remember that this is not a how-to manual.

Larry Ingle

13.VI.18

UNIVERSITY OF MISSOURI
Columbia

ISBN 978-0-8262-2042-4
Library of Congress Control Number 2015940295

∞ This paper meets the requirements of the
American National Standard for Permanence of Paper
for Printed Library Materials, Z39.48, 1984.

Interior design and composition: Richard E. Farkas
Typefaces: Minion Pro

Dedication

To
Charles E. (Chuck) Fager
James A. Ward
without whom. . . .

Contents

Acknowledgments

The list of those who put me in their debt for assistance with this book is nearly unbounded, for writing about a Quaker as notorious as Richard Nixon unleashed a torrent of first-, second-, and thirdhand stories, rumors, and hearsay about him; almost all such tales came from Friends who sought to distance their sect from his reputation. Although most such stories could not be documented and do not appear here, many suggested things that might be searched out and always led to interesting conversations. I highly valued such contributions and the motives of the kind folk who passed them along.

The same thing goes for all those who lent their talents and expertise to my search. Gary S. Smith and I exchanged research on common interests. Greg Hinshaw passed along valuable bits of information and pictures as he delved into a parallel topic for a different book altogether. Retired librarian Neal Coulter remained a fount of information, and Jim Bowman, an electronic whiz, either gave directions over the telephone or came over periodically to tweak some inexplicable quirk on my computer. The staff members of numerous libraries archives were exemplary: Swarthmore College's Friends Historical Library, Guilford College's Friends Historical Collection, Earlham College's Friends Collection, George Fox University's Archives, the Whittier College Library and the Archives of the American Friends Service Committee in Philadelphia. Non-Quaker facilities whose staffs were equally helpful included the Richard Nixon Library, now operated by the National Archives and Record Administration, in Yorba Linda, California, the Herbert Hoover Library at West Branch, Iowa, also run by the NARA, the Lupton Library at the University of Tennessee at Chattanooga, especially the interlibrary system and its highly efficient staffers, the Chattanooga Public Library, and the McKee Library at Southern Adventist University. Librarians and archivists are the best friends of historians. Gary Kass and other staffers at the University of Missouri Press were encouraging, efficient, and exacting, as were their anonymous reader and Randall Balmer. They all helped make the book better.

The people who enabled me to fill gaps and offered encouragement or read early versions of the preface, which I used to try to sort out how I

ix

would grapple with a man utterly lacking in transparency, are so numerous and far-flung that I know before I start that I will miss some: Thomas Hamm, Hayden Wetzel, Meredith Terretta, Zoie Clark, Gwyn Ingle, Free Polazzo, Ben Dandelion, Paul Watson, Jaan Troltenier, Ralph Bowden, John Everhart, Adlai Boyd, Don Rhodes, Paul Buckley, John Huffman, Wallace Henley, Brian Yaffe, Jim Icard, Errol Hess, Clint Cooper, Peter Bien, Arthur Roberts, and Ronald Burnside. Staff members of East Whittier Friends Church also responded to requests for information.

The person who was the constant prod behind the book was Charles E. (Chuck) Fager, a snoopy but friendly journalist with an acute eye for a good story and an instinct for getting the historical one right, based on the whole and full picture. Chuck preformed yeoman's service and continued to push whenever my interest in things Nixonian sagged. Likewise, my colleague James A. Ward, though his interests ran to more mundane matters, like trains and automobiles, than religion, read more drafts, especially of the preface, than I should have asked him to endure. He groused, yes, but he always came through in good time to render fair, telling, and uncommonly helpful suggestions. This book's dedication to the two of them assures that they are appropriately recognized for their inestimable good ideas and encouragement.

In a broader background not directly related to the content of the book that a reader holds now, Chattanooga Friends had to hear more of Nixon and his implications for modern Quakers than they would have desired, but we all persevered--and survived. My wife, Becky, maintained a loving and supportive home, a place conducive to work, even as she reminded me that a part of writing was to keep my study tidy and free of stray notes and piles of books; she has not won yet, but as I write this note the book is not out either.

Finally, it goes without mentioning, though the conventions require it, I remain responsible for what is inside these covers. As I've mentioned above, I had heaping levels of help, but I sought out the sources and put them together in what I hope is a coherent form with the purpose of shining light on a Friend who displayed little during his life. I trust the reader benefits.

Nixon's First Cover-up

Introduction

I also have had to remind myself that we cannot reliably know the outward signs of inward grace even among American presidents.[1]
—Jack M. Holl

In the first and also the final analysis the author of any book about Richard Milhous Nixon must wrestle with the basic question "Who was Richard Nixon?" Some of those who will read this book are young enough to know little of the man and will want to learn about him; some will want to see how his peculiar religion, the one called Quakerism and of which he was formally a member his whole life, had an impact on his life; still others may want to see if their previous judgments, even prejudices, can be confirmed by the evidence. In a broader sense some may want to see what impact religion has on a politician, the sphere of politics usually being considered separate and distinct from religion. The question of defining Nixon is a difficult, a very difficult, one, and one that has no easy—certainly no quick—answer.

One way to gain insights into one of the century's most important political figures is to look at his religion. Nixon's religious world, however, remains to this day the least studied part about him, partially because of the ways he expressed his religious views and partially because of his desire for privacy when he was asked about them.

In addition, as a scholar of the print media has emphasized, this lack of attention to a public figure's religious life is hardly limited to historians and political scientists. Former newspaperman Doug Underwood allowed that journalists and those who comment on politicians for public consumption shy away from dealing with religious issues, not wanting to question the kind of benign statements that people like Nixon made. This inattention, occasioned partly by ignorance of religion, partly by a reluctance to challenge something that appears wholly subjective and can seldom be quantified precisely, helped produce a public that was ill-informed about the religious dimensions of a candidate's stances on issues.[2] With no attention being focused on a political figure's religious commitments, it becomes impossible to know what role one's religion might play in public decision-making or even in that person's life more generally. Every voting citizen is handicapped to some extent when going to the polls by having so little information to dispel the ignorance of the roles of religion and religious presuppositions in a candidate's life.

Nixon, if not a natural politician then at least one who learned quickly, was aware of this reality and built his political career by refusing to offer any specifics about the nature of his religion. Yes, he said on occasion, I have a heritage of Quakerism from my mother—he seldom mentioned his father in this respect, even though his father was as active as his mother among Friends. He omitted important information, including his own conversion at a young age in a Los Angeles revival, even as he mentioned being taken to various revivals there. Instead he emphasized time and time again the utterly personal and private nature of his Quakerism; this approach allowed him to sidestep any questions that might prove politically embarrassing. To mention or explain specifics about his variety of Christianity left him, he wrote, feeling "uncomfortable."[3]

A typical example involved the lack of specificity and the dissembling that he mixed with the truth in answering journalist Garry Wills in 1968. They were on a flight from Wisconsin when Wills, a former Catholic seminarian, sat with Nixon and tried to draw him out about how Quakerism had influenced him. "Oh, I suppose it is the stress on privacy," the candidate answered. "The Quakers believe in doing their own thing," he said, making them sound like a centuries-old forerunner of the 1960s student movement, "in not making a display of religion." Wills came back by noting that some Quakers had open prayers, but Nixon quickly retorted as he dissembled and covered up, "Yes, but that's not our branch. We have silent prayer—even the silent grace. . . . I'm an introvert in an extrovert profession."[4] However accurate that last evaluation of himself, the truth was that his church, new and evangelical to the core, had very little silence.

For this author, the most fertile approach to Nixon emerged in the memoir of one of his three speech writers during his first term, William Safire, a self-proclaimed apologist for Nixon, later a columnist for the *New York Times*, a political commentator of conservative bent, and a word maven (a phrase he coined). His recollections of his time with Nixon appeared in 1975—*Before the Fall: An Inside View of the Pre-Watergate White House*, a 704-page volume. Published only a year after Nixon's resignation in August 1974, it was one of the earliest, if not the earliest, memoirs of Nixon, and it vibrates with observer Safire's astute insights, making it one of the best overviews of the thirty-seventh president and his first term.[5]

Approximately 100 pages into his recollections, Safire asked his reader to take "a metaphoric leap: think of Nixon as a layer cake." He goes on to present eight discrete layers that make up the cake: progressive politician, pugnacious scrapper, power player, hater, realist, observer-participant, risk-taker, and loner. Observers and commentators, friends and foes, choose one of these layers as the epitome of Nixon, making that one the "real" one and ignoring the others or at least passing them off as temporary aberrations. But, Safire insisted, one must take the layers all together if the real Nixon is to be known; to separate and isolate one is to open oneself to be surprised and shocked when another aspect of the man suddenly appeared. Safire admitted that he did not know all the possible layers that might appear and make the total person. Being as skillful as he was, Nixon could play these layers off against each other, emphasizing the one that was the most politically useful at a given time. All this meant that it was practically impossible to know the real Nixon.[6]

This book will examine one such layer, one that Safire never mentioned, Quakerism. I do not claim that I have isolated the essence of the man—far from it, for I do not believe that the evangelical Quakerism that Nixon knew growing up played a large role in determining how he approached life and its problems. It may have reinforced aspects of his personality that helped determine how he responded to those problems. The fact, however, that he never rejected it, fairly often made reference to it at different times during his years in office, and went to his grave as a member of East Whittier Friends Church all suggested that at some level he sensed that Quakerism was part of his basic makeup. He learned to draw on aspects of the Quaker faith to allow him, at times, to deflect criticism or give him, on other occasions, some positive benefit, even as he distanced himself from its demands and often went against its tradition.

To understand Nixon, we are, it seems to me, required to make the kind of suppositional leap that Safire recommended. We can also usefully carry his metaphor one step further to view our Quaker subject even more clearly. A layer cake is always held together with an attractive icing, one that may entirely conceal the cake. A chocolate cake, for example, may have a white icing, but let one cut down through it and find what the icing hides, a dark surprise. The fact that I have described what is commonly called a "devil's food cake" is particularly delicious when it comes to understanding the eight-layered cake Safire set before us—Richard Nixon.

So, as an icing, let's consider the following: In 1977 the British media personality David Frost interviewed the disgraced former president before a national television audience eagerly tuned in to the first of a series of post-resignation interviews. On this occasion Nixon asserted definitively in answer to a question about Watergate and the crimes associated with it, "If the President does it, that means it's not illegal."[7]

The clear import of such a statement was that the president lived above the law, able to avoid its demands whenever he deemed it necessary, for whatever reason he might decide; that is precisely what he did during the notorious and infamous Watergate affair that ultimately led to his undoing. He followed a similar path in the secret bombing he ordered in Cambodia and Laos to support U.S. efforts in Vietnam. He made no such similar comment about religion, Christianity, or his Quaker faith to Frost or anyone else. Never asked, he could easily assume that if no one cared, he did not have to either. So he simply left that matter alone, covering up and hiding any transcendent religious values that might guide his life. As a lifelong politician he operated as though his religious beliefs were not as important to him—or to his listeners—as his public actions. (His neglect speaks profoundly of religion's irrelevancy in our society, at least its visible political aspects.)

Yet that Nixon's religion was not as important as his actions is a grievous misconception. A striking example of overlooking what is important came shortly home to me in early 2011 when I looked at the website of the Nixon Presidential Library in Yorba Linda, California. For the benefit of researchers the library staff has helpfully furnished convenient lists of books and articles about Nixon. Upon looking at this listing, I found only three items, two dissertations and one article, under the topic "Religion," while what looked like hundreds crowded many in the other categories, especially such popular and "important" matters as Watergate and foreign policy. I felt daunted by the massive work that had been done on most aspects of my subject's life, yet reassured that I was plowing almost virgin ground when it came to my interest in his religion.

One's convictions about life, other human beings, one's obligations to those others—the things that often, but not always, grow out of one's religion—determine a person's values. To ignore these values, some rational, some more emotional, results in an inability to fully understand others. Such values go a long way in determining how a person will choose to act, particularly if that person is part of a religious community that places obligations on its members. Nixon was a birthright Quaker, a traditional phrase that defines a person whose parents are both members of a Friends meeting at the time of the birth. He was reared in a Quaker atmosphere and community that valued birthright membership; the concept represented continuity within the traditions of the Religious Society of Friends, the formal name of Quakers.[8] That he treasured this heritage and referred to it on numerous occasions and that he retained his membership in East Whittier Friends Church all his life revealed, at least, his wish to honor that continuity.

Friends have adopted no creedal statements, no words to bind a person to their faith.[9] Yet that history and tradition honor what Quakers call "testimonies," which set standards for members' lives. These testimonies vary over time, change, and are sometimes dropped; traditionally, until the evangelical sweep toward the late nineteenth century, they defined not belief but actions. Thus, when Quakers originated in the mid-1600s, they refused to accept those who claimed to be their "betters" with what Friends called "hat-honor," doffing their hats to nobles, even a king, who expected a man's head covering to be removed to recognize their status. By the time Nixon was born in 1913, this "peculiarity" (as well as some others) among Quakers had disappeared, replaced by the broader testimony of equality.

The testimony against participation in war, like equality, remained a commitment to which all Friends were called, even if some chose to violate it; to non-Quakers, this became the most obvious characteristic of the Society, for this one set the group apart from the vast majority of its fellow citizens. The same was true of the requirement to always speak the truth, a testimony that became known as integrity; the Quaker community wanted to be known as a group that valued truth and expected its members to do so, too. Historically, Friends had stressed living plainly, in dress, carriage, and domicile, without ostentation or showiness; also by the time of Nixon's birth, this testimony had evolved into something Quakers called "simplicity" or now "simple living." In the past, meetings and churches had enforced these testimonies by "laboring with" violators, a process that might lead to the ultimate penalty, disownment, but such an approach declined and gradually disappeared for practical purposes.

I have written this book so its readers and I could come to understand a man who was extremely important to twentieth-century American political and social, even constitutional, history. I have had to use words about a president crafting his religion because, given his tradition, he could never, never permit them to pass his own lips. His Quaker heritage, not to mention that of his mother, would not countenance such a public stance.

Hence a statement like the one that Nixon did not make—that he, and only he, defined his religion—would have put him beyond the pale of Quakerism, and, knowing that, he refrained from uttering the words. So after he got into politics, Nixon instead chose to act as though he had created his own religion without formally repudiating Quakerism. That stance made him, in the phrase of Quaker journalist Milton Mayer, a "dormant" member.[10] In the 1650s, when Quakerism was emerging and becoming a political force in England, Nixon's posture of defining his religion himself would have been denominated as "ranterism," by Quakers and others. Ranters held that God's salvation had freed them from human-created restrictions and that they hence were not bound by any kind of outward laws, rules, and regulations, as ordinary people were. They were accordingly free to do as they pleased, limited only by their own wills. This notion was known theologically as antinomianism, a refusal to be bound by outward, human law. To the popular mind at the time, ranters became especially notorious for their disregard of normal sexual morality. Without knowing it, Richard Nixon adopted the ranters' position, ironically one that seventeenth-century Quakerism's critics had used to blacken the reputations of members of the Society of Friends. Needless to say, the earliest Friends rejected any such characterization, believing they were restoring first century primitive Christianity.[11] Flouting the testimonies of the church of which he was a life-long member, Richard Nixon became a twentieth-century ranter who fashioned his own religion. To attach the label this way is not precisely accurate in a theological fashion, but it is apt enough.

In his absorbing memoir of working with Richard Nixon up to his own resignation in March 1973, Safire made the point that Nixon created himself, though he seldom mentioned religion and of course did not refer to ranterism. Quakerism and evangelical Christianity, both factors in Nixon's life, did not appear in the book's copious index. Safire did not mention religion, that is, until page 599, when a six-plus-page chapter on Nixon the private man and his complex and convoluted character appeared; here religion played a revealing role, perhaps more important than Safire knew or intended. The index referenced two pages as "Quaker(s), RN and," and that was it, for the entire book. But those two pages, 600 and 601, led into one of the most enlightening chapters of the book for this reader. Entitled "There Is a There There," a play on Gertrude Stein's 1920s comment about the lack of substance in Oakland, California—"there is no *there* there"— Safire's chapter ventured that there *was* something in fact at Richard Nixon's center. And he referred twice to Nixon's so-called Quaker statement, unindexed, "Peace at the center," as playing a major role.[12]

The problem for one who would understand Richard Nixon was that Safire's famed lucidity failed him here. A careful reading of chapter 1 of part 9, this section titled, "The Private Man," leaves one seeking the essence of Nixon as befuddled as when the search started. Part of the reason is that Safire liked to play with paradox, as his chapter title signaled. He ended the chapter with these two sentences: "So he presented what he thought was the safest, most dignified, most respectable side as his whole front; after a while he came to believe that was the whole front. Which is why, to the real Nixon—the one who inspired trust in his associates and love in his family—

what Nixon saw to be the real Nixon was not the real Nixon." It is as though the reader is left to infer that the "front" (or icing) as erected or applied by Nixon and defined by Safire carefully obscured what the essential Nixon really was—someone who is not "the safest, most dignified, most respectable" person but the opposite of those much-desired adjectives. Too, if the "front" were a lie, obscuring yet another lie, Nixon's critics ought to be forgiven if they denominate the man a liar and spoke of the sudden appearance of a "new Nixon"[13]—or a ranter, as I have done.

To use Safire's words, his "real Nixon" was the one who "inspired trust in his associates and love in his family," a person who must have existed, somewhere behind and beyond one of the fronts he (the "real Nixon"?) carefully constructed so he could hide. The Nixon who maintained his lifelong membership in East Whittier Friends Church and referred fairly often to his "Quaker heritage from my mother"—yes, that same Nixon—would hardly have built a "front" that would obscure who he was. A Quaker, member of the Friends of the Truth, one of the original names of the Society of Friends, simply could not have justified or rationalized taking such a position. Granted that no one is transparent and open in all aspects of life, Nixon was singularly opaque when it came to revealing to others who he actually was; he worked to keep himself hidden so that others could never glimpse any of the complications, even contradictions, that made him the complex human being he was. Safire's analysis, which might have been revelatory, was almost as opaque. Whether intended or not, it amounted to part of the Nixon effort of trying to keep the "front" firmly in place and hiding the real man.

Once or twice, Nixon himself confessed, obliquely, to the kind of dissembling—or cover-up—Safire described here. During the taping of his first interview with David Frost after his resignation, Frost played a clip from the president's resignation speech. It contained the line in which Nixon said about his mother, "Yes, she will have no books written about her. But she was a saint." Frost recorded, "I had been watching Nixon closely. His eyes were glued to the monitor. They became red. He was clearly stirred, moved. 'That was very much you speaking there, wasn't it?' I asked, hoping that Nixon would now share some of his deeper thoughts and emotions."

"'Yes, it was,'" he answered. "'Yes,'" he continued, adding revealingly, "'and very unusual.'" Then Frost watched Nixon's countenance freeze up and become stern as he suddenly realized what he had inadvertently blurted out, and his emotion was "systematically removed."[14] It was as though he consciously took hold and got a grip on himself lest he reveal too much. Then he replaced the revealing "front" with the one that covered up the "real" Nixon, the one that Safire had written about. Similarly, on a flight to

California in April 1971, Nixon told an aide that when describing the president he should say he was "like the iceberg, you see only the tip." The visible did not represent what was going on, for the "real power is below the surface."[15]

Nixon wanted it this way because he knew that he was always under scrutiny, likely to be observed, wherever he was, even at something as routine as funerals. Tom Wicker, the *New York Times* columnist, related the time he visited Stockholm to interview the Swedish prime minister Olaf Palme. Before Wicker could ask a question, Palme told him that he had met "your President Nixon" at the funeral of French premier Georges Pompidou only the previous April day in 1974. Thinking to get the interview off to a good start, Wicker asked what Palme had thought of him. Palme's eyes widened, he leaned forward, and in a conspiratorial whisper revealed, "He was wearing pancake makeup!"[16]

Others who knew Nixon commented on his personality and also emphasized how complicated and complex he was. John Dean, counsel to the president, explained that once he began viewing the president as a man rather than an occupant of an exalted office, he "saw somebody who operated on lots of levels; there are many Richard Nixons": "There is somebody who is caring . . . and there is somebody who is mean-spirited at the other extreme; who will do anything he has to do to accomplish what he wants to accomplish; he is all those people—a complex person."[17] Others agreed. Chief of staff H. R. Haldeman described him as a "quartz crystal with all kinds of facets; some of them deep and dark, some of them bright and shiny." He could be enjoyable and pleasant and then suddenly become miserable to be around.[18] Cabinet member Maurice Stans considered Nixon a "warm and religious person under a cold-appearing shell."[19] White House assistant John Ehrlichman doubted "seriously that there are many people that have seen the complete Richard Nixon."[20] The astute journalist Garry Wills, who later became a Pulitzer prize-winning historian and university professor, decided that "Nixon could never be really accessible" and then concluded, "I think he is inaccessible to himself."[21] Without using the term, Wills was describing a Nixonian cover-up.

Let us sum up Nixon with Henry Kissinger's careful if poignant assessment. (Kissinger knew him probably as well as anyone else. They were never emotionally close, but professionally they worked hand in glove, particularly on foreign policy matters.) "It would take a poet of Shakespearean dimension," Kissinger wrote in his memoir, "to do justice to the extraordinary, maddening, and debilitating personality of Richard Nixon—at once thoughtful and quirky, compassionate and insensitive; sometimes fiercely loyal, at other times leaving in his wake the casualties of old associates."[22]

It is here that Nixon's "principle" of "peace at the center" can be used as a way to lend meaning to our search. Safire referred to it first as a "Quaker principle," a designation that he must have borrowed from Nixon given its absence among most Friends, and then as Nixon's "ideal." As a principle, it meant that Nixon sought to be alone, where he could hunker down, even hide or cover up, in "the most secure place in the midst of a storm"; as his ideal, it meant the absence of disagreement at the center, a place where he was able "to draw a tighter circle around himself."[23] They were the very last words of Nixon's final memoir, *In the Arena*, and seemed to signify that he had finally reached a place where all conflict was over.[24] Nixon told an inquiring reporter just before the 1972 election that he was "steeled for conflict" by his Quaker heritage of peace at the center, "with an inner security and calm."[25]

Another of Nixon's expositions of his concept of peace at the center demonstrated how closely it fit whatever definition he wished; in other words, he found this notion valuable to give him whatever leeway he might desire. Toward the end of the Watergate crisis, when others of his supporters were fast peeling away, he told Jewish rabbi Baruch Korff, one of his staunchest, how it allowed him to face down his opposition. "[I]t gets down to what the Quakers call peace at the center," Nixon explained; "peace at the center means that whatever the storms are that may be roaring up or down, that the individual must have and retain that peace within him, and that will see him though all the adversity." He went on to emphasize that in his political career, "I have always been usually at the very center of controversy. I would be fighting for and talking for what I believed was right."[26] "Peace at the center" could be both a place to cover up and a place that gave security.

The concept even had policy implications as the president drew upon it. He explained to American Broadcasting Company television correspondent Howard K. Smith in 1971 that it not only gave him poise and perspective, but it also kept him from being knocked off balance by momentary crises and passing stories, gave him the confidence he needed to carry on. Having peace at the center allowed him to "make decisions, decisions in regard to our foreign policy, decisions in regard to the lives of men you have referred to, in a way that will be in the best interests of the country."[27] Nixon had latched on to a concept, not widely known among other Friends, one that gave him a sense of deep security and religious well-being. It allowed him to move through the vicissitudes of life, even the processes that buffeted him in the highest office of the land. There was something suspiciously ranterish about it.

Perhaps Nixon's fullest definition of the concept came in an interview with his friendliest biographer, Jonathan Aitken, a member of the British Cabinet; his words demonstrated also the nature of the religion he had constructed and how far it differed from either traditional Christianity or the faith of Friends, evangelical or otherwise. The date was mid-March 1992, and as Aitken told it, his reflections came right after Nixon planned and pulled off a foreign policy extravaganza, sponsored by the Nixon Library from far away Yorba Linda, California, at a Washington hotel with the nation's foreign affairs elite, including President George H. W. Bush, all present. Aitken and Nixon talked three days after the acclaimed conference, and the former president was in a rare mood, one nourished by his triumphal reemergence as a farsighted analyst. It was not absolutely clear from the account who first brought up peace at the center, although Nixon may well have. Our biographer asked him point blank what the phrase meant and how he thought it applied to him.

"Deep down," Nixon admitted as he looked back on a life that had been filled with ups and downs, conflict and strife, "I am basically a fatalist." Peace at the center "means a private calm in the eye of the storm," the ability to "fight all the way but you never soar too high and you never allow yourself to sink too low." It was not exactly stoicism, nor serenity, nor destiny. Instead he defined it as fighting, something he could do by himself without God or any kind of divine intervention whatsoever. During the "worse time after Watergate, I never gave up." He was always sure the pendulum would swing: "And it has, it has [no doubt thinking of the just-concluded conference]. . . . I think that my fatalism did help me weather the storms of the past . . . and yes, I do feel that 'peace at the center' has come to me."[28]

Such explanations showed how Nixon had created his own religion, one that permitted him to seek a place of inner security, safety, and guidance he could locate nowhere else. It allowed him to dispense with whatever in Quakerism gave him problems or heightened any insecurity. Then he could substitute for those problems the quiet solitude that he valued so much—indeed, that he could not do without. In the 1950s when President Dwight Eisenhower and evangelist Billy Graham, seeking to help Nixon expand his political appeal, recommended that he include references to God and his religious convictions in his speeches, he consistently rejected their advice. He took that position because, he said, "mine is a different kind of religious faith, intensely personal and intensely private"; it would have been, he went on, "demagogic" for him to insert religious passages into his speeches.[29] So he covered up or slapped another dab of icing on a widening opening in an effort to make sure the gap stayed hidden. (Interestingly, he never made any *public* comment about this reticence until after he resigned the presidency and had removed himself from the political arena: this "front" of Safire's was seldom swept aside to reveal what lay behind it.)[30]

What Nixon left those of us who want to understand his religion and the role it played in his life, then, was a faith unique to himself—and himself alone, a kind of ranterism. It was hardly Quakerism, either in its traditional or in the evangelical form that nurtured him as he grew up; his faith partook something from Quakerism true enough—how could it not?—but in his hands it transcended his heritage, even as it reflected and merged with the needs of his personality and his personal and political goals. In the sense that it lent meaning to his life, this intensely personal religion served the purpose of others' traditional faiths, including Christianity. Yet in a deeper sense, the one that might have tied him to Quakerism's history and traditions and made him even into an exemplar of that history and tradition, it was like a ship without a rudder: there was simply no way to move it this way or that or to steer and maneuver the vessel, which was accordingly destined to be caught by whatever current, shoal, or wind it happened to encounter.

It was no wonder that there seemed to have been more than one Nixon, for he had constantly to recreate himself as, under the press of events, his definition of "right" demanded modifications, some major, some minor. Then journalist Garry Wills, Nixon's first and in many ways his most insightful commentator, subtitled *Nixon Agonistes,* his book about the man, *The Crisis of the Self-Made Man.*[31] What Richard Nixon's religious life reveals is ultimately tragic, a simple warning against a self-made religion, a variant of ranterism, a tendency all too tempting to modern Quakers, whether their label be Evangelical or liberal. Evangelicals jettisoned the Quaker emphasis on peace, and those called "liberals" tossed Christ out; both consequently embrace a devalued faith.

At least one other thing needs to be said about the role religion plays in a prominent American politician's life, especially that of a national politician. Unless a politician's views were especially controversial and considered completely beyond the pale of respectability—I am thinking of a thoughtful deist like the nation's third president, Thomas Jefferson,[32] or the first two Roman Catholics to run for high office like New York governor Alfred E. Smith in 1928 and Senator John F. Kennedy in 1960—religion was seldom commented upon during campaigns. (Historians and religious commentators have been a bit more adventurous, especially with a president like Abraham Lincoln, who, despite his failure to join a church, attracted attention because of his open espousal of Christian themes, such as in his second inaugural address.) Until the advent of the so-called Religious Right in the 1980s after Nixon's public career was over, religion apparently made little difference to the electorate. And politicians, who, like Nixon, tended to secrecy, preferred it that way. It was as though religion operated in one sphere, politics another, and they seldom intersected or overlapped.

A recent well-respected analysis of evangelical Christianity in the antebellum period, by the English scholar Richard Carwardine, now teaching in the United States, argues that in the years immediately preceding the American Civil War, evangelical Protestant denominations became the dominant religious force in the country and formed the base of the era's politics. One might expect that these evangelicals would look for candidates of the same stripe who would help achieve evangelical goals and further evangelical ends. Yet Carwardine catalogs eight leading politicians of the period—five presidents, John Quincy Adams, William H. Harrison, James K. Polk, Franklin Pierce, and James Buchanan, and three senators, William Seward, Henry Clay, and William Marcy—none of whom were serious Christians by any evangelical definition; some did not join a church until the very end of their lives, others explained that they had no experience of a "second birth," a prerequisite of membership in any evangelical church.[33] Still by the standard of winning elections to high office where they could influence policy, they did exceedingly well, even as they lacked evangelical credentials.

These examples suggest that Richard Nixon's religious affiliation probably made little difference politically. Yet to understand the man and his church and how it influenced him, as well as his responses to the political system in which he operated, an examination of his religion is in order. More broadly, his worldview was inevitably colored, to some extent, by what he often referred to as his "Quaker heritage from my mother." (Even if that prepositional phrase was his own way of distancing himself personally from that heritage, his use of it bespoke something of his assumptions about what he conceived of as its usefulness in the political system in which he acted.) It may also throw light on some of the policies that characterized his administration between 1969 and 1974. The penultimate purpose of this study then is to isolate what Safire referred to as "the cake layers" that Nixon put in place so that something of the "real" Nixon will stand out and become clearer. Or, to put it another way, in a term that people only passingly familiar with him will immediately recognize, I will isolate the first cover-up of his faith as a model for the later ones, including the one involving Watergate.

My ultimate purpose is to instill a bit of honesty and candor into discussions of religion and politics. I did not like Nixon when he was vice president, I did not vote for him in 1960 when I first voted, and I did not cast my ballot for him in either of his two later races for the White House. But I still think I can deal, and have dealt here, with him fairly. Public commentators and journalists usually shy away from seriously including religion in political discussions; perhaps many of them know little about it and are willing for it to be kept purely private. Richard Nixon ignored religion as a campaign issue as though it would plague his best efforts; he engaged in a cover-up. As a Quaker myself, I believe religion has a role to play in the public arena, one that can be defined and defended intellectually and practically. In his decision to avoid all religious discussions in his campaigns, Nixon was being, I think, untrue to the very heritage he claimed. And the electorate, kept ignorant of a vital facet of a candidate's life, was impoverished by this dereliction as well. His campaigns could conceivably have been more contentious, but at least they would have been honest. If he were embarrassed by that heritage—say, because of its public association with pacifism—he would have been more honest, more Quakerly even, had he embraced a more mainstream and less sectarian faith, an option he occasionally considered. In that way he could at least have avoided a twentieth-century ranterism and another dishonest cover-up.

Given all of these things, the truth probably is that Richard Nixon simply could not have avoided the mess he made of his life. At its best religion has the ability to lift people above the mundane and the usual, to inspire its adherents to be better than they ordinarily and normally are, and to give them a vision of greater and broader possibilities as divine grace infuses their lives. Nixon's evangelical Quakerism did not move him toward these goals probably because after he got involved in politics he distanced himself from it and unconsciously embraced what I have styled ranterism. Except for political purposes, he did not need Quakers anymore and left them behind. Yet he continued to insist on his Quaker heritage all of his life, almost as though he never dared explore at a deep level what he sensed was religion's utility and hoped to experience God's grace. So let's conclude for now by permitting another journalist like Safire—but not one as close to his subject, who watched the president at a greater distance—to have the last defining words: Lou Cannon, a Californian, a reporter for the *Washington Post* during the years of Watergate, watched the president from that vantage point. In 1987, he etched in the essence of Nixon in words that cut and damn anyone with a Friendly heritage, "Nixon just regularly and relentlessly lies. He lies through fulsome praise. He just has no inner sense of what the truth is."[34]

Try writing a study rooted in the life of such a ranter.

1

Richard Nixon's Evangelical Quaker Heritage

[Nixon] told me one time that he intended to go through his presidential papers by a fireplace; he would go through them one by one, and cull out the things he didn't want history to notice. . . . He was going to destroy things, so that what was left to history would be his selective version.[1]

—John Ehrlichman

During his political career, Richard Milhous Nixon would occasionally cite his Quaker heritage when called upon to explain or defend controversial actions. Perhaps the most startling example was in 1971 when, in an interview with the *New York Times,* he was asked about the bombing of neutral Laos he had secretly authorized during the Vietnam War. Commenting on his action, Commander-in-Chief of the Army and Navy Nixon told a *Times* reporter, "I rate myself a deeply committed pacifist, perhaps because of my Quaker heritage from my mother."[2] As president he exercised more raw power than any other of the world's Quakers during the twentieth century, in truth more absolute power than any Quaker in history. This was the same "deeply committed pacifist" whose "Quaker heritage" did not prevent him from enlisting in the navy during World War II and serving in the south Pacific.

Such anomalies might cause some head-scratching among critics, but they did not seem that surprising to those who knew anything about the world of evangelical Friends in the western United States from the 1890s onward. Unfortunately few did—or do. Perhaps the most egregious example was in the biography of Nixon by the much-acclaimed historian Stephen E. Ambrose, author of numerous historical works on a variety of topics. Describing the kind of Quaker meeting that he said Nixon attended, Ambrose had Nixon and the Quakers at his East Whittier Friends Church "[s]itting quietly together . . . without intermediary rites, church, creed, or priesthood . . . or hymns sung together."[3] There was no written creed at East Whittier, true enough, but the rest of the description was totally inaccurate for Friends churches in California. Other scholars who have described Nixon's Quakerism have not been as oblivious as Ambrose to the realities of Friends' history, their tradition, and practice, but most have been bad enough.

Such mischaracterizations make one wonder why this myopia existed. It was no Nixonian conspiracy. Indeed, a major source of ignorance about his religion is the neglect of the question by most historians. A very small group, Quakers in the United States are sharply and often bitterly divided and have been since the 1820s, nearly a century before Nixon was born. Many of those who have written about him have been natives of the eastern states, have lived there, or have earned advanced degrees in that area of the country; their knowledge of Quakerism has been colored by the brand that they are most familiar with, the eastern, or what Friends call the "unprogrammed," type, in the United States the one with the fewest actual adherents. Hence relatively few historians have been willing to go beyond Nixon's nearly-always-bland comments about Quakerism and probe into what he was saying—or avoiding. The same goes for his mother's, Hannah's, statements about her faith, a primary source for historians' accounts of their religion.[4]

Toward the end of his life, with less political need to avoid reminding people of his Quakerism, Nixon could occasionally be more forthcoming. Always somewhat fearful and wary of those who wrote about him, in 1989 Nixon told Aitken, the only biographer he half-trusted, that the others were "second rate," but that one of them, Stephen Ambrose, was at least "close to the truth when he said, 'The impact of RN's Quaker heritage on his personality has been underestimated.'"[5] Yet, paradoxically Nixon never corrected the public record: in his own memoir, he limited discussion of his own Quaker background to three short paragraphs. He certainly made no effort to indicate how Quakerism had the significant impact on his personality that he implied in his comment to Aitken.[6]

In truth, Nixon's Quakerism differed little from the conventional versions of Christianity that marked the religious commitments of most American politicians. To understand why, the history of the Quaker experience in the United States is instructive. Quakers, or Friends of the Truth and Children of the Light as they were first known, began in seventeenth-century England at the height of the English civil wars. Sparked by the charismatic preacher George Fox, they represented one of the radical sects spawned by the revolution and became notorious for their insistence that Christ spoke to all manners and sorts of people and commanded them to testify to the truth they experienced from their divine Teacher during their silent meetings.

Sometimes they were hardly civil, invading churches—which they derisively called "steeple houses"—to demand that their hearers come out from the apostasy that the church had followed for better than sixteen hundred years. On more than one occasion, they went "naked for a sign" in the streets of English towns to demonstrate that sinners should similarly strip themselves of their wrongdoing in penance before the Lord. They disdained social niceties, such as tipping their hats or bowing and curtseying to their "betters," used "plain language" such as "thee" and "thou" to aristocrats and parents who expected the plural "you" from inferior subordinates such as children, and refused to pay tithes or swear any kind of oath. For the last two offenses, they filled up the jails, children, men, and women indiscriminately, particularly after restoration of the Stuart monarchy in 1660. Just gathering in groups over five in number now amounted to a violation of the law and sent them to jail, but their numbers continued to increase accordingly. Undaunted by legal restrictions on getting together and unlike their opponents and rivals the Baptists, they insisted on meeting openly, even advertising their meetings. They made few distinctions between men and women, allowing both to speak in their meetings. While not at first opposing slavery—it did not exist in England—their insistence on equality led them in that direction rather early.[7]

After 1661, the sect officially insisted that members refuse to participate in "outward wars" with "carnal weapons," a position that, with the group's other peculiar testimonies, emphasized its differences with other Christian groups. The Quaker mentality stressed these differences. Friends saw themselves as differing fundamentally from their worldly neighbors. When members became more prosperous and somewhat more acceptable to the larger community, they maintained a different dress—wearing outdated, slightly quaint clothing well into the nineteenth century—and many tried to live in rural separation from those around them. In fact, they "disowned" or cut off members from participating in Quaker business affairs any who married outsiders and did not confess their error to their meetings.

The astute reader will notice that I have not dealt directly with what Friends believed. In contrast to most religious groups, Quakers did not focus on what might be termed "right beliefs," ideas about the Bible's inerrancy, Jesus' virgin birth, the trinity, whether Christ was divine or not or when he became so, the substitutionary atonement, and the resurrection.

Not that such matters were unimportant; it was only that the Friends limited their witness to what they themselves knew by personal experience. They accepted fully, for example, that Christ had been resurrected after his death because they felt his presence in leading and speaking to them during their meetings when they gathered for worship: "Christ was come to teach people himself," Fox proclaimed. So they testified to that reality; the rest they left to others to debate. They were concerned more with right actions than right beliefs, responses to God's leadings rather than theoretical theological discussions. To a group of secular leaders who insisted that the "Gospel" consisted of the first four books of the New Testament, Fox reminded them that "the Gospel was the power of God, which was preached before Matthew, Mark, Luke and John were printed or written." Such power sufficed for him.[8]

These differences between Quakers and other Christians began to lessen with a series of schisms that took place in the United States in the first third of the nineteenth century. These splits occurred within five yearly meetings—annual governing bodies in five regions—between groups of mostly urban-oriented evangelicals who desired to substitute the Bible as a rule and guide for the leadership of the ineffable Spirit of Christ and those who identified with a farmer-minister from Long Island, Elias Hicks, who wanted to somehow recapture what he thought was the purer Quakerism of the seventeenth century; inevitably these latter became known as "Hicksites." The evangelicals who accepted the label of Orthodox, backed by English Quakers, did not have much use for the Quaker "distinctives," so that among them there was a gradual slide toward more integration with the larger Christian world. Over time, some even disdained use of the word *Quaker,* preferring Friend instead; that preference continues until today when the term "Friends Church" is widely used, especially in California. After the Civil War, the midwestern Orthodox part of this world was swept by waves of revivalism, and within twenty years the Quaker meetings in Indiana, Ohio, Kansas, and Iowa, as well as those on the west coast replaced silent meetings with churches led by paid pastors, a departure previously unheard of in the world of Friends.[9]

Over the thirty years preceding 1897 when orchardist Franklin Milhous, Nixon's grandfather, decided to move his family from southeastern Indiana to southern California, midwestern Quakerism had undergone a revolutionary transformation. Before the Civil War, midwestern Quakers differed strikingly from their neighbors of other faiths: they met in silence, in plain unadorned meetinghouses, with no clergy as leaders, following no order of service, and with few distinctions between male and female members. All of them testified against slavery—many of them had moved to the

Midwest from southern states because of personal and religious opposition to the peculiar institution—and enough supported abolitionism and the underground railroad that Indiana Yearly Meeting split in the early 1840s over acceptable tactics to use against slavery. Support for women's rights was also normal among these Friends.

After the Civil War, this situation changed dramatically, at least in the Midwest. "Programmed" meetings pushed aside unplanned programs based on silence. The first cause of this replacement occurred in the late 1860s when revivals, led by visiting evangelists—some Quaker, some not—swept through these quiet meetings. Revivals became annual events for many meetings, now almost always denominated "churches," with "mourners benches" where the newly converted could forsake their sins amid pleas from the preacher for the unredeemed to repent. A new theology, one calling for an instantaneous "sanctification" after conversion, promised both immediate holiness, a "second blessing," for the converted and a perfected new life in the future. This altered focus among Friends mirrored the Methodists' holiness emphasis of a few decades earlier. So close were these holiness Quakers to Methodism that one of them explained matter-of-factly that first Friend George Fox's real successor was not another Quaker but Methodist founder John Wesley.[10]

By the 1880s, many Quaker churches had started employing paid ministers, a startling departure for a movement that had always insisted that any person could speak at a meeting and regarded paid ministers as unscriptural. These new leaders planned services resembling those of other Protestant churches: music, spoken prayers, a choir that led hymns and sang anthems, a formal sermon planned by the pastor, a collection, and an invitation to unbelievers to convert. Some Quaker revivalists advocated adopting—and a few personally embraced—what earlier Friends had disparaged as the "ordinances" or sacraments: outward water baptism and the "supper."[11] In the broad Protestant context, it was hardly a new world, but it differed markedly from the one Quakers had lived in before. The new moves brought these midwestern Quakers into line with many of their fellow evangelical Protestant believers, even as they separated them from most traditional eastern Friends or, as some called them, "silent Quakers."

As they drew closer to other evangelicals and emphasized the need to embrace right beliefs, midwestern and West Coast Friends dropped many of the peculiar testimonies that had long marked the Religious Society of Friends. Before the Civil War, many Friends had worn what they called "plain clothes"—long dresses and bonnets for the women, grey clothing with broad-brimmed grey or straw hats for men—they had spoken the "plain language," peppering their talk with "thee" and "thy" and naming the months and days as "seventh month" (for July) and "fourth day" (for Wednesday). Such peculiarities all but vanished after the Civil War for Quakers in the Midwest, except occasionally within family groups. Furthermore Quaker opposition to war had been severely compromised by the Civil War because, once viewed as a war against slavery, the conflict between 1861 and 1865 led to numerous defections from the Quaker heritage of opposition to war for any reasons whatsoever. Before the war, "disownment" from meeting was the ultimate penalty for infractions, but afterward most Quaker veterans were welcomed back as though nothing had been changed by their violation. As a result disciplinary measures in other areas declined after the war: Quakers who married non-Quakers escaped being "dealt with" by their meetings, so yet another longstanding distinction between Friends and their neighbors went by the wayside.[12]

Whether they consciously intended it or not, these new-departure Quakers had inched toward the evangelical mainstream of Protestantism, forming groups that were much like other churches, especially those that stressed that members should remain "close to Christ." They never defined this closeness specifically, other than demanding that adherents embrace the Bible as the final authority above the immediate direction of the Holy Spirit, while eschewing swearing, drinking, dancing, and other immodest acts; Christianity consisted primarily of requiring upright personal behavior. By surrendering their sectarian theological distinctiveness, they inevitably began also to merge into the broader population and take on the majority's secular worldviews. Hence it became more difficult for Friends to maintain their commitments to opposition to war, insistence on women's equality, and living in ways that stressed simplicity and wholeness. All this change happened rather rapidly—within the course of a bit more than a generation, in fact. The end result was that evangelical Friends' churches became for all practical purposes little different from those of their neighbors. "I saw no difference whatever [between Methodists and Quakers]," one woman remembered.[13] Neither apparently did most evangelical Friends.

Let us call Walter C. Woodward, evangelical editor of the *American Friend*, to help us understand. In 1918, for example, this leader of the new departure carefully drew the distinctions, based more on practice than theology, between his variety of Quakerism as compared to "the strict sect." Woodward named the differences "we Western Quakers can scarcely appreciate":

"Our evangelistic and revivals methods . . . wherein rather a fixed order of religious experience is prescribed; . . . the use of a 'hireling ministry' to which we apply the more euphemistic term of pastoral system; a 'programmed' service of worship; . . . we eschew the plain language, say 'Friends Church' and ever refer to our ministers as "Rev." and "Bro. . . ."

These were, he concluded, a result of facing the frontier and confronting new conditions, so most of the "old customs and ideas were accordingly sloughed off." Woodward lamented that some of the good in "the true Quaker perspective"—he failed to name any—had been lost, but, on balance, "Quakerism must always be truly evangelistic."[14]

This shift toward the broader mainstream was extremely important within Quaker history, not to mention Nixon's own life. With this new emphasis, a Friend could, almost without noticing, slip into a conventional religion, allowing an adherent to divide life into segments, in one of which, for example, a religious setting such as a church, one was expected to act one way, and in another area, like a sporting event, another kind of activity would be appropriate. The temptation of conventionality had always been present among Quakers, of course, but living apart within their own communities, oversight offered by elders within meetings, and strict discipline had made it less likely that members would succumb to the lure of the broader world. And if they did surrender, they would be dealt with, be required to confess their error to the congregation or even be disowned. But with disownment becoming more unlikely, one was free now to be more conventional—and less Quakerly.

Members of Nixon's own family help illuminate these dramatic changes that transformed the Quaker world, even as they embodied the changes themselves. Jessamyn West, a novelist of some note and Nixon's second cousin who grew up in the same community and attended the same church, recalled her (and Nixon's great-) uncle, the dynamic Lewis Hadley. A Quaker evangelist from Whittier with red hair and a long red mustache, Hadley had once served as pastor of East Whittier Church. He would become so energized by the emotions he engendered in his preaching that he would skip across the platform, tossing his songbook to the ceiling with a loud bang and clapping his hands as he held forth. The congregation intoned songs in ragtime and "listened to sermons long on rhetoric and short on reason." Hadley was not, West concluded, "anyone's picture of a Quaker minister"; he was more like what she labeled a "shouting Methodist." She correctly opined that Philadelphia Quakers found this kind of Quakerism "horrifying," but as a child she got gooseflesh listening to him preach.[15] Nixon's mother, Hannah, never once referred to the antics of her Aunt Edith's husband, Lewis Hadley, when biographers and magazine reporters dropped by to interview her. She could hardly have forgotten him because he presided at her wedding.[16] To hear her tell it, Quakerism was inward, staid, quiet, restrained, and private, far removed indeed from anything like her Uncle Lewis's cavorting when he preached. The first cover-up had begun.

California Quaker churches were part of the staunchly evangelical California Yearly Meeting. As they moved into the broad mainstream, these evangelicals even rejected the once-scandalous word *Quaker* to describe themselves, instead designating themselves officially the "Friends Church."[17] Coached by Nixon's mother after her son became prominent on the national level, outsiders who came to Whittier to search out his heritage inevitably went away to cast it in the broader historical Quaker stream and let it appear more traditional than it actually was. Historian Ambrose did not dig deeper than mother Nixon's comments. In fact, the Quakerism Richard Nixon grew up with and took for granted did not even exist fifty years before he was born in 1913. Thus, his own personal religious heritage was, as religions go, very new indeed.[18] In a very concrete way he embodied part of the first generation of evangelical Quakers. However outsiders and scholars might misread churches like East Whittier, more informed Friends appreciated all the nuances that bedeviled Quakers and knew that Nixon represented "what might be called the evangelical core of Quakers. . . ."[19]

California Yearly Meeting, founded in 1895 right in Whittier with 1,248 members,[20] reflected a regional evangelical mood, culture, and stance that permeated the southern part of the state. So enveloping and so ecumenical—a word that no Quaker in the yearly meeting would dare speak, lest in derision—was this evangelicalism that some historians have argued foreshadowed and fed the theological and political underpinnings of the mid- and late-century "Religious Right." Religious spokesmen like evangelist Billy Graham and fellow Baptist Jerry Falwell as well as political leaders like Nixon and President Ronald Reagan used its foundations to build a powerful coalition.[21] The Nixons' family decision that their sons should attend Los Angeles revivals, contrary to historical Quaker tradition, pointed up the ubiquity and power of this evangelicalism, even among people who might otherwise have rejected it. Militant anti-communism replaced a strong commitment to peace, an emphasis on personal piety came to trump social activism, and support for well-off local movers and shakers supplanted a concern for the underprivileged.[22] Hence it also made them prime candidates for the kind of conservatism espoused by the Religious Right. So when Nixon's mother died in 1967, no one commented publicly on the fact that her son invited the nationally acclaimed Baptist evangelist Billy Graham to officiate at her funeral in the family's Quaker church. No one said anything because it was not exceptionable in the circles they traveled.

However united Quakers might be in their evangelical faith, serenity did not always reign, at least when it came to nuance of doctrine among the third of the state's Quakers in and around Whittier and westward to Los Angeles. Whittier's leaders had planned a college almost from the beginning of the town's founding in the 1880s and quickly set about making their dream a reality. A board of trustees, organized in 1887, began building an institution in fits and starts that would teach a full range of courses in most disciplines, including even the fine arts. But doubting the need for students to learn about the arts, not to mention science and foreign languages, a group of more fervent evangelicals started an alternative in 1900, the Training School for Christian Workers, essentially a Bible school for turning out pastors and missionaries; its emphasis was not liberal arts in any kind of collegiate sense but narrower biblical studies. (It would be anachronistic to call those who supported the Training School "fundamentalists" because that word had not been coined in 1900; they were clearly determined evangelicals and intent on seeing that students would have a guarded, Bible-based education.) In 1907 it moved to Huntington Park, a short streetcar ride from Whittier, where it could easily compete for students. Whittier College already had close ties to California Yearly Meeting, but with officials of the yearly meeting also associated with the Training School, it was unclear which institution enjoyed the large body's preference. Uncomfortable with this kind of rigid sectarianism, evangelical though it might be, Hannah Milhous, Richard's mother, entered Whittier College in 1902, a decision that telegraphed her prominent family's preference as well.[23]

The Nixon family was associated with two Friends churches in the area—one at Yorba Linda, where the family lived when Richard was born in 1913, and East Whittier Friends Church, founded in 1907,[24] which they joined when in 1922 they moved the ten miles that separated the two towns. Both illustrated sharp differences with traditional Quaker practices, for members at each considered their church to be a "community church," a concept totally new to Friends, but perfectly acceptable to the new evangelicals that had emerged as all-powerful within California Yearly Meeting. Such a church was almost "chameleon-like" in its plasticity of adapting to the larger community, averred one historian of evangelicalism.[25] A community church set low standards of membership, normally welcomed almost anyone without requiring much beyond a verbal confession of belief in Christ's saving atonement and simple personal standards of conduct such as refraining from drinking. For over two centuries, most

Quakers had lived in isolated communities set off from the larger society; they expected members to adhere to strict standards—wearing plain clothing, using plain language, paying debts, foreswearing war, and discouraging participation in public affairs, except those of the local area—and enforced these rules by "dealing or laboring with," even "disowning," those who violated the norms.

At the beginning of their history, Friends had understood their movement as one that called adherents from other churches into a new and gathered community of believers. In the polity of seventeenth-century Friends, expressed by their founder, George Fox, Quakers were "a royal seed . . . redeemed out of kindreds, kingdoms, peoples, and nations," an elect few fortunate enough to have experienced the leadings of Christ's spirit and called to live as a people redeemed and fashioned anew. Friends thus became a separated "peculiar (or chosen) people," consciously different from those of the world's people they lived among.[26]

The rise of evangelicalism among Friends changed this approach forever. Few evangelical Quakers looked backward; however, that did not mean that they that they looked ahead; instead, glancing off to the side, they took their guides from the Wesleyan holiness groups that flourished in the nineteenth century. Later an historian of Evangelical Quakerism and an activist among them pulled no punches in his summary evaluation of the shortcomings of evangelicalism: his fellow believers gave to the Quaker heritage of pacifism, for example, a very minor role indeed, George Fox University professor Arthur Roberts wrote, "because . . . social ethics had low priority in the ethos of the Wesleyan holiness movement." So it was no wonder that evangelical Quaker practice and terminology "came to be nearly completely Wesleyan." Most evangelical Friends, he wrote, knew little else.[27] Roberts might have been describing Richard Nixon.

Thus in 1962, in an article for evangelist Billy Graham's monthly publication, *Decision*, Nixon used evangelical terminology that emphasized how the historic Quaker views of the nature of the church had changed dramatically. The defeated presidential and California gubernatorial candidate described matter-of-factly for Graham's readers his place of worship in his "small village" as "our little community church,"[28] words that came easily to him and suggested how he, too, probably without being fully conscious of its import, had picked up the Wesleyan evangelical influence.

Apparently this terminology was commonplace among his branch of Friends. A former pastor of the church explained that East Whittier had fewer birthright members as compared to other Quaker churches in the region; it obviously drew not from the Quakers who had come west but from newer residents with no background as Friends. This reality made it a community church serving a broad variety of people.[29] A couple recollected that they had never attended a Quaker church before arriving in Whittier, but everyone, regardless of background, fit in well together at East Whittier because it was, they explained, "really a community church."

No one objected if a new member from another tradition wanted to substitute a private outward baptism with water rather than the one experienced in meetings with Christ's spirit, contrary to the customary and historic practice within the Quaker tradition; community churches easily dispensed with such denominational oddities and operated just like other evangelical churches.[30] Such activities might make the church more "alive," as two other members attested, and a place to which young people would naturally be attracted and feel more welcomed, but they made it less, not more, Quakerly, at least in a traditional historic sense.[31]

The dilemmas that confronted a community church as compared to one that saw itself as separate from the world's people became obvious at Yorba Linda Friends Church during World War I. Mrs. Cecil Pickering, who had been raised a member of the United Brethren and was a good friend of Hannah Nixon's, began attending the Yorba Linda Quaker group, which was started also as a community church, boasting a steeple, as in steeple-house; that feature—not to mention an actual pump organ— shocked some visiting Ohio Quakers there for its first services in August 1912. It welcomed members from all denominations, including Roman Catholics. In 1918 Pickering wanted to put an American flag in the main room of the church to honor local soldiers serving in the armed forces—"you know," recalled she, "that's what they did in those days." Friend Hannah, more attune to Quaker traditions, refused to be publicly associated with the flag but, helpfully, offered to pay for it. One Sunday morning Pickering put it up with tacks behind where William Marshburn, a doctor and lifelong Quaker usually sat on the platform. As he sat down, he glimpsed it, turned around, and asked of no one in particular, "Who dared to put that thing up there?" then ripped it down. Everyone knew that the man who tore the flag off the wall was the dominant figure—the "weightiest Friend" in traditional parlance—in the church and had a major say in what happened.[32] In this instance he was trying to preserve traditional Quaker testimonies in the face of pressures to conform to outside community wishes.

But the struggle was a losing one, at least when it came to what had traditionally set apart Quakers as distinctive. Once the idea of a community church captured the ground there was no going back. In Kansas, where evangelical Friends made up the vast majority of Quakers, as they did in California at the time Nixon was growing to manhood, the head of the yearly meeting's peace committee for fifteen years, from 1933 to 1948, lamented the decline of teaching in local Quaker churches against partic- ipating in war. Anna Jane Michener explained in 1945 that many Friends "felt their meeting is really a community church and they therefore hesitate to give much place" to pacifism.[33]

Organized early in the new century, the Nixon's East Whittier Friends Church partook of these new directions. It met in a wood-frame build- ing that was modest, even austere, particularly when compared to the stolidly brick First (and larger, more affluent, and locally more influen- tial) Friends Church.[34] The rural area from which its founders thought to draw members was dotted with orange and lemon orchards stretch- ing off in the basin to the east, and the church was one of the first estab- lished between Whittier and La Habra; its leadership naturally saw it as a place of uplift and morality for the region among people of every denom- ination. In this respect it reflected the values that evangelical Quakers brought to Whittier: the town had no bars where men might while away their valuable time, pool halls were nonexistent, and liquor was legally banned. Riotous living was thus kept firmly at arm's length. One observer noted only two or three "dismal cafés" that served a few transients who happened by; citizens themselves seldom dined out, content to remain in their quiet homes to eat simply and think loftily.[35] As late as the end of the 1960s, remnants of this atmosphere were evident to those who looked closely. A cynically inclined commentator like Garry Wills vis- ited and detected a suffocating "locker-room smell, of spiritual athlet- icism" that assaulted him after only one day in town.[36] Though not far physically from the First Friends Church, attended by the Quaker mov- ers and shakers of the community, East Whittier Friends Church was like "another world" to them, one admitted—a kind of plebian enclave within the larger Quaker enclave that was Whittier itself.[37] East Whittier Church differed markedly from First Church in its obviously lower-class social and economic characteristics.

Despite its lower-class congregation, East Whittier was not welcoming to Mexicans and other scattered minorities in the area. One Mexican lad came "a few times" to Christian Endeavor on Sunday afternoons.[38] Few African Americans resided in the Quaker-dominated town with whom its insular, aloof, and strait-laced citizens might interact. One lone black domestic who stayed in the home of the Michigan-born editor of the local newspaper in the early part of the century left his employment after only six months. She was not welcomed in any of the stores nor could she find a sin- gle place to go to church: "The people did not seem to *see* her" was the word she relayed to the family when she departed Whittier for good.[39]

Looking back on it from the vantage point of his senior year at Whittier College in 1933, Richard Nixon characterized the church's members and his parents as what he called "fundamental Quakers," who "ground" into him "all the fundamental ideas in their strictest interpretation."[40] This easy characterization was more than a little unfair, truth be told. For one thing, he was not an easily molded hunk of soft clay on which his church and parents had written what he now believed; he was, after all, a highly intelligent person. His very astuteness was part of the reason Nixon wanted to impress his professor, also dean of the college who would grade his effort, with how much Whittier had changed him. And by definition, a community church like East Whittier Friends Church offered broader latitudes of belief to its members than would have been afforded by Quaker meetings of a previous generation. Finally, his parents were both humane and sensitive. As we shall see in the next chapter, neither was the type to have "ground" into him views that a sensible youth would find unattractive or unacceptable.

All that being said, the twenty-year-old Nixon who chose the word *fundamental* to describe his theological upbringing was making a valid point. His church was more concerned that he as a member have a certain set of beliefs—about a literal interpretation of the Bible, the sinner's need for Christ's atonement, and the requirement that he experience a second blessing of sanctification—than that he grow slowly to redemption over a lifetime of opening himself to the divine and struggling with his lower nature. The latter was the traditional Quaker view of how to slowly achieve "wholeness," the one that evangelical Friends had moved "beyond" when they embraced Wesleyan concepts of holiness. It was unclear that Nixon was even aware of this historic shift, for he wrote nothing about it in his essays and said nothing about it in later life. But East Whittier Friends Church certainly stood as a sentinel to the shift— right there on its little rise overlooking Whittier Boulevard—its members remaining content with and unquestioning about what their forbears had done when they embraced the changes that the very term *community church* conveyed.

Nixon came of age and graduated from college at the age of twenty-one when evangelical influence in the larger community was at a low ebb; it would remain so until after World War II. The struggle between science and religion, highlighted by the struggle over Darwinian evolution and the Scopes trial in Tennessee, and the loss of evangelical influence within the mainline denominations during the 1920s both drove evangelicals underground and gave more literal-minded fundamentalists and revivalists a chance to gird themselves for coming battles.[41]

In Whittier, as we shall see, a mid-twenties revision of the curriculum at Whittier College underscored this evangelical decline in the small Quaker-dominated community. The end of this decline after World War II coincided with a turning point in Nixon's life, when he decided to enter the political arena, moved away from Whittier, and became less and less involved in religion and the church.

2

Quaker Upbringing, to 1934

What we have in mind is primarily a religious attitude that recognizes the insufficiency of man as a finite being and seeks to orientate itself through some transcendent guidance, so that man can come to terms with himself, his fellowmen, and the universe.[1]

—Hans J. Morgenthau

Richard Milhous Nixon was a Quaker, not just any Quaker but a life-long, birthright Quaker. His mother's Milhous ancestors had an American Quaker lineage that stretched back to the early eighteenth century when the first Milhouses went from Ireland to Pennsylvania; from that colony the family's descendants moved to Ohio, Indiana, and nearly two centuries later to California. Neither socially nor politically prominent, the family eschewed public attention and contented themselves with cultivating a life of faithfulness to their occupation as farmers and their faith as members of the Religious Society of Friends. They succeeded. They gradually accumulated more than modest wealth, and their Friends meetings recorded some as ministers, that is, people deemed gifted enough to speak under the immediate guidance of the Holy Spirit at Quaker gatherings.

Richard Nixon was also a politician. It was a role not represented on either side of his family tree; he had to carve out his own career with little guidance from those of his relatives who had gone before. Elected twice to the United States House of Representatives and once to the Senate, he served eight years as vice president of the nation and was elected twice to the presidency, the last time, in 1972, overwhelmingly. As a political figure, Nixon had to win elections—he lost two, for the presidency in 1960 and the race for California governor two years later—so he had to learn and cultivate and use the wiles of politicians to succeed. Be all that as it may, his final impressive success was quite short-lived: in August 1974, less than two years after his reelection, President Nixon resigned his position—the only

American president ever to do so—lest he be impeached, likely convicted, and then removed from his office. He lived another twenty years, but however much he tried, he never regained the luster, the trust, and the leadership that had accrued to him as president.

Born into a modest Quaker household in Yorba Linda, California on January 9, 1913, Nixon could not fundamentally change who he slowly became as a person and what he gradually made himself into as an adult. He had to find ways to present himself as a person palatable to an electorate with the power to choose between him and a competitor. One problem was that there was an inherent conflict between his religion and his political career. His religion held up before him ideals that required him—at least to some extent depending on the specific issues—to distance himself from the larger world; the other, the political arena, had as its essence the need for him to compromise, to vacillate, and to temporize in order to be identified with that larger world, if he were ultimately to win. Richard Nixon had to find ways to live in two starkly differing worlds with sharply competing demands.

What Nixon did was to use Quakerism as a kind of shroud to hide a personality quirk that demanded—perhaps needed—silence and quiet. For political purposes this often seemed useful, and he held onto it, even as he convinced people who came into contact with him that Quakerism was inherently the same way. Examples of how others adopted this tactic abound. For one, Bryce Harlow, Nixon's liaison with Congress as Watergate deepened, exclaimed over his boss's warm, engaging personality and speculated that he kept it well hidden because of his "Quaker indoctrination."[2]

The broad outlines of Nixon's inherited faith have long been known, for our politician used them almost from the beginning of his political career. As a birthright Quaker—that is one whose membership in the Religious Society of Friends was automatic because both of his parents were Quakers—Nixon had a rich heritage. (To be absolutely accurate, birthright membership among evangelical Friends had been abolished by the time he was born, but the term continued to be used informally.) His maternal family, the Milhouses, had Quaker roots going back to Ireland and the early-nineteenth-century Ohio and Indiana frontiers; his father, formerly a Methodist, joined his wife's church soon after they were married in 1908."[3] The Milhous family history was replete with members who had been recorded as ministers by their meetings. This status was hardly honorific, and one did not opt or train to become a minister, as Nixon's earliest biographer implied.[4] Quakers designated people for ministers who demonstrated a clear likelihood that they could speak God's word out of the silence in their meetings for worship: they occupied places of some prestige on the "facing benches" in meeting houses and were expected to offer leadership by way of "spoken ministry" to their meetings.

Both Nixon's great-grandmother, Elizabeth Price Milhous, who spoke in church almost up to her death at age ninety-six in 1923 and was one of the founders of the Nixon's church, East Whittier Friends, and his grandmother, Almira Burge Milhous, were such ministers.[5] His mother did not enjoy this status, perhaps because the introduction of paid pastors in evangelical Quaker churches made the old practice a bit redundant. Great-grandmother Milhous, a very quiet person, delivered her messages without the fire and brimstone that might be expected in an evangelical church; she also engaged in such missionary activity as establishing Sunday schools. She always spoke "sweetly" and "nicely."[6] And she may well have been responsible for establishing the Friends mission station, with a Spanish-speaking pastor even, among Mexicans in Whittier's "Jim Town" neighborhood.[7] Though her roots ran to the late 1820s and a time before evangelicalism had triumphed, she obviously adapted to it easily. Describing a revival before leaving Indiana, she wrote of how "the Holy Ghost was acknowledged throughout as leader" by a congregation of Methodists in Butlerville after the same evangelist moved to the Quaker meeting for similar "good service."[8]

Nixon described his grandmother Almira Milhous as a "very devout Quaker pacifist, as a good Quaker should be," indicating that he was aware when he uttered these words in the 1980s that pacifism should identify a Friend. She also spoke in what Quakers called the "plain language" with everyone she met, stranger or not, so when she addressed him, she would say, "Richard, is thee going?"[9] An active member of the Women's Christian Temperance Union, she displayed its sign at her home on the old Milhous homestead next to the highway.[10] Perhaps to her grandson her commitment to peace, like her use of plain language and her support of temperance, was a quaint hangover from a previous age, something he could discard.

This earlier Indiana era became almost legendary among the Milhouses, and Nixon referred to it on more than one occasion. For example, he coached an early biographer, Earl Mazo, what to write so as to emphasize the Quaker heritage that symbolized "opposition to human injustices" he inherited from his great grandfather who ran a station on the legendary underground railroad.[11] In a late-night telephone call to speechwriter William Safire, he confided that "my mother's grandfather ran an underground railroad."[12] His ancestors arrived in Jennings County in 1853, joining Friends in that region of southern Indiana who had taken a strong and determined stand against slavery, even splitting with the larger body and forming a short-lived Indiana Yearly Meeting of Anti-Slavery Friends.[13]

The novel *The Friendly Persuasion*, by Jessamyn West, brought this story to a wider audience when it was published in 1945. Nixon's cousin wrote the book about the fictional Birdwell family and the dilemmas forced upon them by their Quaker pacifism and opposition to slavery before and during the Civil War, basing it on the experiences of the Milhous clan; it became a popular Cold War-era movie starring Gary Cooper in 1956.[14] Two decades later another film by the same title with an expanded focus, produced this time for television, gave a boost to the tale and added details to Nixon's Quaker heritage.

By her retelling, Nixon's mother took the dominant role in her son's religious development. By Nixon's own account, his mother was regarded by those who knew her as "a Quaker saint."[15] Relatives, like Jessamyn West's brother Merle, attested to her saintly bearing: "if there was ever an angel on earth, it was Hannah Nixon. I've never known a woman as sweet. . . ."[16] Locals who needed a confidant or just a shoulder to cry on sought her out.[17] The pastor of Whittier's First Friends Church, not the Nixons' church, also described her in 1959 as "a Quaker saint—patient, loving, quiet, unassuming, understanding." Nixon's second biographer, Bela Kornitzer, who based his book on her recollections, called her a "great and dedicated woman," "the greatest inspirational force" in her son's life, and warmly dedicated his book to her.[18]

Nixon remembered her as intensely private, willing to praise the achievements of her sons yet seldom using negative criticism. Hannah Nixon was almost too good to be true. She was a no-nonsense woman, he recalled, none of this "sloppy talk and even more sloppy kissing and hugging. I can never remember her saying to any of us, 'I love you'—she didn't have to" because everyone who came into contact with her knew that she did. The man famous for never wanting to be caught casually dressed, without a coat and tie, clearly did not like sloppiness—nor displays of affection—and could follow his mother's example. He meant his description as a compliment to her, but it could suggest also that she put a lot of distance between herself and others, that she was aloof even from her children. He considered that her pacifism grew naturally out of her Quakerism, demonstrated by the fact that her Indiana forbears violated the law by using their home as a station on the underground railroad for escaped slaves. When they lived in Yorba Linda, she was also a charter member of the local Federation of Women.[19] At the end of his own life he described her as "a thinking woman. Finding meaning in life for her was never beyond finding meaning in God."[20]

Though he always depicted her as broad-minded and tolerant, Hannah was concerned when she found him devouring the novels and treatises of

Leo Tolstoy one summer when he was in college.[21] Both his parents held to a literal interpretation of the Bible, Nixon recalled, though this recollection may have been an exaggeration.[22] She was evangelical enough to frequently attend the Easter Sunrise Services organized by Fuller Theological Seminary in nearby Pasadena at the Rose Bowl.[23] Nixon defined his Quaker faith, minus its pacifism of course, through her. He once reportedly told a friendly journalist that she was the only reason he remained a Quaker; otherwise, he would have joined the Presbyterians, whom he found more congenial.[24] Her moral authority was very powerful in his life. As late as 1950, when he was forty-seven and celebrated his victory in the senatorial election, he asked the publisher of the *Los Angeles Times* to add some bourbon to his milk so his parents would not detect him drinking alcohol. It may have been unseemly, but he did not want his mother to know that he was sipping bourbon.[25]

Nixon's father, Francis Anthony Nixon, whom everyone called Frank, came from a different background than his wife-to-be, Hannah Milhous. Born in Ohio in 1878 and reared a Methodist, he was a more voluble character, something that may happen when an ill-educated person is forced to grow up in a hardscrabble fashion. He missed out on almost all formal education because his father, a sometime schoolteacher himself, carried the family from their home through the South looking for a climate more suitable for his wife's tubercular condition. After she died and was buried in Mount Pleasant, Ohio, Frank, a teenager, essentially dropped out of school, supporting himself and helping his family. Working as a potato farmer—a job that won him the accolade "Potato King" from his friends—he went west to Colorado, then returned to Ohio and worked as a conductor on a streetcar in Columbus around the turn of the century. He dabbled in union affairs. In 1906 he won a promotion to motorman, but he had to control the car from the open vestibule at either end, not an especially warm prospect in the middle of winter; once his feet froze. So the following year, aged twenty-nine, he was off to California, where he secured a job with a Los Angeles street railroad. There he found weather a lot less frigid, not to mention romance.[26]

The street railroad ran from the big city eastward to Whittier, a distance requiring about fifty minutes to cover. Nixon met Hannah Milhous at a Valentine's Day party in 1908, and despite some serious misgivings from her family—Hannah had not finished Whittier College, and Frank was clearly a step below the Milhouses socially—the couple married four months later. Needless to say, Methodist Nixon embraced his wife's faith and lived for a time with his in-laws, where he no doubt received a generous dose of what Quaker life was like at the family level. Despite the blunt assertion of one Nixon biographer,[27] nothing ever emerged to indicate any differences between Frank's Methodism and Hannah's evangelical Friends church. The couple became active in East Whittier Friends Church when they moved back to Whittier after Frank tried his hand, unsuccessfully, at growing lemons in nearby Yorba Linda; Richard, their third son, was born there in January 1913. Frank was certainly different from many of his Quaker neighbors because some remembered him, somewhat inaccurately, as "mean," apparently because he yelled at the boys, but all knew him as a "good fellow," whose bark was certainly worse than his bite.[28]

Frank was a likeable chap, and people responded to him. In Yorba Linda, he kidded around with teenagers, teasing them and trying to get them to come to the Friends church, the first and for some years the only one in town, and the Sunday school class he taught. With so little to do in the small community, some would go to class but not hang around for church, but then they would come back for daylong hayrides into the surrounding hills or even go on an occasional trip to the ocean. It all built up a sense of wellbeing and community, and Frank was part of it.[29] His social life consisted of discussing religion after church on what the Quaker family called "First Day" and, his youngest son remembered, politics at the store during the week.[30]

After Richard became famous, inquiring reporters seldom interviewed Frank, either because he did not want to speak publicly or because he was more reticent about his faith than was his wife; hence he was almost never quoted on matters involving religion or Quakerism—or anything else for that matter. One of the few who talked with him penned an article that appeared in a national evangelical publication shortly before his death in September 1956. Contrary to those who saw his Quakerism as being somewhat below the standard set by Hannah, when he said that he wanted to teach young people to know that human beings "have been made in [God's] image and that we all have the light within us," the former Methodist was expressing traditional Quaker views in traditional Quaker terms. In the same interview he also revealed the evangelical side of his faith: he preferred to attend a Friends church, but if none were available, he found one where he "worshipped in the name of our Father, Son and Holy Ghost."[31]

Especially in the 1950s, when Richard was vice president, Hannah Nixon took pains to see that biographers and the public got a positive view of her son's religious heritage. She all but dominated the personal side of Kornitzer's biography, granting him ready access to her recollections, personal pictures, and relevant letters. The picture she drew of Quakerism may have been theoretically accurate, but it comported more closely with the eastern "quiet" tradition than the evangelical variety actually on display

each Sunday at East Whittier Friends Church: "There is little outward man-
ifestation in Quakers," she related. "To us, worship requires no churches,
no ministers, no sacraments, not even services." No doubt aware of her
son's reluctance to speak of his religious faith except in the most general
terms and demonstrating her own preference for privacy, she explained,
"a good Friend does not wear his religion on his sleeve."[32] Her church featured, regardless of what she might tell the interviewer busily taking it all
down for his book, "a hired preacher whose [prepared] sermons were as
pulpit-thumping as anything a Baptist or a Methodist could deliver." These
words came not from some hypercritical outsider but from as good a witness as Hannah Nixon, a relative and member of the East Whittier, Jessamyn West.[33]

Hannah also failed to add that in the past Quakers had in fact looked,
spoken, and acted differently, particularly when it came to participation
in war and living the truth they had found in their experience of Christ.
Indeed the evangelical movement of which she and her church were a part
distinguished itself from the practices of eastern Quakers by stressing that
the earliest Friends had carried the faith into the "steeple houses" of those
Quaker founder George Fox scathingly called "professors," people content merely to profess faith rather than possess it. Thus they had no com-
punction about interrupting church services, debating the ministers right
there in their sanctuaries, demanding that those present repent of their sins
so they could become empowered to speak the truth they had just now
encountered.[34] The implication evangelical Friends drew was that modern Quakers should not disdain such an approach in the present age, but
instances of such activities on their part were difficult to find indeed. These
Quakers limited themselves to proclaiming from their pulpits, as a modern
Evangelical Friend phrased it, "the centrality of Jesus Christ including His
exclusive claims as the only way to salvation."[35]

Once her son Richard entered the 1960 political campaign for president, Hannah repeated the claim that he went to church three times each
Sunday, for Sunday school, church, and the evening service and once more
on Wednesday night.[36] (When he wrote his memoirs many years later,
Nixon added his church's unit of the interdenominational youth Christian
Endeavor in the afternoon to his mother's Sunday attendance list.)[37] In the
same June 1960 article for *Good Housekeeping*, mother Nixon commended
her son and his wife for bringing up their daughters by "the strict Quaker
principles" she had used in raising her own children, though now those
principles did not include going to the local Washington Friends meeting
even once on Sundays. She apparently never expressed any disappointment
to her son about his family's decision to attend another church in Wash-

ington.[38] On another central issue, she likewise indicated her willingness to accept Nixon's compromises. Acknowledging her personal commitment to pacifism, she nevertheless emphasized that she had not tried to convince him to invoke his Quaker heritage and seek conscientious objector status after the nation entered World War II; instead she watched, with no evident expression of pain or disappointment, as he violated one of the central tenets of their faith.[39]

In writing his memoirs, Nixon devoted three short paragraphs to his religious heritage, giving only the barest substance to it and emphasizing its tolerance, something that was not obvious to those who observed evangelical Quakerism. The only thing he mentioned of real significance was that his parents, presumably his mother with her Quaker heritage as well as his Methodist-reared father who became a convinced Friend before his marriage, were not content to leave their sons' religious development to the Quakers in Whittier alone. Both parents were "fascinated"—his word—with the evangelists who came to Los Angeles, a relatively short streetcar ride away, and took the boys there to hear them. Thus he listened to the notorious Aimee Semple McPherson at Angelus Temple and her rival Robert Shuler at Trinity Methodist Church.[40]

Nixon did not hear anything different back home at East Whittier Friends Church. Its teachings were biblical, evangelical, and conservative. To join the church, unless one was a birthright member, one had to demonstrate a "new birth." Sunday school classes might explore missionary activities in Central America or Alaska, sites where evangelical Quakers had dispatched workers to convert others. Unlike more traditional Quaker services, there was almost no silence, calling into question Nixon's 1972 assertion that in his family "worship was always a very private matter." The evening worship included rousing gospel singing and testimonies from attenders about what God had done in their lives. By contrast, the more formal morning service seemed rather "plain" just like those in other nearby churches—a printed order of service, preselected hymns, a collection, a prepared sermon, sometimes an altar call—everything except there were no sacraments. For all these, the Quaker emphases were not entirely lost: there was a stress on peace and solving problems without violence, as well as a focus on spiritual realities rather than on superficial ceremonies—hence no outward sacraments—although if a new member insisted on baptism, no one stood in the way. At one point after the Nixons moved to Whittier, Frank pushed for creation of a youth choir with its own director to get away from the more staid, older choir.[41]

By the time young Richard went to college in 1930, East Whittier Friends Church had 161 members, even though they held no evangelistic services that year. Its members contributed $771.58 to missionary work, 42 percent of the $1,830 they paid their minister. Only 20 percent of them "habitually" attended the midweek prayer meeting.[42]

So as Jessamyn West remembered later, California Quakerism was hardly quiet, like the variety that existed on the other coast. The Quakers she grew up with, she wrote, "were not offended by a pulpit-thumping preacher or an amening audience." She herself was convinced that Quakers' too easy acceptance of revivals, something foreign to historic Quakerism and another example of how evangelical Quakers in California had succumbed to the practices of the larger community, was an example of "religious nonsense." She recounted how she had been "saved" twice, once when she was seven, again at sixteen—too often, her family believed, because, like her cousin, she was a birthright Friend and did not need to be even once. At home her Milhous mother taught her no prayers and never listened to hers before she went to bed, never read the Bible aloud nor required her to read it. Still, as she looked back on her childhood, the whole family, parents and children, had informal discussion of practical Christian living that left her knowing that they were part "of a God-loving household."[43]

The Nixon household differed from that of their relatives the Wests, at least as mother Hannah reported it. One of the boys read a text from the Bible or a "scripture lesson" each morning before breakfast. Nixon's mother, alert to Richard's quick mental development, once asked the youngster if he would like to enter the ministry, but he seemed less than enthusiastic about the prospect, so she dropped the matter. She claimed that she would not have minded if he had chosen to enter the ministry of another church: "Whatever denomination he might have chosen would have been all right with me, because he would have been in the service of God."[44] Such evangelical sentiments suggest that, for Hannah Nixon anyway, community church notions had trumped traditional Quaker ones, for no Friend, evangelical or not, believed that pastors had a monopoly on service to God.

Such theological and practical changes introduced a wide, sometimes unbridgeable gulf between eastern and western Quakers, one that Nixon was forced to navigate when he went into politics and moved east. The popular American image of a Quaker partook from those rather exotic silent Friends in the East instead of the more rambunctious evangelical variety of the West, much to the latter group's chagrin.[45] Not only did eastern Friends have a longer history, going back to the early colonial period, but they were also associated with radical political causes, such as determined opposition to war, a principled stand against southern slavery, and support of the

rights of women. They had also been more successful in lodging the peculiarities of their brand of the faith in the public mind. Bearing the Quaker
label, Nixon could in some quarters occasionally find himself the beneficiary of the broad, rather tolerant, sometimes radical tradition of the East,
one that had encompassed his Indiana Milhous ancestors before the Civil
War; if he desired, this history allowed him to identify with internationalism, the United Nations, and the longing for peace, as well as with civil
rights for African Americans.[46] Especially in his early days as a national
politician, he took advantage of this part of his heritage.

The future president drew also on the traditions that only he himself
experienced growing up. As he related in his memoir, as a child he went to
East Whittier Friends Church four times every Sunday. A fine pianist, he
played at various services during the week, including Wednesday nights,
even, he remembered, when he was a Whittier College student.[47] One of the
most popular songs he played in Sunday school was "Jesus Loves Me, This
I Know."[48] At some point he also began teaching Sunday school classes,
even leading the young married couples' class when he was a freshman
at Whittier.[49] Despite this regular activity and despite his church's evangelical emphasis, Nixon did not mention any conversion to Christianity and apparently never felt called to profess his faith in Christ's saving
power. He did recount going with his father and brothers, and, occasionally, his mother, into Los Angeles to hear various evangelists.[50] During the
bulk of their history Quakers had insisted that one should heed the living Christ, but until the revolution in midwestern Quakerism they held
that this encounter, or more aptly *encounters*, took place gradually over a
lifetime. Hence before the birth of revivalism toward the end of the nineteenth century Quakers discounted sudden conversions while holding that
sanctification was gradual and took place throughout one's life. While Nixon's evangelical Quakerism, the kind proclaimed in East Whittier Friends
Church, supposedly embodied the new emphasis, he still found no reason
to mention any conversion.

No need to mention his conversion, that is, until 1962, when Nixon was
in his fiftieth year, and, for some reason, in the same month that he lost his
race for governor of California. He chose to write briefly of his conversion
in evangelist Billy Graham's magazine at the request, said the article, "of
Decision's editors," undoubtedly at his friend's suggestion. Despite remembering the incident "vividly," he had never referred to it before, even when
he assisted two of the earliest biographers, James Keogh and Bela Kornitzer, in getting the facts of his life straight. In the fall of 1926, at age thirteen,
he had just entered high school. He accompanied his father, Frank, and his
two brothers to a Los Angeles to hear Paul Rader, a renowned Chicago radio

evangelist who espoused a perennial revival. "We," he related, neglecting to indicate whether the plural pronoun included his father, "joined hundreds of others that night in making our personal commitments to Christ and Christian service." The editors placed a subhead—"A Night of Personal Commitment"—at the beginning of this paragraph to signal its importance, but it is not clear from Nixon's failure ever to mention this experience again that he saw it as more than generic. That his father, with his Methodist background, was responsible for overseeing his sons' conversion is hardly surprising, but that his mother approved demonstrated how far she had moved from her traditional Quaker upbringing.[51]

One popularizing biographer placed his account of Nixon's conversion at the Rader revival in a chapter entitled, "Richard the Apostate" and drew startling conclusions. Leonard Lurie, who demonstrated that he knew little about the kind of Quakerism practiced at East Whittier Friends Church, says that Nixon's conversion marked him ever afterward as a hybrid in religion, "a Quaker fundamentalist, more anxious, in later life, to follow Billy Graham than [Quaker founder] George Fox." Nixon, Lurie asserted, "never deliberately rejected Quaker ideals. He simply sloughed them off, one at a time, as the need arose." The example Lurie selected to prove his point was Nixon's support of dancing when he was running for president of Whittier College's student body. He depicted Nixon believing that dancing "led to carnal abuse," without presenting any evidence of how his subject perceived dancing, one way or the other.[52]

Nixon's religious heritage was therefore quite conventionally Christian, betaking of nothing especially Quakerly, at least as outsiders regarded that faith. Grandmother Milhous did encourage him with a high school graduation present, a biography of the Indian nonviolent revolutionary Mohandas Gandhi, and he claimed later to have read it.[53] When he entered Whittier College that fall, he served as president of his church's Christian Endeavor,[54] but that fact alone indicated little beyond his willingness to serve. No one left any evidence that the youngster got a plumb line from his frequent attendance at East Whittier's services by which he would be enabled to judge—or even stand tall against—the larger society. Of course, as a boy he did not have the ability to consider such abstract questions, but little in his later life suggested that the values he carried away from East Whittier Friends Church had much impact on his views. Later he could and did talk about "peace," especially when he reached the national level of politics, but every public officer, not excluding generals and other military leaders, used that very word to justify actions that they considered necessary for other perhaps unstated reasons. Such sentiments certainly did not reflect the historic Quaker position running back to what during Nixon's life came to be known among them as the "peace testimony" against war.

The most extensive account Nixon gave of his own religious thinking occurred when he was a senior at Whittier College, up the hill from his family's home, store, and church on Whittier Boulevard. Nixon entered Whittier in 1930, "a successful politician from the first moment he set foot" on campus, one of his professors, drama instructor Albert Upton, from whom he took more courses than from any of his other professors, recalled.[55] It was just as the college was riding the crest of its own curriculum reformation and struggling against fundamentalist attacks. It needed reformation if the description of Jessamyn West, who graduated seven years before her cousin entered, is to be believed: "a college of under two hundred enrollment whose women students became teachers, missionaries, or wives—and sometimes all three. None, as far as I know, ever wished to be anything else."[56]

With a new president and a new dean, J. Hershel Coffin, arriving in 1922, the college reordered its curriculum and implemented a senior-level course called "The Philosophy of Christian Reconstruction," taught by the dean. Coffin had a Quaker heritage to match his name, one going back to Nantucket and including Lucretia Coffin Mott, one of the renowned Quaker feminists of the nineteenth century. With a 1907 doctorate in psychology from Cornell, Coffin was a thoroughgoing modernist; his required course offered soon-to-be graduates a way to integrate their vocational interests into an education imbued with the spiritual insights that Jesus might offer were he in southern California. When the dean's book, *The Soul Comes Back*, was published by Macmillan in 1929, nearby evangelical Friends churches took exception to it, and one withheld a proportion of its assessment in protest the college's "liberalism."[57] Nixon signed up for the course his final year, the third time it was offered.[58]

The 1920s was the age of controversy over Darwin's theory of evolution and a time of challenge from religious conservatives to that idea. It was clear from the twelve essays that Nixon was required to complete for a course aimed at "reconstruction" that modernist Coffin had not shied away from confronting the issues raised in this dispute. (In February 1930, a roving Methodist evangelist, Guy F. Phelps, came to town and before week's end had challenged Coffin, among others, to debate on whether evolution was "Unscientific" and "Absurd"; he went on to "review" Coffin's book, labeling it "unorthodox" and "contrary to the teachings of the Bible." Needless to say, his services were packed with curious students and wondering townsfolk, most of them probably Quaker.)[59] Nixon's essays, a kind of log or journal of his reading and reflection, bore the overall title,

"What Can I Believe?" Reading them now, one can see that Nixon took the route of many students and echoed what he thought his professor wanted.[60]

Senior Nixon may not have realized it, but the course was an integral part of the administration's efforts to respond to the modernist-fundamentalist controversy that riled evangelical churches in the 1920s. The administrators of Whittier College, despite control by the rigidly evangelical California Yearly Meeting, wanted the college to be an accredited and recognized liberal arts institution in the world of higher education. The "Exploration of Christian Reconstruction" course was part of a broader "Whittier Idea" that included up-to-date examinations of religion, philosophy, and psychology in a functionally democratic and Christian context. There were no textbooks, just assigned readings from various works looking to help students form a Christian philosophy that would synthesize religion and science.[61]

In his first essay, Nixon described his parents, somewhat unfairly from what we know about them, calling them "fundamental Quakers," grounding him, with the aid of his church, in "all the fundamental ideas in their strictest interpretation[:] The infallibility and literal correctness of the bible, the miracles, even the whale [sic] story." At the beginning of the second semester, half way through the course, Nixon finally confessed that he had entered this study "practically a fundamentalist" too; the only thing he hazarded a doubt about then was the "absolute infallibility of the bible." Despite admonishments to beware college professors "too liberal in their views," he had watched as many of his childhood ideas had been "destroyed" while he was at Quaker Whittier. He might surrender notions of human depravity and predestination, but he could not give up the idea of God, the first cause, who somehow, he wanted to affirm, directed the destiny of the cosmos. What he still sought was to "find my place in life." Such sentiments must have warmed the heart of his modernist professor, even as it offers insights into Nixon as pretty much adrift when it came to a personal religious anchoring in 1933. He did hope that his studies in philosophy during the year would offer more direction than the mishmash "absurd collection of science, religion and philosophy that I now have!"[62]

Dean Coffin not only lectured in class, but he also assigned extensive outside reading to help the students formulate their essays. Two weeks later, on October 23, Nixon waded into the evolution debate. He did not reject gradual development—one wonders if any of the students did—but he insisted that evolution would not destroy one's belief in God if one "accepts God as the great power behind all creation and development." Humans were greater than animals, said the young man, as he took a swipe at behaviorists who would reduce people to the level of their responses to the physical world around them. A month later, November 29, he delved into the human soul, a subject special to Dean Coffin, a topic that led Nixon to exclaim that his own religious beliefs were "surprisingly strong for a college student."[63]

After Christmas, in January, Nixon reminded his professor that he had entered the course "practically a fundamentalist," but all he could now safely say about God was that the divinity was the "first cause, the great mover," who created the world over time and by some evolutionary process. He made this aspect of his faith sound almost Unitarian. He believed "in the philosophy of Christ. . . . I have gained an immeasurable amount of tolerance, because I have learned that men make mistakes because they are striving for something better." But Nixon, probably prodded by his professor, could not escape fundamentalism and returned to it repeatedly. He had been warned since early childhood, he confessed in March 1934, against the allures of science that deceived people and enticed them away from believing what was in the Bible. Almost as early he had learned that the Bible was "not *one* perfect book," and no amount of fundamentalist logic could make him believe it was. Yet he turned again to the anchor that had proved firmer than either science or logic: that God existed, a fact he finally rested on his faith that God was the creative force "forever driving men onward in an *evolutionary* realization of higher values." If human beings reverted to a more primitive level of behavior, then they had sinned.[64]

What was more strikingly contrary to strict fundamentalism or even evangelical Quakerism was Nixon's failure even to allude to a substitutionary role for Christ's death on the cross. He agreed that Jesus was the son of God, reaching "the highest conception of God and of value that the world has ever seen." His perfect life mingled his soul with God's, and he taught a philosophy that revealed these values to human beings. Without mentioning it—perhaps without even knowing it, for there seems to have been little relating specifically to Quakerism within this course—he had come to a central feature of traditional, but not evangelical, Quakerism: "The important fact is that Jesus lived and taught a life so perfect that he continued to live and grow after his death—in the hearts of men." Nixon believed in Christ's resurrection, not as a victory over death, "but symbolically it teaches the great lesson that men who achieve the highest values in their lives may gain immortality."[65] We may not know what Paul Rader preached specifically in his crusade nearly eight years before, the exact wording that moved young Nixon to go to the front and grasp the evangelist's hand, but we can be sure that it was not something as abstract and personally meaningless as that bloodless formulation.

Yet our senior Nixon could go on and flagellate the church for rejecting Christ, fighting over the meanings of words, quibbling over doctrine, while blessing wars and an economic and social order that had brought depression—a word he did not use.[66] There is no evidence that Jessamyn West read his essays, but if she had, she would have thought of cousin Richard's father, Frank. She went to his Sunday school class, the one that was so popular with the teenagers that it had to be moved out of a room and onto the larger platform where during church services the preacher and choir performed. She considered him an excellent Sunday school teacher, in fact, one of the best teachers she had ever had at any level, including at Whittier College. His cheeks red, his voice trembling with emotion, Frank Nixon flayed away at the injustice of the status quo, so much so that West concluded that his sense of probity "pointed, as far as I was concerned, straight to Norman Thomas," the fire-breathing six-time Socialist candidate for president. And son Richard, she said, had learned at his father's knee: in the second grade at age seven he instructed a group of his fellow students on which candidate was the best. One of them, Rusty, not comprehending, asked her later where young Richard could have gotten such strange notions, strange at least for a seven-year-old. Why, "Frank, of course," she knew.[67]

Nixon—the son, not the father, a died-in-the-wool Republican—proceeded to castigate those who took America to war in 1917, yet he applauded the president who presided over that war, Woodrow Wilson, a Democrat. Wilson, Nixon insisted, held up ideals of world peace and friendship that suggested that every soldier's death was a step toward those goals. Nixon wanted to see what he called "the kingdom concept" in human hearts, then armaments, racial hatred, and the walls between people would disappear.

In his final essay, Nixon admitted that he had "not resisted the heresies of college professors" and consequently was "no longer a fundamentalist." "Through studying the religion of Jesus I have become a believer in social, political, and economic democracy." We cannot know exactly what Nixon meant by these words, but, taken as they read, they indicate he had moved, probably without knowing it, quite close to what might be called a "liberal Quaker" position. He was disgusted with politics as they had always been, as well as with diplomacy and the legal system. Nixon the politician-to-be was still practical: "Yet I feel that it is necessary that we use these methods at least for the time being." He had to live within this system regardless of his future profession, a bit of sleight of hand if there ever was one, for he knew as he wrote that he was going to Duke Law School that fall. He was, however, still affirming that he wanted to apply his understanding of the "religion of Jesus" to his life. Demonstrating that he understood the contradictions between his stated religious views and the practicalities of life,

Nixon more aptly thought his essay should have been entitled, "What shall I do with the religion of Jesus?"[68]

Giving his words their clear meaning, we can surely believe Nixon when he said that he was no longer a fundamentalist, if he had in fact ever been one except for rhetorical purposes. We can also appreciate the contradictions between his religious convictions, as he stated them, and the need to make a success of it in the larger world. What is astounding, however, is how abstract, theoretical, even un-Quakerly, it all was. Nixon's words convey almost no passion, not a strong sense of commitment, certainly not the commitment that might be expected of a Paul Rader convert, not the desire of a Quaker youth to live a life of faithfulness in a corrupt world. If his words are taken as a standard, he was not a fundamentalist. He was willing to entertain utopian ideals, true enough, but there is no indication that he was willing to die—or even live—for them. The adjectives that spring to mind are "conventional" and "bourgeois," perhaps more generously "well-rounded" and "thoughtful." Nothing suggested Nixon could rise above what was expected of an honors graduate of any comparable liberal arts college, not to mention a Quaker one with an innovative curriculum.

Cousin Jessamyn West, nearly forty years later and before Watergate, offered a kind of capstone summation of Nixon's life to that time. She did not find any kind of great depth in his Quaker faith, true enough, but she knew *something* was there nonetheless, if for no other reason than that she experienced much the same thing he did in the same town in the same church. The two—she and the interviewer—were about to explore whether a Quaker could be commander-in-chief of the armed forces as the U.S. Constitution defined one of the roles of president. "And furthermore," she said, "I think [it is] likely impossible for someone who had the training and example of his mother, his father, my father [who had taught Nixon in the East Whittier Friends Church Sunday school], or who heard, day in and day out, what we heard, for him not to have deep inside him a very Quakerish core." She doubted that the American electorate would ever choose one she called a "totally-practicing" Friend to be president; instead they would select someone, she implied, like cousin Richard.[69]

Though for all this second guessing, it is necessary to admit that Richard Nixon's convictions, as described both in his essays and seen in his life, fail to suggest that he had the religious grounding to face successfully the world that would unfold before him. His religious views marked him as totally conventional and banal. Perhaps the same thing could be said for most college graduates. In fact few students as young as twenty-one, by definition, have had to face life outside the sheltered environs of academe. Each amounted mostly to an act-in-waiting, a possibility yet to be. But Nixon's intensive Quaker upbringing, his conversion at age thirteen—even if it took almost forty years for him to mentioned it publicly—and a college education designed purposely to give him a secure grounding in the Christian faith, should have provided him a major edge. Perhaps it would, but the observer would only know as time went on and the vicissitudes of life caused the young man to respond.

In his *Memoirs*, written forty-four years later, Nixon looked back and summed up his thinking as he recalled it at the time of his graduation. Interestingly, he did not refer to his religious training at all, detailing instead the "populist elements" of his father's politics, the "Progressive influence" from his history professor, the "iconoclasm" of his drama instructor Albert Upton, and what he labeled the "Christian humanism" of Dean Coffin. These all gave him, he recalled, "a very liberal, almost populist, tinge."[70] In another context he remarked on what he supposed was Upton's agnosticism, but he followed the drama professor's advice to dig into the works of Russian author Leo Tolstoy; one summer he read nearly everything the novelist had written, becoming practically a Tolstoyan interested in peace and good will for all.[71] That he neglected religious influences, except Coffin's Christian humanism, which was more rational—what the earliest Friends would have dismissed as "notional"—may be illustrative of the lack of real impact his faith had on him. Or it may reflect where the aging former president honestly placed religious authority in his life. Or again it may simply have displayed his assumption that his readers would be more interested in a politician's political evolution than in whatever role religion might play. When he wrote those words he had been, when all was said and done, an active politician much longer than he had been actively religious.

It was certainly more "rational" for a political figure to see religion, even his own personal faith, as a kind of "sideshow" to the main event. Throughout recorded human history, men and women have been impelled by their religious convictions to perform acts, good or bad, uplifting or degrading, meritorious or demeaning, that could hardly be called "rational." When such acts are seen by their fellow human beings as worthy of emulation, the actors are labeled "saints"; when the opposite, they are named sinners, hypocrites, or worse, monsters. Hence Nixon's mother, Hannah, was regarded as a saint by those who knew her, Nixon himself as far, far less, when measured on the same scale. Having graduated in 1934 from a Quaker college, he now faced the possibility of building his own life and leaving his own legacy.

3

A Pivotal Decision:
Nixon and the Military

Quakers have formally opposed war and advised Friends to refuse to use outward weapons since 1661. Yet individual Quakers have ignored this counsel and fought in every war since then. During the first two centuries of their history, the usual response of meetings to those who violated this testimony was to disown or "read the member out of meeting," meaning that he might attend Quaker worship but could not contribute to the group or take part in business meetings.[1] After the American Civil War, when hundreds of Quaker young men chose to go to war against slavery rather than claim exemption, the tradition of disownment for participating in military service was weakened; gradually, over the years, it disappeared. By the time of American entry into World War II when Richard Nixon was twenty-eight years old, the choice of fighting was a matter for the individual, who was expected to consult his conscience and make a decision based on his own judgment. Still, the disciplines advised young Friends to reject military service.

Chicago Quaker Paul Douglas, almost fifty years old in 1941, when the United States formally joined the fight against the Japanese and their European Nazi allies, decided to join the marines as a private. A member of Fifty-seventh Street meeting, Douglas informed his fellow Quakers of his intentions and offered to resign his membership or accept their discipline, even disownment. The meeting refused to adopt either of these courses and asked Douglas to remain. What makes Douglas relevant to our account here was that he became a United States Senator from Illinois in 1948—two years before Nixon joined that body—and continued there until 1966.[2] His decision illustrated how another prominent politician, with the concurrence of his meeting, balanced his membership with what he believed was his responsibility to his country.

In contrast, commenting in *Life* magazine nearly three decades later on his February 1942 decision to join the navy rather than submit to the draft,

Richard Nixon claimed that the idea of asking for an exemption from military service as a conscientious objector "never crossed my mind."[3] Nor did it cross his mind when he wrote his first memoir, *Six Crises*, in 1962. There is not one word in the book about this major break with his religious tradition.[4]

It was the one most momentous religious decision that the young Nixon was called to make during his lifetime, but, astonishingly, he claimed that the possibility of asking for exemption never occurred to him. If his claim in 1970 was truthful, he was not even tempted to weigh his Quaker heritage seriously and seek conscientious objector status. Of course thirty years was a long time, and Nixon had risen from small town lawyer to president of the United States and commander-in-chief of the armed forces, engaged in a bitter war in southeast Asia. As a successful politician, he knew almost instinctively that admitting he had ever considered claiming the right to object on Christian grounds to participation in war could be anathema at the polls. There exists no contemporary evidence to affirm or refute his decades-old recollection, but one thing is clear: what might cross another's mind is always indiscernible, either the next day or in thirty years.

Richard Nixon had reached the pinnacle of American power by 1970, yet he continued to value his Quaker heritage. Friends often admonish one another and themselves to be alert to the promptings of love and truth in their hearts lest they miss God's call. As we saw in his essays as a Whittier College senior, Nixon had sensed such movements and had come down in support of his religious tradition. Yet on December 7, 1941, the Japanese navy treacherously attacked American military facilities at Pearl Harbor, Hawaii, and a new era opened. Nothing from that period survived to allow us to see what Nixon's immediate reaction was, but we do know that within two months he volunteered for the United States Navy and left his Quaker testimonies behind as he sailed away to the South Pacific theater.

In his decision Nixon failed to reach the moral plateau that his cousin Jessamyn West etched out for their common ancestor in her novel *The Friendly Persuasion,* as discussed in the previous chapter. Depicting the Milhous clan before they moved westward to California from southern Indiana, the movie script called for the hero Jesse Birdwell (played by Gary Cooper), carrying a rifle, to be threatened by a Confederate raider. Two of Hollywood's acclaimed directors, William Wyler, who directed West's movie, and John Huston, who had read the script, thought that Cooper, a Quaker above all, should not be shown even handling a rifle.

This discussion angered West, employed as a technical advisor on the film project, and she put her foot down firmly at this possibility of changing her vision. "Jess is a good man," she coached Wyler, "but a man with a flaw. He must be tempted to violence; and we must see him tempted," see, in other words, if he would follow the course he knew in his gut was right. She insisted that what Wyler and Huston, both of whom she respected, had missed was that Quakers were not "rule-followers"; merely obeying some human-made rule against violence, however hallowed and lofty, amounted to imitating someone else's standard. That, she was convinced, would remove the moral content from Jess's decision to do what God had led him to know he must do—refrain from killing another human being even at the risk of his own life.[5] The divinely endowed but human Nixon failed to heed similar promptings of love and truth in his heart. With other priorities, he chose not to be like his fictional relative Jess Birdwell.

Yet the promptings still came every once in a while over the years. "I don't want to kill anybody," Nixon cried aloud one day in December 1941, "why do we have to have wars?"[6] Nor, once he enlisted, did he like the military or its routine or its standardization, realizing that he was not working toward "any future goal." He admitted after five weeks in the navy that he had met some fine men of his age, but his wife made the family aware that military life did not appeal to him.[7] Later, after becoming president, he came to agree with near-pacifist author H. G. Wells that the military mind was by definition mediocre because no one with a whit of intellectual talent would willingly submit to the military regimen.[8]

Nixon had already decided to go into politics[9]—his advisor at Duke told him that if he wanted a political career he should go back home rather than moving to New York to make lots of money.[10] He realized that claiming conscientious objector exemption could very well interfere with being elected. Of course, he could not make such a statement publicly, lest he be seen as out-and-out repudiating his religious faith. When most other young men were joining in an extremely patriotic conflict, one that seemed to have been forced on the nation, opting out would redound to any politician's disadvantage. Nixon did not run for office immediately after finishing law school, true enough, but he certainly built a presence in the Whittier-La Habra communities, speaking to almost any civic club that would invite him and becoming city attorney in La Habra and the assistant in Whittier. Such activities would certainly make his name known and assist him in any future campaign. Rumors circulated in early 1940 that he was going to vie for a seat in the state assembly if the Republican Quaker incumbent decided not to run.[11]

In fact, Herman Perry, the Republican power broker who recruited him for Congress in 1946, pushed him to run for the safe Republican seat in the state assembly, when it appeared the incumbent would not enter the race.[12]

Later he calculated his "political lifetime" as having begun in the Roosevelt years.[13] He pursued his options with typical Nixon-style circumspection, only casually mentioning to his wife in 1941 the possibility of running for the assembly; he did confide to her, again in general terms but ones she remembered later, that one of the main reasons he had moved back to Whittier was to heed the advice of his Duke professor.[14]

As a member of one of the "historic peace churches," Nixon had four options under the law. (Perhaps, though a lawyer, he did not know or care to examine the range of legal choices available to him.) He could allow himself to be drafted and serve in the ranks as the overwhelming number of Americans young men did—and as a clear majority of Quaker men did. (A report presented to the Quaker American Friends Service Committee in 1947 found that nearly 60 percent of young Quakers from 750 meetings served in the military during World War II; only 26 percent claimed the pacifist position, nearly half of those were deferred for farm work or were deemed physically unsuitable for active duty.)[15] To take this route, however, would be contrary to the formal position that the Religious Society of Friends, the Christian group of which he was apart, had taught and encouraged its young men to choose since its beginnings in the mid-seventeenth century. Quakers, the name by which Friends were commonly known, had a long tradition of stressing their peculiarity, their differences, from their fellow citizens, especially when it involved military service.

The other three options were variants of opposition to the military. Nixon's lifelong membership in East Whittier Friends Church in Whittier, California, would allow him to ask for noncombatant service, that is, being drafted but not being forced to carry weapons or be armed, and serving as a medical corpsman. Or he could ask for what was known as alternative service. Such a request would grant him the right to serve in a Civilian Public Service camp overseen by various religious organizations, such as the American Friends Service Committee, and work as a firefighter in national parks, an orderly in a mental institution, or perform similar work of national importance. The third option, taken by relatively few men, involved resisting the draft system entirely and, having openly violated the law, being sentenced to prison.

The *Discipline* of California Yearly Meeting, of which East Whittier Friends Church was a part, was unambiguous at the time of member Richard Nixon's decision to enlist: "We feel bound explicitly to avow our unshaken persuasion that all war is utterly incompatible with the plain precepts of our divine Lord and Law-giver, and the whole spirit of His gospel, and that no plea of necessity or policy, however urgent or peculiar, can avail to release individuals or nations from the paramount allegiance to

Him who hath said, 'Love your enemies.'" Its section of queries, questions that aimed to guide members in their decisions on matters of how their faith related to their practice, was likewise clear: "Do you endeavor to make clear to all whom you can influence and especially our youth that war is utterly un-Christian and cannot be reconciled with the spirit of Christ?"[16] When Nixon told his interviewer nearly thirty years later that the matter of asking for an exemption from military service never crossed his mind, he was certainly suggesting that he had not considered this query and the implications it had for his life. About the only reasonable conclusion to draw was that he had excluded his Quaker heritage and teaching from his mind.

After graduating from Whittier College in June 1934 and enrolling in the fall at Duke Law School in Durham, North Carolina, Nixon did not have to consider the question of war. The nation might be suffering the worst depression in its history, but it was at peace—and not an uneasy peace either. The widespread reassessment of American involvement in the Great War in 1917 made another draft almost inconceivable at the time. Any more foreign adventures ran sharply counter to popular sentiment. Showing how commonplace these views were, Nixon gave voice to them in one of his Whittier College senior essays: War, he wrote as he looked back to 1917 and 1918, "has always seemed to be the most insane of man's many vices. . . . The glory of war, patriotism, heroism, bravery and a hundred other virtues call us away from what we know is right."[17] These sentiments came near to echoing, consciously or not, the misgivings and prohibitions of California Yearly Meeting's *Discipline* regarding war. Friend Nixon had apparently forgotten the views he expressed in his essay.

Almost forty years after he wrote those words, in a conversation with Jessamyn West on Air Force One as they flew back to the United States from visiting the Milhous last home in seventeenth-century Ireland, Nixon reflected on patriotism in a way that suggested his maturity had caused him to reevaluate his collegiate views on patriotism. Here, thousands of feet above the autumnal Atlantic, the conversation between the president and his Democratic cousin—West had not voted for her kinsman in 1960 but for Kennedy—the conversation turned to patriotism. West quoted British novelist E. M. Forster's famous comment, "if I had to choose between betraying my country or my friend, I hope I should have the guts to betray my country."

"Forster was not in a position to be called upon to betray his country," the president responded. Was Nixon suggesting that he was?

West asked, "If Forster had been President, you think he wouldn't have said that?"

Without a moment's hesitation, Nixon came back empathetically, "I think he shouldn't have."

West did not ask Nixon whether he had himself faced that dilemma, but after a minute or two in which he looked out the plane's window, down toward the invisible swirling sea, she related that Nixon said in a calm voice, without complaining or asking for pity, as simply as stating a fact, "I haven't a friend in the world." Was Richard suggesting, she thought to herself, that he could avoid Forster's problem by not having any friends? So she mentioned two or three men whom she supposed were close to the president. "Companions," he countered, causally dismissing her choices.[18] The entire incident was poignant and telling, the kind of revealing conversation this particular president normally studiously avoided.

West was a keen and straight-eyed observer of her cousin and of her own Milhous family. In a revealing oral history interview conducted in 1971, she threw light on the Milhous Quaker heritage and the less-often-commented-upon contributions of his father to Richard's make-up. Many Friends tend to exhibit retiring, even introverted, personalities—not the kind that normally produced politicians—a fact that West drew upon as she reflected on her cousin, who, she thought, trusted her and could be "quite funny, quite open," with her. Her grandfather Jesse Milhous was the typical kind of Quaker who never took a chance, never stepped out of line, never tried anything new, always followed the received straight and narrow. But Richard's father, Frank Nixon, bequeathed him the kind of genes—"of openness and optimism and belief and willingness to take a chance and make a new move that a President would need"—that overrode those from his mother's line. The Milhouses produced "plenty of character and steadiness and intelligence," but not having the get-up-and-go from the Nixons was like "having a warhead without anything to propel it."[19] But West went on to say that she did not think that a "totally practicing Quaker" could possibly be elected to serve as commander-in-chief. She speculated that a black or a woman would win the White House before a real Quaker.[20]

While at Duke, Nixon gave some attention to his religious life, enough to leave the impression with a fellow student that he was a "quiet little Quaker boy."[21] No Quakers gathered in Durham, which except for Duke University was pretty much a working-class town devoted to refining tobacco products; the closest meeting was in Raleigh, the state capital, more than twenty miles away. One classmate remembered that the Californian went regularly on Sundays either to the Raleigh Friends gathering or to Duke Chapel.[22] Raleigh Quakers had joined with two other small groups, the Congregationalists and Christians, to form a United Church, whose minister sympathized with Quaker testimonies and conducted worship services that generally reflected the simplicity of Friends programmed worship, but the distance to Raleigh made it unlikely that Nixon attended very often, if at all; certainly the Quaker dean of Duke's chapel and the Divinity School, who did join the United Church, almost never made it to Raleigh.

The dean of the newly built (in 1932) soaring Gothic chapel was the scholar, social activist, and historian Elbert Russell, who was quite controversial in evangelical Quaker circles. No evidence exists that he and Nixon ever encountered each other.[23] In fact, though he appreciated the architecture and atmosphere in the chapel, Nixon confessed that he did not go often and "didn't get much out of the service" when he did attend. Still, Nixon was impressed enough with two of the sermons he heard that he kept sketchy notes of their content.[24] He did claim in one of his memoirs, undoubtedly erroneously, that he went "every Sunday to the magnificent Duke chapel" to hear either Russell or the Methodist minister with whom Russell alternated services.[25]

Nixon recollected later that he found the racial segregation in working-class Durham off-putting, even immoral, but there is no contemporary evidence of this sentiment if it existed at all. He claimed no memory of either of the regular speakers at Sunday services in the chapel having mentioned race—not much of a surprise in 1930s depression-era Durham. The only time he saw African Americans was on the rare occasions when he was downtown and watching the workers at shift-changing time streaming out of the cigarette factories on their way home and separating by race on either side of the street. No one regarded blacks as individuals, only as members of a despised racial group. A former classmate remembered that Nixon did not remain silent in the face of such discrimination and condemned it in terms strong enough to cause some of his southern fellow students to refuse to talk to him about such matters.[26]

Upon graduation in 1937, Nixon returned to his hometown, studied for the California bar examination, and took a job with a local Quaker-founded and -dominated law firm. His mother had visited the office of Wingert and Bewley in April or May to see if they needed an additional lawyer. When Nixon came in for an interview, he mentioned going into politics. After being hired, he often commented on political developments or national and international problems.[27] He resumed the religious activities that had marked his life before going away to law school but with some differences: befitting his new status as a professional in the small community, he occasionally attended the prestigious First Friends Church of Whittier, even sometimes going early enough to participate in Sunday school there.[28] He still taught a Sunday school class once in a while at East Whittier; on February 27, 1938, his pupils met early for their Bible lecture, and then they trooped off to the mountains to see the late-season snowfall.[29] He attended some Friday evening meetings of the Men's Brotherhood, as well as serving on various committees, but the very sparse records indicate little of what he was saying or hearing. Just his attendance, though, made him an active and energetic member of his church.[30] Notes for a talk on "The American Way" to the church's Brotherhood that attracted fifty-one auditors in February 1938 had him lamenting that religion was "no longer so strong" and included a notation that he would address "Quakers—War." Under the heading "War," he planned to say, "Truth was the first casualty," a sentiment echoing what he had written in his senior essays in college.[31] The following year he explored how to get more men to attend church.[32]

Nixon's membership in East Whittier Friends Church did not mean that it would be the venue of his marriage to Thelma Catherine (Patricia) Ryan, the schoolteacher he met in Whittier at a play tryout in February 1938. One scholar described her as an "agnostic"; that Nixon was surprised to discover this vital detail more than two years later as they planned their wedding suggests that religious beliefs were not something the two lovers had found important enough to discuss before becoming engaged.[33] Another biographer said that as a not particularly religious child she occasionally attended a Christian Science Church.[34] The groom-to-be had his eye set somewhat higher than his own small modest wood-frame church overlooking Whittier Boulevard, namely the presidential suite at the Mission Inn in Riverside, about forty miles eastward. The afternoon wedding on June 21, 1940, was itself small, with mostly close family members present. Garry Wills, Nixon's most acerbic critic who actually visited the site, derided it as the kind of "fluff" that a person with no style and no commitments would choose for a wedding.[35] But Nixon boasted enough class or clout among local Quaker worthies that Whittier College president and Quaker minister Orville Mendenhall consented to preside over the brief ceremony.[36] Until his marriage he lived at home.[37]

All in all, the few records remaining of his personal life sound as though the young professional was finding his way in the world without the need for deep religious obligations. His daughter Julie related the story of a party the newlyweds had when a visiting Duke graduate and his wife went with them to a fancy nightclub in Los Angeles. The club advertised that its floorshow included "the most beautiful girls in the world," and the men were invited to see which one could toss the most garters onto the outstretched legs of the cancan dancers. (How the garters were supposed to stay on their legs remains unclear; perhaps a dancer would catch one with a foot and then pull it up by hand.) Richard Nixon, it turned out, was "the most agile garter tosser" in the club and won a bottle of champagne for his table.[38] The future president probably did not spread word of this feat around the plain wooden East Whittier Friends Church, although it might have been heartily appreciated uptown at the more urbane brick First Friends.

A year and a half after the Nixons were married, the Japanese bombed Pearl Harbor, an attack that led America to enter World War II. More than a year before this, Congress had created Selective Service to oversee the first peacetime draft in the country's history. This development did not turn East Whittier Church into a beehive of Quaker antiwar activity, but its leadership, sparked by the pastor, did organize a meeting for men of draft age in the congregation to discuss conscientious objection. The denomination's monthly paper also suggested that young men should write the AFSC for a booklet on their options in being guided by their "Christian consciences."[39] How such proposals affected Nixon we do not know—he was certainly in the correct age range—for he left few contemporary records of his sentiments about the war or his reason for volunteering for the navy. He did keep up with the news. There is one story that after the war began in Europe in September 1939, he remarked to his parents that the United States would be drawn in. On another occasion, reading the newspaper in his law office, he said out loud to no one in particular, "I've surely met a lot of the blue-eyed German types I'd hate to have to shoot."[40]

What Nixon wanted to reveal came in his memoirs, published in 1978, after he had left the White House. In December 1941, after Pearl Harbor and through the efforts of one of his Duke professors, he got the offer of a job in Washington with the Office of Price Administration. The salary was lower than the combined salary of the two Nixons, but the offer would allow him to "observe the working of the government firsthand," a rationale that suggested he had been considering some kind of political career at the national level. (This intention was reinforced when the periodical of Orthodox Quakers lent national prominence to his employment "for the duration.")[41] Working for such a crucial agency on the home front would enable him to avoid compromising his Quaker principles yet contribute to the war effort, or that's what he speculated his mother believed about his and Pat's moving across the country. It was clear that when he wrote he understood how the war undercut his family's adherence to a central testimony of their faith.

He spent about eight months on his new job. Typical of his tendency to dissemble a bit in his memoirs, Nixon remembered that "[m]any men in OPA were able to get draft deferments and spend the war in their offices. Despite my Quaker background and beliefs, I never considered doing this." An honest Quaker, he implied, could never do such a thing. He thus was able to occupy the high ground, while implying that he was more principled than his fellow OPA workers who stayed behind to work at their desks. Instead he took advantage of the fact that the navy was recruiting lawyers and commissioning them as officers, and so he enlisted in February 1942 and went for officer's training to Quonset Point, Rhode Island, in August; now he would not have to be drafted into the army as a buck private.[42] Even after he signed up, it was not clear that his heart was entirely in it. He wrote home in March that he had been out with FBI "boys" and navy fliers and soldiers. "All are willing to do their part, none are thrilled about it, and all are convinced that the big boys are going to have to come along too. It seems that the old 'college try' just isn't there this time."[43]

Nixon told one of his first biographers that he decided to enlist in the navy because of his conviction "that the fate of all mankind was involved in the last war, and not only that of religion." Despite the strength of this conviction, he insisted that he had not forgotten the religious training from his parents and grandparents; he had decided only to choose differently because the "fate of all mankind" in World War II trumped that training. Patricia Nixon confided to the same interviewer that her husband had done "much soul-searching" about the matter, but Nixon himself never referred to any kind of momentous struggle.[44] Much later, in a memoir, he justified his decision by noting that Quaker pacifism might work fine with a "civilized, compassionate enemy" but not ones like the German Nazi leader Adolph Hitler and Japanese premier Hideki Tojo in World War II.[45] He did tell one interviewer, for a Youth for Christ publication in 1957, that following his decision, he made a long-distance telephone call to his mother and told her, "I've come to a serious decision. I've decided to join the Navy." Hannah Nixon accepted her son's decision with no more comment than, "God gave you your life to live as you understand the truth—."[46]

Truth be told, Nixon had few role models either within his family or his Quaker church for requesting exemption and asserting the supremacy of conscience over government demands. His uncle, Oscar Marshburn, had gone to France during World War I under the auspices of the American Friends Service Committee and worked with the Red Cross, but nearly all western Quakers had already distanced themselves from that Quaker group as too left-leaning.[47] California Quakers of the evangelical stripe simply did not emphasize that aspect of their centuries-old version of Christianity. East Whittier Friends Church's young minister in 1941 did register as a conscientious objector—apparently the only member to do so—but he already enjoyed a ministerial exemption. As a Nixon cousin told an interviewer several years after the war, "I don't specifically remember anybody in the family being a conscientious objector." He admitted that this situation was "unusual since we were all Quakers," but that was the way it was among these evangelical Quakers, and everyone accepted it as a matter of course. Few objectors were members at East Whittier Friends Church or even First Friends Church of Whittier, both of which practiced freedom of thought and allowed the utmost tolerance for individual decisions. Still there was a lingering animosity toward Quakers for their historic testimony: at least one person did not attend East Whittier Church because he did not want to be associated with a group that even vaguely allowed conscientious objection.[48]

Throughout his life, Nixon liked to emphasize that he made decisions because they were right and comported well with his sense of values rather than because they were popular. For example, when interviewed by a committed supporter, a Jewish rabbi no less, only months before he resigned the presidency in 1974, he explained that he had often been near the center of controversy during his career: "I would be fighting for and talking for what I believed was right. And consequently, I attracted opposition, as any individual does who stands up for unpopular positions, what may be unpopular, but which later may turn out to be right and popular."[49] In this vitally important instance, Nixon's assessment of what was right did not include giving much thought to how his volunteering for the navy might conflict with his Quaker heritage.

Nixon's decision, made with no indication that his religious convictions had any impact on it, illustrated the curious disconnect that existed between religion and life (or "faith and practice" as Quakers usually phrased it) within the Nixon family—indeed, among too many Friends more generally, especially among evangelicals in the West or even the quiet Quakers of the East. To a favored interviewer, Hannah Nixon explained that she had not tried to impose her views on her young son about becoming a minister. Instead Quakers, she went on, favored counseling or the use of what they called "advices." They "are gentle and tolerant people, but they are also stubborn in defending their opinions and high-minded in pursuing their ideals." Nixon told the same interviewer in the late 1950s when he was vice president that "there isn't any question that my Quaker background, in which I was thoroughly indoctrinated in my early years, has had a very great effect on my outlook on life."[50]

For all of this, however, that Nixon, by his own admission, had not allowed the idea of becoming a conscientious objector to disturb his thinking demonstrated that his outlook on life had not affected the question of whether he should join the armed forces or not. It was as though he could have an "outlook"—or, in his mother's phrasing, consider an "advice"—rooted in the Quaker faith, that would have no impact on a decision to enter the navy, a move violating the very essence of that faith. In religious terms an "outlook" uninformed by one's religious faith and commitments was hardly to be trusted; or a "conscience" untaught by one's religious tradition and teachings did not produce, in Quaker terms, the kind of "leading" that should be followed.

To adopt Hannah and Richard's explanation of their faith was to reside in a never-never land in which words lost their meaning and religious faith was removed to the sidelines where it made no difference. To illustrate, let us consider an incident thirty years in the future after Nixon had become president. As commander-in-chief of the army and navy, Nixon in the early 1970s unleashed an unprecedented secret bombing campaign against Laos, a country with which the United States was not at war. He had decided that this was a way of preventing the movement of supplies and men to the insurgency into South Vietnam. When commenting on his action in March 1971, Nixon frankly told *New York Times* staffer C. L. Sulzberger, "I rate myself a deeply committed pacifist, perhaps because of my Quaker heritage from my mother. But I must deal with how peace can be achieved and how it must be preserved."[51] If words mean anything, it seems impossible for a "pacifist" with a Quaker heritage to order and oversee the bombing of innocent people, even if the goal was to achieve peace and preserve it. A looming abyss separated "outlook" from practice here.

It was just such dilemmas as the ones Hannah and Richard Nixon grasped that had led Friends historically to forsake public office and politics. The compromises required of officeholders and politicians were simply too much for all but a few Quakers to tolerate, and the higher the office, the greater the likelihood of having to countenance too many compromises. The most dramatic example of this tendency was the 1756 decision of Quaker legislators to resign from the Pennsylvania Assembly rather than impose taxes for fighting the French and Indian War.[52] But unlike the Amish, with whom they were sometimes grouped in the public eye, Friends never eschewed total political involvement: not all voted, true enough, but many did, and all tried to influence public officials to do what was right. Following the resignation of the Pennsylvania assemblymen Quakers were reluctant to stand for public office, especially national ones. Notable exceptions to this stricture were Herbert Hoover and Richard Nixon, both of whom were elected to the presidency, neither reluctantly. Accepting conscientious objector exemption might be permissible, even a benefit, for a Quaker attorney in a small town dominated by them, but for a person with wider political aspirations it was death itself. Four years later, Nixon underscored his perception of this reality when he commented to a political supporter that the local congressman, against whom he was being touted as a candidate, would be hurt by his lack of a military record.[53]

Her son's decision left Hannah, as well as the rest of the family, "troubled," at least that is the way Julie Nixon Eisenhower reported it. Hannah's brother-in-law, also a Quaker, would become director of one of the Civilian Service Camps for conscientious objectors in Oregon, demonstrating that there were ways to serve the country other than joining the military.[54] Her son had not chosen this route, one more consistent with Quaker faith and training. Years later, Nixon told a sympathetic interviewer that both Hannah and his grandmother cried when he went to war;[55] during his presidential campaign in 1960 he related to an audience that both were "very much opposed" when he volunteered for the armed forces.[56] Hannah may have cried privately or when only other close family members were present, but she kept her emotions under control when the family saw Nixon off at the Los Angeles train station for his naval service. It was the emotional Frank Nixon, less controlled than his wife and clearly touched by his Quaker son's leaving, who wept visible tears on that occasion.[57]

Publicly, Hannah always put a good face on Richard's decision. "Though I am a pacifist," she wrote in a national women's magazine in the midst of the 1960s presidential campaign, "I didn't try to stop him."[58] Earlier, she had directed a biographer friend that "I didn't advise Richard what to do when he decided to enlist in the Navy. He was always guided by his convictions, which I never questioned nor discouraged."[59] His mother's reasoning here coincided with Nixon's own continued insistence after he entered public life that Quakerism was private and allowed an individual, led by conscience, to make choices without referring to Christian, Quaker, or scriptural traditions. As we have seen, this position may have been convenient for a politician, but for a Quaker it had numerous problems. Another Friend, Nixon's law partner Tom Bewley, put it bluntly when he reminisced more than fifteen years later: "The Quaker does not bear arms, but some of us feel that our loyalty to our country is greater than our loyalty to our church."[60]

Nixon's momentous decision marked a break with his religious tradition, one to which the Milhouses had adhered, as he told an audience in Ireland in 1970, "going back as far as we know."[61] The brave words he had inscribed about peace in his senior essays remained only on the paper he wrote on. He would not drop the Quaker language entirely. On occasion he would hearken back to parts of it as a way of limning in the secular ideals behind the words—peace, internationalism, civil rights, even free trade and globalization—but the religious faith and practice that nurtured these ideals vanished from his personal life. One Friend remembered that he and Nixon did not learn about liquor—it was hard to get in Whittier, after all—until they both went into the navy.[62] He had become as conventional as the rest of his fellow citizens because all his Quaker distinctions had evaporated. And he would still mention his Quaker heritage, tying it to his mother, but that amounted to a rhetorical flourish. It had little concrete meaning, though it might remain useful for political purposes.

Garry Wills, Nixon's most persistent, even razor-tongued yet fair, critic, did not believe that Nixon was born a liar but decided that he sacrificed whatever measure of goodness and decency he had when he decided to become a politician. "He had once, perhaps," decided Wills, "been too good to be a politician."[63] As early as 1968, interviewing Nixon as he campaigned for the Republican nomination, Wills asserted that the candidate had substituted politics for religion.[64] Wills was suggesting that Nixon had once been his mother's Quaker heir but in taking up politics had gradually become something far removed from that.

An insightful associate, Leonard Garment, who practiced law and traveled with Nixon during the mid-1960s and went to work for him once he became president, came away with the same impression. Once in Miami for a speech, the two Wall Street lawyers, carrying their leather briefcases, arrived after the midnight witching hour of their host and found the walled compound locked tight. So over the wall they climbed and found two single beds in the pool house inside. Nixon simply could not stop talking and did so until he fell asleep. Garment described their experience that night as a kind of "summer-camp confession." Until Nixon drifted off, he ruminated about numerous things, including foreign policy, and about why he had decided to go on in politics. It was not, he insisted, because of partisan rivalries or the ideological commitments surrounding domestic affairs—the things that defined conservatives like the 1964 Republican presidential candidate Senator Barry Goldwater—but because of his "pacifist mother's idealism and the profound importance of foreign policy."[65] But after deciding to commit himself to such idealism—the operative word here is not *pacifist*, let it be noted, but *idealism*—Nixon, Garment concluded, became disillusioned and realized that "success in politics usually required values quite different." So he grew contemptuous of "high-minded ideas"[66] and presumably discarded and left them behind. Even Nixon's most sympathetic and favored biographer could not avoid conscientiously remarking on his subject's "dark side in which mendacity, deviousness, and personal disloyalty could come to the fore,"[67] displaying what young associates like Garment bluntly called "the nakedness of his opportunism."

John Sears, another of the firm's youthful associates who traveled with Nixon as he prepared to run for the presidency, admitted that the senior partner came across occasionally as "a complete phony." Sears told an interviewer about a trip to New England where Nixon related to an audience some "pretty awful lies" on some substantial issues. To justify his duplicity later, Nixon told Sears, "John, I can say things that when other people say them, they are lies, but when I say them people don't believe them anyway." Sears concluded that he was dealing with a "very complicated person," but this man was more—without putting it into these words, he had rejected his mother and her values.[68]

It is impossible to document exactly when Nixon made the decision to turn his back on the idealism that he spoke to Garment about and get involved in politics; he never said. We know he decided to run for Congress in 1946 after he got out of the navy—that's a story that has been told many times. The decision, it is safe to say, was not a spur-of-the-moment thing, even if we cannot know exactly when the decision was made. He probably had been thinking about going into politics long before 1945, perhaps even as early as 1941 when he decided to pull up his Whittier stakes and move to Washington, D. C. Or perhaps those rumors in 1940 about running for the state assembly had some basis in fact.

What we do know was that in volunteering for the navy, Nixon was cutting his ties with his "Quaker heritage." Looking back on the decision later, he responded to a question as to when he realized that the modern world differed from the one in which he had been raised. "I think the war was probably the breakpoint," the mature man admitted, "I could have engaged in other activities during the war, such as my uncle and others did during World War I, Red Cross and other activities. But I just had a different attitude."[69] He directly confronted this reality in one of his memoirs. Writing of his skill at poker while serving in the South Pacific, he explained that "any kind of gambling had been anathema to me as a Quaker" in Whittier. "But the pressures of wartime, and the even more oppressive monotony, made it an irresistible diversion," clearly worth turning his back on his heritage as a Friend. His skill brought him "substantial" winnings. He described that he once beat odds of 650,000 to 1 at stud poker with an ace in the hole and a royal flush in diamonds. He not only made money, but he learned that those who bluffed usually talked loudly and long, while one who had the cards kept his counsel, a lesson that reinforced his tendency to cover-up—he maintained a "true poker face" to win.[70] The exact amount he took home remained as closely held as that royal flush, but estimates run from $3,500 to $10,000, either a princely sum.[71] But he did not fire a weapon in hostility.

Nixon did not know—could not know—what would come next, but a political career for an accomplished young lawyer was not beyond the range of possibility, particularly after he had put in his time as a naval warrior. Quaker it was not, but the stage was set for his next act.

4

Two Friends and a friend

It is not at all chance that both the Chamberses and the Hisses, arriving over very different routes, should at last have found their way into the community of Quakers.[1]

—Whittaker Chambers

Until Watergate, the most important development in Richard Nixon's public life was the 1948 controversy occasioned by Quaker and former Communist Whittaker Chambers, an editor at *Time* magazine. Chambers testified before the House Un-American Activities Committee that friend of Friends Alger Hiss had been a member of a Communist espionage ring during the 1930s when he served in the government. Friend Nixon served on that committee and spearheaded the effort to document the truth of Chambers's charges; without Nixon's persistence in championing Chambers and his allegations, it is safe to say that Hiss would have escaped conviction, for most members of the committee would just as soon have dropped the matter. It was no wonder that the story of this incident and its implications formed the leading feature of Nixon's first book, *Six Crises*.[2] The affair finally ended with Hiss's 1949 conviction for perjury after he denied that he was a Communist and gave classified documents to Chambers. Without this seminal development, Nixon would have remained just another congressman: it made him a major political figure and gave him a national reputation as an anti-Communist.

Such matters, as well as religion, were not issues or major factors in the 1946 congressional race in California's sprawling twelfth district, but Nixon's Quaker background helped assure him the support of an influential group of Whittier's Republican movers and shakers. Herman L. Perry, a birthright Quaker—things like that mattered in Whittier—manager of the local Bank of America branch and Republican activist, first suggested Nixon's name. Perry thought Nixon had all the qualifications for taking on the five-term Democratic incumbent who seemed to have a lock on the district, Horace Jerome (Jerry) Voorhis. A young veteran, reasonably well known, a good debater, a lawyer of some local repute, and a "Quaker of good stock," Nixon seemed an ideal candidate to contest with an overly confident Voorhis and put the seat in Republican hands. Perry and Nixon's old law partner, Thomas Bewley, had to first maneuver Whittier College's former president out of the running, but their task was made easy; he died from a heart attack a year before the election.

Perry took umbrage at the editor of the *American Friend* for an August 22 editorial that applauded a Voorhis resolution to deplore wasting grain. Labeling Nixon's opponent a hypocrite who appeared before church groups and then went off to Washington and supported radical causes, Perry demanded the editor back down.[3] After his candidate won the election, however, Perry backed down himself and admitted that his first letter had been "sharp"; he also insisted that Nixon "still clings to many of the traditions of the Quakers," a fact that justifies keeping an eye on the "very able and progressive young man with *high ideals*." Rather defensively, for Nixon's wartime service was a departure from the main Quaker tradition, Perry justified his man's wartime military service by pointing out that he had followed the path of "ninety percent of our Quaker boys."[4]

Such matters added nothing to the electioneering in the Golden State; they amounted to internal Quaker concerns reflecting the thinking of those inside the campaign. Thanks to California's unique primary laws, Nixon and Voorhis squared off in both Democratic and Republican primaries in June 1946—Nixon coming in about 8,000 total votes shy of his opponent— but in November's general election he proved victorious by gaining 56 percent of the ballots against Voorhis's nearly 43 percent.[5] Politics had served to pull him back to East Whittier Friends Church, for on October 8, a Tuesday, he spoke to the Men's Brotherhood there following a covered-dish supper, which wives of members also attended.[6]

Upon leaving California and its evangelical Quakers behind and entering the national stage as a member of Congress in 1947, Nixon cut whatever ties he had with the Religious Society of Friends. There were no evangelical or programmed Quaker churches in Washington, D. C., the only meeting in the capital being unprogrammed and nonpastoral. This reality had not prevented evangelical Quaker Herbert Hoover, president from 1920 to 1933, from attending regularly when he was in office; in fact, the Hoover family contributed substantially to financing the building of what was known as the Florida Avenue Friends Meeting and importuned a Stanford University professor to move east so he could occasionally minister from its facing bench.[7] Nixon did visit the Washington meetinghouse once for a midweek forum to report on an overseas trip he took as a relatively new congressman.[8] With no comment then or later to attract attention to the matter, he left his Quaker involvement behind forever.[9] Years later, in 1981, a newspaper reported that the Nixon girls occasionally attended First Day school there with their visiting grandmother while Nixon was in the House, but no contemporary account has surfaced.[10] Except on rare occasions, such as his mother's funeral at East Whittier Friends Church in 1967, when evangelist Billy Graham officiated, Nixon never again attended a Quaker gathering of any kind.[11]

Nixon could not, however, escape Quakers entirely, for they seemed to pop up, sometimes in the oddest places. The editor of the *American Friend*, the major periodical of the middle-of-the-road Five Years Meeting, dropped by for an interview with the new congressman and told his audience that he found his visit "very rewarding."[12] Nor could anyone have expected that they would be central players in one of the most dramatic and politically divisive cases of Communists in government that the Cold War produced. That they were different kinds of Friends from the new congressman from California's twelfth district made no difference in the popular mind, for nearly everyone automatically assumed that all Quakers were peaceful, always truthful, and pillars of personal integrity and rectitude. The past histories, not to mention the future careers, of the three principals called all these popular assumptions into question, but the story was never couched that way; what was involved in the Chambers charges and the Hiss denials was the question of Communism and espionage that gave the opening Cold War a dramatic and early domestic push.[13]

Whittaker Chambers, a heavy-set, slightly disheveled individual, and his entire family were members of Pipe Creek Friends Meeting, a small rural unprogrammed meeting near Union Bridge, Maryland, twelve miles from the farm that he operated in his spare time. Born in 1901 in Brooklyn, Jay Vivian Chambers was raised in Lynbrook on the south shore of Long Island in a family whose father, a newspaper graphic artist, all but deserted his wife and two sons. Grandmother Chambers came to visit them often after she moved from Philadelphia to Brooklyn and related tales of her Quaker mother to her grandson, who came to relish her stories of "plain Quaker clothing" and peaceful hilltop meetinghouses, so far removed from his suburban experience. A bookish sort, the young Chambers devoured Victor Hugo's *Les Misérables,* rereading it so many times that it doubled as his Bible; then he taught himself German and Spanish, too. When he enrolled in Columbia University in 1920, he substituted his mother's maiden surname Whittaker for Vivian, which he hated, and became his own man.

Never graduating from Columbia, Chambers got a job with the public library. On the advice of a professor he went down to Philadelphia to see if he could get an appointment as a relief worker in Russia with the American Friends Service Committee. But word arrived there that he had written a notorious if sophomoric atheist play, and the prospect of serving with the Committee evaporated immediately. He joined the Communist party at about the same time (1925) that he, unsure of his sexual orientation, began experimenting in homosexual trysts. (Chambers included more than a four-page analysis in *Witness* on why people chose to join the party; significantly, for himself he wrote simply, "I was one of those drawn to Communism by the problem of war."[14] Despite his later refusal to call himself a pacifist, a factor making him hesitate before becoming a Friend, his distaste for war may have been one of the things that made the Quaker faith attractive to him.) Soon he was a staff writer for the Communist *Daily Worker*. From about 1928 to 1932, he got involved in translating children's books, including *Bambi* from the German; before long, translating dozens of books, he was making a living in the bourgeois world and had become enough of a literary sensation to publish his own stories in the Communist *New Masses* and become the editor there. Relatively prosperous, in April 1931, he and Esther Shemitz, an artistically inclined radical, were married.

The party, though, required its members' talents in other pursuits, so Chambers was directed to go underground and essentially became a secret agent and a courier. It was in this capacity that he and Esther got to know Alger Hiss, his wife, Priscilla, and her son by her previous marriage, Timothy Hobson. According to Chambers's later testimony, they visited the Hisses in Washington quite often, the Hisses came to Baltimore to see Whittaker and Esther, who lived for a time in the Hiss apartment; they all took meals together and generally shared their lives; they were close, as close as friends. Hiss gave him copies of documents that he had taken from his office in the State Department and Priscilla Hiss had retyped, and Chambers took them to his contact in New York for shipment to Moscow. By early 1938, Chambers had decided that Communism, while it might represent the right side of history—he never totally escaped this conviction—was heinous, and he could no longer be part of it, even if he had to choose the losing side. He defected, going underground again, not for the party this time but for himself and his family of three others, a virulent anti-Communist. A year later he had a job with *Time*, and from there his career as a writer for that magazine flourished; he wrote cover stories, book reviews, all thoughtful and insightful pieces, and he became a favorite of the publisher, Henry R. Luce, himself a noted anti-Communist.

Chambers gravitated toward Quakerism after his faith in Communism disappeared. "I stand," he wrote later, "within no religious orthodoxy."[15]

Nor was he committed to pacifism. The first may have attracted him to Quakers, for those he knew were not orthodox Christians; the other made him think Quakers were not the group for him. But he found the silence of their meetings intriguing and then profoundly moving in its ability to transcend the outside world and introduce him to, as he put it, "the silence of the creature" and connect him with God. This inward experience "beyond any power of the mind" reached him and never let him wander again. In 1952 his twentieth-century classic, *Witness*, appeared. The philosopher Sidney Hook labeled it "one of the most significant autobiographies of the twentieth century" and a "minor classic in the history of religious conversions."[16] A best-seller unfortunately neglected by many because of its sometimes strident but intellectually astute anti-Communism, it was a memoir of and reflection on a meaningful life, his own. As such it fit comfortably into the mold of Quaker journals going back to the mid-seventeenth century. It was a genre that Quakers had often used successfully, including Chambers's favorite and the most famous one, the 1694 posthumously published journal of the English reformer George Fox, founder of the faith.[17]

Overlooked by most people who commented on Chambers and *Witness,* including his biographer, was the fact that his book, like those earlier Quaker journals, represented a kind of dialogue he had had with events in his life. Without his religious faith, it was impossible to understand what meaning he had extracted from life. As he confided to one longtime friend, "I am first and foremost a religious person."[18] His memoir, essentially a twentieth-century Quaker journal, amounted to more than a dried description of where he had been and what he had done. It was that, but it was more. He came to his Quakerism slowly, just as one lives a life and watches it gradually unfold, day-by-day, step-by-step, opening up and carrying him on. Conversely he integrated those steps into his life, and they informed each subsequent step he took as he went along; as his religious convictions developed, he came to understand them as informing and reminding him where he had been and what he had experienced, as well as what all of it meant in the grand scheme of things.

Chambers never entirely relinquished a cynical side of his nature, even when dealing with his Quaker faith, something of major importance to the ex-Communist. (He was lionized as a "conservative" after his defection from Communism, and conservative he was, but his political views were tempered by Quakerism.) He once shocked a "weighty" Friend—one whose spiritual insight gave added importance (or weight) to the person's views—with the idea that the prize-winning *From Here to Eternity* by army veteran James Jones, a novel about the coming of World War II, was essentially moral. Observing his auditor's surprised reaction, Chambers decided that such Quakers were so focused on the "the light [that] shines in the darkness" that they did not realize that the illumination acted to dispel a murkiness of dirt and ooze that was as natural as the light itself. Such "good, fatuous, mischief-making Quakers," he concluded, need "nothing so much as a touch of humanizing sin."[19]

Nixon, participant in an unusual symposium devoted to a single book in the literary journal *Saturday Review* in May 1952 after *Witness* first appeared, did not see this side of Chambers's memoir and misunderstood the book's significance. Nixon called it a "great book" because Chambers had made a "plea for an Anti-Communist faith" that echoed his own views, absent the religious underpinning. For the ever-serious Republican politician, Chambers was hardly more than a welcome recruit in the Cold War battles.[20] Nixon the Quaker did not notice the most important truth of *Witness*: the story it told represented the culmination of a man's search for meaning in life, a search affirming the primacy of divinity, that could touch a human being through mystical means, that had finally triumphed over his previously held secular faith of Communism and materialism. Secular intellectuals, like the liberal historian Arthur Schlesinger Jr., who led off the symposium with the longest contribution, and many of the others, were put off by such openly religious and Christian assertions, a main reason they disdained the book and found it unconvincing.

Chambers understood that Quakerism and Christianity were at their base a rejection of much of the modern world, a scandal to moderns if there ever was one. For him this was the central issue, the main question of the twentieth century, which suffuses the book much like the ink that makes the words. He saw "the original Quaker witnesses"—perhaps he selected the very title of his book from this central mission of the earliest Friends—as bequeathing the means that each "should make his own person a living testimony against the world [and] should therefore protest mutely that those things which the modern world holds dear and indispensable are at the root of its despair." There was anti-Communism here, true enough, but only because Communism was part of the fallen modern world.[21]

All this was four years into the future, a long way from August 3, 1948, when a "mystery witness" was called to the witness table at the House Committee on Un-American Activities. Whittaker Chambers was almost unknown to most of the nation when he took the oath before the committee on which Nixon served. His monotonously delivered and understated revelations would, however, presently make him famous. For all that notoriety, he never escaped what one scholar aptly described as "an unconvincing Quaker meekness with the grumpiness of the prophet without honor in his own land."[22] He charged that among others he had known when he was a member of the Communist Party cell and a courier for information stolen from the State Department was the current president of the Carnegie Endowment for International Peace and a former official in the Agriculture, Justice, and State Departments, Alger Hiss, himself little known outside elite legal, diplomatic, and intellectual circles. Hiss's relative obscurity with Americans beyond the East Coast was no more; from then on, the names Hiss and Chambers would forever be associated. (Nixon later reported that Chambers's testimony was the first time that he himself had ever heard of Hiss.)[23] Born in Baltimore in 1904, Hiss studied at Johns Hopkins University, and received a law degree from Harvard Law School; he topped off his legal education by clerking for the renowned Supreme Court Justice Oliver Wendell Holmes in 1930 and 1931. His most influential post was as Secretary-General of the United Nations Conference on International Organization, which drafted the United Nations Charter in mid-1945.

Hiss's religious commitments, if there were such, remain a mystery. He was not a Friend, although by the time of Chambers's testimony he had moved for some time in Quaker circles, enough to elicit strong support within the American Friends Service Committee, the best-known Quaker organization in the country and named as their representative to receive the Nobel Peace Prize the previous fall. He served on a committee to evaluate that organization's peace activities and occasionally spoke around the country at AFSC peace seminars, one way the group sought to expand its influence among the populace at large. Its executive secretary, Clarence Pickett, testified as a character witness for him at his second trial. Hiss's wife, Priscilla, a graduate of Bryn Mawr College, a Quaker-related institution outside Philadelphia, was much closer to Friends. After 1947 she and their infant son Tony regularly attended the Twentieth Street Meeting in New York, ironically where Chambers had first worshipped; her husband occasionally went with them. In 1953, while Alger was serving time in prison, the mother and son applied for membership in that meeting. Apparently following her wishes, she and Alger commonly used the old-fashioned Quaker plain language when they addressed each other.[24]

Coming as they did in the midst of the 1948 presidential campaign, Chambers's charges against Hiss, a Democrat like the incumbent president, were bound to rivet the nation's attention. Hiss, in his rebuttal testimony two days later, on August 5, denied everything, so each side's supporters lined up to do battle; Hiss publicly threatened to sue Chambers for libel if he repeated his statements outside the hearing, so the charges and refutations escalated. Nearly six weeks later, on September 16, Clarence Pickett of the Service Committee met with Chambers at the Homewood Friends Meetinghouse in Baltimore to see if he could move toward some reconciliation between the two disputants. Though he emphasized that Chambers impressed him as a bit unstable emotionally and perhaps in need of further conversation with two or three Friends, Pickett wrote that the family was active in Pipe Creek Meeting. Chambers was surprised that Priscilla Hiss was considering joining Friends because he could not image how a Communist would be allowed to join; he could not believe that she was so cynical as to have her religious affiliation used for Communist purposes.

Pickett's primary purpose in visiting Chambers was to see if he could effect some kind of meeting between the men and forestall a libel suit, perhaps even *two* libel suits, one from each side. Chambers and Hiss, Pickett ventured, might be able to draw up a joint statement that would preserve their mutual integrity. Chambers did not see how Hiss could agree to any kind of document given the adamant position he had already taken. He insisted that he was telling the truth. When Pickett suggested that to help clear the air the two wives might meet, perhaps at the Pickett residence at Pendle Hill near Philadelphia, Chambers readily agreed. Pickett promised that there would be no publicity, but he related in his memo—though apparently not to Chambers—that he doubted the likelihood of such a meeting; he did assure the editor that he would talk to Hiss and, if necessary, Priscilla about it. (There is no evidence that he did.) He confided in his memo that two or three Friends might be found who were willing to meet periodically with Chambers and Hiss separately and "repeatedly" if they wished.

Pickett then explored with Chambers the role of Nixon, who had taken a major role in the whole affair. When he told the former Communist that Nixon was a Friend and gave him some detail about Nixon's "religious connections in Whittier," Chambers "was surprised," Pickett recounted, "to find that Congressman Nixon is a Friend." Stressing that he was not critical of Nixon's role as a member of the committee, Chambers "did not feel that he approached it in any sense as an understanding Quaker, but rather as a lawyer and Congressman as contrasted with a person of religious life and understanding."

Chambers's surprise at discovering Nixon was a Friend contradicts Nixon's recollection. He had gone to see Chambers at his farm in Westminster, Maryland, sometime during the week of August 7 to 14, more than a month before Pickett informed Chambers of Nixon's religious affiliation. During their informal conversation, marked by a growing sense on the part of the congressman that, contrary to rumors, Chambers was not a drunkard, disreputable, or unstable, Nixon became convinced that he was talking to a man both sensitive and intelligent. At one point the conversation turned to religion, and Nixon informed his host of his own Quaker background, "that I was a member of the Society of Friends." Chambers explained that he and his family attended a local meeting and mentioned, incorrectly, that Priscilla Hiss, at the time he knew her, was also a Friend and then, snapping his fingers in sudden recollection, recalled that she used the plain language when she and her husband spoke to each other. This revelation served to confirm Nixon's opinion of Chambers's veracity, for he remembered from his own family situations that Quakers sometimes spoke this way.[25] But the problem remains: either Nixon misdated the Westminster meeting by more than a month, which is unlikely, or over the course of a month Chambers had already forgotten learning of Nixon's Quaker ties from the man himself. Or perhaps the journalist, for some reason, lied to Pickett.

Pickett ended the conversation quite depressed, for he saw no way of preventing a long court battle, something Friends tried always to avoid. "It may be that Hiss will win," he wrote, "but I am afraid that it will be a hollow victory. So much bitterness will be engendered, I am afraid, that it may impair the usefulness of both men." He did not think Quakers should even try to find every last shred of evidence possible; locating evidence was the job of the authorities, including the congressional committee. Instead Quakers should, he implied, devote themselves to finding a way to reduce the animosity likely to result if reconciliation proved impossible.

A couple of days later, Pickett met also with Nixon. It was a good session, the AFSC secretary told his journal, but his account of his conversation with the California congressman was not nearly as detailed. Nixon was concerned that both men were going to injury themselves, but he was more critical of Hiss than he was of Chambers because he surmised that the former had not been "completely open and frank." Nixon also offered to show Pickett the records in the case, but his visitor opted to wait until later. Open and cooperative, Nixon stressed that he was always ready to talk with Pickett and he should feel free to come at any time.[26]

From this point on, the controversy moved inexorably forward. Hiss was indicted on December 15, 1948, and ultimately tried on two counts of perjury for denying that he had given State Department documents to Chambers in the 1930s; this trial ended in early July of the following year with a hung jury, unable to reach a decision on the charges. The government almost immediately retried him—it was at this trial that Pickett testified as a witness to Hiss's good character—and he was convicted in November 1949, a legal and political vindication of both Chambers and Nixon. He received a sentence of five years in prison—he proved to be a model prisoner—and after being released in 1954, spent the rest of his life

affirming and trying to prove his innocence. He died in 1996, still proclaiming that he had been framed.

Unlike the other two actors in this almost cosmic drama, Hiss never
successfully played the card of religion. There was simply too little to go
on. When Chambers disputed his contention that he had actively attended
church during the 1930s, Hiss named several ministers to corroborate his
testimony, but, questioned by agents from the Federal Bureau of Investigation, none of them could produce evidence to support this claim. One even
denied that he had ever seen Hiss in his church.[27] Hiss attended an Episcopal Sunday school when he was a child, something that may have contributed to his being—his word—"a Prig"; he remained a member of the
Episcopal Church.[28] Yet his harshest academic critic conceded his idealism
and fanatic commitment to his goals. Hiss exemplified, wrote University
of Virginia law professor G. Edward White, an "instinctive altruism," coupled with a "strong faith in his own competence" and "single-mindedness
and self-control," all qualities that made him a perfect secret agent.[29] In this
way he was much like Klaus Fuchs, the German-English Quaker, who confessed in 1950 to spying for the Soviet Union and served a prison term for
his crime.[30]

Before Chambers's allegations, Hiss was primarily a bureaucrat who
toiled behind the scenes and had little opportunity to reveal his ideas; afterward because of his adamant determination to assert his innocence and
clear his name, an unsuccessful effort to which he dedicated the rest of his
life, he had no time for anything else. Until his last post as president of the
Carnegie Endowment, he was not prominent enough to be invited onto
the speakers' circuit, and the only things he wrote afterward for public consumption were books and articles that sought to prove his innocence. The
upshot was that Hiss, outside the case that made him famous, remains to
this day something of an unknown and his thinking rather much a blank.
One objective scholar avers that he always stood for "a multilateral foreign
policy rather than the unilateral exercise of American power" of the sort
that drove the nation into the Vietnam War, but she adduces no evidence
to prove her assertion; perhaps she extrapolated from Hiss's life's work,
which is perfectly acceptable, but her point would have been strengthened
with a salient quotation from something Hiss wrote or said.[31] Great parts of
his life, including whatever religious sensibilities he possessed, if any, were
like a closed book mislaid on a shelf in some old archive.

What makes Hiss of such interest here is that he seems almost a mirror
image of his antagonist, Richard Nixon, the man who was, next to Chambers, most responsible for keeping the finger of suspicion pointed at him
and seeing him convicted and sentenced to a term in prison. Nixon's biog-

rapher Stephen E. Ambrose made this point toward the end of his third volume. As old men out of the limelight, both Nixon and Hiss sought rehabilitation from their fellow citizens. But, too proud, neither could bring himself to admit that he had done wrong, Nixon about Watergate, Hiss about being a spy. Moreover, to heighten the irony, each had been the victim of his own words, Nixon on the notorious tapes, Hiss by notes in his own handwriting and typed stolen government documents, hidden away by Chambers.[32]

In his final summary assessment of Hiss, on the last page of his book, G. Edward White concluded that his subject was "a complex, troubled, ingratiating, formidable personality. . . . [one] ideally suited to maintain a secret life." With the exception of being ingratiating, Richard Nixon exemplified those same personality traits. White posited that Hiss was a man for whom spying for the Soviets and spending the rest of his life lying about it gave meaning to his existence: it "was a way of demonstrating his multiple loyalties, channeling his altruism, and achieving self-fulfillment." White thought that Hiss sought "psychic integration through spying and lying" and predicted that there would be others likely to follow him who would take similar paths.[33]

Richard Nixon did not seek "psychic integration" through spying, of course; neither did he articulate that he sought it through lying. Nor would Hiss have described himself in the devastating terms White chose. But throughout Nixon's public life he pictured himself—as well as allowing himself to be pictured—as a Quaker with all the baggage that label implied, good or bad, but then he distanced himself from the practice of a Quaker, from waiting on God's leadings in worship, the thing that distinguishes a Quaker, to even attempting to live the faith's testimonies. We do not know for sure, but it was highly unlikely that a man with a "Quaker heritage" like Nixon's could overlook the fact that one of the original names of the Religious Society of Friends was "Friends of the Truth." One comes away from looking at his career wondering where the Truth had gone.

Considering Hiss and Nixon side by side, I find it difficult to dodge the conclusion that they were alike in at least one basic way. In 1962, in *Six Crises*, Nixon proposed that Hiss had replaced God as the "sole judge of right and wrong" for the party of the workers, meaning that his "morality could be reduced to one perverted rule: anything that advances the goals of Communism is good."[34] Over the course of his life Nixon allowed himself to become the sole judge of what was right and wrong and decided that anything that advanced his political career was permissible. Nixon, unaware of what he was doing, had defined a ranter and implicitly justified covering up. And, like Hiss, he went to his grave never admitting publicly what he knew he had done.

5

First Quaker Vice President

Let a good Quaker stop this fight.[1]

—Richard Nixon

After the conviction of Alger Hiss for perjury, Richard Nixon was the most prominent Quaker officeholder in the country. His religious faith was not something he often dwelt on, except in the slightly ironic sense he used to describe breaking up a fight between the muckraking Washington journalist (and nominal Quaker) Drew Pearson and Wisconsin's anti-communist senator Joseph R. McCarthy. The setting for the fight was a dinner-dance at Washington's elite Sulgrave Club the evening of December 13, 1950. During an intermission, while couples were dancing, McCarthy accosted Pearson, who had been writing columns about the senator's finances, and warned him that he was going to "put him out of business" with a speech on the Senate floor the next day. When Pearson retorted by asking him if he had paid his overdue taxes yet, the infuriated and younger McCarthy invited him to step outside. Others, including a congressman who had had polio and used crutches, convinced him to sit down and avoid a fight.

Later as the partygoers were leaving, McCarthy confronted Pearson again in the more private cloakroom downstairs. Pearson claimed the burly senator kneed him in the groin, but when Nixon came down to get his coat, he found McCarthy with his hands around his nemesis's neck and the journalist struggling to breathe. Seeing Nixon, McCarthy slapped Pearson across the face so hard that his head snapped back and then said, "That one was for you, Dick." Nixon then placed himself between the two, with the words, "Let a good Quaker stop this fight." Pearson snapped up his coat and scurried out of the room while McCarthy rebuked the recently elected senator, "You shouldn't have stopped me, Dick." However grateful Pearson was for Nixon's timely intervention, he did not halt his anti-Nixon columns nor those attacking McCarthy.[2]

Despite Pearson's best efforts in his columns, Nixon's reputation as an anti-communist led him to victory in 1950 over Helen Gahagan Douglas in the race for California's open United States Senate seat. Hence in a real sense, Alger Hiss assured that his archenemy Richard Nixon would gain the vice presidential nomination of his party.

Some Quaker concerns other than Pearson overlapped with Nixon's post-Hiss career. The principle one involved the American Friends Service Committee (AFSC), an organization whose very existence raised the temperatures of most western and all evangelical Friends. That its secretary had testified to Hiss's good character did not help its reputation in such quarters. The AFSC, founded in Philadelphia in 1917 to give Friends of all persuasions who were conscientiously opposed to participation in World War I an alternative to military service, had been controversial among evangelical Friends since the 1920s.

Yet some of Nixon's relatives had served under its red and black star during the first war, and well-known evangelical Quaker Herbert Hoover had raised funds for the group both during and after the conflict. Like many such institutions that originate for a specific purpose, once that purpose was achieved or the conditions requiring it ended, the organization had to search around for something to justify its existence. It became a major relief agency, serving to feed and clothe hungry and ill-clad Germans and Russians after the war ended. By the 1930s it became involved in domestic relief among miners and their families in the Appalachian coalfields, in working to assist southern tenant farmers, and in seeking to improve racial relations. During the late 1930s, as European nations began to inch toward war, it sponsored "peace caravans" of college students to go up and down the countryside discussing foreign policy and engaging in efforts to prevent American involvement in a European war. These efforts eschewed partisan politics and championed moral and religious approaches to the topic of peace.[3]

At about the time Nixon went to Washington, AFSC was preparing to unveil a new strategy. The year 1947 was important in three respects in its life: it was the thirtieth anniversary of its founding, an apt time of reassessment; it (with its British counterpart, the British Service Council) received the Nobel Peace Prize in the name of all Friends; and the Cold War was just getting under way with all that would portend. With the Nobel Prize to validate the activities of Quakers, the Committee enjoyed more prestige than ever before, an influence that it could put to good use by developing and flexing its political muscles, or so many within the group believed. By early 1948 AFSC Secretary Clarence Pickett had opened discussions with Secretary of Commerce Henry A. Wallace, a critic of President Harry Truman's emerging Cold War policies, about supporting him in a possible run for the presidency that year.[4] Such moves inevitably set evangelical Friends' teeth on edge.

As early as the 1920s, evangelical Friends had begun distancing themselves from AFSC; this was a period of intense theological polarization between fundamentalism and modernism, and AFSC helped propel modernism into the Quaker world. The Committee did not proclaim that Christ was the Savior and win converts to Christianity and Quakerism. Instead, it relied on its good works to impress people with how Christians and Quakers followed the Prince of Peace. This deafening silence on what evangelical Friends believed was the central mission of Quakerism quickly alienated yearly meetings in the far West and the Midwest, and they began withholding what was already lukewarm support. Because evangelical Friends associated AFSC with "liberalism," and they considered themselves to be opponents of this approach, they determined to hold AFSC at more than arm's length. Evangelism—winning the world for Christ—came first for these Quakers.[5] Though never noted for supporting such evangelism, Nixon still had major reservations about AFSC, which by his time seemed tinged with a questionable leftwing approach likely to lose any of his supporters mainstream political support.

Nixon expressed his personal views regarding the AFSC about this time in a letter he wrote to Tom Bewley, his former law partner in Whittier. Nixon sent him an editorial that appeared in the New York City *Daily Compass*, which he described as an "uptown edition" of the newspaper *Daily Worker* and obviously a Communist paper. "You and I, of course, know that Quakers are not Communists, but they are certainly being used by the Communists." Nixon said he had been put out by AFSC's invitation to Hiss to address a seminar in New Hampshire scheduled in the middle of the second trial, an announcement trumpeted in the New York press right next to news of the trial; it surely influenced the jurors. "The obvious effect, of course, would be to build up Hiss in the minds of readers who had confidence in Quakers." Nixon said he had been bombarded with letters about why "Quakers have allowed themselves to be sucked in by the Communists" and he had had a hard time answering them.[6]

A fine example of such concern was Nixon's principal Quaker political supporter back in Whittier, Herman Perry, who had been keeping an eye on AFSC since at least January 1948. That month the southern California unit of AFSC sponsored the appearance of Scott Nearing, an independent radical economist, to speak at Whittier College, First Friends Church, and the Lions Club. The business-oriented Lions were particularly incensed by Nearing's record, which they had investigated, and his talk. Perry warned the chairman of AFSC's local office that unless he could clear up the questions about Nearing the organization's fund raising would be damaged in the region.[7]

Four years later he mailed his senator a letter containing a story from the American Legion magazine on the Katyn forest massacre of Polish Army officers by Soviet forces in 1940. Perry scribbled a note to the story: "Stalin is certainly a fine fellow. American Friends Service certainly must admire him for this effort."[8] In one deft swoop, Perry linked Soviet dictator Josef Stalin to AFSC, a reflection of wider evangelical Quaker distrust for both; Senator Nixon could hardly avoid Perry's point.

Neither Perry nor the AFSC was through. In late March 1948, the AFSC announced the speakers at its annual "International Relations Institute" in Whittier; they included such notables as sociologist Ruth Benedict, former Communist Bertram Wolfe, University of Chicago economist Maynard Krueger, journalist and pacifist Milton Mayer, and Disciples of Christ minister and peace activist Kirby Page, as well as an Indian scholar and a Russian émigré; the thing that most of them had in common was being critics of American foreign policy from a leftist point of view. Perry suggested that Nixon have an investigative staffer on the House Committee on Un-American Activities check them out; he also informed a friendly Washington journalist, Walter S. Steele, of these "pinks" and asked him to look into their backgrounds also. Word came back from Steele that all were "extreme leftists," some fellow travelers with the Communists, and others Socialists and pacifists. Mayer had once even written for leftwing Negro publications.[9]

Nixon's response to these revelations included a five-page report from his investigator on Nearing, as well as information he had collected on the others. He warned Perry to keep the source of these reports confidential because they were designed for members of Congress and were not supposed to be released, except to people like Perry, "who can use the information for conducting a further investigation of the organization or individual involved." In another context, Nixon observed to Perry that intelligence such as this "makes me wonder about some of our Quaker friends." Perry promised that he would only show the information to the chairman of Whittier College's faculty committee and added, "It looks as if American Friends Society is being improperly used by those interested in the welfare of the Bolsheviks." A week or two before Hiss's first trial for perjury, Nixon sent Perry a copy of a letter sent to another congressman about a mid-May AFSC conference outside Philadelphia. Nixon included a handwritten note asking if Perry had heard that AFSC had asked Hiss to speak during the summer at a conference in New Hampshire, another indication of the group's political intentions.[10]

Nixon's stance got mixed reviews from his fellow Quakers. After speaking at Earlham College in May 1949, Nixon was lauded by the president of the college, Thomas Jones. "I have never felt more proud," he penned four days after Nixon's appearance, "of my Quaker connections." Any doubts "liberal Quakers" might have about the congressman were removed. "Your Christian democratic understanding and your method of handling difficult problems of state were most impressive." But another Indiana Friend, an H. J. Bourne, had a different take on Nixon. "Your Quakerism is putrid," he wrote in a telegram Nixon promptly sent along to Perry. He noted on it: "*Herman*. Here's another one. Did you know that [recently convicted German-English atomic spy for Russia, Klaus] Fuchs was a Quaker too? Maybe *we're* wrong! Dick."[11]

Perry took the hint and wrote a long letter to Bourne, explaining that as a native of Westfield, Indiana, he was a God-fearing, law abiding, "rugged individualist" Quaker. Claiming that for twenty-five years he had studied the trends toward socialism in religion, education, and government, he ended by echoing Nixon's comment to him on Bourne's telegram: was not Fuchs a Quaker? When Nixon got his copy of Perry's letter, he agreed: "too many Quakers of his type are holding themselves forth as representing the viewpoint of the majority." He promised to dispatch Perry's letter to people in New York and Washington to detail where Quakers stood on Communist infiltration of the nation. And he suggested Perry send a copy to Fulton Lewis Jr., the noted anti-Communist news commentator; Perry promptly complied.[12]

Such concerns bubbled up during Nixon's campaign against Helen Gahagan Douglas. One correspondent, a man the Republican congressman knew well, wrote to tell him that on the evening before the election, a Quaker had spoken on the radio in behalf of Douglas, a fact he linked to AFSC. He thought that this "propaganda machine [was] hiding behind the Quaker faith and known as 'AFSC' should be stopped in its tracks. Their methods are clever, well-planned, and dangerous." Nixon agreed that the actions "of certain Quaker groups" were not designed to help him; he suggested that his correspondent contact Perry who was in a position to do "some good" inside the church. Perry, of course, had long since concluded that AFSC was "too friendly" with Communists.[13]

During the campaign Nixon and his supporters moved to shore up his support among friendly Quakers, especially after a Douglas ad trumpeted that her "work had not passed unnoticed by . . . fine people known as 'Quakers.'"[14] Perry wrote Nixon's campaign manager Murray Chortiner to inform him that local church members in Whittier—presumably not Friends—were bombarding Quakers to inquire if they were supporting the

Republican candidate "whole heartedly." Soon a press release from head-quarters spread the word that 100 Quakers had signed a statement supporting Nixon. They charged that the Korean conflict had been brought on by the State Department, seeking to appease the Soviet Union. "As Quakers, we are pacifists," they reminded Californians who might have doubts, "but not pacifist [*sic*] to the extent of being pushed around."[15] With support from such Quakers, Nixon went on to defeat Douglas.

Two years later, as it turned out, the residual benefits of Hiss's conviction for perjury, as well as Nixon's reputation as an internationalist, redounded to his political benefit. His support for American economic rebuilding in Europe gave him a reputation in Congress rather different from that of the usual anti-communist there. Thus he became the candidate of the internationalist wing of the Republican Party for the vice presidency with former Supreme Commander of Allied Powers in Europe Dwight D. Eisenhower heading the ticket. But Nixon's subsequent nomination was not enough to guarantee his spot on the Republican ticket.

Two months after the convention, the Californian's place seemed again up for grabs, as controversy swirled around him. Sensational news that a group of wealthy Californian businessmen administered an account consisting of approximately $18,000 broke on September 18 in the *New York Post,* edited by a 1930s Communist, James Wechsler, now a liberal who supported the Democratic presidential candidate, Adlai Stevenson, even writing some of his speeches. Nixon was the beneficiary of the fund because, the fund's recruiter explained, he exemplified a politician who rejected "socialization" and supported the "free enterprise" system that the donors valued and wanted to promote. Though he had known about circulating rumors of the fund as early as September 14, when he appeared on the television program *Meet the Press,* the news of the fund in headlines panicked Nixon, and, said one historian, he became a virtual "whirligig."[16]

Revelation of this secret fund captured the attention of the nation for a few days that autumn as Republican politicians scurried privately to settle on a solution. Some wanted Nixon to leave the race outright so they could find a new running mate for Eisenhower, others wanted to gauge public opinion, and some of his staunchest supporters simply advised lying low until the storm died down. The presidential candidate had the major say of course, and he vacillated, one day on Nixon's side, the next equivocating. His most enduring comment was that to remain on the ticket, Nixon had to prove himself "as clean as a hound's tooth." Nixon may have overdramatized his own struggle in his account, *Six Crises,* but he clearly comes across as overwrought in his first national campaign. He was all but cut off because when the to-do started he had just begun a whistle-stop journey up the West Coast into Oregon aboard his campaign train, the Nixon Special. The long-distance telephone calls kept up fast and furious for about five days as Republican leaders tried to find a face-saving way out for all concerned.

With short talks required of him most of the day, Nixon grew more and more weary, a state matched by an increasing testiness, which was in turn produced by the conflicting advice from all the phone calls he had to deal with. He even heard from his mother, staying with the Nixon girls in Washington; she promised, "We will be thinking of you," her Quaker family's way of saying that they were praying for him. He literally cried when he got her telegram. He arrived in Portland, Oregon, on the same day, Saturday, September 20, with the prospect of having Sunday off, which would give him some time to sort things out and calm down. That night in the Benson Hotel he convened a meeting of his advisors; they were almost uniformly pessimistic about his chances of remaining on the ticket. They did agree that he had to find a way to go over the heads of the press, perhaps with a television talk, to fight for his place. The conference broke up at 3:00 a.m. with the candidate staying behind to ponder the options. Not surprisingly, he soon decided that he was the final and ultimate decision-maker himself and went to bed, dead tired after a grueling two days. The clock read 5:00.[17]

However troubled his sleep might have been, Nixon was up and about before 9:00, but he certainly exhibited no ebullience. He foresaw, he said later, "another long day of ordeal." His former law partner in Whittier, Tom Bewley, had flown in and remembered that the Nixons left for church about half an hour later. Nixon and his wife planned to attend Portland's First Friends Church, where several of Nixon's relatives were members, with a few members of his staff. His attendance went unannounced to the media because, reported a Nixon spokesman, "Dick doesn't believe in political religion."[18]

When the party returned to the hotel, Nixon seemed transformed, virtually a different person, according to Bewley. Earlier, Nixon had seemed tired, remote, and lacking in energy as though the struggle to decide how he should respond to the fund crisis had drained him of energy and his usual decisiveness. Now, back from church, he grabbed Bewley's hand and convincingly confided, "I'm not worried anymore," as though he had reached clarity on what to do next. There is no way to know if something Pastor Charles Beals said in his sermon had had this impact or whether it was merely being at First Friends Church, but Nixon definitely seemed changed and more sure of himself upon his return. Nixon himself did not mention going to church but stressed that Bewley's arrival with word that the relatively small electorate in Whittier supported him "100 per cent" was a major morale booster and buoyed him immediately.[19] It was the only time in his entire life that another person commented on the impact of a specific religious episode on Nixon's actual bearing. That made it a landmark well worth noting.

Now sure of his path, Nixon conferred with advisors, took telephone calls from eastern leaders of the Republican Party, including Eisenhower, and decided to go on nationwide television to give his side of the story. It would be the way to sway public opinion and convince Eisenhower that he should remain on the national ticket. The upshot was the famous "Checkers Speech," which produced a ground swell of support for the embattled vice presidential candidate. It demonstrated not only Nixon's political capabilities but also his mastery of the relatively new medium of television and, of course, cemented his place on the ticket next to Eisenhower.[20]

The fund crisis and his television address had little impact on the popular vote, but the "Checkers Speech"—its name came from one his daughters had given the dog a supporter had sent—became legendary in Nixon's political career. In fact, for years some men in Washington and California who wore three-piece suits, a mark of well-off gentility, sported gold chains carrying a polished tooth across their vests. These symbolized membership in the Nixon loyalists' Hound's Tooth Club, named after Eisenhower's comment.[21] Tired of the presidency of Harry Truman and his Fair Deal, the electorate gave the Eisenhower-Nixon ticket its endorsement, and in January 1953, the two men took the oaths for their new positions.

Nixon, of course, could not know that he would serve two terms when he won in 1952. His religious activities over the next eight years involved two basic developments, the weakening of his ties with his Quaker background and, later in the decade of the 1950s, his growing closeness with evangelical leaders. These included particularly preachers of note, such as famed evangelist Billy Graham, a North Carolinian and Baptist, whose fame preceded Nixon's only by a little, and Norman Vincent Peale,[22] who, though raised a Methodist, became pastor of Marble Collegiate Dutch Reformed Church in New York City. Political considerations moved Nixon to these two courses.

A bit over two years after the Nixons first moved to Washington, in April 1949, the secretary of the Washington Friends Meeting on Florida Avenue, an unprogrammed group, quite different from East Whittier Friends Church, wrote Representative Nixon. He asked him to consider the Washington meeting his "home meeting" while he and his family lived in the capital.[23] Instead, the Nixon family chose to attend Westmoreland Congregational Church near their home, but they did not become members. In January 1954, Nixon, now vice president, gave a formal talk to the youth at the same church, giving his impressions of the young people he had met on a recent world tour.[24] Later, in 1957, when they moved their residence to Wesley Heights in the northwest part of the city they started going to the nearby Metropolitan Memorial Methodist Church. Although its pastor, Edward G. Latch, gave the invocation on the last day of the Republican National Convention in 1960 and was introduced as "Mr. Nixon's minister," none of the Nixons were members of the church, the vice president's membership remaining at his California home church.[25] A neighbor of the Nixons in northwest Washington observed that the vice president was not ostentatious about his religion, though he and his wife saw that the girls attended Sunday school regularly.[26] They went to Latch's church for four years.[27]

Religion was not a high priority for the Nixon family. It was important enough that they wanted their two daughters to attend a Sunday school where they could learn something of the basis of Christianity, one of the roots of morality in their middle- to upper-class neighborhood. Pat had affiliated with a "community church" back in southern California, its doctrines and theological premises—not to mention its formal name and even exact location—unknown,[28] and her husband seemed less disquieted by the whole matter than willing to acquiesce in whatever the minimum of outward observance required. He told a journalist with whom he was close that he would not have formally remained a Friend had it not been for his mother; otherwise, he confided, he would have probably become a Presbyterian like the Eisenhowers.[29] In 1952, invited to attend a men's dinner at his own church, he even inquired of political advisors in Whittier as to whether he should go while he was in town.[30]

Like Eisenhower, also, Nixon could speak of religion in broad, generic terms, ones that enlisted it in the ongoing struggle against communism, the vice president's signature issue. On February 1, ten days after the inauguration, the American Legion, the nation's main organization of veterans, initiated its "Back to God" crusade over the radio with both the new president and vice president as speakers. Eisenhower had recorded his statement because he could not be present in New York where the crusade was broadcast—he was baptized for the first time that day at the National Presbyterian Church in Washington—so Nixon spoke to the 1500 people in the studio audience. Warning against "moral decay," he applauded the president's "private prayer" that he had used to open his inaugural address, pointing out that such an act would not be possible in half the world. He also endorsed "the privilege of free worship." "Our spiritual strength," he intoned, "is our greatest advantage over those who are trying to enslave the world."[31]

Words like these were part of the litany of the just forming "American National Religion," as one scholar, T. Jeremy Gunn, named what later came to be tagged as the nation's "civil religion."[32] Gunn more aptly tied its tenets of government-endorsed theism, militarism, and free enterprise capitalism to the Cold War struggle against communism that consumed Americans in the 1950s. This faith was designed to unite Americans religiously in a seemingly never-ending battle against implacable atheist foes represented by the Soviet Union and the People's Republic of China. The most salient public statements of this new faith were inserting the phrase "under God" after "one Nation" in the Pledge of Allegiance in 1954 and Congress's declaration two years later that "In God We Trust" was the national motto.[33] The president also let it be known that he expected all cabinet members and their families to attend church, something that most probably had had an impact on Nixon's own decisions.[34]

The vice president, however, gave no public indication that he understood this new emphasis. The family attended church but not the church of his heritage. Instead the principal personal contact the Nixons had with Quakers outside the family while they lived in the East was that both girls attended Sidwell Friends School, a Quaker school that was becoming a popular educational institution for the District's social and political elite. (As a proprietary school, its ties to Quakers were not typical because no local meeting controlled it.) Going to Sidwell allowed the girls to attend a school with a minimum of African American students—the "few" in the first grade in 1958 were three grades below ten-year-old Julie; the exclusive Sidwell had no "colored teachers," as Nixon himself phrased it—rather than a public school with possibly more black pupils. Following the 1954 Supreme Court decision desegregating public school, the question of where elected officials sent their children could be explosive, so Sidwell would permit the vice president's office to take the high road and claim, correctly, that the girls were going to an integrated if private school.[35]

With Nixon as their father, the girls would have received a good education whatever school they attended. His office provided him broad contacts with important people always interested in cultivating his good side by giving their attention to his family. For example, Israeli leader David Ben-Gurion came out to their house when he was visiting Washington during Nixon's vice presidency. Tricia was studying what Nixon referred to as the "Hebrew-Christian religion" at Sidwell, and Ben-Gurion took over half an hour giving her his views on the differences between the Old and New Testaments. It may have been over her head, but her father was quite impressed that such a man of importance would take so much time with his daughter; whatever Tricia learned, Nixon was taken with Ben-Gurion's thoughtfulness with a young and inquisitive girl.[36]

Friends beyond Sidwell School tried to influence the vice president; the most prominent, Richmond P. Miller, executive secretary of Philadelphia Yearly Meeting, dispatched repeated letters after 1955. Suggesting that Nixon "find thy way" to woo voters by convincing them "that thy Quakerism is very much a part of thy convictions," he sent a directory of meetings in the Washington area, invited him to attend the liberal Friends General Conference in the summer of 1956, asked for a signed photograph, which Nixon forwarded, and volunteered to accompany him to Friends meetings when he campaigned in Philadelphia. Miller went down to Washington to meet Nixon, returning to write a laudatory article on his candidate for *Friends Journal* before the 1956 election. After that, he even proposed that Nixon affirm when he was inaugurated in January to testify to the Quaker belief that one could be truthful without swearing. Nixon's procrastination and coolness toward Miller clearly suggested he did not agree that publicly identifying with Quakers would benefit him politically.[37]

His involvement with Miller and Quakers at Sidwell Friends was much less problematic than dealing with those at the AFSC. Nixon the politician had long ago learned how to be circumspect when it came to dealing with AFSC and its leaders directly. He might criticize it (and the Quakers it represented) and agree that it was "pinkish" in its political tendencies to a close Friend like Herman Perry, but when he talked or wrote to its leadership he was careful to refrain from blanket condemnation. He did not particularly care for Clarence Pickett, executive secretary in March 1950—probably because Pickett testified to Hiss's good character during his second trial—but neither did former Quaker president Herbert Hoover. As Hoover told a Friend in 1957 "[t]hat Pickett fellow was too much of a politician—more of a politician than a Quaker ought to be unless he's in the business."[38] No slouch as a politician himself, Nixon thanked Pickett warmly when he commended the vice president's kitchen debate with Soviet premier Nikita Khrushchev during his acclaimed trip to the Soviet Union in 1959.[39] Of course, by that time Pickett was safely retired and not in a position to use Hiss in AFSC's Institutes of International Relations.

Lewis Hoskins, executive secretary of AFSC after Pickett resigned and during the rest of the 1950s, was another matter. Formerly a pastor in New York Yearly Meeting, Hoskins proved quite diplomatic, and before long Nixon was addressing him on a first-name basis. The executive secretary was especially careful to keep Nixon up to date on AFSC activities in the Middle East regarding the Arab-Israeli conflict, an area where AFSC was quite active, and in 1957 the Russian intervention in

Hungary; Nixon responded positively to these efforts, even conferring with a stellar delegation from the board of directors—Harvard professor Henry Cadbury, Pendle Hill luminary Anna Brinton, and Hoskins—in his office. Even when he was unable to see a group because of other commitments, he invited them to confer with an aide. One thing Nixon avoided was discussing desegregation in the south or proposals for federal intervention on that explosive domestic topic with AFSC. At one point, Hoskins sent a telegram to the president asking him to go on television and speak to southerners regarding the need to uphold black students' rights in Little Rock, Arkansas, and proposed that Nixon support their plea; he responded by commending the committee's activities in racially torn Levittown, New Jersey, without mentioning the Little Rock crisis at all. Nixon was quite willing to remain open to the AFSC so long as discussions dealt with far-away foreign-policy matters, but he held himself aloof from hearing the leadership out on racial issues. His "no" was blunt and final to Hoskins's request for a meeting on the southern situation.[40]

Making it more difficult to easily characterize Nixon's position on Quakers and racial matters was a half-hour conference he had with a delegation of three staffers from AFSC shortly after he became vice president. As the number one Quaker in the city, Nixon was one of the first public officials they called on. Designated by the national Community Relations Division to help end segregation of public facilities in the nation's capital, the three young people spent six months in Washington interviewing public officials, business leaders, and newspaper editors, among others, about their willingness to move forward on the question of open accommodations. Nixon impressed the three with his seemingly honest interest in their cause, giving them his personal telephone number, introducing them to his private secretary, and promising to take the matter up with members of the Senate Committee on the District of Columbia. Cordiality infused the meeting. As they stood peering out the window of the vice president's office, Nixon told them that if it could be done without publicity and if they needed a place for any of the team to stay, that he would be glad to open his home's guest room to one of them.[41]

Such a convivial gathering was behind the scenes and under the radar, and Nixon never called attention to it in a way that would garner him either political support or injury. Similarly in the spring of 1955, on a trip to Cuba, the vice president met in Havana with the clerk of Cuba Yearly Meeting who lauded him for his courageous friendliness and as "a smiling optimist of the power of love."[42] He also never publicly revealed that when he purchased a new house in northwest Washington in 1957, he refused to sign the restrictive covenant attached to the property that would have prevented it from being sold to African Americans.[43] Yet after becoming president, he told his special assistant on domestic affairs at least twice that blacks would not benefit from federal programs because they were "*genetically inferior* to whites," the classic definition of a white racist.[44]

There was a more telling and concrete example during his presidency of the same notion. In his memoir Columbia Broadcasting television correspondent Roger Mudd recounts a comment Nixon made at the 1970 annual meeting of the Radio-Television Correspondents Association black-tie dinner. As president of the association, Mudd sat at the head table with Nixon, whom Mudd described that evening as "socially geeky" and unable to banter. When black singer Diana Ross entertained the gathered worthies, Nixon turned to Mudd and remarked, revealing more about him than he probably intended, "They really do have a sense of rhythm, don't they?"[45]

Such remarks highlighted the distance Nixon had put between himself and eastern "liberal" Quakerism. In March 1954, an exchange of letters with an Oberlin College student, Helen Steere, daughter of the prominent Quaker professor at Haverford College, Douglas Steere, also illustrated the same point. (It was not clear that her correspondents knew whose daughter she was.) Steere had averred in her letter that the Quaker notion that God was in every man implied nonviolence in action and expression. Nixon diverted the letter to his old sponsor and surrogate Herman Perry for a reply. It went through two or three drafts before both the vice president and his Whittier Friend had polished it enough that they thought it ready to be sent. Perry identified himself as a Quaker "who believes that since the dawn of the New Deal, the socialistic trend and the communistic era, our church has slipped down the road of socialistic thinking." He did not fancy Quakers preaching the idea of "peace at any price, which is tinctured basically with communism and socialism or whatever you call it," mentioning Whittaker Chambers, Klaus Fuchs, and Alger Hiss among Quaker "left-wingers" of the last ten years. The letter ended with Perry questioning whether Steere was truly a member of a Quaker church in Oberlin because he had been unable to find one listed there (there was not one; there was an unprogrammed meeting). Thus, he wondered if she was just a member of some sort of organization allied with AFSC, clearly below the mark of Quaker for him or Nixon.[46]

By the end of the 1950s, relations between AFSC and Nixon had warmed considerably. Perry had almost disappeared as a regular correspondent, at least in part because the vice president was not as beholden politically to him as he had been when he was a congressman and a senator. Hoskins's good relations with Nixon gave the former some basis for pushing, and he did. In January 1958, Hoskins wrote an aide in the vice president's office how he appreciated Nixon's busy schedule while insisting that the AFSC's board still wanted to meet with him. They "wanted to share some Quaker concerns in a way that we are sure Richard Nixon will understand." In other words, they would not take "no" for a final answer: and they didn't, for Nixon met with them two weeks later, although there was no indication of what transpired, whether racial matters were discussed or not.[47]

Nixon occasionally got letters complaining about "subversive activities" of the AFSC, but the warmer relations that had developed with that Quaker organization did not cool much. He thanked Hoskins for a note endorsing his upcoming trip to the Soviet Union and expressed the hope that discussions with the Soviet leadership would redound to everyone's advantage. The AFSC secretary had decided to take a job at Earlham College, so Nixon took that opportunity to extend his best wishes on the job he had done and the prospects for the future. When an AFSC staffer sent along a report of the All-African People's Conference that had just concluded in Tunis, the vice president, now a presidential aspirant, averred that he maintained an interest in such proceedings and was glad to see these observations. He even sent best wishes to AFSC's 1960 Santa Barbara Institute for World Affairs, asserting that the USSR's closed society was the principal impediment to world disarmament.[48]

Nixon continued to take this more nuanced view of AFSC as the 1960 presidential campaign neared. A Quaker in Pennsylvania protested to him about its seventy-two-page pamphlet *Speak Truth to Power*, the most incisive pacifist publication ever issued in the United States. A frontal attack on the Cold War and a call for civil disobedience to prevent international conflict, the pamphlet appeared in 1955 and was widely commented on in the nation's press; its very title, created by the committee that produced it, proved so compelling that it began to be adopted by many others who wanted to stress that not just the powerful could define major issues.[49] Nixon explained that since its creation the Society of Friends had been opposed to war and pursued peace and understanding and had accordingly won the Nobel Peace Prize in 1947. "There is no question," he wrote, "but that this philosophy colors all their activities." While he might not agree with all their approaches, he did applaud their work with refugees and displaced persons. "For this reason alone," he ended, "I would continue to support them."[50] But there is no evidence that he did.

Nixon's determination to downplay religion during his 1960 campaign against Senator John F. Kennedy, a Roman Catholic, was a personal choice, one made despite contrary advice from the president and leading evangelicals, including Billy Graham. A major part of the decision grew out of his reluctance to delve into matters of faith on the hustings. He was not prepared to divest himself of all remnants of Quakerism—otherwise he would have resigned his membership in East Whittier Friends Church, to which he sent a greeting on its fiftieth anniversary in 1957[51]—but he could never forget that his Quaker background was a mixed blessing, unlike, for example, the civic Presbyterianism that Eisenhower had embraced when he entered the White House.[52] To outsiders, even those who knew little about it except what they learned in school, Quakerism had a long and generally honored history. This was particularly true in the United States, where it was associated with William Penn, founder of Pennsylvania, venue of much of early American policymaking, as well as the struggle against slavery in the eighteenth and nineteenth centuries and for women's rights.[53] All these were positive attributes that could benefit a candidate who could associate himself with them. But as the unpopular reputation of the AFSC demonstrated, Quakerism had a downside for a candidate who sought acclaim for his strong stand against Communism, a stand that might result in war, a conflict that could quickly go nuclear. The pacifist side of Quakerism was the cross our California Friend had to bear. Indeed, strong evidence suggested that pacifism among Quakers themselves was declining.[54]

It had certainly declined with Nixon. Not only did he enjoy a reputation as a vigorous anti-Communist, a heritage of the Hiss case, but he also was just as vigorous in his espousal of strong military forces to counter the nation's enemies. He avowed support for massive military strength at home and the system of "vital" armed alliances against communism abroad. Yet there was another side to the man, one that perhaps was based on Quakerism—a grounding that was not clear because he refused to mention his religious convictions even when they positively influenced his thinking. In a commencement address at Lafayette College in Pennsylvania in June 1956, one reprinted in the *American Friend*, the magazine of Five Years Meeting, the voice of "moderate" Friends in the Midwest, he made these points clear. Surveying the postcolonial world, he explained how the people there valued intellectual and religious achievements even above material ones. "The intellectual is not dismissed as an egghead. The artist is not called a long-hair. The minister of religion is not considered an impractical idealist." He deplored that abroad "Americans are considered anti-intellectual, deficient in culture, and superficial in religion." Americans must, the vice president insisted, win hearts and minds, by treating previously colonial people as "our moral and spiritual equals." This stance was as important as military prowess.[55]

A bit later, as he prepared to run for the presidency in 1960, he amplified on this central point and tied it directly to his background as a Friend. Nixon told one questioning journalist, writing for the mass-circulation *Saturday Evening Post*, that he was not necessarily a respecter of the status quo when it came to external relations, even the stands marking the foreign policy of the Eisenhower administration. "I am a chance-taker in foreign affairs," he boasted. "I would take chances for peace—the Quakers have a passion for peace, you know."[56] Thus, not speaking of religion *per se*, he could call on his background as a Quaker to reassure any voter who thought him some kind of rigid anti-Communist conservative.

A fascinating example of how Nixon's Quaker background could be used to cast him in the best possible light came in notes apparently prepared for talks that Nixon's Whittier legal secretary, Evlyn Dorn or others, might be asked to give about his religion. There were seven points: "Religion—very reverent—Quaker background." "Tolerance." "A man's religion has a considerable effect on his approach to all problems. . . . Quaker background, in which he was thoroughly indoctrinated in early years, has had a great effect on attitude toward world & national problems." "Emphasis on peace & mutual understanding that was drilled into him at home, in school and particularly in church affairs in early years. Great interest & concern for less fortunate people in many lands." "Civil rights field— Quaker background responsible for his strong convictions in this field." "No talk of prejudice, social or religious—a great moral issue." "A Quaker who does not have to be thanked for what he does." Since these notes were relatively early in his political career, it is likely that Nixon himself had a hand in drawing them up.[57]

This approach had an important impact on the African American leader Martin Luther King Jr. King, who had met the vice president at the time Great Britain granted Ghana independence in 1957, found him "absolutely sincere" about his racial views and convinced that the race problem in the United States was injuring America's reputation abroad. "Nixon," King explained to an early Nixon biographer, "happens to be a Quaker and there are very few Quakers who are prejudice [*sic*] from a racial point of view." A superb diplomat who "has a genius for convincing people that he is sincere," Nixon totally disarmed King with his "apparent sincerity."[58]

Nixon tried to emphasize the politically positive side of his Quaker heritage by constantly reiterating that Quakerism was a faith that was tolerant—hence he could not attack his 1960 opponent because of his Roman Catholicism—and intensely private—hence, because he was a Quaker, he had to keep his convictions to himself. Thus Nixon the politician could benefit from the history that Quakerism bequeathed him, a history that came to him neatly wrapped in the flag, and yet he wanted to say nothing that might rebound and inadvertently embarrass him. He took umbrage when Adlai Stevenson, Democratic standard-bearer in 1952 and 1956, was quoted in the press as "wondering out loud" why people did not make Nixon's Quakerism an issue, for the simple reason that "many Quakers are pacifists."[59] The 1960 Republican candidate, to be sure, would not make it an issue.

Neither in his memoirs nor his recounting of the 1960 campaign in *Six Crises* did Nixon allude to his reticence about religion. This seemed a curious omission indeed considering that he responded to numbers of entreaties from both his friend Billy Graham and President Eisenhower to be more forthcoming about religion and his faith. But these responses were private, and no one outside those who commented to him was made aware of his thinking. In October 1969, just prior to the National Prayer Breakfast, over which the president was to preside, Nixon was faced with the need to say something about his religion and the role of prayer in his life. To dodge this expectation, he decided that Graham should be delegated to tell the press about the president's view that religion and prayer was a "private personal matter." Graham acceded to the plan.[60] Near the end of his life, in 1992, he told his assistant Monica Crowley, again in the privacy of his study, "I read the Bible, but I don't go out there preaching about what I know or think about it. That is mine to hold on to."[61] It is difficult to believe that someone as politically astute as Richard Nixon and attune to public thinking as he was would intentionally remain silent unless he believed that his silence would benefit him in some way.

Nixon's interpretation of Quakerism—as being an essentially private religion, best left to the solitary individual—not only allowed him to avoid revealing anything about his personal faith, but it gave him a sturdy cloak to hide behind, one that would justify his penchant for secrecy and withdrawal from normal human contact. This was an aspect of the man that did not become obvious in the 1950s but only emerged after he was elected president and the pressures of that political office built up. His closest associate in his administration, the individual with whom he probably spoke most often and most deeply, the person with the greatest authority on foreign policy who served first as national security advisor and then as secretary of state, Henry Kissinger, described Nixon's odd reaction after he rode his reelection sweep to a convincing victory in 1972. Though he might have been expected to exhibit a sense of victorious pleasure, he "withdrew into a seclusion deeper and more impenetrable than in his years of struggle." "Isolation," Kissinger went on, "had become almost a spiritual necessity to this withdrawn, lonely, and tormented man who insisted so on his loneliness and created so much of his torment."[62]

Kissinger depicted him as a "loner," almost a recluse, who, to quote historian Robert Dallek, "would hole up in his hideaway office, slump in a chair, and write notes on a yellow legal pad. For hours or even days he would shield himself from outsiders, allowing only a small circle of aides to join him in his rambling ruminations."[63] This was a person, so determined in his isolation, with no counterpart in the whole sweep of Quaker history, going back over three hundred years. Of course, as a politician with immense power, similarly unmatched in the long history of his faith, Nixon was unique.

Quakerism, whether in its evangelical or traditional unprogrammed variety, had never tried to produce people like the one Kissinger described, telling as it is. To Quakers, "spiritual necessity" never required isolation from other human beings. To the contrary, though they firmly insisted that God spoke to individuals, Quakers held that truth came to individuals gathered together in a community of believers to await the divine voice. That was why their gatherings for worship were central to their faith. Their meetings were "gathered" under or "covered" with Christ's presence when a worshipper or leader spoke the words that God—and the speaker—knew the congregation required at that particular time and place; an advice from 1753 summed it up well: they were then in a "united dependence on the power and Spirit of Christ."[64]

Billy Graham, world-famous Baptist evangelist, served for over three decades as one of Nixon's closest personal friends and advisors. They met not long after Nixon came to the senate in 1951; he was thirty-eight and Graham, thirty-three. Eating in the Senate dining room with his North Carolina senator Clyde R. Hoey, Graham indicated to his host that he had met Nixon's mother during one of his crusades in southern California, so Hoey introduced him to Nixon. The two hit it off immediately and were soon playing golf together. Graham confided in his autobiography, published after Nixon's death, that, looking back on their histories together, he might have exaggerated Nixon's spirituality. Nixon was ready with references to the Bible and his mother's faith—he rarely spoke of his own— so that Graham decided that "it was not always easy to tell the difference between the spiritual and the sentimental." And when Nixon "spoke about the Lord, it was in pretty general terms." In retrospect, Graham considered that he might have been manipulated more than a little by his political "Quaker Friend."[65] Nixon's reticence did not necessarily honor the privacy of his Quaker heritage but may simply have accurately reflected a void existing at the heart of his own faith.

The passage of time, of course, always makes a person wiser, something Graham knew as well as anyone. He admitted that he was evaluating his

Quaker friend's faith from the vantage point of forty-five years and after the turbulent events that had transpired over that period, including the revelations that the Watergate affair laid bare. Given the ultimate importance that the evangelist publicly placed on the need for salvation through one's belief in the sacrifice of Christ's death on the cross, Graham's failure ever to inform Nixon of his doubts before he died is striking, even shocking, in its apparent inconsistency. For within his frame of reference—not to mention Nixon's supposed evangelical one—what was involved was not the vice president's temporal political success, important as that might be, but his eternal destiny. Making his reticence even more startling was Graham's avowal to his friend in 1962, "There are few men whom I have loved as I love you."[66]

By mid-1955 Graham had learned that Nixon, like most politicians, responded to such positive stroking. Following a vice presidential speech in Boston, Graham wrote, "Your sincerity, strong convictions, and humility are evident and catching." He confessed to having "quietly" passed the word to assorted religious leaders to invite Nixon to address them. Nixon, he thought, could gain wider attention by accepting invitations to speak to various Christian assemblies around the country, a summer mainstay for southern denominations whose members flocked to the cooler mountainous region in western North Carolina where the evangelist lived. In his first hint of reluctance, Nixon responded that he had received some invitations already, but that he had declined to accept any.[67]

The next summer, Graham's quiet words and advice paid off. Nixon agreed to come to the Carolina mountains to speak to Southern Baptists at Ridgecrest, southern Presbyterians at Montreat, and Methodists at Lake Junaluska. It was clear that Graham saw these speeches as a way for Nixon to break out of his narrow political thinking: "Very frankly," he confided, "you are in need of a boost in Protestant religious circles." People wanted to know about the vice president everywhere Graham traveled. "There is nothing like personal contact." These religious leaders "will become completely sold on your sincerity and ability as I have been." Graham had already written drafts of the speeches the vice president was to give and would introduce him on all three occasions. The audience at Junaluska was, according to Graham, the "warmest" of the three that day, though the words the vice president uttered seemed more like platitudes than substance: "No nation that despises justice can long succeed—it may have enormous military power, but if it lacks spiritual principle, it will not survive." Nixon stayed at Graham's mountaintop home near Montreat, just east of Asheville, and found Billy and Ruth Graham's hospitality "perfect in every detail." He wished Pat and the girls could have come along to experience it.

The hospitality was good for the Graham-Nixon relationship as well, for in his very next letter, Billy began addressing Nixon for the first time as "Dick."[68] The following summer, when he was conducting one of his crusades in New York City, Graham convinced Nixon to come up to Madison Square Garden on a Saturday afternoon, sit on the platform, and say a few words that could be televised. Graham was exultant about Nixon's appearance and the telecast. The letters poured in to the vice president's office.[69]

Through actions like Nixon's appearance at the Garden, the relationship between the two evangelicals deepened and grew closer, at least on Graham's part. In November 1962, after Nixon lost his race for governor of California, Graham assured him that their friendship was not because he was vice president or an international figure: "Dick, I have thousands of friends but very few close, intimate friends. There are few men whom I have loved as I love you." Indicating that he knew something of Nixon's temptations, he went on to admonish this intimate friend that he should not turn to drinking and recommended a Presbyterian church near his home to attend.[70]

Graham was very concerned with racial relations and tried to get Nixon to comment on this topic to demonstrate his leadership among moderates. In the fall of 1957, when the Little Rock, Arkansas, Central High School crisis erupted, Graham invited the vice president to come to Miami to speak to 12,000 Presbyterian men. Graham was convinced that the church was "the most powerful influence on public opinion in the South" and that the moderates in Miami were "men of considerable influence, not only in the church but in their own communities." He suggested if Nixon spoke to them as he had at the Presbyterian assembly in Montreat the previous summer, adding a few paragraphs on love and race it would "be extremely helpful" in influencing southern public opinion. Graham invited Nixon to attend the "fully integrated" crusade that he was conducting in Charlotte, North Carolina, the following autumn, but once again Nixon pled the burden of being needed elsewhere during the congressional campaign season.[71] Nixon turned his friend down, unconvinced that the Little Rock crisis and race were something he wanted to take on to that extent. Christianity, racial relations, and politics were three things that simply did not mix in the vice president's thinking.

6

A Quaker and a Roman Catholic for President, Again

Before 1960, the only time in American history a Quaker ran against a Roman Catholic for the presidency was in 1928. Herbert Clark Hoover, a Friend who strongly supported Prohibition—a "dry"—with deep roots in the rural evangelical Quaker movement, carried the Republican banner. Opposing him was Governor Alfred E. Smith, a Roman Catholic and Democratic "wet" from New York City. (Jessamyn West's parents feared their daughter, a lapsed Republican, might vote for Smith; she assured them that she would not—she kept her promise, instead casting her ballot for the Socialist candidate, Norman Thomas.)[1] Hoover defeated Smith decisively, even doing the unheard of—winning the electoral votes of five traditionally Democratic southern states. Hoover's impressive victory margin assured that neither party would again consider a Roman Catholic as its candidate for president—until the 1960 campaign when the Democrats nominated John Fitzgerald Kennedy, a Roman Catholic from Boston and a United States senator. His opponent was Richard Milhous Nixon, the Quaker vice president.

Unlike 1928, religion in the 1960 campaign was a subterranean issue, the kind seldom spoken of publicly by the candidates yet one that had the potential of influencing countless voters. Nixon aptly referred to it later as a "boiling cauldron of embittered anti-Catholicism." The focus of the issue that season centered, of course, on the Democratic candidate. Almost no one commented on the possibility that a Quaker like Nixon could not reasonably serve as president if elected—not only because he was a safe Protestant but also because his reputation and record failed to suggest that he would endanger national security by taking the pacifist position generally associated with his faith. Religion did emerge occasionally, as when North Carolina's governor Luther Hodges told a crowd in Charlottesville, Virginia, that Americans had selected a Quaker over a Catholic in 1928 and lived to regret it: "if you vote for a Quaker this time, you will regret it hor-ribly."[2] But such comments, uttered in the midst of the campaign, proba-bly amounted to little when it came to Nixon's religion and certainly not its specifics.

The well-known self-help pastor Norman Vincent Peale, a strong Nixon supporter, airily dismissed any religious liability when he commented on his candidate's Quaker faith, "I don't know that he ever let it bother him,"[3] a nice summary of the way most politicians operated at that level. Religion was there all right, lurking in the background, but it made little difference. Others who knew him had similar assessments. A commentator for the *Los Angeles Times,* Bill Henry, had attended church with the vice president but said he had never heard him speak of his faith. And a Nixon aide reported that his boss never mentioned Quakers or Quakerism in the three years he worked for him, but he still judged that he had a "deep religious feeling," even if he never expressed it openly.[4]

Kennedy's church affiliation was an obvious target for intense oppo-sition among Protestants in the South and Midwest, those areas of the country likely to respond to evangelists like Billy Graham, the people who seemed to have the most questions about Catholicism. Presbyterian L. Nelson Bell, Billy Graham's father-in-law, and an editor of the evangeli-cal magazine *Christianity Today,* informed Nixon that there was a "slow, completely integrated and planned attempt to take over our nation for the Roman Catholic Church," and the election of Kennedy was part of the plan.[5] Some board members at *Christianity Today* were even convinced that a Kennedy administration might revoke its tax-exempt status.[6] Given such sentiments, one chronicler of the campaign stated flatly that the reli-gious question was "the largest roadblock on [Kennedy's] path to the Oval Office."[7]

Because of the Hiss case, Nixon already possessed a reputation as an anti-Communist. Now he carefully cultivated a reputation as an inter-nationalist and slightly left-of-center Republican politician. While in the House, he had served on the so-called Herter Committee on foreign aid and had come home from a 1947 trip to Europe an avid supporter of eco-nomic assistance to Europe and of the Marshall Plan. He had enjoyed the support of the eastern Thomas E. Dewey wing of the Republican Party that had pushed him as Eisenhower's running mate in 1952. Most important of all, for the 1960 campaign he assiduously tied his less than conserva-tive political approach to his "Quaker heritage." He ticked off only three examples—central ones to his political career as it turned out—to illustrate the values "drilled into us at home, in school, and particularly in church in my early years": his "great interest in international affairs," "the problems of millions of people in the less developed areas of the world," and his "strong convictions on civil rights." He had been reared in a family, he testified, "always free from prejudice, whether racial or religious." So these were moral issues for him, growing out of "the traditional Quaker attitude of concern for less fortunate people."[8] Thus he deftly used some of the concerns of unprogrammed "liberal" Quakers as arrows in his political quiver.

It was fascinating that Nixon got strong political support for this maneuver from evangelical Billy Graham and from Thomas E. Dewey, long a leader of moderates within the Republican Party and its presidential candidate in both 1944 and 1948. Graham sent word that in a conversation with Dewey, the latter had wanted him to relay to Nixon that he considered the vice president one of the most able men in the party, but he worried that "you may be taken over unwittingly by some of the extreme right-wingers." Dewey and Graham united in believing that Nixon had to remain in the center if he was to carry the banner of the Republicans in 1960. Graham promised to use "what influence I can to show people that you are a man of moral integrity and Christian principle." Nixon agreed that Graham's political advice was "right on the beam," adding that he had been trying to follow it; there is no evidence, however, that he began attending church more often.[9] Practically all his life he retained a positive view of Graham's "rare perspective and insight. This is one of the reasons his predictions of political trends usually prove to be strikingly accurate," but he obviously did not always follow his recommendations.[10]

There was another side, however, to evangelical Quaker Nixon. For all his feet-on-the-desk ruminations about his Quaker heritage and his barely left-of-center political stance, Nixon associated with people who did not much care for the kind of Quakerism that could inspire pacifism, international cooperative institutions like the United Nations, or aggressive civil rights practices that might lead to breaking laws, all likely possibilities in the period. A sterling example of such a minion was Peale, pastor of the Marble Collegiate Dutch Reformed Church in New York and publisher of numerous books devoted to mind-curing self-help. A political bumbler, former Methodist Peale was also very much a theological lightweight. Boasting a fifteen-year record of cozying up to out-of-the-mainstream groups, he admitted invoking God's presence in the opening prayer for a WWII meeting of a far-right, nearly fascist, political pressure group, and he associated himself with Facts Forum, a creation of the ultra-conservative Texas billionaire H. L. Hunt in the mid-1950s.[11]

At the end of the war, Nixon was stationed briefly in New York. While there, he encountered Peale and attended his church.[12] Correspondence during the 1950s showed the two drawing close politically. Peale, a conservative who appealed to business leaders, developed a self-help theology with undertones of populism—something that appealed to the status-conscious Nixon—and he had a devoted following thanks to his *Guideposts* magazine (created in 1944) and his enormously popular book *The Power of Positive Thinking* (1952). He also wrote a syndicated newspaper column and was much in demand as a speaker at inspirational conferences. Businessmen were one of his target audiences and one that brought continuing acclaim. By 1957, Peale was estimating that he enjoyed an audience of fifty million people weekly, most likely the largest ever collected by a single American religious figure; it certainly surpassed that of his only rival, evangelist Billy Graham. Together he and Graham exemplified two aspects of the 1950s religious revival.[13]

Peale's notoriety, though, was not accompanied by any corresponding political shrewdness. His acumen deficit when it came to politics became starkly evident in the early days of the campaign, much to his embarrassment and Nixon's chagrin. Peale saw himself as something of an informal advisor on political realities, as he revealed in a long, informative letter to the candidate on August 1, 1960. Nixon had earlier asked him to distribute copies of journalist Bela Kornitzer's laudatory biography among opinion leaders, a task the New York preacher eagerly executed; Peale pledged, "Anything I can do to help your campaign is all too little." He thought it "incredible" that voters might choose a man like Kennedy, who had, compared to the vice president, so little experience and character, and he reported that in a recent conference with Billy Graham the two had agreed to "do all within our power to help you."

Peale then passed on some specific advice regarding people he had encountered in his travels who might be of help. He included a New Yorker, whose name and address he supplied, he had met recently in Austria who promised to mobilize millions of foreign-born Americans to support Nixon. (An alert Nixon wrote in the margin that one of his aides should note this information.) He also relayed the news that he had talked with Israeli leaders like Ben-Gurion and Abba Eban, whom he found supportive of the vice president, and also conferred with Arabs, who were also responsive, particularly after he related "that a real statesman is running against an insatiable opportunist with vast sums of money at his disposal."

Peale considered "the idea that Kennedy has more 'glamour' than you is rubbish," and advised Nixon to get out among the people—the Bills, Johns, Marys, and Berthas—so that each could say on returning home, "I saw Nixon today—you know, he is a good guy, just like anyone." He also wanted Nixon to be seen in church every Sunday, the same advice Graham customarily gave, as a way of appealing to the loyalties of "the great honest masses of our people." Returning to his populist theme, he emphasized that "America is still folksy, not Madison Avenue-ish." He wanted a "walking, man-to-man campaign down the streets of America" so that "the dim and ill-defined personality of a distinguished figure in Washington becomes simply Dick Nixon, who came from where we all started, among the humble, decent people of the land." "And your personality," Peale wrote, "never fails to communicate when people get close to you." From his notes in the margins it was clear that candidate Nixon was happy to garner such news, even if subsequent events were to prove that Peale's advice did not match his political know-how.[14]

Billy Graham was much more the political pro. His choice of Nixon was not much of a secret. By his own admission, his hardly circumspect endorsements of the vice president on radio and television—"the best qualified and best trained man in America for the presidency"—by mid- to late 1959 had already captured headlines. He pleaded with Nixon again to attend church regularly. Writing on November 19, Graham reminded his friend that he already had the support of "the overwhelming majority of the religious-minded people" of the nation. That support was precisely why he needed to be seen in church every Sunday, for his political enemies would trumpet any inconsistency discovered in his actions. Graham claimed to have received letters from concerned Christians criticizing him for endorsing a man who chose to absent himself from religious services; the evangelist did not mind such letters himself because he had taken his stand and would stick by it, but he did not like what they implied about the softness of Nixon's religious support—something the vice president could remedy easily, merely by going to church every Sunday. He had to prevent his Protestant support from going soft, even disappearing.[15]

Nixon simply did not want to put himself in situations where his religion was on display. He instructed Graham that the Quaker way was to keep piety private: "We sit in silence," he explained,[16] even though evangelical Friends seldom did. To him, ostentatiously going to church also smacked of injecting the issue of religion into the campaign, as a Kennedy supporter had complained he was doing once when the Nixons were photographed returning from church. "This shows that you just can't win on that issue!" he all but exploded to Graham. The most effective thing ministers could do with church members was to urge them to vote.[17] Graham already knew that. In October 1959, a full year before the election, he told a crusade audience in Indianapolis that "Christians ought to get into politics. Mr. Nixon . . . is certainly every inch a Christian gentleman."[18]

Other fervent evangelicals made the same plea to the vice president. L. Nelson Bell wrote Nixon in July 1959 that he thought Graham had offered timely advice. He acknowledged the validity of the Quaker's concern that his "Christian faith" not become a matter of "political exploration." "At the same time," Bell went on, "it is vitally important that the Christians of American have a sense of direction when looking to their national leaders." Before the 1960 campaign revved up, Nixon "will be in a position to make an affirmation of your faith which could be a background of comfort." Bell suggested specifically that Nixon should write an article for *Christianity Today* and thus reach a "great majority" of Protestant ministers in the nation.[19]

When it came to the presidential campaign of 1960, the issue of religion, specifically Catholicism, was never far from the evangelical mind. Graham's contacts were extensive, something others realized and used to their advantage. In early June the preacher to politicians went by the Senate office of Majority Leader Lyndon Johnson and found him with Speaker of the House Sam Rayburn, both Texans. Johnson had already decided to try to get into the race to deny the nomination to Kennedy, so the Texas allies used Graham to send a message to Nixon, the likely Republican nominee. The Texans were convinced, reported Graham, that if nominated, Kennedy would probably garner nearly 100 percent of the Catholic vote. Graham echoed Johnson and Rayburn and suggested that Nixon had to find a way to solidify the Protestant vote behind him; he opined that the surest way to do so was to select Minnesota Congressman Walter Judd, a former missionary doctor in China, as his running mate. This kind of political advice went so far beyond what Graham usually proffered that he instructed Nixon that the letter was strictly confidential and advised that he should destroy it after reading it.[20]

Graham had reason to remain circumspect, for he simply did not want to appear to be overtly involved in political affairs, even if distancing himself from the political arena might produce a Roman Catholic president such as Kennedy, something evangelical Protestants found difficult to contemplate. Hence there was a sleight-of-hand aspect to his political actions during this period. On the one hand, he knew how to cultivate politicians, as when he told Nixon in a letter marked "Personal and Confidential" that "God is giving you supernatural wisdom in handling difficult situations." Graham related that he rose at three in the morning in Europe to listen to the nominee's acceptance speech at the Republican convention in Chicago.[21]

On the other hand, after encouraging Peale in August to attend a September 7 gathering in Washington that focused squarely on the issue occasioned by a Catholic presidential candidate—a get-together that proved to be quite controversial and damaging to all involved—Graham looked back on the affair and admitted in his autobiography that he was "privately glad" that he could remain in Europe and did not have to attend.[22] Hence, though remaining behind the scenes, as was his preference where political controversy was likely, Graham was involved in setting up the conference. All three of these men, Peale the front man, Graham the maneuverer, and Nixon the candidate, found themselves scrambling to explain and make excuses for what others saw as their roles in interjecting the religious issue into the campaign.

A Swiss gathering in Montreux, on the scenic shore of Lake Geneva, remains to this day shrouded in mystery.[23] But there is no doubt it helped lay the groundwork for the subsequent and explosive one-day conclave in Washington on September 7. We know that Graham planned his Montreux meeting for Thursday, August 18, of a group of between twenty-five and thirty evangelical leaders, but less than a third of those who attended are known. Nor do we know how long they were in session. They met for what Graham labeled an "evangelism strategy conference," sounding rather more theological than a confab designed to focus on issues raised by a Roman Catholic candidate for president of the United States. Aside from Graham, the best-known person there was Peale, who, despite his fame, was definitely not on par with Graham as evangelical spokesman. Graham had invited him at the last minute after Peale, vacationing in Europe, requested to speak to Graham about publicly endorsing Nixon for president, a step he had already taken.[24]

The few names we do know suggest that some of the most politically involved evangelicals took part. L. Nelson Bell was one of these prominent secondary figures. A medical doctor who had served as a Presbyterian missionary to China before World War II and the Communist rise to power, Bell was an active member of the southern Presbyterian church, helping start the *Southern Presbyterian Journal* in 1942 to combat "liberalism" and "modernism" in his church. His daughter Ruth married Graham in the following year. In 1956 he encouraged his son-in-law to back his idea for an evangelical counterweight to the more established—and liberal—*Christian Century* magazine; they dubbed their creation *Christianity Today*, and it quickly became quite influential. The fact that its founders based it in the nation's capital underscored their intention that it should have the maximum national political impact. It carried a major burden in the campaign against Roman Catholic Kennedy in 1960. Bell served as the magazine's executive editor until his 1973 death.[25]

Other participants were just as politically involved, if in other ways. Graham said about one of them, Harold Ockenga, the gentlemanly pastor of Boston's Park Street Congregational Church, "I never made a major decision without first calling and asking his advice and counsel." Boasting a doctorate from the University of Pittsburgh, Ockenga did not permit his academic achievement to overshadow his evangelical convictions or piety and served as founding president of the National Association of Evangelicals, among other positions.[26]

Two others at Montreux, Baptist Clyde Taylor and Congregationalist J. Elwin Wright, were also involved with this group, a rival of the ecumenical and liberal Federal Council of Churches. (The association, founded in 1942, made the term *evangelical* more acceptable than the previously used *fundamentalist* to describe those who adhered to biblical inerrancy and literalism. Evangelical was also more appealing than fundamentalist to the increasing numbers of upwardly mobile and better educated Christians after World War II; Quakers shared this preference, for fundamentalism implied a more literal theological position that had never been popular among them. Thus it was natural that those who led California Yearly Meeting would embrace the term *evangelical* to describe themselves.)[27] Both Taylor and Wright were vigorous anti-Catholics and deeply involved in promoting the Washington meeting of the "National Conference of Citizens for Religious Freedom" dealing with church-state separation the next month.[28] Daniel Poling, a vocal opponent of pacifism, had been pastor of Marble Collegiate Church in the 1920s and now edited the *Christian Herald*.[29] Samuel Shoemaker, a fiery New York City Episcopal priest, was noted for his association with Alcoholics Anonymous; some described him as its cofounder.[30]

With such politically involved evangelicals predominating, it was impossible to avoid the unfolding presidential campaign in the United States, even if the participants in the "evangelism strategy conference" had wanted to. "We have just had a conference with twenty-five outstanding American clergymen," Billy Graham began his account of the gathering in a letter to Nixon on August 22, a date suggesting that the meeting had not been a one-day affair. They discussed "at great length" the implications of the political campaign, "particularly as related to the religious issue." Graham described for Nixon seven "observations" that resulted from the deliberations:

1) "A highly financed and organized" Washington office was going to open on September 8 to supply information to American religious leaders. It would operate at the "highest level" and would be free of "bigotry and intolerance," which, he seemed to suggest as an implied criticism of previous fundamentalist forays, sometimes hampered efforts to highlight Catholic threats to church-state separation.

2) A just-concluded survey revealed that 76 percent of Protestant cler-

gymen were supporting Nixon. By the election, more than two months away, the percentage would be "greatly increased."

3) "It was generally felt" that there would be "an overwhelming Catholic block vote" for Kennedy, but it was not expected to be as massive as earlier estimates. The participants agreed that the Catholic vote was as large as it would ever be, but the Protestant vote, presumably for Nixon, would gain momentum and increase.

4) Those participants who were from the South did not believe that Kennedy's choice of Senate Majority Leader Lyndon Johnson as his running mate would necessarily succeed in wooing voters from the South and the border states to the Democratic side. All, whether from the North or the South, thought Republicans should emphasize their "more conservative platform" and the religion issue, both of which could overcome southern questions about civil rights.

5) The conferees "commissioned" Peale and Graham to urge Nixon to be more outspoken about his religious views, which remained murky and gave concern "throughout Protestantism." Graham had attempted to explain Nixon's reticence when it came to talking about religion, but the others present insisted that the people had "a right to know of a candidate's religious convictions." Graham urged him once again to speak out on the subject. (This was also Bell's position.)

6) Graham confided that he had just written a letter to his mailing list of two million American families to organize their Sunday school classes and churches to get out the vote. (Beside this news, Nixon wrote "good.") He also reported that most of his following was in the Midwest, California, Pennsylvania, and New York, but that his mailings went to every post office in the United States. "We are getting other religious groups throughout the Nation to do the same," and hence expect many millions would be contacted.

7) "Dr. Peale is coming out flat-footed for you in a sermon on or about October 9." Though this move might be costly and provoke personal attacks on him, he "feels he must speak out at all cost."

Graham concluded his three-page letter with the wish that Nixon could come to North Carolina during the campaign, a move he expected would "dramatize the religious issue throughout the Nation without mentioning it publicly" and tip the Tar Heel State into his column. The next day, Graham wrote again to add that the attenders at the meeting were agreed that Nixon's campaign was not as well organized as Kennedy's; he amplified that from his own observation that the Democrat seemed much more able to get his name in the press and before the electorate than Nixon. Nixon was impressed enough to call an aide's attention to Graham's observation.[31]

This letter placed in Nixon's hands the obvious intelligence that he had a loyal cadre of supporters among prominent evangelical clergymen, leaders with the will and means to mobilize millions of their fellow believers. And they were willing to act on their own with no direction from him or financing from Republican coffers. Even if they sniped at him for not speaking out on religious matters, they still supported him firmly and warmly. The letter also made him aware that, despite what such clergymen might say publicly about tolerance and laying aside bigotry, they were willing to use widespread Protestant concern about Roman Catholicism in a way that would benefit him. In this sense he could personally take the high road and refrain from using religion as a campaign tactic, while allowing his evangelical backers to fan anti-Catholic sentiment that would rebound to his political advantage, perhaps even victory. There was no conspiracy here—a community of interest grew out of the shared assumption that the Republican and Quaker Richard Nixon would make a better president than the Democrat and Roman Catholic John Kennedy.[32]

Because the Montreux meeting confirmed, privately, what Nixon knew but did not have to mention publicly—that he enjoyed the avid support of evangelical leaders, both lay and cleric—it was vitally more important than the notorious September 7 National Conference of Citizens for Religious Freedom in Washington that grabbed newspaper headlines. This was the gathering, let it be recalled, that Graham at Montreux had pushed Norman Vincent Peale to attend, the same one about which decades later the astute Graham would write he had been "privately glad that I would still be in Europe and therefore unable to attend."[33] Hence when the news of the meeting hit the papers on September 8, Graham was safely an ocean and half a continent away. Nixon likewise was not involved, probably knowing nothing of it; he was hospitalized at Walter Reed Army Medical Center for an infected knee that he hit against a car door while campaigning about the time of the Montreux meeting.[34]

The most prominent person present, Norman Vincent Peale, agreed to preside.[35] This proved a serious mistake because he was a latecomer to the effort and knew little of what was going on. And his role as public spokesman for the meeting caused it to be dubbed the "Peale Group" immediately and forever. It would have been more accurate to call it the NAE, for the National Association of Evangelicals, group, but that title would not have tripped off the tongue quite so flippantly. Nor would it have caught the attention of the pubic the way Peale's name did. Except for sectarians, however, few knew anything about the NAE, while Peale had millions of readers and fans.

The man principally responsible for putting this meeting together was a young NAE staffer and contributing editor for its periodical *United Evangelical Action*, Baptist preacher Donald Gill. Gill was apparently granted leave from the NAE at the behest of the seventy-year-old J. Elwin Wright, generally credited with coming up with the idea of the NAE in 1941. Clyde Taylor, who among other positions—Graham identified him as secretary of the World Evangelism Fellowship[36]—sat on the board of the NAE and embraced Wright's idea. The NAE, a relatively tiny organization of evangelical churches whose members disliked any hint of centralization, had Roman Catholicism near the top of its list of the world's evils.[37] On this occasion Taylor worked out an alliance with Protestants and Other Americans United for Separation of Church and State, a group with secular and religious representatives who organized to protect the First Amendment's promise; it published tracts, supplied speakers, and bought advertisements to raise the specter of Catholic threats to First Amendment guarantees of religious freedom.

The meeting convened in private at the Mayflower Hotel with about 150 in attendance, mostly Baptists; only a tiny number of Presbyterians and Methodists were present; no Episcopalians took part. An energetic reporter from Long Island's *Newsday*, Bonnie Angelo, showed up to cover the proceedings, only to learn that it was closed to the press. She promptly found a room wired for sound adjacent to the meeting room and listened to the proceedings from there; for the afternoon session she brought in a *Washington Post* reporter with whom she shared her notes from the morning after he agreed that his paper's story would not appear until after *Newsday* hit the streets.

Gill had planned well. Each person received a "manual" containing sample tracts and suggested resources for organizing local groups; the manual also included a copy of the previously prepared statement that Peale was to read to the press at the conference's adjournment. A soloist sang all verses of "I Want to Be a Christian in My Heart." There was an appeal for funds to carry on the work, an offering being something of a necessity among evangelical Protestants. The speakers, including Harold Ockenga, who was, after Peale, the most prominent clergyman present, delivered a boilerplate warning of the inability of a Catholic president to withstand pressure from the Roman hierarchy. Graham's father-in-law, L. Nelson Bell, reminded his auditors, "Pseudo tolerance is not tolerance at all but merely ignorance."[38]

Following the afternoon session Peale, Ockenga, and Gill met with the press for nearly an hour outside the meeting room. It was this give and take with the reporters that caught the headlines because the casual Peale was clearly unprepared and showed poorly. He admitted to an early questioner that no Roman Catholic was present and that almost all the attenders were evangelical Protestants. While hardly a surprise, it was a reality that called into question the press release's statement that participants had "fairly" discussed "facts." He conceded that prominent theologian Reinhold Niebuhr had not been invited because nothing would have been done had he come. One reporter wanted to know if Kennedy's voting record had been discussed; Peale denied that it had, but the *Washington Post*'s story the next day contradicted this denial by noting that his vote on aid to parochial schools had drawn attention. Asked if there was any way that Senator Kennedy could reassure him about his ability to meet the demands of his faith and be president, Peale was blunt, accurate, and impolitic: "Not unless he renounces his church's doctrines,"[39] something impossible if Kennedy were to remain a Catholic. It was on this occasion, too, that Peale inadvertently if honestly denigrated Nixon's Quakerism. Asked if the vice president's Quaker background gave him pause, the New York cleric was candid, "I don't know that he ever let it bother him."

The whole affair was an unmitigated disaster for the evangelicals. If they wanted publicity, they got it—in spades. The person who gave the invocation, George Docherty, pastor of the New York Avenue Presbyterian Church in the capital, bailed out the next day by declaring he supported Kennedy. The nation's press was universally hostile; Billy Graham was astounded at the twist the media administered.[40] Niebuhr, professor at Union Theological Seminary in New York, and a colleague there, John C. Bennett, both leaders also in New York state's Liberal Party, leveled charges of "religious prejudice" at Peale and the "Peale Group." Peale withdrew from Citizens for Religious Freedom three days later, and, chastened, he and his wife went into hiding. This speedy about-face marked him as a coward to evangelicals, a situation helped not at all by his public true confession that "I was not duped—I was just stupid." He even formally resigned the pastorate of Marble Collegiate Church, but its governing board refused to accept his resignation. Citizens for Religious Freedom petered out presently. Amid all this folderol Graham was in Europe, carrying on his crusade against sin, not Roman Catholicism in the United States.

By the following Sunday, September 11, Nixon was out of Walter Reed and raring to take on the issue of religion in the campaign. Scheduled to be interviewed on *Meet the Press,* he was ready when a question came about the Peale Group. He did not jump on Peale, but he refused to associate himself with the statement the conference of Citizens for Religious Freedom and Peale had issued. Then he went on to affirm that he believed with "no doubt" that his opponent "would put the Constitution of the United States above any other consideration"; by implication, he would do the same. It may have been what a candidate for the highest office in the land had to say, but it was not what a serious Quaker—or for that matter what a serious Christian of any sort—would say so absolutely. He did not want the election "determined primarily, or even substantially, on religious grounds." "As far as I am concerned," he stressed as firmly as he could,

> I have issued orders to all of the people in my campaign not to discuss religion, not to raise it, not to allow anybody to participate in the campaign who does so on that ground, and as far as I am concerned, I will decline to discuss religion and will discuss other issues in order to keep the minds of the people on the issues that should decide this election and to keep them off of an issue that should not enter it.

He hoped Senator Kennedy would do the same.[41]

Nixon's stance had the added advantage of freeing him from discussing any embarrassing questions about his own religious convictions or even revealing anything substantive about them. Very few people believed that his Quaker heritage might interfere with his responsibilities if he were elected. He was not a pacifist—that was quite clear from his naval service during World War II—and his record of supporting measures to push back militarily against the communists was beyond question also. Clearly, he could envision no conflict between his faith and his responsibilities as a future commander-in-chief. By refusing to discuss religious issues he would be able to set aside any aspect of Quakerism or Christianity that anyone might interpret as requiring actions that would prevent him from taking the presidential oath to "to preserve, protect, and defend the Constitution of the United States," as required in Article II.

Earlier in April, months before he was nominated, Nixon had told the American Society of Newspaper Editors that he could envision only one way that religion could legitimately be part of the campaign and that was if a candidate for the highest office claimed no religion at all. Fortunately that was not the case in 1960. All potential candidates, he said, "recognize and cherish, both in their personal and public lives, the religious and moral principles which are the very foundation of our American ideals." He was no more specific than those nonpartisan and noninflammatory words. As far as he was concerned, the campaign could now proceed happily by ignoring the candidates' religion as an issue.[42] Thus he embraced a kind of natural religion that he saw underpinning American society, rather than a revealed faith from the Bible, championed by most evangelical Christians, or, in the case of historic Quakers, from the inward promptings of Christ. Unwilling to acknowledge that an agnostic and especially an atheist could qualify for president, Nixon with his statement drained away the kind of religious commitment that flowed from divine demands that traditional prophetic religion laid on its adherents.[43]

Although Citizens for Religious Freedom was fatally injured by the Mayflower conference, the National Association of Evangelicals soldiered on in its stead. In October, its board of administration issued a "Statement of Concern" condemning the failure of the American Catholic hierarchy to repudiate and abandon its interference with policies that threatened private conscience. Going a step further, it also took aim at pro-Kennedy Americans who used the word *bigot* as a way to describe those who were concerned with the political power of the Catholic Church.[44] After the election, Clyde Taylor and the NAE's executive director in an interview outlined a strategy for the 1960s in the group's monthly magazine. They repeated a call for evangelical Christians to get involved in politics so as to counter Catholics at the local level.[45] Evangelicals would use this overt political approach for the next few decades, even after they changed sides and made common cause with Catholics on issues like abortion and anti-Communism.

There were costs to the evangelical strategy, psychic ones anyway, such as being aroused from a good night's sleep. J. Elwin Wright, founder of the NAE and early backer of the Citizens for Religious Freedom, complained bitterly that his efforts "to present the religious issue fairly and without prejudice or invective" through the Washington conference had resulted in heaps of abuse, anonymous midnight telephone calls, crudely written postcards, and publicity "with an unfavorable slant."[46] And purely functionary Wright, unlike the Quaker Republican Richard Nixon, was not running for national office.

True to his word, Nixon remained mum on the issue of religion during the rest of the campaign. He correctly surmised that it was a double-barreled issue and likely to damage him regardless of how he might use it. So he decided to stand aside, encourage his ardent evangelical supporters to get out their vote, likely to go for him and collectively larger than the Catholic poll would be, but not dwell on the religious issue himself, less he be pilloried as a bigot. (Interestingly, Graham endorsed this approach.)[47] Too, Nixon had to hold on to a good proportion of the Catholics who had voted for Eisenhower in 1956 if he were to defeat Kennedy, something difficult to do unless he could get his opponent's pledge to forego religion as an issue. It was altogether a difficult task.

Fortunately for his campaign effort, Senator Kennedy was not so hampered. Indeed, any hint of Protestant opposition would likely unite Catholics behind him and put the larger, northern, and urban states more firmly into his column, helping him and preventing Nixon from holding on to part of the Catholic vote. The Democratic campaign acted with alacrity. Kennedy's brother Robert thought religion, despite all protestations to the contrary, was the number one issue; already he had tied Peale to Nixon, suggesting that the clergyman's effort to distance himself from the failed effort could not obscure Republican attempts to use religion as an issue. Only days after the now notorious September 7 meeting, the Massachusetts senator apprehensively accepted the invitation of the mainly Protestant Greater Houston Ministerial Association to address them on September 12 and answer questions about religion in the campaign. Kennedy gave a masterful performance, especially appealing for tolerance, causing Texan and Democratic House speaker Sam Rayburn, keenly aware of the power of evangelical preachers in his state, to chortle, "he ate 'em blood raw."[48]

A few days later, on September 17, during a press conference in Minneapolis, reporters tried unsuccessfully to corner Nixon on the religion issue again. One asked him about Kennedy's promise to resign the presidency if his duties interfered with his religious beliefs; would Nixon make the same pledge? Side-stepping neatly, the vice president said he could not comment lest he make religion an issue in the campaign. Would it violate your pledge, persisted another reporter, to respond to Democratic vice presidential nominee Lyndon Johnson's remark that he was getting letters questioning your ability, as a Quaker, to discharge the duties of president? It would, averred Nixon: "I will not comment on it." Well, then, the unidentified reporter bored in, "Have you gotten any mail of that kind?" "I have had letters from Quakers complaining about the fact that I am not a pacifist, and I have had letters from non-Quakers complaining about the fact that I am a Quaker. So, I am in both sides of this issue."[49]

The campaign was not over, of course—the first-ever televised presidential debates still lay ahead—but religion as an issue addressed by the candidates all but disappeared. Nixon occasionally mentioned Quakers in his campaign speeches, but only in passing and only in ways to set himself off from Quaker testimonies. For example, in Canton, Ohio, home of staunchly evangelical Quaker Malone College, in early October, he asked an enthusiastic audience what the country should do to "keep the peace without surrender." He answered his rhetorical question: "First, we've got to begin with the greatest military strength in the world." "I say this, speaking from my own Quaker background," he went on, "because I know that there are many who are concerned because American [sic] maintains military strength."[50]

Later that month, at a breakfast in Los Angeles, Nixon expanded on this position a bit, to make clear to any doubters that he was not the kind of Quaker who would weaken the nation. He agreed that those who opposed his candidacy also wanted peace. The question was how to achieve it, what means to use. Many of his friends, he said, his Quaker friends, were his strongest critics. They wanted to know why he was not more supportive of disarmament and why he could not be more trusting of the Russians and their proposals on disarmament. It hurt him, he claimed, to hear criticism from people who were committed to peace so strongly. Why do I, he asked, differ with this longing for a way to achieve peace? "I know," he said, "that when there are men in the world who are on the loose who are not for what we are [for], who are out to conquer the world, by any means, if necessary, by war, if possible by any means, if necessary, including war. . . ." Facing people like Chinese leader Mao Tse-tung, who believed that a third world war might bring a communist world, "we have to have a strong force which can be a guardian for peace."[51]

Evangelical Protestant churches were awash in anti-Catholicism, publicized by sermons, magazine articles, and numberless religious tracts that were cheap to print in lurid colors, easy to distribute, and filled with the latest diatribes from questionable sources. In many ways the 1960 campaign offered, as it turned out, a last opportunity before television took over completely to depict overweight red- or black-cloaked medieval-looking Catholic bishops, carrying hooked shepherd crooks grasping for political power while subverting the Protestant-created U.S. Constitution.[52] Many articles in *United Evangelical Action* carried notes listing the prices of reprints for distribution, such as the one the executive director of NAE George Ford wrote in May entitled, "A Catholic President: How Free from Church Control?"[53]

The same kind of material even went to the Quaker candidate's mother, Hannah Nixon; presumably she could get to him if anyone could. Someone from Harrisburg, Pennsylvania, sent anti-Catholic tracts entitled "Lincoln's Assassins" and "To Kill Protestants." A person who addressed her by her given name and described himself as a Friend wrote that "we dare not" elect a Catholic, regardless of what "they" say. And another letter's author expressed shock about his discovery that Rose Mary Woods, Nixon's longtime secretary, was a Roman Catholic.[54]

Graham was still in Europe and would remain there until the first week in October, about a month before the election. He continued to counsel Nixon on the campaign from afar, advice that the candidate told an aide "makes a hell of a lot of sense." Graham was convinced that the Democrats were using the religious issue to solidify the Catholic vote behind their man and split the Protestant vote. And Graham went on to reiterate the word he had from Lyndon Johnson in June, that "Kennedy can be elected solely on the religious issue." The truth in this assessment, Graham insisted, must be repeated over and over but "*not by you*," he emphasized. Instead President Eisenhower must repeat it on the stump: "It would not hurt him in the slightest and it would dramatically turn the tide by showing both Protestants and Catholics that they had been led into a political trap." Get prominent Republicans like Nelson Rockefeller, Thomas Dewey, and New York senator Jacob Javits, the evangelist recommended, to say similar things. As for Graham, he did not want to get involved, lest he be crucified—"we have already witnessed what the Press did to Peale"—and that would rebound back onto Nixon. As the campaign progressed, he might reconsider, but not yet.[55]

At the same time as the kerfuffle over the Peale Group, another mostly ignored and internal Quaker to-do nearly surfaced for all to see. It involved the AFSC and commemoration of the 300th anniversary of the Quaker declaration against war, the single most defining testimony of Friends. Let AFSC's pursuit of peace thrust Quakers and their supporters into public view in a way that might prove embarrassing to the vice president, and the velvet gloves would come off. In mid-August 1960, word reached staffers in Nixon's office that Quakers were planning something they called a "Friends Peace Pilgrimage" at the Pentagon the weekend of October 23 and 24, a little more than a week before the election. In a close election such a dramatic public affair could easily direct attention to an aspect of Quakerism that Nixon would much rather keep under wraps. Religion was already involved in the campaign, and Nixon wanted to make sure that no public attention came to rest on controversial Quaker testimonies, like pacifism. As planned, the pilgrimage certainly had the potential for doing just that.

Stanley McCaffrey, executive assistant to the vice president, called in D. Elton Trueblood, a Quaker well known in the broader religious world who had served as chief of religious affairs in the U.S. Information Agency during the first four years of the Eisenhower administration, to see if he would assist in getting the pilgrimage postponed until after the election. Trueblood and his wife interrupted their vacation to come to Washington on September 7—the same day the Peale Group gathered—to discuss the matter with McCaffrey and E. Raymond Wilson, head of the Friends Committee on National Legislation, the Quaker lobbying group in the capital. Trueblood took the lead in the hour-long meeting, arguing strenuously against the pilgrimage, while McCaffrey occupied the high ground by stressing that the vice president only wanted to supply information to any who needed it. McCaffrey's information consisted of raising questions about the wisdom of holding such a gathering just prior to the election, a view with which Trueblood agreed. McCaffrey reminded Wilson of the possibility of injecting religious issues into the campaign. He referred specifically to Nixon's membership in the Friends Church, presumably as a reminder that Nixon would be tarred by this Quaker action. The next morning, September 8, he received a telephone call from Wilson saying that he had conferred with those planning the event and that it had been rescheduled for the weekend following the election. McCaffrey dispatched a telegram thanking Trueblood for his efforts in helping secure this "wise decision."[56]

The pilgrimage did take place from November 12 through November 14, attracting over a thousand participants from all over the country. They walked from downtown Washington to the Pentagon, where whole families stood in silence, holding signs in two-hour shifts until 3:30 p.m. on Monday. There were no catcalls or shouts from uniformed or civilian workers, only respectful glances as people entered the five-sided military building, and stares from the windows during the day. Some Quakers claimed it was the most successful demonstration that Friends had ever mounted, but it came after the ballots had been counted—too late, thanks to the efforts of Nixon's staff, to have any impact on the general population or the election.[57]

Graham returned home during the first week in October and was soon galvanized by the politics around him. Nixon's chances seemed doubtful, and Kennedy's popularity was growing daily. His talk of sacrifice and boldly facing the challenges of the 1960s even appealed to Graham. The next week he visited Republican Henry R. Luce, publisher of *Time* and *Life* magazines, and told him that he favored Nixon but did not want to get involved in politics, lest he fall afoul the press and receive the Norman Vincent Peale treatment. After a long and inconclusive conversation Luce suggested that Graham write a personal evaluation of Nixon and that he would run it in *Life*. Burdened with misgivings, the evangelist agreed, went back home to Montreat, and, inspired, dictated a bit more than 1,200 words in an hour, "the easiest article I've ever done."

The article bespoke close friendship and admiration for Nixon, relating how they had met a decade before and had grown close by golfing, swimming, and engaging in long earnest talks. Nixon, said his friend, "holds a deep conviction that we must make every effort toward a spiritual revitalization of the western world." Yet despite a noble goal that Graham shared, he had determined to remain on the sidelines "especially when religion became an issue in the campaign."

Yet, evangelist Graham went on, he was a citizen too, just as were all the movie stars, labor leaders, and columnists. Even ministers—he instanced Niebuhr and Bennett of Union Theological Seminary—were speaking out in favor of Senator Kennedy. He cited world leaders, none by name, who had told him that Americans were electing a leader of the free world; hence the average American voter should realize that as "you vote you will be voting for scores of little people around the world." "I believe that the vice president has the qualities and possibilities of being another Abraham Lincoln to lead us in these years of crisis ahead. He is already a world figure of whom Chairman [Nikita] Khrushchev [of the Soviet Union] is afraid." Graham could not understand charges that Nixon was cold or calculating or how people could say they did not know why but they just did not like him. "Richard Nixon, to me," he said, "is the epitome of warmth, affability, and sincerity," with "qualities found in few people." But "his outstanding quality is sincerity." "His mind doesn't seem to reach for political gimmicks. . . . I can testify that he has a deep personal faith in God springing from devout Christian parents yet he is reluctant to speak publicly about it. . . . I know him to be a deeply religious man."

He concluded by emphasizing that the 1960s "could be the world's decade of decision," a word he customarily used in his crusades. Graham was not saying all this because he was against Kennedy; "I'm simply for Mr. Nixon." Of course, he would support Kennedy were he to be elected, but "[w]e need to decide this election on our knees." "As for me, I will vote for the man I believe to the best qualified, for the man who has given us every reason to be proud whether before a belligerent Khrushchev in Moscow or a howling mob in Venezuela."[58] Glowing and politically astute, it was a recommendation that responded to many of the charges made during the campaign and, had it appeared, might well have influenced and won votes for the Quaker from California.

(The reference to Khrushchev in Moscow offered telling insights into both Graham's and Nixon's fundamental presuppositions. It referred to Nixon's famous "kitchen" debate with the Russian premier in Sokolniki Park, site of the American National Exhibition, where there was a model American home costing around $14,000. A celebration of the latest fruits of American materialism, with a new color television set in the living room rivaling fancy gadgets in the kitchen, the exhibit saw the two leaders tossing around claims about which nation supplied its people's need more adequately. Soon they were disagreeing on which side presented ultimatums to the other. Back and forth the debate went, but the discussion never got beyond the purely material to dwell on deeper spiritual or religious values. Neither Nixon, who recognized that the debate would have a political impact back home, nor Graham, whose faith should have led him to rise above the material, seemed to understand the broader implications of the kitchen debate; instead they gloried in the very materialism that President Eisenhower had hoped to move the debate with communism beyond.)[59]

Graham was still troubled and called three friends for advice, all Nixon supporters: Republican Senator Frank Carlson from Kansas, journalist David Lawrence, editor of *U.S. News and World Report,* and radio newscaster Paul Harvey; none, of course, had read the article. Carlson was doubtful but on balance thought the piece should appear. The other two were adamant that it should not, but Graham remained unsure. The night before *Life* was to go to press, he and his wife, Ruth, got on their knees and prayed that God would use the article if it did appear, *"and if it was His will that it not appear that He would perform a miracle and stop it!"* By the next morning they had resigned themselves to its coming out—until the telephone rang and three miracles occurred, one right after the other: Florida Senator George Smathers, North Carolina Governor Luther Hodges, and Tennessee Governor Frank Clements, Democrats all, called and expressed "deep concern" about the article. Clement told him out right, "I love you no matter what you do, but I hope you don't publish it." And Hodges added that he would be "getting into politics."[60]

Mystified—though that was how miracles leave those to whom they happen—Graham had no idea how they knew anything about it, until publisher Luce telephoned at 10:00 A.M. to tell him he had called Kennedy during the night about the article. Appealing for fairness, Kennedy asked if he could get a prominent Protestant supporter, someone like Reinhold Niebuhr, to prepare a similar piece for him. (Kennedy must have called his three southern supporters; otherwise they would not have known what Graham had agreed to do.)

Luce wanted to go ahead with the original, but Graham got him to agree to await the arrival of another piece, one that simply asked Americans to go to the polls to vote. Though doubtful, Luce agreed to wait. When the nonpartisan one arrived, Luce liked it and agreed to run it. Graham interpreted this all as an example of God's "strange and mysterious way."[61] Graham said later that he had tried to reach Nixon personally to talk the matter over with him, and his staff seemed so indecisive that his own misgivings multiplied. Only after he and Luce had agreed to withhold the first article did staffers approve running it, but then it was too late.[62]

Nixon himself responded ten months later, after the ballots were all in, admitting that at the time "we were simply at a loss as to how properly to handle the religious issue." On the one hand, Kennedy and other Democrats—he mentioned Governor Hodges of North Carolina as a prime example—used religion "shamelessly" against him. He now believed that the original Graham article would have been "a definite plus," but he also remembered, on the other hand, how Peale had been mishandled by the press; he had not wanted Graham to face the same "savage attacks." He wrote nothing that could be considered a rebuke.[63] In *Six Crises*, he claimed to have "vetoed" Graham's article, but there is no contemporary evidence that he did so, and Graham never mentioned that Nixon had anything to say about it.[64]

Kennedy's victory margin on November 8 was just over 100,000 votes nationwide out of a record 68.8 million ballots cast. Kennedy only barely carried Texas where Baptists and members of the Churches of Christ were strong and apt to be anti-Catholic. In analyzing such a close election it is possible to isolate any single issue as tipping the scales one way or the other, so one cannot finally conclude that religion was decisive. But Nixon's refusal to discuss religion at all or take forthright stands on matters of concern to Protestants—such as the flashpoint issue of aid to parochial schools, which he tried to sidestep by saying that Congress might give aid to states, which could in turn dispense the funds to schools as they chose—clearly hurt him among those who wanted a sturdy wall between church and state and feared Roman Catholic influence. Unhampered by a self-imposed ban on discussing religion, Kennedy appealed for tolerance, opposed government aid to church schools, and rejected sending an American ambassador to the Vatican, the last two counter to the wishes of many in the Catholic hierarchy. One historian concluded that Kennedy's Catholicism hurt him with devout Protestants while winning him massive numbers of Catholic voters. In short, Nixon lost his gamble when he tried to leave religion on the sidelines.[65] Popular radio commentator Paul Harvey, friend to both Nixon and Graham, remarked on the air as though to Graham, "your personal friend lost by the margin you could have delivered."[66]

Historian Sean Casey concluded his book on the religious issues in the 1960 campaign by asking a relevant question about John Kennedy: What kind of Catholic was he? This is not the place to explore that question, but it reminds us that a similar one has never been asked about Quaker Richard Nixon. A Texas Baptist editor in an article published less than a week before the election expressed shock that "a Protestant candidate for the presidency whose church has always supported separation of Church and State" could be so "vague, evasive, and ambiguous" about aid to parochial schools. *Baptist Standard* editor E. S. James wanted "a clear, unequivocal statement [that] Protestants had a right to expect" from such a candidate. He did not receive one, for Nixon ignored his plea.[67]

More broadly, Nixon's insistence on silence about religion during the campaign served to deprive the electorate of valuable insights into the basis for his values and his stand on the issues. His stance not only hid Nixon's faith from view, but the consequence also left voters to doubt whether there was anything religious about him. Hence it was no wonder that he sometimes seemed to be a one-dimensional person. Insofar as his views on issues grew out of his religious convictions, religion was highly relevant. Discussing it could only reveal some of the root assumptions that a candidate would bring to the political office for which he was contending. Historically Quakers had always held that what was important was how a Friend lived, not so much what he or she believed. So Nixon might have ventured into explaining how his faith had an impact on his understanding of the world without getting into esoteric discussion of fine points of faith.[68]

Neither did the Quakers who organized the Peace Pilgrimage to the Pentagon a week before the election receive support from their fellow believer, the vice president running for president; to the contrary, that candidate's executive assistant persuaded them, aided by a prominent Quaker, to postpone their demonstration until after the election. Nixon was the kind of Friend who elevated his conscience to such a level that it gave the immediate needs of his political career supremacy over commemorating 300 years of the sect's opposition to war, its defining characteristic. Unlike Kennedy, Nixon never had to address this striking anomaly, because, already having excluded religion from the campaign, he never explained how he might differ from the faith and practice of his church. Too, Protestant religious groups allowed much more theoretical latitude to individual believers to chart their own course than the Catholic Church permitted, and Quakerism rested at the extreme individualistic end of the Protestant spectrum, giving Nixon more leeway than another Protestant might have enjoyed.

Three decades later, in a volume of his memoirs, Nixon detailed why he could not personally have responded positively to Eisenhower's plea that he introduce references to God and his religious faith into his speeches. Interestingly, in describing his reaction to the president's plea, he never gave any specifics about his own religious convictions, but only to those of his mother and his family. "It should have been easy," he wrote, "to follow [Eisenhower's] advice. No one could have had a more intensely religious upbringing. . . . [M]ine is a different kind of religious faith, intensely personal and intensely private." For the rest of the paragraph, however, he wrote not of his faith but of his mother's: she prayed regularly but privately; her religion was sacred, but she refused to speak familiarly about sacred things, yet she never had questions when others spoke of their faith. Hence, Nixon concluded, it would have been more than out of character for him to have spoken of his religion on the stump—it would have been demagogic.[69] One of his critics, yet a close observer and social friend, conservative Catholic Washington journalist Walter Trohan, offered another reason: compared to Kennedy, prone to "beat drums on his religion to attract sympathy," Nixon had "less religious bias than any man I have ever known with the possible exception of another Quaker, Herbert Hoover."[70] Being mostly devoid of deep religious sensibilities made the vice president more tolerant.

No one can ever know how a choice by Nixon to honestly and publicly grapple with the implications of his faith for military and foreign policy, say, would have played out in the political arena. It would certainly have added a perhaps refreshing ingredient to sterile discussions of Quemoy and Matsu, two contested islands claimed by the Nationalist Chinese off the coast of mainland China, or whether in fact a "missile gap" existed between the United States and the Soviet Union, as Kennedy asserted. On military and defense questions Nixon was already the "peace candidate" in 1960 because Kennedy had to appear more aggressively determined against the Communists in Cuba and the Soviet Union than the Eisenhower administration, which Nixon was bound to defend.[71]

Secretive and introspective, Nixon was simply not the kind of politician to take chances in public. It was the tried and true for him. Because a candidate's religion was something that could be set aside (unless it was deemed somewhat exotic like the Roman Catholic variety), he sought to do so. This attitude also helps explain his decision not to associate himself with any Quaker congregation other than East Whittier Friends Church. He was the kind of Friend who, except for the funeral of his father in September 1956, had not darkened the door of a Quaker church or meetinghouse in perhaps a decade. Indeed, in 1956 he wanted so little to do with Friends that he could not find fifteen minutes to meet with a political science class from Quaker Haverford College even though he had his picture taken greeting a group of *Minneapolis Tribune* newsboys the same year.[72]

Judging by the amount of space he devoted to it, Nixon considered the campaign of 1960 the most important crisis of his career up to 1962, even more important than the Hiss case.[73] He gave little impression that his loss troubled him very much. Instead he looked at it as an opportunity to learn and to persevere, quoting a fellow Duke Law School student in another context, "You know what it takes to learn the law? An iron butt," which turned out to be one of Nixon's nicknames.[74] Perhaps his cultivation of what he sometimes termed the Quaker principle of "peace at the center" may have given him equanimity about the loss that enabled him to rise above it, at least for the immediate moment.[75]

As far as religion was concerned, it was Kennedy who came out the shining knight with the cross emblazoned on his banner; he played his religion much more carefully, more expertly, and proved victorious.[76] Nixon's silence on the issue meant that he could neither benefit from the advantages of his Protestantism nor take from Kennedy the crucial number of

Roman Catholics that Eisenhower had counted in his victory in 1956. In this way, the religion issue proved to be exactly as Nixon predicted: it neither helped nor hurt. In as close an election as 1960 proved to be, Nixon's failure to demonstrate how his religion would influence his policies proved to be vitally important. Although he never put it quite this way—indeed, it is not even clear that he realized this truth—his inability to convey the depth of whatever religious, nay Christian, commitment resided at the center of his faith worked against his election. At some instinctive level, Nixon must have realized all this, for from now on he practically ignored religion.

In the broader sense though, Nixon's loss did redound to the benefit of his long-range cause, for he won the support of many evangelical Christians. Astute observer Garry Wills, looking back on the defeat, wrote in the *New York Times Magazine* in August 1976 that the Californian had "achieved a rare empathy with fundamentalists"; they worked with and for him to put aside the threat of a Catholic candidate for the presidency. In the process they not only became more familiar with a political process that had seemed alien to them, but they also became convinced that Nixon was "more evangelical than Quaker in his outlook." "Nixon remained the beneficiary of that presumption," Wills concluded, "and of evangelicals' willingness to separate the good Christian from his political views, to stand by a brother despite disagreement, to comfort him under attack, growing more loyal as the siege mounted."[77] Such a lesson would certainly be useful in the future.

The picture was taken in 1954 when Richard Nixon took a break from campaigning in southern California to eat at the home of his parents, Frank and Hannah. Few unrehearsed pictures of Nixon exist; this may be one, though the Nixons seem rather too dressed for a drop-in meal. Courtesy of the Richard Nixon Presidential Library & Museum

Nixon's East Whittier Friend s Church, where Richard Nixon was a lifelong member, 1960. Courtesy of Gregory P. Hinshaw

Nixon and Billy Graham on the podium at the Graham Crusade, Neyland Stadium, Knoxville, Tennessee, May 28, 1970. Nixon spoke to an overflow crowd at the Crusade's "Youth Night," the first time a President had ever spoken at an evangelistic rally. Courtesy of the University History Collection, Special Collections, University of Tennessee, Knoxville, Libraries

Richard Nixon welcomes the "congregation" to his presidential church in the East Room of the White House, September 12, 1971. The preacher for that day was Ben Haden, pastor of the First Presbyterian Church of Chattanooga, Tennessee, seated behind the lectern. Courtesy of the Richard Nixon Presidential Library and Museum

Pictures of Richard Nixon with fellow Friends are rare indeed. This one, taken on May 17, 1971 at the White House, includes the President shaking hands with Landrum Bolling, President of Earlham College, and D. Elton Trueblood, also of Earlham and a loyal supporter of the Chief Executive. Courtesy of the Richard Nixon Presidential Library and Museum

The Wilderness Years, 1962–1968

The campaign of 1960 marked a major turning point in Richard Nixon's life. It was his first political defeat, a fact that left him, nearing forty-eight, facing a double loss: not wealthy, he had to find something to do professionally, and he was out of politics at least until the next election. Yet he exhibited few signs of bitterness. He hurriedly reassured two of his evangelical Christian supporters, Norman Vincent Peale and Billy Graham, that he did not hold them responsible for his defeat, but the extensive coverage he gave to the issue of religion in his postelection book *Six Crises*, published in 1962, suggested he had serious doubts about the way he had handled the matter at the time.[1] He did not, however, move to change either how he presented his faith or how he embraced his Quaker heritage, both of which remained inscrutably hidden. Nor did he return to his Quaker-dominated hometown of Whittier, although he went back to California, taking a job at a prestigious Los Angeles law firm, one more befitting a former vice president than his old small Quaker firm. Early on, the Nixons attended the Wilshire Avenue–Westwood Community Methodist Church when they were at home.[2]

Nixon's defeat, narrow as it was, did not end his political ambitions. In his August 1961 letter to Graham in which he absolved the evangelist of any responsibility for his loss, he confided that he was being heavily pressured to enter the California gubernatorial race against the popular incumbent, Democrat Edmond G. (Pat) Brown. (Both Dwight Eisenhower and Whittaker Chambers urged him to run.)[3] He did take on Brown and lost heavily after the governor charged that Nixon, if elected, would use the Sacramento governor's mansion as a steppingstone to another run for president. Nixon's religious commitments were not widely commented upon, although his campaign committee got an occasional letter from a voter concerned about the candidate's avoidance of all religious matters. One wrote that he accepted Nixon as a moral man with a fine religious background but added that he would like to see him entering a church every once in a while, either his own or the writer's Methodist one.[4]

Remembered afterward was not so much his defeat—it was not massive, nearly 300,000 votes out of some 6 million ballots cast—as his televised and notorious "last press conference" early on the morning after. He was bitter, having ruefully remarked coming down on the elevator that losing California after having run for president was "like being bitten by a mosquito after being bitten by a rattlesnake." Tired, disappointed, and overwrought, Nixon stared down, then shook his fist, and lashed out at the reporters present, who, he surmised, were "so delighted that I lost." "You won't have Nixon to kick around anymore," he told his audience, "because, gentlemen, this is my last press conference."[5] He later confessed that his remarks were "a great mistake."[6]

Nixon's words of course garnered wide attention. The press attacked him with unvarnished glee, and his closest friends feared for his mental stability. Billy Graham wrote immediately that he was praying for Nixon "almost continually." "It would be very easy," Graham suggested in a way that implied he knew his correspondent well, "for you to become bitter, to draw up in a shell, and even to exclude those who love you the most." He suggested that Nixon should wait a week or two and call another press conference. "Make it a great social occasion with food." Then he could confess that he was exhausted at his last press conference from staying up all night analyzing election results. He advised Nixon to act like "a big man" and "say three words: 'I am sorry,'" and promise not to engage in politics again. Graham advised that such a move would stop criticism of Nixon for being a poor loser and give him "a tremendous advantage."

Finally, evangelist Graham wanted Nixon to "start reading the Bible," hinting that he did not believe he had been doing so before, and begin "learning the value, power and secrets of prayers, and attending church with new faithfulness." He recommended that the Nixons might attend the nearby Bel Air Presbyterian Church, pastored by Dr. Louis Evans, whose wife was a former screen actress. Graham ended the letter by warning the defeated candidate against any "turn to drink or any of these other escapisms," which he did not name. Nixon marked "RN saw" and the date on the letter, but there was no response, or none was kept—perhaps Graham's advice simply cut too close to the quick in the defeated candidate's wounded psyche.[7]

The 1962 California gubernatorial campaign and its aftermath, Nixon's "last press conference," marked an observable change in the former vice president's personal style and approach to politics. During previous campaigns, Nixon had won a reputation as a tough, hard contender, one who did not pull punches and sometimes tiptoed up to the unethical and sensational but did not too often cross the invisible line into the totally unscrupulous. And there was little that was actually too far out about his efforts. True, he used the issue of Communism to tar those he ran against—his first opponent, Congressman Jerry Voorhis in 1946, he depicted as a socialist leaning dangerously leftward toward Communism;[8] his second, Senator Helen Gahagan Douglas in 1950, he averred on a number of occasions was "pink right down to her underwear"[9]—but the tar was no darker and no stickier than other politicians customarily used when they were determined to win.

But an earthy, even obscene, side of Nixon appeared during this campaign and would never entirely go away; in fact, judging from the number of "expletives deleted" that popped up in the White House tapes later on, such expressions increasingly became part of Nixon's daily vocabulary. Most of them were spoken to a few intimates and sometimes overheard by others but never publicized until his enemies wanted to point them out or his resignation sullied his image. One reporter from the *Sacramento Bee* recalled that in a café during Nixon's campaign for governor, a fellow journalist suggested he might talk to a man from the McClatchy chain of papers; rejecting any such notion, Nixon shot back, "I wouldn't give them the sweat off my balls."[10] Another reporter repeated a story that in the same campaign he was talking with Nixon about a poorly organized and attended rural rally when the candidate explained, "Oh well, that's what you have to expect from those fucking local yokels."[11] Such verbiage surely did not represent the Quaker heritage from his mother; more than likely it came from his navy experience during the war. No matter, one doubtful journalist thought he "swore expertly."[12]

Later stories about his drinking habits also surfaced. Nixon admitted a low tolerance for alcohol, so he normally avoided drinking in public altogether and kept any private imbibing to a minimum. But aide John Ehrlichman told one historian-interviewer that the former vice president was drunk at the 1964 Republican convention in San Francisco.[13]

Nixon's major decision was whether to carry out his implied promise in his press conference, to leave politics for good. Within weeks of his loss, which among other things demonstrated that he had no political future in his home state, he tipped his hand, deciding to move to New York, an ideal place to relaunch his political career. The success of his first memoir, *Six Crises*, which covered his political activities from the Hiss case through his last defeat, assured him continuing and hefty royalties as well as an enhanced reputation. He took a job with a major law firm on Wall Street, one that gave him plenty of time for making and keeping contacts, bought an expensive and commodious condominium, and placed himself at the geographic center of the nation's opinion movers and shapers. One visitor thought his law office looked like a trophy room. Lining the walls were pictures of world leaders whom he had met; on a small table by his desk, a bit too obvious and incongruous for a normal law office, there lay a big book about the Society of Friends. It all seemed designed to win over any skeptic who might happen by.[14]

The same intention seemed to guide the Nixons' choice of a church in New York. The family, to quote the man himself, "regularly attended" Norman Vincent Peale's Marble Collegiate Church and got to know better one of the most famous and influential religious leaders in the country; there is no way now of knowing whether "regularly" translated to weekly, monthly, or whenever something else did not prevent him from going.[15] The entire family's relationship with Peale deepened during this period, so much so that the pastor became Nixon's closest spiritual advisor, as he recalled it, more influential than Billy Graham.[16] The evangelist had in fact suggested Marble Collegiate to Nixon, a recommendation he thought a good one, because Peale "never fails to give an inspiring sermon."[17] Nixon made periodic contributions to the church, particularly around Christmas and Easter. He requested a copy of an occasional Peale prayer that impressed Pat and then sent a copy along to his mother. Just before Christmas 1963, Peale asked the Nixon family to drop by his study after Sunday services so his family could meet the Nixon girls; Nixon responded and presented a picture of Pat and himself to his pastor, who gave it a permanent place of honor on the wall of the study. In late November 1963, following the assassination of President Kennedy, Nixon even convinced Peale to stand in for him at the annual meeting of the National Association of Manufacturers lest his own appearance be considered too political. Peale, always attuned to business and its interests, readily agreed.[18]

Peale's approach to the Christian faith inevitably reinforced Nixon's own tendency to identify worldly and political success with religion. This emphasis was not part of Nixon's Quaker heritage but came from the emphasis Peale gave to his theology. As the title of the minister's best-selling book suggests, "positive thinking," especially tying one's thinking and prayer to one's worldly desires, had the power to bring material success. One reason Peale was so popular with businessmen was that he told people that prayer could make them millionaires because God would spread his grace around them and reward them. One Sunday in the summer of 1968 he explained in his sermon that even the presidency was available to those who adopted his method, although he probably neglected to mention that it was open to only one person at a time. That being an election year, Nixon, sitting in the congregation, undoubtedly understood the lesson Peale intended.[19]

It is impossible to know for sure now—there are always such unknowable contingencies in history—but it seems likely that sometime within these wilderness years when he was out of power, Nixon began to draw on those parts of his religious heritage that he could use to feed and nurture his political ambitions, an example being the book on Quakers displayed in his law office. Except in the broadest and most general terms, Nixon seldom spoke of his Quaker religious faith, leaving the serious and cynically inclined observer to wonder if he had any. The last time, for example, that he openly attended a Friends church was at the funeral of his mother after her death in September 1967. Graham led the service at the East Whittier Friends Church where Hannah Nixon's son had played the piano as a youth; the emotions provoked by his mother's death brought back memories that drew sad public tears from the usually well-controlled Nixon.[20] There is no record that he ever attended an unprogrammed Friends meeting for worship.

Nixon did write a warm note to his aunt and uncle by marriage, Olive and Oscar Marshburn, who called to greet the Nixons when they passed through New York on their way home to Whittier from working with Quakers in Africa. The Nixons had taken a trip to Mexico to celebrate their twenty-fifth wedding anniversary and missed his relatives. "You both deserve unlimited credit of your selfless dedication in the service of less fortunate people," Nixon inscribed in his note.[21]

Certainly, judging from Nixon's lack of specificity about it, his faith seemed to have had little content. One exception exists to this generalization, even though it was also shrouded in mystery and generality. Sometime before 1972, perhaps in this wilderness period, Nixon referred to his Quaker upbringing and heritage in terms that referred to something specific, concrete, and commonly referred to among members of the Society of Friends. "My Christian creed," he said, "includes the noble thought of Quaker Founder George Fox: 'There is that of God in every man'; and therefore every man the world around—regardless of his race or religion or color or culture—merits my respect."[22] It was a sentiment that eastern liberal Friends could certainly appreciate and applaud.

Despite such remarks, few and isolated as they were, Nixon remained an inconsistent and complicated person. When it came to political considerations, it proved impossible for him to act as if those with whom he disagreed merited very much respect—from him or anyone associated with him. Two and half years into his presidency, he sat ruminating in his office in the Executive Office Building about the need to attract union members to the Republican cause and his reelection effort the following year. He picked up on one of his common themes, the spinal weakness that he believed marked the educated and elite class. The two-thirds of the nation who never darkened the door of a college, he averred, could readily understand the need to be strong on drugs, crime, defense, and the country's national position in the world; the elite had no character and could not be depended on even to comprehend these needs. The uneducated people, plus those in the farm heartland, were all that remained of the character of the nation. We Republicans, said he, recognize that the country is in a great moral crisis, but we "won't get leadership from our class"; we will have to draw the uneducated masses to our side, if necessary by going over the heads of their nominal leaders.[23] Respect for those he opposed could not be found in such tirades.

Such a comment, unique as it was, suggested that Nixon's faith actually reflected something more than his customary generalities. If not as specific, a similar one, included in a book he published in 1982, proved more valuable in showing how Nixon was able to merge his Quakerism with his political career. *Leaders* was a work in which Nixon described what he had learned about leadership by looking at people he had met or knew about from study. His concluding chapter gave him a chance to summarize the lessons he took from his observations and reflection, including those from his own career.

Near the beginning of the chapter Nixon harkened back to President Charles de Gaulle of France, explaining that the general was supremely sure of himself and entertained no doubts about the correctness of his decisions. He was as close to being a monomaniac as could be found outside an insane asylum and seemed to have an open pipeline to God. Nixon picked up on this aspect of leadership and amplified it. "That inner voice," Nixon wrote in terms that George Fox would have understood, "is something that a leader's ear grows attuned to." The inward voice was trained, he insisted to give the thought his own, non-Foxian, twist, by "the exercise of power." Real leaders like de Gaulle did not second guess themselves or fret about decisions later, for they knew they were right.[24]

What Nixon did here was to use a central tenet of classical Quakerism and the synonymous phrase embraced by liberal, eastern, unprogrammed Friends, the "inward light" or "inner teacher." His conscious decision to use the synonymous term *inner voice* in this way suggested that he knew broader Quaker history, for evangelical Friends—by the time he wrote, they had even rejected the term *Quakers* to describe themselves—had long since ceased using the phrase, "inward [or inner] light." The earliest

Friends had made it central to their preaching: they knew from their personal experience that Christ spoke inwardly to human beings, convicted them of their sin, and endowed them with divine power to live righteous lives. But the universalism implied in such words seemed to evangelicals to preempt and make unnecessary what they saw as the saving work of Christ on the cross. Indeed in 1887, the standard statement of evangelical Quakerism, reprinted in most books of discipline of programmed Friends, the Richmond Declaration of Faith, absolutely repudiated any notion of a concept like the inward light, despite its deep roots in Quaker history: "We own no principle," it affirmed, "of spiritual light, life or holiness, inherent by nature in the mind or heart of man."[25] East Whittier Friends Church's members never owned this principle either.

Thus the very thing that traditional Quakers believed made human beings unique and unified them in a common humanity allowed Nixon to justify what might, in other contexts, be considered stubbornness or even arrogance to justify decisions in using power. His "inner voice" may not have grown from formal religious training at his church, but his use of it here in a political sense and to teach a political lesson meant he had gotten it somewhere. The earliest Friends, who knew they could be led by the inward light, did not preclude its use by political figures and for secular purposes, such as the ones to which Nixon was putting it in his book. When they appealed to a Lord Protector Oliver Cromwell or a King Charles in England, they spoke to this notion. Fox advised Cromwell in 1655 to subdue and be "still and silent from thy own wisdom, wit, craft, subtilty [sic], or policy what would arise in thee, but stand single to the Lord, without any end to thyself."[26] Putting such an inward guide to use inevitably gave Nixon a self-assurance about his own decisions that could make him appear determinedly unbending when someone questioned his course of action.

Such an understanding was apparently fairly common among those who exercised power at the highest level in the United States. For example, Abraham Lincoln told an associate that he was acutely conscious of the leadings of "the Almighty" when he had decisions to make. "I have had so many evidences of his direction, so many instances when I have been controlled by some other power than my own will, that I cannot doubt that this power comes from above." But Lincoln, perhaps uniquely, particularly when compared to Nixon, was able to maintain a sense of saving humility about this divine and outside guidance that came to him when he had to choose between courses of action.[27]

Ironic, too, was the fact that Nixon's stance here lent him some of the same self-assuredness conveyed by the title of the American Friends Service Committee's well-known mid-1950s statement on pacifism, *Speak Truth to*

Power: A Quaker Search for an Alternative to Violence.[28] Although it had a historically and authentic Quaker sound to it, the wording of the title in fact originated from within the committee with the Friends who wrote the pamphlet. They hoped to move American policymakers to reevaluate the Cold War and end the conflict between the United States and the Soviet Union. Widely commented upon in the secular press when it was published, it did not change American foreign policy, but the words of its title came into the language to justify those who spoke plain and simple truths to those in positions of power and influence.[29] Nixon's reference to the strength the "inner voice" gave a leader to impose his will on history grew out of this same milieu.

For all of these reflections on leadership and how they related to listening to the word that sounded within, Nixon wanted no part of any kind of formal Quakerism. Elton Trueblood, a professor at large at Earlham College and a leading moderate Republican Quaker, wrote in 1964 to see if Nixon would like to affiliate with another of the groups that Trueblood started. This one would be called the National Monthly Meeting of Friends designed for people in public life who could not normally attend meetings but wanted to maintain some connection to the Society of Friends. As a good Friend of Herbert Hoover, Trueblood believed that the former president's two sons would be interested and thought Nixon would also.[30] Nixon did not respond, and nothing more came of the National Monthly Meeting.

Yet for all his disdain for Quakerism, Nixon could recognize its impact even if he avoided mentioning the word or faith itself. His friend journalist Walter Trohan related the story of the former vice president's June 1967 appearance at the annual gathering Hoover had created for movers and shakers at Bohemian Grove in the redwood forests of California. Invited to deliver the closing Saturday night address that had always been reserved for Hoover when he was alive, Nixon unburdened himself of an oratorical tour de force. Speaking with few notes, Nixon surveyed the world, suggesting conservative solutions. Drawing only on his memory, he included a stirring tribute to Hoover. The deceased president, then gone for three years, would be remembered, said Nixon, above all else as "a man of great character." He did not, however, mention the role Hoover's Quaker background played in forming his character. "Deserted by his friends, maligned by his enemies," and vilified viciously by all, Hoover "was a triumph of character." "Two thousand years ago," he concluded, "when these great trees were saplings, the poet Sophocles wrote, 'One must wait until evening to see how splendid the day has been.'" His words brought men lolling on the grass to their feet cheering his presentation. Trohan advised

Nixon to give that speech on the hustings, saying that if he did so he would win the presidency.[31]

On the question of whether he would run for the presidency a second time, Nixon obviously listened to more than the inward voice. His close friend and increasingly political confidant Billy Graham played an important role. Six months after his Bohemian Grove address, at the end of December 1967, Nixon visited his close Florida friend, Bebe Rebozo; Graham and his associate T. W. Wilson joined the duo Saturday through Monday (December 29-31). The conversation on Saturday ranged over political and theological issues, including what Graham described as an "interesting" discussion of Romans 1 and 2, interspersed with prayer. The next morning no one went to church, but Nixon and Graham walked about a mile and a half on the beach, deep in conversation all the way. In the afternoon they watched the Super Bowl. On Monday, before breaking up and going their separate ways, Nixon asked Graham what he should do about announcing his candidacy for president. The evangelist did not have to think long about that and replied, "I think you should run. . . . You are the best prepared man in the United States to be President." Graham saw that Nixon was torn about the decision and, perhaps to encourage him, predicted that Johnson would not run based on some conversations he had had with the president, also a close friend. Nixon scoffed at that unlikely possibility. They left it there, though politician Nixon recalled for *Good Housekeeping* the following July that Graham had a great deal to do with his final decision.[32]

In this period, Graham and Nixon grew even closer in political terms. Graham kept up with what Nixon wrote or said and sent him comments about what he observed in his travels, as well as quoting the former vice president in his radio program (broadcast over 900 stations, Graham reminded him). He also fed Nixon political intelligence when he encountered other politicians. In early February 1964, following a meeting with Lyndon Johnson, he came away "terribly depressed" because the president had shown "such complete ignorance of foreign policy." He stroked Nixon's ego, too, as when he reported that Tennessee's Democratic governor Frank Clement had been so charmed by Nixon when they met in Nashville that he had completely changed his mind about the Republican. (In the same letter, he asked for Nixon's thoughts and prayers for the "fully integrated" crusade he planned for June 1965 in Montgomery, Alabama.) Nixon could stroke also. Thanking Graham for his political advice, he expanded, "you have one of the best political minds in the country and the nation lost a potentially great political leader when you went into the ministry."[33]

The two confidants even discussed political candidates, Democrats as well as Republican. Nixon heartily agreed with Graham in September 1966 that the massive media build-up of Senator Robert Kennedy was "a fantastic one," one likely resulting in his being elected to the White House in 1968 unless some "counterforce" occurred. Knowing his man, who likewise knew his correspondent, Nixon underlined his own misgivings about another Kennedy in the White House, "I can imagine that your reactions to such an eventuality are similar to my own."[34]

One foreign policy issue—American policy toward Vietnam—and one domestic issue—questions of race, which included urban rioting and desegregation—dominated the presidential campaign of 1968, and both bore on what a Quaker candidate like Nixon might advocate. He was in no danger of being seduced by a consultant who cautioned him not to threaten to use atomic weapons in Vietnam, advice posited "not on moral grounds, but because they won't work on any rational scale of costs vs. benefits."[35] Trueblood advised him to be neither hawk nor dove on the question and to avoid specifics or any kind of plan, saying only that the present policy was a "disgrace and a failure."[36] Nixon basically followed this strategy during the coming campaign, in March bluntly confiding to advisors in private that "I've come to the conclusion that there's no way to win the war." But he knew he could not dare be so open in public during a political campaign, lest diplomacy be adversely affected. "In fact," he went on, "we have to seem to say just the opposite, just to keep some degree of bargaining leverage" with the enemy in Vietnam and their supporters in the Soviet Union and China.[37]

On August 1, he presented a statement to the Republican Platform Committee, the gist of which was captured in the first definitive sentence after the introduction: "The war must be ended." It should be ended "honorably, consistent with America's limited aims, and with the long term requirements of peace in Asia." But to indicate that he had not joined the "peace-at-any-price" crowd, whom he disdained, he stressed that "it must be waged more effectively." There should be no further escalation on the military front but a "dramatic escalation of our efforts on the economic, political, diplomatic and psychological fronts." The war requires a "new strategy" because it was a different kind of conflict from those the United States had been involved with before. He concluded his general recommendations by averring that the nation had to "require a fuller enlistment of our Vietnamese allies in their own defense." Let a new administration bring a fresh eye.[38] Here were, unfleshed out, the fundamental ingredients of his administration policy toward Vietnam. The press and the opposition immediately labeled his views as too "dovish" and remarked on the change they showed in his hardline reputation.[39] Yet he said nothing later to take away or add much to this seminal statement.

When the Republicans convened in early August, Nixon had clearly not ruled out the possibility of a peace campaign; he even tempted Mark Hatfield, Oregon's Republican junior senator with the idea of becoming his running mate. Hatfield, a Baptist evangelical whose public doubts about Vietnam had made national headlines, was Billy Graham's favorite for the slot, a choice Graham had made known to Nixon months before.[40] A longtime political associate of the Californian, in 1960 then-governor Hatfield had placed Nixon in nomination for the presidency. This time around he was tapped to make a seconding speech for Nixon, one to appeal to the "religious and peace communities," Nixon's minions advised. Befuddled, Hatfield sought out Nixon's campaign manager John Mitchell for guidance on what to say. Mitchell tried a Nixon tactic, responding that Nixon's mother had been "a wonderful Quaker." The still-puzzled Oregonian evangelical came back, but "she's not the candidate. . . . I have to speak to his issues, his beliefs, his actual involvement." So Mitchell retorted with another typical Nixonian diversion: "Like Quakers, you know, he's kind of reticent to speak about his faith." This one served no better, for Hatfield had known Hannah, "and she's not at all reticent to speak about her faith. She's quite loquacious, in fact." Responses were no better when he sought advice on what to say to the peace community. Hatfield knew he did not intend to change his position on the war, a reality that chilled relations between the two politicians. The rest was history: Spiro Agnew, governor of Maryland, got the nod.[41]

Graham did his part too. Immediately after the Republican convention, evangelist Graham, conducting one of his crusades in Pittsburgh, invited the victorious candidate to appear. His introduction of Nixon was almost fawning in its generosity: not only did the Republican standard bearer exhibit a "tremendous constraint of temper" and the utmost "integrity in counting his golf score," but Graham also hailed him as more "realistic" than Jesus. Of course he asked his congregation to pray for his politician friend, in the name of the less realistic Jesus.[42] It was no wonder that upon leaving, Nixon looked solemnly into the waiting TV cameras and intoned to the faraway audience, "This was one of the most moving religious experiences of my life." He made no comment about the likely political impact of Graham's comments on his fate or the voters' choice.[43]

The Democratic candidate, Vice President Hubert Horatio Humphrey of Minnesota, had a liberal record within his party going back to 1948 when he had stood forthrightly against the segregationist southern Democrats. The issue of what kind of policy could extract the United States from Vietnam was the easier of the two for Nixon to address, even if the question remained volatile. President Lyndon Johnson, with whom Humphrey served, had been committed to carrying on and winning the war in Vietnam since his first days in office and had overseen the introduction of massive American ground, air, and naval forces; by the end of 1968, about half a million American troops had been sent to Vietnam. Most of those on the ground were draftees, a fact that made the draft very unpopular even as it forced every young man either to accept or to finagle a way around selective service—the latter by entering college, going to Canada, or simply not registering. The Democratic standard-bearer had only an extremely limited range in which to disagree with his patron Lyndon Johnson, whose pride did not permit him to brook serious opposition from his vice president.

The increasing unpopularity of the Vietnam War made the issue quite iffy for Nixon. His refusal to be specific about his plans, for example, got him into trouble with people like Oregon senator Hatfield, who agreed to help the campaign by speaking for his friend before student and peace groups. But Nixon simply would not detail his anticipated approach toward the war. Hatfield wrote him pleading for candor and openness; in return he was informed that he was being dropped as a Nixon surrogate.[44] Nixon could not simply rush out in front as a leader of the war's opponents. He was hampered by his record, one stretching back to his entry into politics in 1946. Related to his history, he tended to see every nationalist uprising anywhere in the world as part of a communist threat, orchestrated from Moscow. An unaltered stance assured him a strong base for support from conservatives anxious about the United States being made to appear weak.

So Nixon tried to have it both ways, each one shrouded in secrecy. His career included a mix of a zealous anticommunism and moderate positions on international relations; these two factors gave him some intrinsic appeal, on the one hand, to conservative heirs of McCarthyism within the Republican Party and, on the other, to moderate Republicans in the northeast. Their spokesman was New York governor Nelson Rockefeller, himself an on-and-off a candidate for the nomination in 1968. Since May, peace negotiations between North Vietnam and the United States had dragged on in Paris, a situation that led Democrats to hope, if not pray, that reaching a peace agreement would surely enhance Humphrey's chances to the White House. The major problem for the Johnson administration was wooing the stubbornly anticommunist South Vietnamese president, Nguyen Van Thieu, into joining the Paris talks, something he steadfastly refused to do. Nixon had to make sure that Thieu stood firm, a stance that would scuttle the chances for a peace agreement and sink Humphrey's hope of donning the mantle of the peace candidate. Keeping the South Vietnamese in Saigon and away from Paris would assure that there would be no peace agreement prior to the election.[45]

A German-born Republican academic who had graduated from Harvard and served as foreign policy advisor to Rockefeller, Henry S. Kissinger, turned out to be a key as far as Nixon was concerned. Distrusted by zealots because he had associated with the New Yorker, Kissinger also consulted with Johnson's State Department and the Arms Control and Disarmament Agency and played a central role in funneling information about the president's intentions regarding the Paris negotiations and Vietnam. He even went to Paris in September where he spoke with members of the American delegation. After returning to the United States later that month, he had at least three conversations with either Nixon or his campaign manager (and law partner), John Mitchell, before the election. Nixon claimed in his memoir that Kissinger never relayed confidential information, though he certainly reported that Johnson planned to halt the bombing of North Vietnam as a peace overture before the end of October—obviously before the election and early enough to sway voters to Humphrey.[46] Hence Nixon had to redouble his efforts to make sure that President Thieu did not send a delegation to Paris and end the war within days.

Nixon had opened a private and unofficial avenue of communication with Thieu as early as July. He and Mitchell met with the South Vietnamese ambassador, Bui Diem, and Anna Chennault, co-chairwoman of Republican Women for Nixon and widow of famed aviator General Claire Chennault who had commanded the World War II Flying Tigers in China. Nixon, to some degree acting as though he had already been elected president, asked his "very dear friend"[47] Chennault to be his channel to Thieu via the ambassador. She readily agreed. When Johnson announced a halt to the bombing on October 31 (a move Nixon was convinced was aimed at his defeat),[48] Mitchell telephoned Chennault to make sure that officials in Saigon understood Republican needs. Chennault reassured Mitchell: "Thieu has told me over and over again that going to Paris would be walking into a smoke screen that has nothing to do with reality."[49] (It is revealing that Chennault's name appears nowhere in Nixon's memoirs.)

Meanwhile, Johnson reacted like a wind-driven blaze on a Texas prairie. Because he suspected Nixon of somehow being behind Thieu's intransigence, he raged that the Republican was guilty of treason as American lives were lost to serve his personal political ambitions. He ordered Chennault's telephone line tapped for national security reasons. This rationale for the surveillance and the fact that Chennault lived in Washington's Watergate hotel made the irony all the more delicious later. On November 2, three days prior to the election, the wire tappers heard Chennault inform Bui Diem that Nixon was going to win, so that the envoy could tell "your boss to hold on" a little longer.[50] In short, a Republican electoral victory would mean that war would continue and that President Thieu would retain the backing of the United States to remain in power himself. It gives no secrets away to say that Nixon did win the election; that the war dragged on until January 27, 1973, when South Vietnam joined in signing the agreement to end it; and that Thieu remained president until April 21, 1975, outlasting Nixon by nine months.[51]

What merits attention to this intriguing episode is that it demonstrates how flexible—not to say duplicitous—Nixon could be when it came to a matter central to his political career, in this case, the only major issue, peace, that also tied directly to his religious background and heritage. If Quakers were noted for anything, it was their commitment to peace, their desire for the peaceful resolution of violent conflict. Up to this point in his career, the emphasis on peace during his campaigns had not been foremost, even though it was always there. The emphasis grew once he too office. As we shall see, the overarching quest during his administration was the search for peace. Moreover during the unpopular Vietnam War, as during the 1968 election itself, support for peace was an issue sure to win popular approval and capture votes.

One prominent Quaker spokesman, Elton Trueblood, who had served in the Eisenhower administration as director of religious information at the Voice of America, visibly tried to establish Nixon's bona fides as a peacemaker. Writing in *Quaker Life*, official magazine of the largest organization of Friends in the United States, he lauded the Republican's "respect for his spiritual background [that] has intensified his effort to find a way to end the war, with the establishment of a true peace." It was no accident, he went on, "that his religious faith is deeply evangelical for the evangelical stream is the major one in Quaker history, particularly in the westward trek."[52]

What is so striking—even inexcusable for those interested in evidence of Nixon's commitment to his Quaker faith, other than Trueblood—was his willingness to short circuit the chance for an immediate peace in order to gain a major political advantage. True, had he refrained from maneuvering with Thieu so that the Johnson administration might achieve a peace settlement, Humphrey might have won the presidency, and Nixon would have had to go back to his law practice in New York and await the next election. That would have meant a major personal sacrifice, but it would have saved many lives, both Vietnamese and American, and not added mountains of treasure to those already expended. What was clear in his machinations was Nixon's apparent concentration on the short term, his electoral chances, and his inability, so far as we know, to let the long term take first place in his consideration. Nixon may well have believed that he alone could create a structure that would make war impossible for the next generation. He never said anything like this in such explicit terms, but his candidacy and the way he undercut the peace process certainly suggested that he thought this way.

If Nixon was going to beat Humphrey, he needed to see that Thieu remained in Vietnam and to take advantage of widespread American opposition to the war. Thus, publicly, he found nothing good in the Johnson war policy, except that the president had not pulled out of Vietnam, not "cut and run," in the parlance critics like Nixon used. He was harsh in his criticisms of Johnson's "gradualism," shorthand for lacking the coherence Nixon deemed necessary. Yet he was convinced that he understood the communist threat emanating from Moscow and Peking and how to meet it better than anyone else, especially Humphrey. He never explicitly said that he had a "plan" to end the war, and certainly not a "secret plan," but his attacks on the Johnson policies—always couched in language like "New leadership will end the war and win the peace in the Pacific"—certainly fed the electorate's hopes that he, a new leader, knew how to solve the problem of Vietnam. That conclusion was one he wanted to promote. He did nothing to disabuse those who thought he had a plan from their perception, for this would assure that his candidacy might well secure their votes.[53]

The domestic question of race was the other divisive and important issue in the campaign and tested the wiles of Quaker Republican Nixon. To complicate the matter there was flamboyant George Corley Wallace, the Democratic (and populist) governor of Alabama, running on the American Independent Party ticket. A fiery opponent of desegregation, school busing to achieve it, and any softness on racial unrest and rioting, Wallace appealed to many white southerners; he also stood a good chance of taking votes away from Nixon (as well as from Humphrey) in white ethnic neighborhoods of midwestern cities like Chicago, Detroit, and Cleveland. Wallace's racial appeal provoked one worried Indiana Friend, Landrum Bolling, president of Earlham College, to offer to hit the road full time on the Republican's behalf during the last four weeks of the campaign. "[T]he swell of Wallace support has quickened the necessity for men like myself to do more than write papers and vote!" Bolling explained. But Nixon apparently did not take the energized Quaker up on his offer.[54]

Nixon's choice of a running mate, Governor Spiro T. Agnew of Maryland, was seen as placating his southern supporters, particularly the powerful Republican senator from South Carolina, Strom Thurmond; yet Agnew had been an early supporter of the other principal Republican candidate for president, the liberal Nelson Rockefeller, a fact that made him a bit more complicated than Wallace. Rather than explicitly trying to undercut Wallace's appeal to those fearful of desegregation, Nixon demanded "Law and Order," a slogan that played well to white suburban voters leery of black advances. (Soon Humphrey was talking about "Law and Order with Justice," a phrase underlining that Wallace was victorious in having defined the terms of the debate in regard to race.) Playing his cards carefully, Nixon might well benefit from a candidate on his left, Humphrey, and one on his right, Wallace, the two of them enabling him to run as a centrist on race.[55] It was a good place to land in a national campaign, by any measurement. Still, he considered himself a "conservative as least as I define it," he explained privately to one skeptic.[56]

With his Quaker heritage running back to ancestors who cooperated with the underground railroad in southern Indiana in the years before the Civil War (something he did not want anyone to forget),[57] Nixon had a reasonably progressive record on civil rights. A decade before, in January 1957, for example, Senator Humphrey had asked him, as president of the Senate, to decide whether the Senate could adopt new rules at the beginning of a session by a simple majority to prevent filibusters against civil rights legislation. Nixon ruled that the upper house might indeed choose to do so and referred the question to the body, which, dominated by the Senate majority leader from Texas, Lyndon Johnson, voted 55 to 28 against adopting new rules. Had the vice president held that the matter of rules was the pending business, the opponents of civil rights legislation would have had to overrule the chair to prevent a victory for those demanding new laws, a much more difficult vote. An arcane question, to be sure, but it was one that he could easily have avoided—because it was arcane—so the fact that he did not sidestep it demonstrated his willingness to come down publicly on the side of civil rights for African Americans. Yet his failure to submit the question immediately saw him temporizing, having it both ways.[58] It was a good place for a clever politician to be.

Nixon was a clever politician if ever there were one, one who knew exactly when he needed to factor his faith into the calculus to be considered by the voters. Just before the Republican convention met, he summed up his view of Quakerism for a newsmagazine reporter in a way that spoke to the major issues of that campaign season. "The three passions of the Quakers are," he explained carefully and authoritatively, "peace, civil rights, and tolerance. That's why as a Quaker I can't be an extremist, a racist, or an uncompromising hawk." That he failed to mention the need to bring salvation to the lost demonstrated that he had long since left his evangelical Quaker faith behind—he sounded like one of those "liberal" eastern Friends.

Another good thing that happened just prior to the election was Billy Graham's announcement, four days before voting began, that he had cast an absentee ballot for Nixon. He had insisted that he did not publicly endorse candidates, always studiously shying away from explicitly indicating his choice before. But having already told a Portland crusade audience, "There is no American I admire more than Richard Nixon," he was determined to sway any undecided folk to select his man. When Graham reversed himself and came out for Nixon, Harry Dent, a South Carolinian and Nixon operative who knew something about swaying the southern voter, boasted to *Newsweek*, "That was all I needed. I used it in all our TV commercials right down to the end."

It worked, if narrowly. Nixon won the election but with a tiny margin of .7 percent over Humphrey, the victor taking 43.4 percent of the vote, the loser 42.7; Wallace's 13.5 percent would probably have been Nixon's had the third party candidate not been in the race. In an election so close, almost any issue can be isolated to prove that it was the most important, so Vietnam could certainly have been the issue that brought the victory, but it is more likely that it was race and racial relations that tipped it to Nixon. For only the second time in American history a Quaker would take the helm as president; whether that would make a great difference when it came to Vietnam or the relationship between blacks and whites, the two most important issues in 1968, was yet to be seen. Interestingly, the questions about his religion that had come up occasionally eight years before were not broached this year. Whether this change meant a decline in religious sentiments or more acceptance of Nixon as a mainstream politician—a role his victory proved he had mastered—was also unclear.

8

Power Corrupts Gradually

Power is not for the nice guy down the street or for the man next door.[1]
—Richard Nixon, *Leaders*, 1982

Upon taking the oath as president on January 20, 1969, Richard Nixon found that the need to convey any kind of public religious commitment was mostly obviated. Except for the likelihood of a second term—assuming that nothing untoward happened during his first—he would probably not have to face the electorate again, so he did not have to worry about the kind of advice that had come regularly from evangelical supporters like Billy Graham in the 1950s. Of course, there were always ceremonial functions of a religious nature, such as the annual National Prayer Breakfast, that demanded his participation, but comments at those were rather general in nature—"church stuff," he off-handedly dismissed it on the occasion of his first.[2] About the same time, shortly after taking office, he described himself simply as a "lifelong" and "believing" Quaker and a "church-going Christian," without offering anything more specific.[3] Using the power that came to him as president, he could also structure situations so as to prevent any public questioning of his religion and faith. A good example of this last approach was the Sunday morning church services in the executive mansion he began immediately following his inauguration. For those content with outward forms, these weekly sermons served to underscore Nixon's religious commitments without placing undue pressure on the president.

More broadly, the kind of rhetoric that characterized most presidential statements, those introducing proposed departures in foreign or domestic policies or explaining and defending old policies, lent themselves to the type of broad concepts of which practically all presidents were masters. Unifying and emotive terms like "national interest," "equal rights," "fairness," and "the will of the people" could often sound almost quasi-religious and easily transformed into political benefit.

"Peace" especially was one such generality that Nixon could use that fell squarely within his religious background as a Friend, a conclusion that outsiders also remarked on.[4] And because practically everyone approved that concept in theory—very few national politicians dared plump publicly for war and violence—he could trot it out on almost any occasion without risking any valuable political capital. As long ago as 1958 when he had been preparing to run for the presidency the first time, he had confided to columnist Stewart Alsop that once in office he would take chances when it came to foreign affairs and peace—"the Quakers have a passion for peace, you know."[5] Years later, six years short of Nixon's death, in fact, New York internist Arnold Hutschnecker, who had treated the Californian since 1951, revealed a similar detail about his patient. A pacifist himself, Hutschnecker told Tom Wicker, one of Nixon's biographers, in the strictest confidence that his patient revealed to him before the election that he had planned an outline for a cabinet-level Department of Peace that he would establish once he were elected.[6]

No one could slight him for this kind of expression, which almost dared anyone to differ with him—or what he termed the Quakers' passion. So Nixon continued to express this passion for peace. He came to southern California a month before his inauguration to explain this emphasis to home folks. Speaking at the Anaheim Convention Center near Whittier, he returned to that theme. "I bring a passion for peace," he told the crowd. "It comes from my father, my mother, my church, and my college. I think it can happen—and we will work to bring it to the world."[7] Soon Nixon— a "church-going Christian"—would be in a position to act to achieve that goal of peace.

One perceptive observer and insightful journalist, Republican Richard J. Whalen, who wrote speeches for the new president, warned against taking such sentiments too seriously. When he came to interview for a position on a Sunday afternoon in September 1967, he was doubtful and skeptical of the Californian for not being forthcoming enough about his goals for the country. After three hours of mutual give and take, however, he went away impressed if not entirely convinced. There was none of the arrogance or sense of self-importance in Nixon that other politicians usually exuded, and the president made no pretense of being a reluctant participant in the political game; instead he dove in and reveled in every minute. He lived for playing the course and took pleasure in analyzing himself and the others who were running. But this kind of stance offered Nixon a measure of protection, Whalen thought, for it focused on individuals and away from ends and goals. So, Whalen concluded, any questioner "hesitated to ask Nixon, naively, just *why* he wanted to be President."[8] If Whalen still had doubts about this particular politician's goals and aims, he could hardly have been reassured when Nixon called him a few days later to see how his decision-making was coming along and sought to reassure him with "Flexibility is the first principle of politics."[9] Whalen, New York Irish Catholic that he was, signed on with his doubts about "centrism" still intact.

So the president-elect worked to unite the country behind him, at least religiously. A "Religious Observance Committee" surfaced well before Inauguration Day to tie the nation's diverse religious groups to this effort. Headed by a former official in the Eisenhower administration who had also served on the South Dakota supreme court, the committee planned one of the few prayer services ever to be part of the official inauguration ceremony. It asked Americans to observe three minutes of silent prayer at 11 a.m. for the "tranquil transfer of authority." It distributed cards depicting praying hands suitable for display in stores and other business establishments with the Nixon slogan "Forward Together." The committee tapped Norman Vincent Peale to read "A Call for Spiritual Renewal" and Charles Ball, former pastor of East Whittier Friends Church, the president's own church, to give Quakers their place. The committee, representing the new president, sought an enhanced level of "spiritual and moral renewal," and to that end it made the first public announcement of Nixon's plans to hold regular non-denominational Sunday worship services at the White House.[10] Judging from such events, religion and a broad nondenominational Christianity were to play a new and enhanced role in the new administration. It was clear how Nixon wanted to buttress his reputation as a "lifelong" and "believing Quaker" and church-going Christian.

With all this advanced religious hoopla, everyone expected Nixon to focus on the issue of peace, given that the war in Vietnam was at its height and in his campaign he had promised that his policies would end the conflict. So the newly sworn-in president proceeded to "consecrate my office, my energies and all the wisdom I can summon" to the cause of peace. It was a statement generic enough to offend no one and contained no specific sectarian reference to the central Quaker testimony. But then Nixon went on to use a phrase, unremarked on at the time, that would come to be embedded in many of the foreign policy statements that appeared during his term in office; he said he wanted to strengthen the "structure of peace" among all nations.[11] Five years later, under siege during the Watergate hearings, he explained to press secretary Ron Ziegler that now was the greatest time in history to build a "structure of peace in the world." "And I'm the only man that can do it," he insisted. "There isn't anybody [else] coming along the pike. Can you imagine Teddy Kennedy making the kind of decisions that I have to make?"[12] And just before leaving the White House, he used those same words in his resignation speech, pledging—for whom is unclear, obviously neither himself nor his successor—that "we must complete a structure of peace."[13] It had become almost a ritual pronouncement, the alpha and omega for foreign policy in his administration, which rolled off his tongue without his giving the phrasing much thought. After his resignation, he was still affirming that this effort "meant more to me than any I have ever been engaged in."[14] "Judging by his words, it was a major emphasis indeed; by his deeds, especially regarding Vietnam, the structure got relatively few bricks and remained weak."

In addition Nixon suffused his inaugural address with Quaker-sounding sentiments. He did not name them in that sectarian fashion of course, but for those attuned to such ideas, their origins were clear. Consider some examples:

"To a crisis of the spirit, we need an answer of the spirit."
"And to find that answer, we need only look within ourselves."
"Greatness comes in simple trappings."
"When we listen to 'the better angels of our nature,' we find that they celebrate the simple things, the basic things—such as goodness, decency, love, kindness."
"The simple things are the ones most needed today if we are to surmount what divides us and cement what unites us. To lower our voices would be a simple thing. . . ."
"We cannot learn from one another until we stop shouting at one another—until we speak quietly enough so that our words can be heard as well as our voices."
"Let us take as our goal: where peace is unknown, make it welcome; where peace is fragile, make it strong; where peace is temporary, make it permanent."
"With those who are willing to join, let us cooperate to reduce the burden of arms, to strengthen the structure of peace, to lift up the poor and the hungry."
"The peace we seek—the peace we seek to win—is not victory over any other people, but the peace that comes with healing in its wings; with compassion for those who have suffered; with understanding for those who have opposed us; with the opportunity for all the peoples of this earth to choose their own destiny."

Even when the new president adopted the kind of concepts that twentieth-century American chief executives customarily used to define larger goals for American foreign policy, they came out sounding more than a little Quakerish. For example, Nixon's statement, "We seek an open world—open to ideas, open to the exchange of goods and people, a world in which no people, great or small, will live in angry isolation," sounded like the description of how to achieve peace rather than merely promoting crass imperial expansion.[15] The traditional Quaker concern for peace gave Nixon an opportunity to find words that in wartime fit admirably with the popular goal of ending the divisive Vietnam War and unifying the people behind his program, the broad purpose of inaugural rhetoric anyway.

All that being said, Nixon fell short of shifting the public mood on peace with his inaugural address in the way that his predecessor John Kennedy had achieved with his June 10, 1963, address on foreign policy at American University, which has been called one of the seminal speeches of a twentieth-century president.[16] (In that address, Kennedy, five months before his death at the hands of an assassin, promised to make the world safe for diversity and pleaded for more optimism on the possibility of ending war.)[17] Perhaps it was simply the failure of Nixon's oratory or doubts about his general credibility with the public, but his words failed to elicit the kind of response he clearly wanted or lead to much popular acclaim. The fact that few contemporaries referred later to Nixon's important phrase, "structure of peace," showed that it never captured the public's imagination nor crossed their minds in any meaningful way.

Nixon's doctor, Arnold Hutschnecker, lobbied the new president about plans for a Department of Peace. The internist came down to Washington—Nixon seldom went to his office when he wanted a medical consultation—but he had to make an end-run around Nixon's top aides in order to see him by getting secretary Rose Mary Woods to take him into the Oval Office unbeknownst to the rest of the staff. In its privacy, he reminded the president of his 1959 decision to create a Department of Peace and suggested that he could now follow through on his plans, but Nixon told him that Congress would not approve a new department for fiscal reasons. Hutschnecker countered by broaching the idea of an "agency for the exploration of the dynamics of peace," something that Nixon thought might be feasible, but nothing came of it.[18]

Nixon's broad generalizations about peace and the need to obtain it, no matter how politically appealing, could not substitute for the specifics of foreign policy in given areas of the world. Whether in Vietnam, the Middle East, where the conflict between Israel on the one side and the Palestinians and their Arab allies on the other continued to fester, or China, the Soviet Union, or Europe, Nixon and his policies would have to get down to specifics with specific leaders. A brilliant strategist admittedly, Nixon would have to put his broad goals to the test on a ground made hard by historic antagonisms, differing conceptions of how to get from here to there, and national interests that inevitably clashed. Nixon no doubt understood this reality, but only time would tell what the verdict would be.

Friends' groups, meanwhile, were busily sorting out how they might relate to the new president. Even before the election, on August 30, the principal publication of unprogrammed Friends, *Friends Journal*, tried to elicit from the Republican candidate details of his religious background, but was rebuffed by an aide. Instead, at Nixon's request, the periodical's editors were referred to Bela Kornitzer's 1959 biography as a source for what they desired. On November 20, three heavyweight Quaker groups, Friends World Committee for Consultation, Friends Committee on National Legislation, and Philadelphia Yearly Meeting, sent Nixon a joint letter proposing a kind of pastoral visit of five or six Friends to seek ways of supporting and upholding him; the letter pledged that no political overtones would intrude into this occasion. The letter also mentioned that the Washington Friends Meeting wanted to explore ways to minister to the newly elected Quaker president, perhaps by holding services after the manner of his own evangelical East Whittier Friends Church, a move in line with its own history after it scheduled similar services for the first Quaker president. An aide regretfully turned the request down by saying that the time of the president-elect was limited.[19]

On inauguration day, Washington Friends Meeting tried again. The clerk of this unprogrammed "liberal" congregation wrote Nixon to inform him of the various meetings in the capital, calling particular attention to the small gathering in the library of Sidwell Friends School that the Nixons might find congenial. "Friends," wrote Robert Gronewald, "are deeply conscious of the heavy burdens placed upon you by your high office and pray that God may sustain and guide you in leading our nation in these times of great trial."[20] A Nixon assistant replied to Gronewald that the president appreciated his letter and would note the information on his "forward calendar." In a memo he attached for a second aide, the assistant, Dwight Chapin, unaware of just how far Nixon had distanced himself from Friends, innocently suggested, "Perhaps this would be a good church service since the President is a Quaker?"[21] He knew little of the permutations that marked Quaker history and life, and he knew even less about his boss.

Some expectations existed in the country for the new chief executive to affiliate himself and his family with a "mainstream" denomination as other presidents had done, or at least that was the way Edward L. R. Elson, pastor of the National Presbyterian Church, read national sentiment. Only days after the election in November, he wrote to the president-elect and his wife, former neighbors of the Elson family eight years before when Nixon served as vice president, that he hoped they would follow Dwight Eisenhower's example and join his church. He extended an "urgent invitation" that they follow such a course. Advising Nixon that "[w]ithout in any way forsaking your Quaker allegiance [and] mindful of Mrs. Nixon's earlier relationship with a California Community Church," Elson informed the couple that it would be "most appropriate for you to be associated with us." An aide noted on the letter that he called Elson on December 12 to inform him of Nixon's "worship plans" after the family removed to the nation's capital.[22]

Except for careful readers of the *New York Times,* few others outside of Elson knew of Nixon's plans. The Quaker president had already decided to hold Sunday services in the White House with preachers and choirs of his choice rather than going to a local church. (The only Nixon biographer with ready access to his subject, Jonathan Aitken, reported that Nixon had considered this innovation at least a year before he was elected and had drawn up a list of likely preachers, but Aitken did not give a source for this information, and no list has surfaced.) When the first service was held six days after his inauguration, it came as pretty much a surprise. If he had already decided to hold these services, nothing had emerged in the campaign about the plans. To Aitken, and perhaps to Nixon, this idea was justified by the Quaker's commitment to his faith and to his desire for "religious privacy," a way to avoid the public clamor that often accompanied presidential visits to churches.[23] Nixon's predecessor, Lyndon Johnson, had occasionally been embarrassed when he attended churches only to have the minister aim his sermon, sometimes on foreign or Vietnam policy, at the chief executive.

Nixon could invite only ministers he trusted to conduct services and any minister invited was his guest and would be expected to preach the word of God in a way that comported with good manners; the congregation also consisted of those the president invited who could not be expected to cause any disruption. The president even exercised veto power over the hymns visiting pastors could choose. Ohio pastor Harold Rawlings, scheduled to preach on November 16, 1969, was asked to submit the names of two hymns he wished his audience to sing and did so weeks in advance. But word soon came back that the president did not know his selections and that he should propose two more. He did so, which the hymn chooser-in-chief now deemed acceptable.[24] Hence Nixon exercised control over the preacher, the congregation, and even the songs in "his" church.

A dramatic illustration of the problem Nixon might face going out to church during an unpopular war occurred on Good Friday in 1971. A last-minute decision to cross the street to St. John's Episcopal Church for afternoon services did not prevent "half-dozen minister types" from greeting the presidential party at the front door chanting "Peace Now." Undaunted, Nixon and the group from the White House stayed for the twenty-five-minute service but, thinking to outfox the demonstrators, left by a side door. But there the anti-war contingent hovered, shouting that Christ had died to save men's lives or some such. Once back at the office, Nixon promptly canceled previously announced plans to go to Gettysburg for Easter services and decided to celebrate at a church in a nearby town when he spent the rest of the weekend at Camp David in the Maryland mountains.[25]

Nixon's decision to insulate church services in the White House also reflected his dislike of going to church generally and gave him a convenient and useful way out. His attendance at religious services over the years had been sporadic at best, and he seldom if ever made any kind of reference afterward to what he might have heard in a house of worship. If he received anything of a spiritual nature from the gatherings, one would think that he would have wanted to have them more often. Instead almost two years into the experiment, word came from the Oval Office that its occupant would like to reduce the services to once a month from twice monthly.[26] Nine months later, in September 1971, a conference of staffers met in the White House to discuss the merits of changing the time of the services from Sunday mornings to 5:00 in the afternoon. Two women who worked for Pat Nixon pointed out to those attending that the purpose of the church services was "to take the sting out of the fact that the President doesn't attend area churches." If the time changed to late afternoon, then he would have to go to a local church in the morning, at least occasionally.[27] The time of the services remained the same.

H. R. (Bob) Haldeman, White House chief of staff, explained the president's decision to hold church services at the presidential mansion as a typical Nixon solution to a dilemma he had to solve. (Associated with Nixon since the 1956 campaign, Haldeman was as close to him professionally as almost anyone else in the administration.) As the chief of staff detailed it later, Nixon did not like going out to church because his attendance caused a "stir" for the Secret Service, as well as the church and its parishioners; yet "he was also uncomfortable, symbolically," allowed Haldeman, "with the thought that the president did not regularly go to church," so holding monthly services at the White House seemed an obvious solution to him.[28] Finally it served a political function—a fact not to be gainsaid by the politician-in-chief—both for those invited to preach and sing but also because the president customarily spent upward of an hour and a half afterward having refreshments and greeting and shaking hands with those he had invited.[29]

Well after the Watergate affair, Billy Graham, Nixon's closest evangelical friend who not surprisingly preached the sermon at the first service, revealed that he had reservations about the departure from tradition, although he carefully remained circumspect in his comments. Watergate had forced him to reassess his own relations with the president, so his evaluation published in the magazine he helped found, *Christianity Today,* might be seen in retrospect as a rebuke. He mused that he thought that a president might set a better example by a pattern of going regularly to a local congregation, though he understood that the assassination of Kennedy had made it difficult for a successor to do anything he might want.[30] Nixon, of course, never compared himself to Kennedy, even in this way.

A year into the experiment and the services were working to Nixon's political advantage and shoring up evangelical support. Religious Heritage of America, an organization with little purpose beyond giving another platform to self-help author and ardent Republican W. Clement Stone, bestowed on the chief executive its "Churchman of the Year in 1970" award partially because he initiated the White House services.[31] A letter from a Baptist minister and graduate of Bob Jones University, the divisively fundamentalist college in South Carolina, explained what the minister told his Denver, Colorado, congregation when he heard the news that another Bob Jones graduate had officiated at the White House: "it is wonderful to have a president who hears evangelical and fundamentalist preachers and not just the liberal men." He recommended that Nixon secure Bob Jones Jr., then president of the university that bore his father's name, to preach at a White House service.[32] No doubt elated about the accolades, Nixon the centrist and pragmatist could not afford to invite any person as aggressively sectarian as Jones. If this letter be an indication, the White House services helped cement evangelical support for the administration.

Nixon's only public explanation for his decision came in his introduction to a collection of the sermons delivered at these Sunday-morning sessions published just in time for the 1972 campaign. With no cynicism, his words still sound like a campaign speech spiced with unifying religious sentiments. He contrasted the bare, leafless trees of winter outside with the coziness the two hundred in attendance experienced in the East Room—"a warmth of spirit engendered by human friendliness, faith in God and country, and the magnetism of" Billy Graham. Avoiding a reference to Quaker history as he defended convening in a building dedicated to worldly purposes—his sect had met in secular and unsanctified places from its beginning—he insisted that those assembled could sense God's presence "in the words of the Pledge of Allegiance [to the flag], 'one nation, under God, indivisible.'" He wanted to meet in the White House to give an

example that would encourage his fellow Americans to attend worship services, and he hoped they would continue in the future. In an earlier time,
he noted, when "the pressures of modern life" were not so overwhelming,
Americans took their religion more seriously. As his references of "God
and country" and the pledge indicated, he saw the services as part religion,
part patriotism.[33]

Even the possibility of political fund-raising in connection with the services, tinged with the reality of social and economic class, underscored the
president's continuing attention. The next March a memorandum circulated in the White House relaying the president's request to aide Charles
Colson that he "develop a list of rich people with strong religious interests
who could be invited."[34]

On the Sunday of the first service, January 26, the *New York Times*
carried a story reporting that Quakers in Washington Friends Meeting
believed the president would not plan to attend their gathering because
some of its members were in jail for evading the draft; they also mentioned
that the Washington Meeting welcomed draft resisters and had sent medical supplies to the enemy in the Democratic Republic of Vietnam, positions unlikely to win plaudits at the White House, even with a Quaker now
resident there.[35]

The president was visibly nervous that first morning, Graham, who naturally was scheduled to preach, remembered. The anxious president rushed
down to the East Room time and time again to peer in to see how many
and who had come, and then ran back upstairs to play the piano for George
Beverly Shea, who would sing later.[36] Nixon introduced Graham as his
"longtime personal friend" to the congregation of two hundred invitees,
including most members of the cabinet and eight White House telephone
operators; some children were in attendance, lending an unusual family
atmosphere to the formal East Room.[37]

A Seventh Day Adventist who attended the first service after Nixon's
second inauguration, on January 21, 1973, left a vivid account of the proceedings. Ron Graybill marveled at how the opulent East Room hardly
resembled a church with its gold draperies and three giant crystal chan-
deliers. The guests rose when the president entered the room to introduce
that Sunday's participants, Rabbi Edgar F. Magnin of Los Angeles, Joseph
L. Bernadine on his way to Cincinnati by order of the pope, and Billy Graham, who had presided over the first such service four years before. The
congregation, even including the rabbi, rose and sang the doxology, whose
lines praised "Father, Son, and Holy Ghost." The Mormon Tabernacle
Choir rendered "America the Beautiful" with its customary gusto. Rabbi
Magnin commended Nixon as "our great leader, our great President, and

a beautiful human being," while jabbing at the "new morality" masquerading as the "old immorality." Graham held the crowd in the palm of his hand as he cited Nixon's election night wish that future generations would look back on the 1970s and unite in "God Bless America" for those years' goodness. Basking in the warm glow of the surrounding spiritualized patriotism by the end of the services, those present retired to the state dining room to greet their jovial host and refresh themselves on sweet treats.[38]

Nixon continually tried to tweak the services to meet a standard he never publicized, but whose implications suggested the fundamental political nature of what he was doing. For example, at the end of 1969, he remembered that on some previous occasions there were as many as seventy-five empty seats, so he passed the word along that he wanted the "house [to] be substantially oversold," even if some had to stand in the back of the room.[39] At another time, prior to the 1972 election campaign and just after Saturday night's annual Gridiron Dinner, he wanted to make sure that those who attended were "friendly to us," either locally or from around the country and that no working press would be invited. No wonder this memo was marked "Confidential," for if it had surfaced, it might have propelled the church services right onto the nation's front pages.[40] Nixon normally permitted press pool coverage but excluded anyone taking photographs.[41]

The services were time-consuming and fraught with scheduling, theological, and political problems, all of which had to be balanced and dealt with, sometimes late on the night before. Take Saturday night, June 28, 1969. At 9:30, a micromanaging Nixon called his chief of staff, Bob Haldeman, to tell him that he had just discovered that the rabbi for the next day's affair was from New York. Did no one remember, demanded the president, that he had wanted Senator Hugh Scott from Pennsylvania to have the honor of selecting a rabbi from his home state to give him some political mileage? Haldeman put in four phone calls to staffers, one of whom was at an all-star football game in Atlanta, and one to Scott, who was not even planning to attend because he was in Philadelphia. Then the president called again to ask if the only Republican Jewish congressman had been invited. Six more calls, and they concluded that he had been contacted but turned them down; Haldeman so advised Nixon. Still not satisfied, Nixon called back to speculate that the doxology might not be appropriate for the rabbi. Two more calls confirmed that that classic Trinitarian song was in fact on the program, so at 11:30 they alerted the printer to stand by to print a substitute. But a call to the assistant who had picked the rabbi up at the airport revealed that he had approved the program as printed. At 12:30 a.m, everything squared away, a rung-out Haldeman got to bed after concluding his diary entry with a weary "Another day at the White House."[42]

Until March 17, 1974, about five months before Nixon resigned the presidency, there were forty-five religious gatherings in the White House, three of them devoted to Christmas music, four times led by Graham and the same number by Norman Vincent Peale, of Marble Collegiate Church. Most of those who participated were prominent religious figures, including three Roman Catholic cardinals, two Jewish rabbis, a lone African American evangelical Baptist from Los Angeles. Only three Quakers, all associated with evangelical churches and two probably not well known outside the Quaker world, got invitations, and each visited only once: D. Elton Trueblood, religion and philosophy professor at Earlham College and a writer of some note, Paul Smith, president of Whittier College and historian who taught Nixon there, and T. Eugene Coffin, pastor of Nixon's own East Whittier Friends Church.[43]

Hardly the kind of men who might seek to embarrass one who had access to his own bully pulpit, these establishment figures do not suggest that President Nixon had ventured far from his community church background. But those invited were selected from a narrow range indeed: no participants who took strong stands on divisive social issues got through the gauntlet of interested Nixon friends and observers. Even a prominent clergyman like Coleman Carroll, Catholic archbishop of Miami known for his strong positive position on civil rights, drew opposition from Nixon's close Florida friend the banker Bebe Rebozo and was dropped from the list.[44] So the published sermons do not reveal that the guest preachers rattled anyone's cage or stepped beyond the range of mainstream respectability. White House religion was certainly not prophetic.

Graham and Peale enjoyed the most acclaim, the former as an evangelist to millions and unofficial chaplain to presidents from Harry Truman to George W. Bush, the latter as a popular purveyor of a self-help gospel of optimism as well as one who dabbled in Republican politics. The congregations each week varied, consisting of a mixture of executive office staff members, diplomats, Supreme Court justices, high-ranking military officers, and occasional members of Congress; the president (or his staff) selected all who attended. With no awareness of the irony involved, Nixon had created church services made up of "peculiar people," a collection called together by the man of house rather than through any divine action. Once, on May 10, 1970, the president even ordered the exclusion of Secretary of the Interior Walter Hickel because he had defended young Americans who had criticized the invasion of Cambodia.[45] And of course no one in any of the gatherings ever simply walked in off Pennsylvania Avenue.

Over Nixon's entire public career, these White House services amounted to the epitome of Nixon's personal actions revealing his religious commitment. They were, collectively, singular expressions of the role that religion played in one layer of his life and how religion became so easily intermingled with patriotism. The ecumenical group of religious leaders who officiated at them were emblematic of the president's discomfort with religious dogma of any kind, whether Quaker, protestant, Catholic, or Jewish, conservative or liberal. The services amounted to a kind of mildly evangelical community church transported from east Whittier to the more diverse national level. He could invite a Conservative Jewish rabbi to speak or a Roman Catholic cardinal just as easily—indeed, perhaps more easily—than, say, a Quaker college professor. The services were controversial in some quarters at their inception—and the renowned theologian Reinhold Niebuhr, hardly a supporter of the president anyway, penned an article attacking them for violating the separation of church and state and charged that they reflected a way for Nixon to promote his private religious views[46]—but they soon faded into routine and were largely ignored.

One cabinet member, Secretary of Commerce Maurice Stans, of course a staunch Nixon supporter, demonstrated how easily the White House affairs underscored the point the president sought to achieve. In his memoir Stans opined that the services illustrated that the president was "at heart a religious man," whose generous sacrifice of time to plan and preside over them indicated only what Stans described as a "spiritual" motive. Just convening the services was enough to extract an affirmation from the uncritical Roman Catholic Stans.[47] On balance they seemed to have had little impact on anyone else involved, or at least nothing concrete has surfaced to suggest that they made much difference. Yet Pat Nixon's social secretary oozed praise in 1971, saying that they are "the most popular thing we have."[48] Nothing said or done at any of them, though, changed Nixon's decisions on major policies regarding the war in southeastern Asia or those leading up to and during the Watergate affair.

Overseen by the nation's Quaker president and after all is said and done, they still remained a curious anomaly. It was significant that Nixon's hope that he had begun something that his successors might imitate did not work out, so when he left the White House, they were all but forgotten. A Republican activist who frequently attended, Anna Chennault, perhaps best summed them up when she casually referred to them in passing as "a ritual introduced by the Nixons," with little more meaning than warmly gripping the hand of the pastor at the door following a service at East Whittier Friends Church. (And despite Chennault's nod in her direction, nothing suggests that Pat Nixon had anything to do with them except dutifully attending).[49]

But let Charles Colson, described as the "most cynical of Nixon's aides" who after his turn in prison following Watergate became an evangelical minister, have the last word. He told an interviewer, "We turned those events into wonderful quasi-social, quasi-spiritual, quasi-political events, and brought in a whole host of religious leaders to [hold] worship services for the president and his family—and three hundred guests carefully selected by me for political purposes."[50]

Nixon defined religious faith, as he informed readers of Graham's *Decision* in 1962, not "in the abstract" but "in the personal, simple terms which I heard in my earlier years." He failed completely, however, to lay out any content to that faith; he did not even define it in ways that would lead the most nominal Christian or Quaker or Jew to understand his meaning: all that was required was "faith," undefined, unexplained, contentless. The problems facing the nation, he insisted, "involved, after all, the moral and spiritual health of the American people." The threat of communism, the balance of world power, the question of guns and butter were important issues, but all paled before the "question of souls." He wanted to recall Americans to "the faith of their fathers," for we, he affirmed, "are a religious people," who "ultimately [go] back to the fundamental truths of the Bible." All Nixon could do at the end was to evince, anemically, a "fresh interest in the days ahead to learning what the Bible says in our time."[51] What the Bible said had changed not at all, just as little had changed for him religiously in the intervening seven years.

Nor did questions about Nixon's personal religious commitment entirely disappear despite the White House church services. During the 1972 campaign, Rose Mary Woods, Nixon's longtime personal secretary and a Roman Catholic, reported to Ron Ziegler, the president's press secretary, that she continued to hear complaints about Nixon's failure to attend church or say anything "along the spiritual line." She explained that one person who spoke to college groups had relayed to her that he got questions like, "Does he believe in God?" or, if from an unfriendly source, "Does he think he is God?" Woods wanted Ziegler to get stories into college newspapers about Nixon's religious background and see to it that in the president's radio addresses, he include a line asking God's help, support "—or however!"[52]

The fact that he was now president did not mean that Nixon could escape obligatory statements at events like the annual National Prayer Breakfast. Begun by President Dwight Eisenhower in 1953, these prayer breakfasts had become a place where leaders like the president could convert religion into a political utility, rather depleting it of its transcendental and prophetic qualities.[53] Nixon's first one came only ten days after his inauguration, on January 30, in the ballroom of the Sheraton Park Hotel.

Giving a nod to the ever-present Billy Graham, the new president was at his community church best: "That theme is religious faith, which despite the differences we have brings us together—brings us together in this Nation and, we trust, may help bring us together in the world." He stood tall, well aware of what his civic religion required as he molded it to shape the nation's need. "You have not lost faith in the religious background that has sustained us," he told the assembled worthies, "and we will be able to meet the challenge which is ours . . . [and] determine whether peace and freedom survive in this world."[54]

Despite his tendency to use such statements, some Americans found the lack of substance in Nixon's faith not at all obvious—indeed just the opposite. To cite only one example, a statement from an Assembly of God Church in the relatively small Portage, Michigan, six weeks into the new administration was mind-boggling because it commended him for leading a crusade of which he was undoubtedly totally ignorant. During his campaign he had never hinted at what the church had found out, somehow; it must have encountered something about Nixon that no one else had discovered, then or later. Its members gave the president "100%" of the signers' support for his efforts to "start a spiritual movement in the United States," something he never alluded to, even by implication. As the days passed, the petition went on, the likelihood of a "Holy Ghost Revival" breaking out grew more and more certain, so the petitioners advised the president to get out in front if he joined them in favoring one.[55]

More than eight months later, in late October, no such revival had occurred, so Nixon presided over the National Day of Prayer breakfast in the White House's state dining room, an event that he had earlier proclaimed. Graham, of course, was the main speaker, but the president made this occasion unique because he revealed more about his Quaker background that he had offered to a public audience before. He even joked that the reason so few Quakers got elected to the Senate was because they were accustomed to being silent, something few had noted about his church in east Whittier. He then explained that his mother and grandmother had grown up within the silent tradition and had told him—suggesting that he did not know from his own experience—that the meetings could last an hour or more with no one saying a word. Before turning the podium over to Graham, Nixon invited the group to engage in a "moment of silence in the manner of the Quakers." There was no indication how long the silence lasted, though the ceremony would have likely made headlines the next day had it gone on for any time near five minutes.[56]

In preparing for the National Day of Prayer, John Ehrlichman, after Haldeman the most powerful staff member in the Nixon White House, suggested that the president needed to address the role of prayer and religion in his life. Nixon's general and slightly humorous comments about Quakerism may well have been provoked by Ehrlichman's suggestion, but he still was not personally able to go as far as his assistant proposed in revealing more about his religious views. So he delegated to Graham the responsibility of meeting the press before the prayer day event and laying it out once again that the president's religion remained a "private personal matter, not a public function." When Haldeman called Graham, the usually agreeable evangelist agreed to do so after he talked with the president.[57] Graham knew what was expected: he had already explained to a national radio audience after the election that Nixon "has a typical Quaker reticence" about speaking of his faith in public, a praiseworthy stance, Graham opined, and a way to refrain from seeking political gain from religion.[58]

The nation's civil religion had been lowered to such a pass that Nixon believed he could legitimately use his religious heritage to evoke snickers from his audience. So this Quaker president could easily toss off jokes about quaint old practices that had once been immensely important to members of his religious group but of which he knew nothing personally. And he entrusted to a certified and compliant clergyman the burden of explaining away the chief executive's public silence about his own personal convictions. He could not do so himself, lest he run the risk of tarnishing a reputation garnered from uttering the right kind of pious religious and patriotic phrases expected of him. In 1659 George Fox, founder of those "in scorn called Quakers," could hardly be charged with perceiving this specific threat but still warned "Friends [to] take heed of blending yourselves with the outward powers of the earth."[59] Quaker Nixon had apparently never encountered this advice, either from the pulpit of East Whittier Friends Church or in any of the Sunday school literature he had taught there as a youth.

9

Withdrawal from Vietnam

Third, . . . no matter what facet of the Nixon Presidency you consider, don't ever lose sight of Vietnam as the overriding factor in the first Nixon term. It overshadowed everything else all the time, in every discussion, in every decision, in every opportunity and every problem, and you have to take that into account as you deal in those subareas and other unrelated areas.[1]

—H.R. Haldeman, 1987

Decisions involving foreign affairs, especially military and defense policy, were the most immediate that might be affected by a Quaker president's presuppositions, particularly one taking office during the Vietnam War. Acutely aware of his oft-referred to "Quaker heritage," Richard Nixon knew that the standard set by the Religious Society of Friends required, if not a pacifist position, at the least one that moved firmly away from the violence of war and toward the establishment of peace. It was a goal broad enough for Nixon to embrace it in theory, even as he undercut it by his administration's tactics. He might publicly honor his mother as a "saint" for the way she exemplified the Quaker testimonies, including pacifism, but he also knew that he certainly could not follow her down that road. He had never done so. It might have been impossible to reconcile his religion with the duties required of a commander-in-chief of the army and navy by the United States Constitution. He had always shied away from publicly hinting at any contradiction, either in 1952 when he won the nomination for vice president, in 1960 when he first ran for president, or eight years later after he won that office.

Though silent in public about what his faith required, Nixon as president was willing to admit, even use, "Friendly" principles if the occasion seemed to him to require them. For one example, consider his conversation with two senators, his national security advisor, and some of his top staffers in April 1971. They were discussing the antiwar demonstration that had occurred during the previous spring weekend. He conceded that the demonstrators were against the war in Vietnam. "My answer to them is, 'I'm against this war, but see where I am, I happen to be, because of my background, which is Quaker, against all wars, and that's why I'm trying to end war in a way that we will have a reasonable chance to avoid other wars.'" He went on to explain that the country in the past had too often won the wars but lost the peace. "My God, we're gonna end this war 'n' win a peace. That's what we are doing."[2] His statement demonstrated how he could embrace his Quaker background and his determination to end the war on his terms, but only in broad and very general terms, such as his pledge to create a "structure of peace."

It might have been less problematic, in fact, for Nixon to be both commander-in-chief and a Quaker if had viewed war as a last resort to be undertaken only if every other effort to preserve the peace had failed. This was not the case with the conflict in Vietnam. He was correct to insist that he had only inherited the war in southeast Asia—as he would iterate in his November 1969 speech—but that was through no fault of his own. Nixon's record as a strong opponent of communism may have led to his tendency to see every nationalist uprising anywhere in the world as a communist threat. In October 1953, with the French battling the Vietminh nationalist insurgency in an effort to save their colony in Indo-China, vice president Nixon offered a toast when visiting Hanoi in which he asserted that the source of the civil war came from outside—"to call it by its name, . . . totalitarian communism."[3]

Back home, exploring what to do about the impending defeat of the French, Nixon demanded that the United States take unilateral action in Vietnam, not even ruling out using an atomic bomb. On April 16, 1954, he told the American Society of Newspaper Editors meeting in Atlanta that he favored using American military forces in Indo-China to prevent any further expansion of communism: "I believe that the executive branch of the government has to take the politically unpopular position of facing up to and doing it [dropping an atomic bomb], and I personally would support such a decision." Such a course would dramatically telegraph to the Vietminh, the Communist nationalists, that the United States would not countenance what its leaders defined as the expansion of communism. His stance made him the most vocal voice for military involvement in southeast Asia within the administration; for the next twenty years he never moderated. Only President Eisenhower, retired general, prevented open military involvement on the mainland of Asia in 1954. His Quaker vice president came down clearly on the other side.[4]

Almost without exception, historians agree that Nixon, of all those whose political careers spanned the years of American involvement in Vietnam, was a—even *the*—central figure. No one was more important. As one historian, Andrew Johns, concluded, Nixon "alone among American political figures contributed either directly or indirectly to every key decision on Vietnam from the 1950s to the Paris Peace Accords as a senator, as vice president, as a clarion voice for escalation, and as president."[5] And Nixon biographer Stephen Ambrose showed that he remained "out in front" of his predecessor Lyndon Johnson whose name seems rather unfairly attached to the Vietnam conflict: "Whatever move Johnson made in the direction of escalation, Nixon was always one step ahead of him demanding more."[6] Keeping a step ahead of Johnson in the warrior's race was certainly an unusual path for a lifelong member of the Religious Society of Friends to find himself treading.

Tom Wicker, the *New York Times* columnist and, surprisingly, a positive interpreter in his book *One of Us,* published in 1991, attempted to relate Nixon's approach to Vietnam through his Quaker mother, Hannah, and undertook a foray into psychohistory. Noting the obvious to all who have tried analyzing him—that Nixon divulged his inner feelings to few people—Wicker located an informant who wanted to remain anonymous and had watched Nixon closely since the Californian came to Congress in 1947. This unnamed individual deduced from their many conversations over the years that Nixon suffered from "guilt feelings" because in his rough and tumble political career he had not followed the example of the mother he often called a "saint." Hence he was driven to achieve peace in Vietnam. Then he could go in spirit to Hannah's side and hope for her absolution, "Mother, I have made peace. I am worthy of you."[7]

In a curious kind of way, Richard Nixon, the determined anti-Communist cold warrior, became the de facto peace candidate in 1968. That was relatively easy, strange as it might sound to those who remember only a bellicose Nixon. Retiring President Lyndon Johnson tied Democratic candidate Hubert Humphrey firmly to his policies lest the vice president find his support from the White House unraveling; when Humphrey strayed a bit, LBJ tugged at his leash to pull him back in line. George Wallace, who bore the American Independent Party's banner, was a screeching and uncompromising hawk when it came to Vietnam, even though his appeal centered more on domestic matters than foreign policy.

Perhaps the closest Nixon ever came to trying to balance the competing demands he felt as president was at a prime time press conference on June 1, 1971, nearly a year and a half after he took office. A reporter asked him about charges that the administration was responsible for bombings that constituted immoral and criminal conduct. The president prefaced his reply by noting that his views with regard to war were well known. (Paraphrasing his attorney general, who once famously stated that to see where the administration stood people should "watch what we do, not what we say," Nixon later allowed that it was unnecessary to read what he had written to understand him, people instead "could observe what I have done and judge for themselves.")[8] "I grew up in a tradition," the president reminded his audience, "that considered all wars immoral. My mother, and my grandmother on my mother's side[,] were Quakers as I have often pointed out to this press corps, and very strongly disapproved of my entering World War II."

But Nixon adamantly refused to see the Vietnam conflict in a moral vacuum, for the consequences of not acting would be catastrophic, meaning not only the loss of freedom for seventeen million South Vietnamese and but also opening the way for a much wider war in the Pacific region and even across the world. "That I believe," Nixon emphatically averred in one starkly declarative sentence. As president he had to take the long view and consider this broader picture. His policy moved toward ending the war, a result that would contribute "to the peace we all want," and to validate, he implied, his Quaker grandmother's and mother's goals by means they would have abhorred and rejected. The immediate tactics of bombing only assured peace for the future, he held.[9] He carefully did not say so, but in the context of Quaker analysis, he sought a noble and glorious end through ignoble and inglorious means.

As he had many times before during his career, Nixon endowed the conflict with a kind of mythic quality as a substitute for what the American people had come to believe about Vietnam. Put simply, by this time they had moved beyond this notion and had long since rejected the war as a reasonable way to prevent countries from falling into Communist hands, like a row of dominoes. (President Eisenhower had first used the domino metaphor at a press conference in April 1954 when American aid to the French in Vietnam was being debated.) Americans probably did not understand the Vietnam conflict as a nationalist struggle against outside domination, but more and more they were rejecting Nixon's analysis; his paced removal of American military forces from Vietnam underscored his awareness of the shift away from his policies.[10]

Over the course of 1969, his first year in the White House, and well into 1970, Nixon faced increasing pressure that the insurgent Vietnamese were bringing on the United States' ally, South Vietnam. He was forced to make decisions and take action regarding Vietnam that ran counter to popular desires to remove American forces from southeast Asia. In February 1969, little more than a month after he took office, Communist armies unleashed a new offensive that sent American troops in Vietnam—then 541,500—reeling. Literally seething, Nixon fell back on basic instinct, according to his National Security Assistant Henry Kissinger, which was "to respond violently to Hanoi's cynical maneuver."[11] Thus, it was no surprise that the president ordered the secret bombing of Vietnam's neighbor Cambodia, beginning in March. When Cambodia's neutralist government fell shortly thereafter, he approved a joint South Vietnamese-American incursion into that country to remove what was referred to as "Communist sanctuaries."

As a gesture to domestic opponents, Nixon announced in June 1969 the first troop withdrawal of 25,000 military personnel, a decision he followed with a speech on November 3 introducing the concept of "Vietnamization," which he claimed had been put into effect in March but not explained fully and publicly. Admitting "deep divisions" among Americans, Nixon had a plan that would train South Vietnamese forces to defend themselves, allowing, he hoped, some 60,000 American soldiers to be withdrawn by December. This was a way to fulfill his pledge "to end the war in the way that we could win the peace" and to secure "a just and lasting peace."[12] Vietnamization allowed the president to set the level of American forces leaving Vietnam and, contingent on countless local factors including the number of American trainers and the willingness of anti-Communist southerners to cooperate, move toward turning the war over to them. It seemed as much a delaying tactic as a plan for Americans to leave the area, a kind of having it both ways. Nixon faulted himself for not preparing the American people by giving adequate background information.[13]

Even when he made the effort to persuade his opponents on a personal level, Nixon faltered. Mark Hatfield, the antiwar Republican senator from Oregon and a staunch evangelical, told of being invited, in a small group of senators, to the White House's east room for a presidential briefing on Cambodia. The president stood at the door to greet his guests. When Hatfield reached the front, the senator tried to ease the tension with a bit of humor by saying, "Well, Mr. President, I frankly don't know what I'm doing here." Shaking this guest's hand only because he had to, Nixon looked at him through "steely eyes" and responded, "It's because . . . we're in the H's."[14]

Such incidents with old friends may have led Nixon to reflect, both on himself and his policies. He was the kind of person who constantly examined and assessed himself but almost always in private. Huddled in his easy chair in his secret office in the Executive Office Building or isolated at Camp David, he covered pages of his legal pad of things he needed to do and how he should change. The beginning of his second year in office, in January 1970, gave him a fine opportunity to look back and evaluate himself and his tenure. The words he jotted down at Camp David on January 14 were positive, but selecting them for inclusion suggested that he thought he had not lived up to them. He divided his goals into ones involving the family and then his own "Personal Leadership" with a section on "Programs." Under his leadership, he listed, "Excitement—Joy in Job—Sharing—Lift spirits of people—Pithy-memorable phrases—Brevity Moving Conclusions Anecdote—Statesmanship—Honesty—Candor—Hard Work Consideration for subordinates Concern for people—Letters—Calls—Intelligence—Effect on Small Groups['] *Vitality*."

What is so remarkable about these personal goals was their "spiritual" nature: with the exception of letters and telephone calls, they went beyond material qualities and sprang from decisions only Nixon could make. If he believed himself dull, a killjoy, or long-winded and prolix, then he had to decide to be excited, joyous, or brief. He would either have to fundamentally change himself, something notoriously difficult to do, or consciously set out to act contrary to his nature. The latter he could more easily do. His old drama instructor, had lauded as "perfection" his ability to cry real tears on command; he foresaw a career in Hollywood or on Broadway for one of his best students rather than a mere political office, however high.[15] When he spoke of lifting people's spirits or a "Moving Conclusion," the president clearly viewed himself as one whose leadership would allow him to help his fellow citizens soar above the mundane. Here was a president who clearly saw his role differently from that of other politically oriented occupants of the White House. Dull Richard Nixon would be charismatic.

Others also noted Nixon's ability to consciously control himself and his emotions. Though he worked for him less than a year as a speechwriter and consultant before the election, Richard Whalen would have agreed with Upton about Nixon's thespian abilities. The difference was that Whalen saw this conscious self-control as something "priceless" the California Quaker had learned so he would be successful as a politician. (It must be pointed out that Whalen, a conservative Republican, hoped for a more principled president than Nixon turned out to be, a wish that clearly clashed with reality.) Whalen detected what he called a "combative impulse" in Nixon's nature, a carryover perhaps of his father's brashness—which the journalist did not mention—and one he trained himself to master.[16]

Nixon's yellow pad notes carried nothing particularly unusual under the heading "Programs," except that "*Reorganization*" (presumably of the executive branch) appeared more than two years before he publicly unveiled it. One surprising subcategory was "Spiritual Quality," which consisted of two items: "1976," referring no doubt to commemoration of the two hundredth anniversary of the Declaration of Independence six years hence, and "National Purpose—goals." Although nearly a year into his term, Nixon was still without a catchy name for his programs. He apparently had no idea what to call his agenda, contenting himself to jot down the names previous presidents had used, such as Theodore Roosevelt's Square Deal and Kennedy's New Frontier; he knew he needed a name, even if he could not come up with one.[17] Four days later, Nixon was back at the overview in the Executive Office Building, analyzing his first year. He gave himself credit for reestablishing dignity and respect for the country abroad, but he believed he was not working hard enough. He needed to buckle down, come up with some kind of bold and gutsy initiatives, and make more telephone calls to his supporters, even as he polished his press conferences, a perennial concern because he simply did not care much for reporters.[18]

These unstructured ramblings indicated not a little disquiet in the outwardly serene bearing of the president. Haldeman's wise advice at the beginning of this chapter helps make sense of one continuing phenomenon of Nixon's first term, his unease as he tried to balance the growing unpopularity of the war in Vietnam with his own firm determination to assure a "peace with honor" in that part of the world. Nixon himself was part of the problem. At the end of April, he announced that joint American-Vietnamese forces would cross the border into neighboring Cambodia and expel the North Vietnamese Communists from safe havens there. With members of his staff questioning his decision, even taking the opposite side, Nixon, convinced it was the right course, was more conflicted about the decision than any other up to this point. His daughter Julie saw him as being "really disturbed" and "quite worried" about it.[19] After protests erupted on many of the nation's campuses over this new departure, Nixon was taped at the Pentagon on May 1, 1971, referring to "these bums, you know, blowing up the campuses." Three days later, four students at Kent State University died at the hands of Ohio National Guardsmen; his descriptions of "bums" came back to haunt him because it elicited widespread harsh comment.[20]

By this time in the early 1970s, even evangelical Quakers had questions about the nation's course of action, even though a Friend like themselves set the policy. No poll was taken in California Yearly Meeting, the larger body of which East Whittier Friends Church was a part, but a 1967 survey of the equally evangelical Northwest Yearly Meeting centered in Oregon and Washington, revealed an equal division of opinion: 45.5 percent favored escalation of military action in Vietnam and 45.5 percent supported "de-escalation of the war even if the North Vietnamese and Viet Cong did not reciprocate." One close observer concluded that the first group feared anarchy and communism and supported the government as a bulwark against both. The other segment of Friends wanted a "greater prophetic faithfulness in calling nations to account against God's standards of righteousness."[21]

In California Yearly Meeting, the superintendent, Keith Sarver, a staunch pacifist, who originated an appeal for a "New Call to Peacemaking Conference" among Quakers in 1974, could not find a way to mention either the Quaker president or, surprisingly, even the Vietnam War itself. The best he could do in the appeal was to recognize "the fact that Friends have been divided in recent years by some actions taken to implement the concern for peace." This heritage of moderation was evident in 1967 when T. Eugene Coffin, pastor at Nixon's East Whittier Friends Church, expressed chagrin at local news outlets that repeated news service reports about Quakers sending medical aid to North Vietnam without first checking with local Friends churches about their attitudes. But then he turned around and condemned the "sterile and static" conformity that characterized too many Friends groups when they seemed to have forgotten that Quakers were called to "obey God rather than man."[22] Without using the name, Nixon may well have been the man Coffin was referring to, for he was the president.

Unprogrammed Friends, the "liberal" ones in the east, the ones that Friend Nixon disdained, were not so circumspect. They brought evangelicals like Coffin up short a few years on when they questioned whether East Whittier Church was exercising appropriate oversight of its wayward member. Journalist Milton Mayer, a Friend with Jewish roots who was originally from Chicago, wrote a monthly column for *Progressive* magazine but made a splash in the pages of *Christian Century* in October 1973 with an article that raised questions about disownment of the president. Mayer conceded that disownment, excluding Nixon from attending the monthly meeting for business and contributing, had fallen into disuse among Friends, but he ventured that the underlying principle, the need to labor with him about his derelictions, had not, not by a long mark. Mayer conceived that a handful of Friends in Nixon's church could topple Nixon from the presidency—this was after the Watergate affair but prior to the House of Representatives taking up impeachment—by moving to discipline or disown him after he "disunited himself from spiritual fellowship." Nixon might avoid such a spectacle by going before the church's Ministry and Counsel Committee to "say that he had found his birthright principles inoperative (perhaps he could think of another term) in the life of statesmanship." A rejection by his own church, Mayer surmised, would be "a serious blow to the religious prop which holds up the President's crumbling image in Middle America."[23]

Unwilling to take guidance from eastern Friends, East Whittier Friends were not about to abandon their member, no matter how wayward. The church's minister contributed an article to the same publication at the beginning of the new year in which he explained that at the time of the bombing of Cambodian incursion three years before, the church had received a number of requests from Friends and meetings to examine Nixon's membership. The Ministry and Counsel Committee, considering the question a "family" matter, then concluded that it "would be unchristian to drop [him] from membership." Now that Mayer had converted it into a national issue, the church had not changed its position: "As an autonomous Christian Quaker fellowship" that sought an alternative to war, Coffin stressed that his "was a caring community and [sought] to restore rather than destroy, to heal rather than hurt, to reconcile rather than divide." Among those who weighed in on the issue was Yale University Divinity School professor Roland Bainton, a Friend, who questioned whether a Quaker could legitimately be president and proposed that Nixon should voluntarily ask for his membership to be terminated.[24]

If such developments in the small Quaker world did not move the occupant of the White House, antiwar demonstrations in the nation's capital certainly did. A dramatic example occurred before dawn on May 9, 1970, in the early morning before a huge demonstration of more than 100,000 protestors was to meet at noon. Nixon acted on the spur of the moment and without seeking advice from any subordinate. The administration was on edge with demonstrations during this period. About the same time, Henry Kissinger had to sleep in the president's bedroom in the White House fallout shelter because he literally could not leave to go home.[25] Watching knots of students gathering at about 4:00 a.m. for the demonstration, Nixon resolved to go out, mix with them, take their measure, and defend his policies in person.[26] One contemporary commentator thought the escapade "no more than a footnote,"[27] but in retrospect it occasioned more significance. Speech writer William Safire termed it the "strangest, most impulsive, and perhaps most revealing night of Nixon's Presidency,"[28] another Nixon aide, David Gergen, thought it "poignant,"[29] and Nixon biographer Herbert Parmet used it as a "teaser" to pull the reader into his book.[30] Egil "Bud" Krogh, Ehrlichman's assistant, present for all but the first few minutes of Nixon's comments, concluded later that he "had seen the man behind the mask" that morning, a "softer" man.[31] Nixon's unscripted and unprecedented visit to the Lincoln Memorial revealed something of the complicated complexity that tore at this tormented man as he tried to be the kind of leader he imagined the nation needed.

Nixon had had a press conference at 10:00 p.m. the evening before and responded to questions about the planned demonstration the next day. He insisted he understood what the students who were coming to Washington wanted: peace, to stop the killing, and to end the draft. "I agree," he told the nation and the press corps, "with everything they are trying to accomplish." Despite the fact that he had just decided to send troops into Cambodia and push the North Vietnamese out of that sanctuary, he promised to continue to reduce American troops in Vietnam and "hasten the day we can have a just peace." He knew, he observed, that the protestors thought the president's decision would "expand the war, increase American casualties, and increase American involvement"; what they did not understand was that he had made his decision precisely "for the very reasons they were protesting."[32] Implicit in his comments was his notion that if the dissidents only appreciated the rationale for his policies they would embrace them and go home, allowing everyone to live happily together in peace ever after. Sometimes impulsive, he decided he had to get through to critical students.[33]

Nixon received or placed some forty-five calls before going to bed a bit after 2:00 a.m. He slept soundly until he awoke about 4:00 o'clock.[34] Although he never referred to it explicitly, the mobilization had obviously left the president keyed up; his instinctive actions suggested that he was searching for a way to get his message out to the protestors. To distract himself, he went into the Lincoln sitting room and did the usual, put on a Rachmaninoff record. His valet, the Spanish-born Manolo Sanchez, heard the piano music, got up, and went in to find out if the president needed something. "I asked him," Nixon recalled, "if he had ever been to the Lincoln Memorial at night." After Sanchez said he had not, Nixon got dressed, and the two men went down and got a car driven by a petrified Secret Service officer; Nixon warned those who remained behind that they were not to contact anyone from his office or the press, but it turned out they ignored his order. The president was loose in the city, although it took only five minutes to get to the memorial. According to Egil Krogh, who arrived from the White House just after Nixon and parked behind the president's idling limousine, there were four Secret Service agents present—not enough for proper security—along with Nixon's physician, Walter Tkach.[35]

Two small groups of students milled around the rotunda. Nixon went over to a group of about eight men, shook hands, and found them "not unfriendly" if a bit surprised and "overawed." He asked them the usual questions, where they were from, how old they were, and what they were studying. Most were from New York, and over half had never been to Washington. He told them that it was an outstanding city, and, after listening to the speakers, he hoped that they would find time to see some of the historical monuments, one of which was the Lincoln Memorial, which he considered one of the most beautiful sights at night. He mentioned his press conference, which two or three volunteered that they had not been able to hear as they were traveling. He was sorry they had not heard it, because, he emphasized, "my goals in Vietnam were the same as theirs—to stop the killing and end the war to bring peace."

Nixon took the lack of response to mean that they did not agree with his position, and he told them so; he hoped that they would give the administration a hearing on other issues and that their hatred for the war would not turn them against the United States and its system. "I said, I know that probably most of you think I'm an S.O.B. but I want you to know that I understand how you feel." Then he recalled for them that after he got out of law school and was ready to get married, he had been thrilled when British Prime Minister Neville Chamberlain came back from Munich and said that his trip meant peace. He also reminded them that he had a Quaker background and was as close then to being a pacifist as anyone could. Hence he had dismissed British Conservative Winston Churchill's criticism of Chamberlain as a "madman." But looking back from this distance, he recognized that he had been wrong after Churchill became prime minister and courageously carried out the policies he believed were right in the face of widespread opposition.

The president then focused on "areas where I could draw them out." He advised them to travel, and, when one of them said that money was scarce, he told of borrowing money to go Mexico with his wife and later to Central America. But they could start with the United States where there was much to see and different people to meet, like the Indians of the southwest. Then he told them the "Negro problem" was a major concern on many of their campuses and that they should always remember that the Indians had been treated just as badly as blacks. He admonished them to keep lines of communication open to Indians, Mexicans, and Negroes.

By this time, a girl had joined the all-male group. Nixon asked if anyone there was from California, and she said she was from Los Altos, which turned out to be one of the president's favorite towns in the northern part of the state. And speaking of the Golden State, he suggested that when they went there, they should notice what "massive strides" were being undertaken on behalf of the environment, "which I knew they were all interested in." He mentioned specifically that one of the best surfing beaches in southern California was Marine Corps property and that he had taken steps to open it to the public so that everyone could enjoy it and its natural beauty. Most seemed to agree with his point, as they did when he advised them to travel abroad, especially to Asia and China whose 700 million people "are one of the most remarkable people on earth." He added that they should not forget India; it was terribly poor but rich in history, philosophy, and with a compelling mystique that they should try to understand.

Moving on to discussing the Soviet Union, Nixon responded to a question of what Moscow was like—"I said grey"—and recommended that if they really wanted to know Russia, they should go to Leningrad; the people there were more outgoing because they "were not so much under control and domination of the central government." Someone—two students were in architecture school—brought up architecture so Nixon advised visiting Prague or Warsaw to see more beautiful buildings than in Moscow. One listener wanted to know about practical matters like visas, which Nixon opined would not be a problem, though he suggested if they had problems they could contact his office for help. That generous offer elicited a chuckle that went through the group.

What really mattered in all these places, though, was not buildings or air or water but people. He offered Haiti as an example, one of the poorest places he had been in Latin America. When he was there in 1955, "the people had a dignity and grace which was very moving." Haiti had neither great cities nor especially good food, true, but the people had character. This allowed him to return to the United States to emphasize the importance of not being alienated from the people of one's own country. He mentioned that blacks and whites had less contact with each other at major schools than when they were not on the same campus. He seemed disappointed when no one responded in specific terms to this comment.

By this time the group had grown to about thirty, with some being more "leader types" and somewhat older. One of these newcomers spoke up, "I hope you realize that we are willing to die for what we believe in." Nixon said he knew they were and that he was trying to build a world in which no one would have to die for one's beliefs but could live for them. He reiterated what he had said in the press conference about overcoming some of the differences with the Soviets to make some progress in limiting nuclear arms, but no one seemed interested in that subject, perhaps "because we moved through so fast and perhaps because they were overawed by the whole incident." Another student pointed out that they were not interested in what Prague looked like but the kind of life they could have in this country. The president replied that the whole point in discussing Prague was not to discuss the city but its people, and he reminded them that the world was getting smaller. He stressed that it "is vitally important" that we know and appreciate people everywhere and particularly in the United States.

It was not altogether clear that Nixon's energy was running out, but he began to wind up his discussion with another attempt to meet the students where he thought they were. The necessity of clean air, water, and streets was obvious, and attempts to protect all three laudable, and the president confirmed that his administration had "very bold programs" to move in those directions. But such cleanliness "is not going to solve the deepest problems that concern us all." Clearing up blotches in the natural world, he stressed, could leave the nation "completely sterile and without spirit." "We must think about why we are here. What are those elements of the spirit which really matter[?]" Seeking a way to identify with his youthful audience, Nixon said they were searching the same way he had been forty years before, when he entered college. Cleaning up, even ending the war, "was not going to solve spiritual hunger which all of us have and which, of course, has been the great mystery of life from the beginning of time." Sounding very much like the Quaker he had been once, Nixon stressed the "elements of the spirit that really matter." Sanchez had already mentioned a couple of times that there was a phone call for him in the car, so Nixon shook hands with a few of the students closest to him and started walking down the steps of the memorial.

Three things happened as the president was getting into his car, striking in their contrast with the president's almost spiritual comments that had come before. A group of women, some of whom identified themselves as students from Syracuse University, had gathered at the base of the memorial, and Nixon went over to them on his way back. The only time that he had not concentrated on consequential national and international topics that evening, he told them that he knew of the Orange, their football team. Perhaps it was one of these women who complained to a reporter that the president was "not really concerned with why we were here." The press later tended to play up this interpretation, allowing his brief comments about football to color their take on the nighttime escapade and lending the whole affair an air of presidential condescension. Even John Ehrlichman of Nixon's staff belittled his boss's interjection of sports into a serious conversation with people who had driven many miles to demonstrate against the war.[36]

The second incident involved a red-bearded Detroit student. He aimed his camera at Nixon as the president started to enter the car, and Nixon inquired if he would like to come over and get into the picture. The guy with the beard moved in beside Nixon, who asked his doctor to take the picture. Delighted, the Detroiter burst into the broadest smile Nixon had seen the entire evening. The still-genial chief executive seized the opportunity to return to a theme he had mentioned earlier, namely that he knew the students were "terribly frustrated and angry" about Vietnam, but he hoped that their ire did not turn into a blind hatred of the country. To dispel any doubts about how good the country was, he suggested a visit to the passport office where no one was lining up to get out of the country, for all its faults. The president shook hands with the visitor from Michigan and got in the car, which pulled away down the Mall to the Capitol building.

The third incident demonstrated how quickly Nixon changed to reveal a different front or "layer." This time he descended from the high spiritual plane he had been on in the memorial down to the lowest level of crass. As they pulled out, a bearded guy—not the fellow from Detroit apparently—ran up and thrust his middle finger into the air at the car's principal occupant. Always conscious of who might see him, Nixon looked around to make sure that no members of the press were in sight, and then he gave the bearded guy the finger back. Turning to his valet with a gleeful smile, he said, "That s.o.b. will go through the rest of his life telling everybody he knows that the President of the United States gave him the finger, and nobody will believe him." And the presidential car sped off up the mall.[37] Krogh's car followed behind, its occupant noting the thousands of students milling around and their makeshift tents dotting the mall, but he left no record of having seen the two obscene gestures moments before.

Sanchez had never been in the capitol, so the four, Nixon's valet, Tkach, Krogh, and the Secret Service man, got a guided tour of the building by one who had first come there in 1947 and had served in both chambers.[38] The Senate side was locked, but they found an attendant who had come to work the same year as Nixon arrived; he opened a House door for them. After entering they encouraged Sanchez to mount the Speaker's chair, and they all applauded. Three black cleaning women came by to shake hands, one asking Nixon to sign her Bible, which she happened to have with her. They left and drove to the Mayflower Hotel's restaurant, where the still-free president breakfasted on corned beef hash topped with a poached egg, the first one he had had, he said, in five years. Outside of official duties, it was the first time since coming to Washington as president that he had eaten at a public restaurant. He signed autographs for any who asked. The group arrived back at the White House about 7:30; they had been away for three hours.

As Nixon reflected on it later and after the press had put the entire episode in a bad light—perhaps because the president had not informed them of what he planned that evening—he became more than a little angry. To counter Ehrlichman's assertion that Nixon had gone to the memorial and acted tired, Nixon wrote Haldeman a memo so the staff would know at least what he was trying to do. The staff, the boss averred, were "enormously interested in material achievements of the administration and what we accomplish in our record," but they represented an inability "to communicate on those matters that are infinitely more important—qualities of spirit, emotion, of the depth and mystery of life which this whole visit really was all about." A staff enthralled with mere material progress and short-term political goals could not understand these students, many of them "middle class and lower middle class" as Nixon remembering himself attending Whittier College. "Perhaps the major contribution I could make to them," the president explained carefully, "was to try to lift them a bit out of the miserable intellectual wasteland in which they now wander aimlessly around."[39] If that assessment was a damning indictment of the nation's colleges and universities, it also hid undertones of his red-haired relative Lewis Hadley's sermonizing of long ago. Then again, however, it may have simply been just another of those layers that obscured the "real Nixon," who lurked behind it all.

Even such spiritual matters had political implications for the country's first Republican, as became apparent in a memorandum he worked on in July 1970, a bit over three months before midterm elections. He pondered how to hang the race issue, liberalism, and the student tag on the Democrats, a stream of thought that allowed him to jot down for his own use anyway that it was a "myth that RN picked up [in the polls] as he became more liberal on race, welfare, environment, troop withdrawal." He told himself to remind aide Haldeman to invite former members of Congress and both cabinet and subcabinet members to Sunday morning church services at the White House and perhaps have a group in the night before. He wanted to find ways to schedule more events where he could excel, such as television interviews, foreign travels, or speaking to audiences with no notes. He even ripped "Dignity" of any transcendental meaning, hinting at the installation of a White House taping system when he explained it as "Every word recorded[,] act Remembered"—and that was six months before he ordered such a system installed.[40]

About the same time that summer Nixon convinced Charles Colson, his chief political operative, in one of a rambling series of conversations, that he wanted to revive what Colson described as "old-fashioned values, something a restless nation could rely on and believe in." "If I do nothing else as President, I'm going to restore respect for the American flag," he determinedly confided to the former marine, as though that piece of colorful cloth materially embodied something of the American spirit.[41]

The man who could curl up in his easy chair in the Executive Office Building, his feet propped up on an ottoman, and ponder putting tape recorders in his offices and on his phone was one side of a controlling, determined Nixon—the side that would lead to his downfall, let it be said. Another layer appeared less than a year later in a conversation he had at the end of March 1971 with Pulitzer Prize–winning novelist Allen Drury.

Musing at San Clemente, Nixon pointed out that the "important thing [in this country] is our will." (We need to keep in mind that only the previous month the president, wearing a different hat, had used his will to order wiring the White House.) Americans needed to believe in themselves and their ability to shape their future. "The problem now," he correctly if too sweepingly averred, "is the American spirit. This is the crisis of the spirit that we face. The most important thing is to restore the American spirit. That is what I would like to do before I leave this office."

When Nixon uttered those words—the kind his mother and most Quakers would have readily understood and approved—he knew that Drury was preparing what would become an impressive book of photographs of and interviews with his associates celebrating the administration. As a politician, Nixon also recognized that those words might well speak to potential supporters and convey to them what he had told those students at the Lincoln Memorial the previous spring, that spiritual concerns dwarfed mere material achievements. Yet, in almost the same breath that he made his comments to novelist Drury, Nixon also affirmed, "The important thing is not our capacity to do things—we have that."[42] Nixon understood, knew deep down where his best perceptions resided—what Christians since the first century had called a person's "bowels"[43]—what was important. But this same man could, as he seriously ruminated about it, somehow cast the word "dignity" over his desire to remember every act and record every word.

More important, his emphasis, as he usually phrased it, was totally secular; it had no expressed higher—spiritual or religious—value. The spirit he wanted restored and renewed was "the American spirit," and he gave it no content. At least when he had spoken to the students at the Lincoln Memorial he had insisted that even something as borderline between "spiritual" and material as traveling in foreign climes took on a humanistic content, learning to appreciate other people, not just the buildings they had constructed; now, to Drury, he did not even broach that possibility. Had he attached some religious significance to this restoration, he would have violated his lifelong stance that discussions of religion were not appropriate in the political arena. That was a place, after all, that he was convinced ought to remain free of anything but the broadest generality and ultimately less meaningful politically phrasing. Publicly it would remain that way.

10

Nixon's Need for Religion

[People] don't have to really read anything [to understand me]. They could observe what I have done and judge for themselves.[1]

—Richard Nixon

The disquiet near Nixon's center—his bowels, to use the biblical term—was clearly highlighted by his private musings and jottings. (Quakers use "center" as a noun pointing to the solid inward seat of a person's being; it had a special meaning for Nixon as can be seen by his use of the term, especially in his last memoir, to encapsulate the overarching goal in life, achieving "peace at the center.")[2] Yet for all his efforts, he remained personally uneasy, even torn. It was an unease that tugged at his unsure center, made him restless, and sent him in search of a security that others seemed to have but which continued to elude him despite his best efforts and the remarkable success he had made for himself in politics. In the days after the shooting at Kent State University in May 1970, as other campuses erupted in protest, Nixon confessed that these "were among the darkest of my presidency. I felt utterly dejected."[3]

The experience he was going through was hardly new. It reinforced what he had confided in his first memoir, *Six Crises,* written nearly a decade before after his defeat in the 1962 California governor's race. "Coolness" or "serenity" at a time of crisis, he reasoned then, was a product of faith. Defining a faith that was totally self-generated and devoid of ties to religion, he demonstrated how far he had drifted from his evangelical Quaker background, whose force he relegated to residual "religious heritage and moral training." He left such influence to the past and thought that faith "comes to an individual after he has gone through a necessary period of indecision, of doubt and soul-searching, and resolves that his cause is right and determines that he must fight the battle to the finish."[4]

Despite such a definition devoid of traditional religion, Nixon took unprecedented steps to be identified with the nation's most prominent churchman, Billy Graham. Nixon could then gain some reflected glory. Talking with one close associate, he even toyed with the idea of converting to Roman Catholicism in the hope of finding the stability and order that somehow eluded him. Judging from his restlessness, an emptiness and void, far from peace, existed at Nixon's center. National Security Advisor Henry Kissinger recalled that the president in that period "reached a point of exhaustion that caused his advisors deep concern."[5]

Only days after his visit to the Lincoln Memorial, Nixon surprised Graham when he agreed to speak at an evening service of the evangelist's crusade in Knoxville, Tennessee.[6] As vice president Nixon had sat on the platform at the New York City crusade in 1957, and Lyndon Johnson had attended the 1965 Houston revival of Graham's, but no president had ever spoken before from the platform of an evangelistic rally. (Nixon liked to crow about the "firsts" he initiated, but he never referred to this one again, perhaps because those dealing with Christianity no longer mattered.) The person who first broached the invitation is not clear—Graham's authorized biographer implied that the invitation originated in east Tennessee, perhaps with the local congressman[7]—but in a telephone call to the evangelist at his home in Montreat, North Carolina, Nixon expressed concern that his appearance might come across as too political. Graham did not think so but was still a bit taken aback, if pleasantly, when the White House announced with no further discussion that the chief executive would attend and speak on Thursday, May 28, 1970, already designated as "Youth Night."[8] Perhaps he believed his attendance would help identify his administration with American young people.

Already controversial on the University of Tennessee campus, the crusade became more so with Nixon's anticipated appearance at UTK football's Neyland Stadium. This would be the first Nixon visit to a university campus since the shooting at Kent State on May 4. It also represented a foray into the still Democratic south into a state where Vietnam War critic Senator Albert Gore was high on the president's list of senators who should go down to defeat. Gore's Republican challenger, William E. Brock, arrived with Nixon on his plane and made sure that he stood right beside the president when pictures were taken.[9] Knoxville was the largest city in heavily Republican east Tennessee, a fact that promised a large turnout for a presidential visit and ensured an eager crowd of ordinary citizens to hear him. Student activists, who had faced off against the university administration that year on a range of issues, from curfews in women's dormitories to selection of a new university president, were prepared to oppose Nixon's drop-by; they enjoyed the support of a good handful of professors, including a professor in the department of religion.

Graham had already tried to make Nixon's visit nonpartisan—certainly "a president," he said in a prepared statement, "should be allowed to attend a ball game, entertainment, or a religious service without it being interpreted as being political"—but in the volatile spring atmosphere that goal was as close to impossible as trying to prevent east Tennesseans from flocking to a Vols football game on a warm Saturday afternoon in the fall. The largest audience ever assembled in the state flooded into the stadium. Close to 100,000 were in the audience, 70,000 filling the seats, better than 25,000 sitting on grassy banks and crowding the parking lots and listening on loud speakers; two-thirds were Baptists, most regular church-goers, many young people for "Youth Night." When a local clergyman prayed for "our beloved president," about 250 protestors, seated in a separate section waving antiwar placards, shouted in angry derision but were hooted down by more vocal Nixon supporters. Nine of these "undisciplined brats," as a local paper described them, were arrested.[10] Security was the tightest east Tennessee had ever seen.[11] The volume of sounds emanating from the two sides resembled nothing so much as a football game between the Vols and their arch rivals the Georgia Bulldogs.

Nixon addressed the clear divisions between the vast majority of people there who were demonstrating their support for him and the much smaller number of dissenters. Graham had told him, he said, that this was youth night and that there would be a diversity of opinion present, so he carefully positioned himself on the side of his supporters while subtly demeaning the minority: "I am just glad that there seems to be a rather solid majority on one side rather than the other side tonight." For the rest of his time, his words sounded like political boilerplate of one addressing a youthful audience; he celebrated the mass of students seeking a good education while committed to (good) causes beyond themselves, and he championed those preparing to be future leaders who sought peace. He commended the nation he led: "this is the kind of country where a young person knows that there is a peaceful way he can change what he doesn't like about America and that is why this is a great country." He concluded by emphasizing that those who wanted a better, clearer, fairer, peaceful world "must turn to those great spiritual sources that made America the great country that it is."

That was as close as Nixon got to anything that contained any sign of the substance of faith and religion. His speech was vapid. He did endorse Graham twice as one who embodied the "spirit" of religion "that each of us needs" or "hungers for," but that was it, nothing more specific, nothing about his own needs, nothing to indicate to the Baptists present that he recognized any of the landmarks of faith, his or theirs.[12] Graham's biographer excepted Nixon as a "government official" who because of his position could "not deliver a religious address" but conceded that other crusade officials present believed "it left much to be desired."[13] Graham, unnamed, was likely one of these. He gave no indication at the time that the evangelical Quaker's remarks fell short of the kind of "forthright . . . witness for Christ" that he wished from the president; instead he confined such assessments to his autobiography published well after Nixon's death.[14] After his talk, Nixon joined his wife and Henry Kissinger, a Jew, on the podium to listen to Graham's sermon. His appearance in Knoxville had no major impact on him; at least he made no reference to it in any of his memoirs.

Nixon's disquiet became clear to Charles Colson, a man whose reputation was covered so completely with vitriol that he was sometimes known as the "White House Hatchet Man." He saw an emptiness in his boss just before Christmas 1973, as the Senate demands for the Watergate tapes increased and just after Colson announced his surprising conversion to evangelical Christianity. Summoned to see the president, Colson had a long, private conversation in the Lincoln sitting room upstairs in the White House because Nixon had come to distrust his West Wing staff. He had begun to doubt the Secret Service, he told his guest, and he did not know for sure that the special Watergate prosecutor had not bugged this very room. Once or twice Colson thought that he should ask the clearly troubled Nixon to pray with him, but, as a new Christian, he felt himself woefully inadequate. They spent most of their time on Watergate-related matters, with the president trying to nail down Colson's memories of various events. That night, shortly after 11:30, the White House operator awakened him with a call from the president, who just wanted to continue their talk earlier that day. The two chatted about this and that, and then, out of the blue, Nixon made his most startling and stunning statement of the day, "You know, Chuck, I get on my knees every night and just pray to God." For one who always seemed self-assured and could never admit weakness, this confession took Colson aback, and he himself prayed for his boss.[15]

Another of Nixon's most startling and revealing comments about his own personal disquiet when it came to his faith occurred in the summer of 1971 at the time Congress was debating federal aid to parochial schools. The president sat down to discuss religion with Colson. After a gathering of his domestic advisors closed and the others had left the Oval Office, Nixon turned to his assistant and confessed a secret need for something of "enduring spiritual value." Colson judged him earnest and sincere as the president confided, "You know, Chuck, I could be a Roman Catholic." He admitted that if he converted, his political opponents would sneer that here is old "Tricky Dicky making a pitch for the Catholic vote." Nixon had apparently mused along these lines for some time, perhaps considering how far his mother's Quaker faith divulged from the less-tolerant Catholicism. Now his voice dropped to all but a whisper, "it's beautiful to think about, that there's something you can grab hold of, something real and meaningful. How I wish we could all have it—something really stable. . . . I believe, I believe," and his low voice trailed off.[16] There was emptiness there.

If journalist Anthony Summers is to be believed, Nixon told his domestic aide John Ehrlichman much the same thing. Sometimes the president would laud the Quaker beliefs of his mother and explain how he considered "the Quaker ceremony was very simple, more authentic." And then at other times he would seem to long for the security he perceived within the Roman Catholic Church: "You know if I were to embrace a religion"—the implication being that he had not done so up to that time—"it would be Catholicism, because they're so well disciplined in their dogma, so well defined."[17] In another context, one having nothing to do with religion, everything to do with Nixon as the complicated human being he was, Henry Kissinger flatly stated, "I was aware of Nixon's compulsive insecurity" because he had so often served as its target.[18] And he knew Nixon nearly as well as did anyone within the administration.

Twenty years later, Nixon was making the same point in another connection and when he could no longer run for office because he was now disgraced. Thirteen months before he died, in March 1993, talking with his assistant, the youthful and eager-to-learn Monica Crowley, he demonstrated the service religion provided by referring to the nineteenth-century French traveler and astute observer of Jacksonian America, Alexis de Tocqueville. Nixon rated his book *Democracy in America* a "masterpiece." Tocqueville cared little for religion as an aid to an individual's spiritual well-being or for the sense of mission or broad concern it often produced. Whether for Tocqueville or Nixon, that variety of religion was virtually useless. No, the role of religion that Tocqueville found appealing and recommended was the same one that attracted our politically oriented former president and the same one that made him long for the stability that he believed Catholicism would underpin: "He considered religion," explained Nixon to Crowley, "even more important for [potentially unstable] democracies because it instills habits, like moral responsibility and conscience. *That* is what is missing today—a sense of conscience."[19] Nixon wanted religion to hold the society together, a kind of social glue, not to serve as a valuable and inspiring end in itself.

Even toward the very end of his life, Nixon remained enamored of Roman Catholicism, for its doctrines, which "have been thought through and examined for centuries," and for "its power to teach right and wrong." People, he was convinced, relate to its endurance and its mystery, which was why he lamented the church's changing "from the traditional Latin for the Mass to English. I know why they did it: so people could understand what was going on, so they could understand the message. But the mystery and the tradition were all part of it." And then he implicitly criticized his own Quaker tradition, for failing to understand that ritual was more powerful than words when they lacked "the power to sweep [people] up even if they're a little weak on the message."[20]

There might also have been a political and anti-Kennedy dimension to the attraction of Roman Catholicism. When he traveled to Europe as a private citizen after his defeat in the California governor's race in 1962, Nixon let it be known when he sought an audience with Pope John XXIII that he expected to be granted an audience as long as the pontiff had had with Catholic President John Kennedy, for, the former vice president explained to his go-between, the U.S. Consul in Rome, "If the truth be told I am a better Catholic than he is."[21]

Such comments as these reveal more about Nixon and his mother's version of Quakerism, as well as his personal need for religious security, than they do about any intrinsic appeal that Rome held for him. Mother Hannah Milhous Nixon, born in 1885 in Indiana at the beginning of the introduction of pastors among midwestern Friends, was a kind of transitional figure. She grew up in a relatively well-to-do traditional Friends setting where the old Quaker world with plain language, traditional silent worship, and the values of a unified community of faith reigned. Her description of Quakerism for her son's biographers partook of these old, now-discarded patterns and practices. Yet she lived most of her adult life in a new and different Quaker environment, one of programmed worship, pastors, evangelical doctrines, and—more important—one that she, judging from the way she depicted her son's religious heritage, was never entirely comfortable with.

Hence when her son described the aspects of religion he longed for, the personal needs that pulled him toward Roman Catholicism, he chose words like "real," "meaningful," "well defined," and "really stable," suggesting that he found these concepts absent from his own religious, evangelical Quaker experience. Historic Quakerism, the kind his mother had known as a child, promised that the believer would come to know these concepts over the course of a lifetime of waiting silently in worship and feeling the gradual unfolding of God's leadings and promptings. The evangelical world Nixon grew up in, in contrast, stressed the need for a one-time salvation experience, the kind he experienced as a youthful teenager in Los Angeles at Paul Rader's revival in the mid-1920s. Making such a one-time decision for Christ keynoted his friend Graham's preaching as well. However this central event might develop in others' lives, in Nixon's case it had failed to produce anything he could now, fifty years later, call "real," "meaningful," or "really stable." (There is no record that he ever attended an unprogrammed, silent meeting for worship.) So he sensed meaning somewhere else, this time in Roman Catholicism, a place nearly totally alien from his evangelical Quaker faith.

According to Kissinger, the Nixon White House was so "emotionally exhausting" that it had robbed the people who worked there of their ability to see or comment upon its occupant's "all-compassing loneliness" because he "needed them as much to fill the emptiness of his life as for their practical advice."[22] An "empty" life was simply not one in which an observer, present or future, could reasonably expect to find much substance of religious faith. Or, as speech writer William Safire put it, quoting Gertrude Stein from the 1920s, when it came to Nixon, "there was no *there* there."[23]

Unlike Safire, who saw Nixon as having many, perhaps countless, facets to his life, Garry Wills—journalist and historian not to mention a Roman Catholic—boiled the man down to one: he was a politician, a complete politician, the composite politician. Writing about Nixon before he became president and created his warped administration, Wills's words were damning even as they summed up and gave a different dimension to Safire's quotation from Stein: "With other politicians," Wills observed, "informality exposes the man behind the office, a range of personality that extends beyond political role. But Nixon does not exist outside his role, apart from politics: take his clothes off, he would be invisible."[24]

Yet for all that—and despite its essential truth—Nixon had succeeded in bamboozling himself and close and insightful observers like Kissinger. At Nixon's funeral services, Kissinger explained in clear view of a nationwide television audience that he had found it "a privilege to have been allowed to help him." Why? Because "Richard Nixon ended a war, and he advanced the vision of peace of his Quaker youth."[25] Perhaps Kissinger wished to refrain from speaking ill of the dead, a common desire at funerals, but more likely his statement here suggests that he had bought into Nixon's self-characterization. Nixon did indeed envision a "structure of peace" and did withdraw American troops from Vietnam, as well as ending the draft, something Quakers had always opposed, but any connection between these achievements and vision he received from being raised a member of the Religious Society of Friends remains tenuous. He always claimed that his heritage as a Quaker played a role, perhaps an important one, as he pursued these policies, but it is extremely doubtful that his membership at East Whittier Friends Church prepared him to advance them.

Many times over the course of his career, Nixon offered a justification for his support of the use of military force. In all of them, he laid to one side the role of religious faith in his consideration. He gave a nod to his Quaker heritage, but he never delved into any kind of nonviolent, much less pacifist position; instead he usually referred to war simply as "immoral," something few would disagree with. Quakers were not pacifists because that position was tactically plausible, even though it certainly could be. Instead they took the position they did because they believed, as the original formulation of the 1661 testimony against war stated,

> That the spirit of Christ, by which we are guided, is not changeable, so as once to command us from a thing as evil and again to move [us] unto it; and we do certainly know, and so testify to the world, that the spirit of Christ, which leads us into all Truth, will never move us to fight and war against any man with outward weapons, neither for the kingdom of Christ, nor for the kingdoms of this world.[26]

One lengthy discussion of his view of conflict and war occurred at a press conference on June 1, 1971, when a reporter asked him to respond to critics who charged that his bombing policies in southeastern Asia were "immoral, criminal conduct." "Well, my views in regard to war are well known," he began and noted that he came from a religious tradition that regarded all war as "immoral." But the Vietnam War, he quickly added as he left morality aside, should not be considered in a vacuum. The freedom of seventeen million people in South Vietnam was involved, as well as the possibility of a larger war in the Pacific and the wider world prompted by "Communist aggressors." "That I believe." He supported ending the Vietnam conflict in a way that would give the South Vietnamese "a reasonable chance to defend themselves against Communist aggression. . . . That kind of ending would contribute to the peace we all want."[27]

The war might be halfway around the globe, but it turned up to haunt him everywhere he turned. When daughter Patricia married Edward Cox in the White House gardens on June 12, 1971, only days after his press conference, five Quakers got police permission to demonstrate across the street in Lafayette Park. Their presence during the ceremony set Nixon off. He demanded of H. R. Haldeman whether "we" had a "long-haired son-of-a-bitch" who could go over there and interview one and find out how long he had been "in a Friends meeting." "There are a hell of a lot of these people, Bob, who are new Quakers." Nixon did not have problems with a Quaker staying out of the war—"because, you know, he was born that way"—but if they joined the Quaker church to avoid the draft—"I'm sick of those pricks." After being reassured by Haldeman that "we" have some of those longhairs, Nixon drifted off into ruminating that "we need some "Long-Hairs for Nixon," some "Beards for Nixon," not like FBI Director J. Edgar Hoover, who "isn't worth a shit. He's got all those crew-cut guys."[28]

A decade later, long after his resignation, Nixon told an interviewer, "As a matter of fact, war compromises principles. War is evil. All war is wrong. All killing is wrong. The question is, for example, when Eisenhower ordered the bombing of Dresden, which was a civilian target, and more than 40 million burned to death in one night, that certainly was immoral, but it would have been more immoral to allow Hitler to rule Europe. That is what it gets down to."[29] Not only were Nixon's numbers grossly inflated—25,000 people died in those February 1945 raids—but also he fell into the common fallacy of those who demean the Quaker position: after the violent deed is done, damning the pacifist because peaceful means seem impossible at that point to stop the atrocity; after the bombs start falling, the pacifist obviously cannot roll them back.

In the same vein, in 1991 he applauded President George H. W. Bush for having the guts to ignore all the State Department and diplomatic types and order the military to push the Iraqi army out of Kuwait. These fancy-pants conciliators, he said, could "not recognize that while war is bad a bad peace is worse, because it will always inevitably lead to a bigger war."[30] This was the kind of *realpolitik* rationale that the German-born and Harvard-trained Henry Kissinger could get away with; it was hardly the policy that a grown-up Quaker youth from Whittier College ought to champion. By the time he was president, it had come to that.

In the privacy of the Oval Office, Nixon illustrated how far he had slipped from his Quaker moorings. Making plans with Kissinger and Haldeman as a spring demonstration against the Vietnam War neared for the weekend of April 24, 1971, the three men surveyed its size, character, and the prospects for violence—Kissinger's favored adjective for it was "disgusting"—and then Haldeman reported matter-of-factly that "your Quakers" were mobilizing 10,000 marshals to keep the peace. With mention of that group, the president perked up, "Quakers." Haldeman explained that they would "make sure they keep 'em peaceful and quiet." Nixon came back blunt and sure of himself: "I don't want any of those damn Quakers over here to see me." Even Haldeman seemed taken aback by this stark reaction and pointed out that "All their literature emphasizes not to be violent." "We'll see," replied the doubtful president.[31]

Nixon never hinted in public of the appeal of the Catholic Church to him or his disaffection with Friends; his conversation with Colson was private and remained so until Nixon was out of the White House. In public he gave the impression that he was entirely comfortable and supportive of mainstream evangelicalism. He publicly identified himself with it and with its best-known proponent, Billy Graham. One of the most dramatic of these occasions was October 15, 1971, so designated in the evangelist's hometown of Charlotte, North Carolina, as "Billy Graham Day." The president stood waving beside Graham in an open convertible as it slowly crept though massed throngs in the city's center to the coliseum. Antiwar demonstrators awaited the entourage, but the notables made it into the building with no problem. Inside Graham spoke first, applauding the city's leadership for setting aside the day to honor him and his work. And of course, he commented on Nixon's impending trip to China.[32] A reporter present labeled Graham's tribute to Nixon "effusive."[33]

Unlike his speech in Knoxville sixteen months before, Nixon this time made only a passing reference to religion and in the broadest terms. Instead, a little over a year before the 1972 election, he designed his words to appeal to Tar Heel voters. For example, when referring to Graham's ties to North Carolina, he brought up his own, his three years, 1934 to 1937, at Duke University's law school; he did not compare the fact that they had both grown up in small towns and were nurtured in evangelical churches. He had "great goals" for America—the way the president pronounced these words made them sound as though he wanted to capitalize "Great Goals"— the most important one being the Quakerish world peace. Toward the end he did mention religious faith, but he limited its meaning to nondoctrinal "moral strength and character." He lamented that such characteristics were hard to preserve once a nation grew wealthy, as the United States had, but he went on to say that such preservation was a task for individuals. He lauded the fine man who had spoken to millions around the world and heaped praise on Charlotte and Mecklenburg County for having produced him. He said nothing about how his own faith differed or resembled Graham's, nor what he might have learned from his friend.[34]

In this taciturnity Nixon did not follow the man whom he and two thousand other people had come to the coliseum to honor. Graham depicted the president as a person who simply had no room to compromise with expediency of any kind: Graham told the story of how once when he made some kind of suggestion, likely a political one, only to have Nixon rejoin, looking him squarely in the eye, "Billy, that would not be morally right." Graham thought about his idea a bit and decided, "At that moment I felt that he were the preacher and I was the sinner."[35]

It is impossible to know whether Graham would have made the same assessment if he had known the preparations that the president's office had taken long before October 15; likely he would have. Haldeman had delegated the White House's chief advance man to go to Charlotte ahead of time to prepare for the presidential arrival. Ronald Walker sent back a "High Priority" memo that Haldeman exalted in taking responsible for. Walker estimated that between 150 and 200 demonstrators would be present: "they will be violent; they will have extremely obscene signs." As he went over the report, Haldeman underlined "violent" and "obscene," and wrote "Good" beside each. The signs, Walker thought, would be directed not only at the president but "also toward Billy Graham," a prediction that Haldeman likewise underlined and scribbled "Great." Using smoke bombs, the dissidents would "blitz" the coliseum in an attempt to disrupt the ceremonies. Haldeman considered it "Good" that the Charlotte police force was adequate to prevent any problems. Walker had recruited twenty-five Veterans of Foreign Wars (VFW) members and fifty to sixty volunteers from Republican ranks to collect tickets, confiscating any from "undesirables" and tossing them aside as "fake"; Haldeman gloated that they were "*not* our people."[36]

The city's newspapers recounted the plights of angry coliseum-goers who were denied admission; the listing seemed endless. A superior court judge's sixteen-year-old daughter and her little brother were both turned back as undesirables. One woman with her fourth grade son made the mistake of stopping to chat with demonstrators, and they consequently were suspected and rebuffed; "he thought," moaned the mother about her disappointed son, "that he was coming down here to be saved," yet we "just got kicked out." Even a group of children from a Quaker Sunday school class could not meet the high entrance standards that October 15. Graham defended such exclusions by saying that no one could blame them on the president.[37] Though this assessment may have been technically correct, the White House certainly had directed and overseen the event's planning. Even the Secret Service responded to White House fears. North Carolina Governor Robert Scott, a Democrat, complained that for some reason its agents would not allow him to fly the state flag on his official car and held him back from wishing the president Godspeed at the airport. "They brushed me aside twice as the President started for his plane," Scott groused to the press.[38]

The care with which the administration planned the Charlotte outing illustrated that Nixon was already, a year ahead of time, thinking of the 1972 election campaign. Graham played a prominent role in advising the president as they anticipated what was needed for his reelection effort. The evangelist, with numerous contacts in the South and among evangelical Christians nationwide, wanted to make sure that Republicans worked to strip the "moderate" image from one of the Democrats who many suspected might win his party's nomination, Senator Edmund Muskie of Maine. Nixon appreciated such counsel, of course, and told H. R. Haldeman that he should call Graham at least every two weeks to get his reading of the political situation. With lots to do and think about, Nixon preferred "not to get into these matters as directly with him," the president explained, but such calls were needed to maintain enough contact that Graham would not come to think that they were ignoring the groups associated with him.[39]

Graham's ties to the country's evangelicals remained extremely important to Nixon. Nixon's cultivation of the nation's foremost evangelist and Graham's closeness to the top Republican served both men's interests. It enhanced Graham's ability to exhibit close ties to policymakers and showed how his advice gave a prominent evangelical access to power figures; it was no mean feat to have the chief executive of the world's most powerful nation take time to speak at his crusade in a rather provincial part of Tennessee or help him celebrate his own day in his hometown of Charlotte. For Nixon, being close to Graham had obvious political importance with a major voting bloc, but, more important here, it helped assuage any doubters who might question his commitment to the Christian faith. Not to be gainsaid either was the weight it added to his own search for personal reassurance about ineffable matters of faith. If, for political reasons, he could not seriously consider converting to Catholicism, he might reasonably expect a level of security from associating with Graham.

Graham's brand of evangelicalism was the kind that easily merged with a politician's need for religion, for it politely stood aside from most questions of governmental policies, particularly the war in Vietnam. Truth be told, there were other varieties, representatives of which occasionally challenged both Nixon and Graham and embarrassed them enough to cause evident discomfort.

11

Watergate:
The White House Warp

For all the efforts to institutionalize the problems of Richard Nixon and
analyze the causes of his downfall, in the end the key to the mystery lies
in Mr. Nixon's character. . . . Chicken thieves should not sit in the Oval
Office.[1]

—William F. Buckley, Jr.

On the surface, the events commonly referred to under the label "Watergate" had little to do with Nixon's religion. In a narrow sense they dealt
with the break-in at the Watergate Hotel where the Democratic National
Committee chairman had his office, but, as the investigation of the criminal offense continued, its focus broadened. Soon the word came to encom-
pass a wide range of activities that ran backward to the very beginnings of
the administration, in the case of Nixon's claims of high deductions on his
income tax to decisions he had made even before his inauguration. By the
time he resigned in August 1974, Watergate had come to define the Nixon
administration itself and covered the president with dirt that he spent the
rest of his life, twenty years, trying to scrub away. Regardless of what he had
or had not done during his little more than four years in office, he could not
escape "Watergate." It followed him to his grave.

Watergate, this broad category of Nixon offenses, inevitably defined the
man, pointed to his basic values, and thus, inadvertently, offered revealing insights into the nature of his religion. The paradox of Nixon's life, one
in which he has always tried to keep private portions hidden from outside
observers, was that he was an intensely private person, an introvert even,
in an profession that appealed to and ladled its advantages on outgoing,
extroverted types. Ironically, the lesson that most people took from Watergate involved the centrality of the cover-up, Nixon's natural, increasingly

frantic, dogged, and tireless attempt to keep the lid on the whole affair so that it would not unravel in public and damage him politically. He had been a cover-up expert all of his life. During the entirety of his political career, Nixon had been personally successful in maintaining an exemplary private life. Unlike many of his predecessors, no sexual dalliances ever tarnished his reputation, he did not inordinately enrich himself or his family through public office, he ordinarily did not drink to excess, and his gambling at the poker table, though highly profitable during World War II, ended when he left the navy. He had a reputation for being something of a fake, true enough—his famous nickname "Tricky Dick" underscored that—but it was earned by his willingness to shade the truth politically, not by any moral sleight-of-hand.

Given his ability to keep his private life hidden from public view, Nixon might have been quick and astute enough to have easily prevented Watergate from becoming the kind of scandal that would damage him or force his resignation. Though he survived for a bit more than two years after the break-in, he ultimately proved unable to weather the storm and was labeled an "unindicted co-conspirator" by a federal grand jury, escaping a jury trial and perhaps even a prison term only through his resignation and the timely pardon granted by his successor. In failing, he could no longer keep closed the cupboard that hid his secrets; they came tumbling out in full view of anyone who cared to look. The most important for this study revealed what values remained of those inculcated by his Quaker parents and others of his church. The summation is not encouraging, for Watergate and especially the cover-up proved beyond any doubt that deep down—in his bowels—Nixon was a person of duplicity and deception, determined to obfuscate and obstruct.

Nixon was, moreover, the president. That mere fact—and it was far from "mere"—gave him tremendous influence, made his word the law, to be carried out without question. Bill Gulley was the head of the White House Military Office, a virtually unknown White House position, and he served in it for eleven years, under four presidents, from Lyndon Johnson to Jimmy Carter. "In the White House," he wrote, drawing upon his experiences with all four of them but especially with Nixon, "you never worry about the law, about breaking the law. . . . My thinking was, If the President wants it done, it's right. I never questioned it. It never occurred to me that some sheriff might show up someday with a warrant."[2] That attitude put an enormous premium on the character of the man who sat behind the desk in the Oval Office. Gulley, a civilian in a military role, was not a political appointee, and if he believed as he said, what must those whose positions depended upon loyalty to the president have thought?

Memoirs by participants in Watergate are nearly as ubiquitous as historians' and journalists' renditions of the grand affair. Almost all the authors are content to account for the affair solely as a reflection of the peculiar personality or political obsessions of the president. Somehow or other Richard Nixon was at the root of the problem. In the sense that he set the tone and was the pattern for wrongdoing, this is an accurate interpretation. But it is not the whole story, true though it be. Nixon's two predecessors, as he constantly reminded Americans after his resignation, had also engaged in "dirty tricks," such as taping visitors and callers, although they, as far as we know, never oversaw criminal break-ins. (The fact that the Quaker president concentrated on taping may well have been his unconscious attempt to defend the one practice that made his downfall sure. The break-ins, the lies about them, and the cover-up to hide them were extremely significant after all, but without the tapes the others could have been explained or argued away. In this sense the decision to surreptitiously tape was the ultimate dirty trick and was central to his defense.)

Only one of those who wrote about Watergate approached it as a crisis embodying what might be called the spiritual malaise that tarnished the executive mansion and Washington more generally by the mid-twentieth century: Wallace Henley, a low-level aide in the White House and a sensible, evangelical, Southern Baptist minister, and former religion editor of the *Birmingham* [Alabama] *News*. The book was *White House Mystique*. Written in 1976, the book attracted scant attention except perhaps in an extremely narrow range of Christian circles. Despite a diligent search in the usual places and exchange of e-mails with its author, I have been unable to locate a single review—though it carried a foreword from Nixon's converted "Hatchet Man," Charles Colson. Yet the riveting insights of its author and its message offer the kind of glimpse at Richard Nixon and his White House that demands close scrutiny.[3]

Henley was one of the herd of younger people Nixon liked to pat himself on the back for hiring. He was twenty-nine years old in August 1970, when he responded positively to Robert Mardian, special counsel in the Department of Health, Education, and Welfare, to serve as assistant director of the cabinet committee on education. Then a month or so later, he followed Mardian to the Justice Department when Mardian became assistant attorney general. Near the beginning of 1971, he bounced to the White House to work with yet another southerner, Harry Dent, Senator Thurmond's former operative from South Carolina, basically overseeing southern political activities, which meant finding ways to woo dissatisfied Democratic whites into the Republican Party.

By the time he left his job in the summer of 1973, Henley had come up with the phrase *White House Warp* to define what he observed among the people who worked at and near the capital's center of executive power. Their view of the real world was distorted, viewed as though through a prism, with blind spots and paranoia dominating, so that they came to believe everyone was against them and therefore likely candidates for inclusion on an untitled "enemies list." Those arriving with principles honed already outside the political arena, for example in a religious or Christian context, were "wise ones who saw the nature of things, and recognized what they should resist," but Henley found precious few of these. Nixon the Quaker loner in the Oval Office who had always been in that arena was surely not one of them; indeed he set the pattern for the White House Warp. Watergate resulted. In creating this culture, internal to the White House, Nixon displayed, as a recent historian has underlined, a 'flaw' that led him 'to convince himself, without evidence, that enemies were conspiring against him, and to use that to justify his conspiring against them.'[4]

A young Irish Catholic journalist had seen the same thing a bit earlier and made the same point in secular terms. Though of course he did not refer to it as "White House Warp," Richard J. Whalen, who worked for Nixon as a speechwriter until the late summer of 1968, described how Nixon's aides, the "Germans," created almost a hermetically sealed bubble around the aspiring president to keep those they defined as undesirable from conferring with him. Whalen published an exasperated memorandum to the president in his 1972 book, *Catch the Falling Flag*. It captured the spirit of an administration whose leader did not know where to stand. Nixon seemed to have no convictions, if indeed he had ever had any. Whalen characterized Nixon the president as making a transition from citizen to monarch, satisfied merely to rule rather than govern. "To be believed," Whalen warned, "you must act on what you believe. As it is, your administration does not appear to have any settled beliefs." To govern required leaders to trust in and act on their convictions—having signed up with him, Whalen had thought that Nixon had once had some—even risking popular rejection by declaring them. But he pointedly and truthfully reminded his former boss, "Every President of the first rank has braved that risk; and every mediocre President has shied away from it." Coping would simply not do, and that was all the White House seemed committed to. Whalen did not mention Watergate because it still lay in the future when he wrote, but, like Henley, he viewed something like it hovering and ready to swoop down on the horizon.[5]

As Henley saw, the warp was the necessary precursor of Watergate because Nixon divided the world simply between those who were for him and those who were against him. One of many dramatic examples was the president's reaction to the Supreme Court decision of June 30, 1971, rejecting the administration's effort to prevent publication of the Pentagon Papers, the internal history of the Vietnam War leaked to the press by Daniel Ellsberg who had helped write it in the Defense Department. In a conversation early the next morning with H. R. Haldeman, Charles Colson, John Ehrlichman, and Henry Kissinger, Nixon let fly at those who would thus undercut good order. He was mad, hopping mad, at what the Court had done. He needed someone who could devote full time to ferreting out leakers, could take presidential calls at, say, two in the morning, and would ruthlessly pursue those passing secrets to the press. Nixon wanted someone who oozed tenaciousness, as he had in the Hiss case: "go back and read the chapter on the Hiss case in *Six Crises* and see how it was done," its author advised his audience, who had heard much of it many times before. They tossed around the names of this congressman and that one—could Philip Crane of Illinois do it? No, he was a talker. Could Bill Brock of Tennessee? No, he was too nice, hardly a Joe McCarthy. He finally decided that John Rousselot of California had the right qualifications—he was conservative enough, a member of the John Birch Society, and, as the president phrased it, he "will be fine. He's mean, tough, ruthless. He'll lie, do anything. That's what we need."[6] He did not say it, but those adjectives indicated he wanted to find someone like himself.

Henley did not resist, at least not while he was on the payroll, but he accurately observed and caught the spirit in the White House. The former "Superaide," as he facetiously referred to himself, sadly confessed his inability to see all this while he still worked in the White House. He was wrapped up in pursuing a kind of "pragmatism," by which he meant the ability to get things done, that is, to be flexible enough to stay in power. So our author pointed his finger directly at the man in charge, the president, who proved quite comfortable in idolatrously using God for his own ulterior purposes, "the mouthing of religiosity": "God could be worshiped in the East Room on Sunday, and lies be told to the press on Monday." Any contradictions that might emerge—none ever acknowledged of course— were simply ignored because pragmatism did not permit them.[7] Henley was probably unaware of it, and, as an evangelical, would not have wanted himself identified with such a radical critic of Nixon's religion anyway, but his analysis was strikingly close to the criticisms theologian Reinhold Niebuhr laid out against those same White House rituals when they started in January 1969, before Henley signed on.[8]

Henley's postresignation assessment of Nixon's main religious practice was devastating, and the fact that his book was ignored when it was published and virtually overlooked by subsequent writers is almost equally telling. Nixon believed, Henley granted, that religion was a vital part of civilization and that he was going to lead in a revival of moral values through a public stress on religion. The White House services were a weekly part of that effort. For the Superaide, they amounted to a different level of stroking, a way to reward one's friends or cool down those who had been offended by something or other. The ultimate in stroking was being invited to a state dinner, while an invitation to a Sunday morning service was well down the list. The worship of God or, in Quaker terms, listening for God's guidance, was not a part of their rationale, only cultivating the famous and powerful. Superaide Henley spent a portion of his time telephoning such people in service to his leader.

Henley did not get to see the chief executive—the "Big Man" as he called him—very often. Once when he did, during the campaign of 1972, the experience was quite revealing. Oral Roberts, a faith-healing evangelist who had settled down somewhat after he founded a university in Oklahoma, was scheduled to see Nixon. Harry Dent normally handled such affairs but had to be out of town, so the task of overseeing the guest fell to Henley, who had already prepared a briefing paper for the president to use with his guest. The half-hour discussion in the Oval Office went well, but at the finish something not in the script occurred. Roberts volunteered that he wanted to pray for Nixon and the president for him, while the three men stood and held hands, forming a circle. Nixon agreed but did not proffer his markedly trembling hand to the lowly Superaide so the circle was not completed. "Oops," Henley ruefully remembered as they stood on the presidential seal woven into the blue rug, "I didn't write the President a prayer." Nixon's prayer, to Henley's surprise, was appropriate, simple, and non-amateurish, sounding practiced.[9]

All his White House experience of being an aspiring Superaide came home to Henley when after the 1972 election he got a telephone call from *Washington Post* reporter Carl Bernstein, the Bernstein who had helped keep the Watergate break-in on the front page of at least his newspaper. Fishing for leads, Bernstein explained that he had heard that Henley had misgivings about Watergate and wondered what information he had. Henley responded truthfully that he had not been involved and knew nothing about the affair. In a flash that startled him he realized exactly what he had become working in the White House. The reason he had not been involved and knew nothing was simply that he had never been asked: had he been he would have been involved as deeply as anyone else. He was not so much Mr. Clean as he was Mr. Lowly, or Mr. Idolatrous, who had himself bought into the White House Warp and was so low on the totem pole that his superiors deemed him useless and unneeded. As quickly as might be, Henley freed himself of Washington and hurried back to Birmingham.[10]

Another young "superaide," almost exactly Henley's age, David Gergen, who worked on the Nixon speech-writing team, saw the same thing, even using the term *mystique* to describe the aura that Nixon introduced to the White House. More of a policy wonk than Henley, Gergen was uninterested in faith and, ignoring the religious implications of what he was observing, found a way to stay on in the White House through Nixon's resignation. But he saw the situation clearly as his own memoir later showed. Gergen wrote that the president bore "personal responsibility for [Watergate] because he created an atmosphere in which his subordinates would logically assume this was what he expected from them."[11]

Like Gergen, most White House and election staffers did not resign—they soldiered on, assuming that standing against the Vietnam War equaled political opposition to the president. Quakers, unlike the one in the Oval Office, were prime suspects in their opposition because they were grounded in their pacifism; indeed, they searched for ways to publicize their view on war as a way, they hoped, of winning adherents to their side. For example, in 1969, right after the inauguration, Friends announced that they planned, as they phrased it, a "witness" or demonstration outside the White House against the Vietnam War. They tried to see the new Quaker president but were shunted aside to National Security Advisor Henry Kissinger, who dismissed them with the words, "Give us six months. If we haven't ended the war by then, you can come back and tear down the fence." In May 1972, Friend Helen Gardner from Bethesda, Maryland, reminded the country through the letters column of the *New York Times* of this earlier commitment; she also bemoaned the recently announced increased bail fine of fifty dollars for those arrested outside the fence, not for tearing it down but for silently praying that the conflict would end—and this while a Quaker president set national policy.[12]

If the country did not take note of Kissinger's promise and Gardner's letter—and no evidence suggests it did—some in the White House did not miss the persistently praying Quakers outside. In early May, six Friends, among hundreds conducting a vigil along Pennsylvania Avenue, were able again to gain admittance to talk with Kissinger, but they came away dispirited, that they were convinced the only "secret plan" around was one to escalate the war.[13] August 1972 found Colson and Jeb Stuart Magruder, deputy director of Nixon's reelection campaign, sending an underling out to infiltrate the Quakers beyond the fence, discern their political intentions, and see if they planned to disrupt the Republican convention in Miami. Although the Friends likely did not wear political buttons, Colson wanted to make sure that the White House operative had a sticker or button supporting the likely Democratic candidate, Senator George McGovern.[14]

Such Quaker activities and the perception of men like Henley, even in the White House, had little impact. Most remembered the immediate and the obvious, seldom going beyond the surface of the affair to seek a deeper explanation, much less its religious roots. Consider the revelation H. R. (Bob) Haldeman, the aide who served the president longest and was closest to him, recorded in his memoir about events immediately after the initial Watergate break-in on June 17, 1972. Nixon was in Florida. The next morning he seemed as "cool" about the whole affair as he had been before it occurred. In Haldeman's recollection, the president decided that those "crazies" at the Committee to Re-elect the President had pulled off a "political prank." "Hell," Nixon said, no one ought to "take a break-in at the *DNC seriously*. There's nothing there."

On Air Force One that evening, heading north, the president sipped a beer and again dismissed the whole affair. "'Silly damn thing,'" he allowed. What that façade of calmness, coolness, even amusement, must have cost the chief executive, Haldeman mused. Sometime later Haldeman talked with Charles Colson, who told him that the president had called the same morning when he was so outwardly calm about that "unimportant" prank. At one point, reported Colson, the president was so angry at those who had broken into the DNC office that he threw an ashtray across the room. Haldeman had witnessed his boss in a "towering rage" many times, but he had never seen him throw anything. Haldeman could only wonder, "Why did he telephone Colson so angrily, yet hide that emotion from me and everyone else?"[15]

Haldeman's question, which occurred to him only in hindsight after the fact, was mostly rhetorical, but the actual answer was simple: President Nixon found it to his advantage right then to conceal his emotions, the area his Quaker faith underpinned and sanctioned. He wanted to hide his real reaction from his top aide because, simply put, he had a different relationship with Colson than with Haldeman, and he did not think it was time for his long-serving aide to be privy to things that political manipulator Colson knew. Haldeman realized, like the lowly Henley had, that he was not being brought into the loop here. His loyalty to the president might be severely compromised if he knew too much too soon. Long experienced, Nixon's approach made sure cover-ups never came to light.

The president did not have to think through the problem in such a logical fashion. Instead, he acted instinctively, the way a politician caught with his hand in the cookie jar will always respond. Of course, this was not the president's actual hand but the hands of people associated with his administration, people for whom he was ultimately responsible. Attorney General John Mitchell headed Nixon's 1972 Committee to Re-elect the President—which popularly and a bit libelously later became known as CREEP—but its director until Mitchell resigned his cabinet position was Magruder, originally one of Haldeman's young go-getters in the White House. On the Saturday morning the Watergate burglars were arrested and the affair came to public attention, Magruder did not think deeply about the cover-up, even though he had good reason to: he had ordered the break-in. In California, where he got news of the arrests, he realized instantly, as he put it, that this crime "could destroy us all." "The cover-up, thus, was immediate and automatic; no one ever considered that there would *not* be a cover-up." With their political power they could quickly erase this mistake, he decided.[16] Of such were the first thoughts of one who lived and moved within Henley's White House Warp.

The affair that the break-in at the Watergate occasioned went on for nearly twenty-six months, until Nixon announced his resignation on August 8, 1974; it took effect the next day. Senatorial hearings and revelations, resignations and firings throughout the administration, up to and including Haldeman and Ehrlichman, the two men closest to the president, press conferences, Supreme Court decisions, votes in the Judiciary Committee approving three articles of impeachment against Nixon, eroding support from Republican members of the House and Senate for the occupant of the Oval Office, and then Nixon's own resignation, all these dragged out Watergate. Even then it was not over because the disgraced former president could not know his fate but had to await his successor's full pardon, on September 8, a month later, for crimes that Nixon had or might have committed.

Any sign of religion practically disappeared during this period. The Sunday East Room services had almost entirely disappeared, pushed aside in 1972 by the needs of Nixon's reelection campaign; after his landslide victory the political reasons for services evaporated because he would never have to face the electorate again. The all-consuming Watergate maneuverings demanded so much time and attention that little remained for something that had always been second level anyway. The only one in 1974 featured Norman Vincent Peale on March 17.[17] The president's reputation was not so shot that he was unable to look into a television camera and attempt to convince his audience that truth and religion were important to him. On April 30, 1973, the day he fired his counsel, John Dean, who had given damning testimony to the Senate Watergate Committee, and H. R. Haldeman and John Ehrlichman resigned, Nixon gave a major speech to try to salvage what was left of his administration. Expressing shock, outrage, and determination to get to the bottom of the affair—and naming a new attorney general to do so—Nixon concluded, "Tonight I ask for your prayers to help me in everything that I do throughout the days of my Presidency."[18]

Even Nixon's close evangelical confidant Billy Graham felt cut off as the full story gradually emerged. As early as Nixon's second inaugural, Graham had sensed a new frostiness from the victor. He and his wife, Ruth, sat directly behind the Nixons at the inaugural concert at the Kennedy Center, but they had apparently had no contact with each other because when the evangelist saw that the two in front of him had no program, he handed them one; the president, apparently not realizing the source of the proffered program, pushed it aside, and it fell to the floor. Pat whispered in her husband's ear, and he turned around and apologized. Graham wrote in his memoir, the president "blocked my access to him during the rest of his presidency." According to his recollection, the two discussed Watergate only once, at San Clemente two or three months after Nixon's resignation.[19]

Nearly six months of 1974 were devoted to the Senate Watergate hearings. From May to August and again from September to November, the story of Watergate tumbled out; must-see television carried witness after witness testifying to assorted criminal and questionable activities. At the end of October, the House Judiciary Committee received the task of examining the varied impeachment resolutions introduced by House members, and its chairman got broad subpoena powers so the committee could prepare for hearings. Though no one could foresee the future, it was apparent to most Americans, including Nixon's most ardent evangelical supporters, that the beleaguered chief executive was in a struggle for the very survival of his administration.

By the end of 1973, Graham had decided to go public with his criticism of the president, something unheard of for him. He came to Washington to preach at the White House for the Christmas service on December 16 in Nixon's East Room church. He told the editors of *Christianity Today*, the evangelical magazine he had helped found more than a decade and a half before, that Mrs. Nixon called him when he was in Switzerland and asked him to speak. (Nixon had always before handled such invitations, so the fact that his wife carried out the task this time likely underscored her husband's other preoccupations.) While in Washington, where *Christianity Today*'s office was located, he submitted to an interview that was to appear in the January 1974 issue. To increase publicity for Graham's views on Watergate and Nixon, the magazine released the interview to the press three days before Christmas, soon after it was done; it was widely publicized.[20]

For Nixon, it was like the proverbial lump of coal in the Christmas stocking. Right up front, Graham responded to the question of whether Watergate was illegal and unethical: "Absolutely," he responded, "I can make no excuses for Watergate. The actual break-in was a criminal act, and some of the things that surrounded Watergate, too, were not only unethical but criminal. I condemn it and I deplore it. It has hurt America." Graham did not condemn the president outright—in fact, he insisted, rightly at that time, that he had not been accused of criminal activities and that Americans should listen to his side of the story—and he also defended his own right to counsel and give advice to the president in private. He conceded that many of Nixon's judgments were "very poor," particularly when it came to the choice of staff members. Asked about the private church services, at one of which he had just preached, Graham said that he wished that Nixon would attend a local congregation but that the assassination of John Kennedy made that less likely. Then he dismissed the charge that his preaching or praying with the president made Nixon seem more respectable and appealing than otherwise. If Nixon wanted to use the evangelist as a tool, Graham asked in a subtle dig, "why has it been so long since he has invited me to the White House?"

Referring to Nixon's "incurable self-righteousness" and refusal to admit mistakes, the interviewer wondered if, as a pastor, Graham should bring such matters up. The "preacher to Presidents" revealed that he had spoken with Nixon privately on this current visit, but he refused to divulge what he had said, though he agreed that it was better to admit to errors than to avoid doing so. Asked what kind of man Nixon really was, Graham significantly spoke of him only before he became the chief executive. "Warm," "gracious," "a good sense of humor," and never "cold or diffident" were his words. As for profanity—rumored before the tapes were released and always of interest to an evangelical audience—"the strongest word I ever heard from him was 'hell,' and that only on a few occasions." He believed Nixon's "passion for 'peace'" came from his "Quaker background."

On the Watergate break-in itself, Graham shifted the blame to Nixon's subordinates, who believed that their boss must be reelected, if, for example, the war was to end. Here Graham took a shot at those who supported civil rights and opposed the war in Vietnam: Nixon's staffers, many of them young, had heard calls for "civil disobedience" in the name of this cause and that cause; they "knew their 'cause' was just" so they naturally concluded that any means to achieve it were legitimate. So Graham also took aim at another favorite target of evangelicals, the decline of absolute standards of right and wrong and their replacement by "situation ethics." Watergate was the "bitter fruit" of such perversities, not the decisions of individuals or a "finite man" like Nixon, he suggested.[21]

Even something normally as free of controversy as the National Prayer Breakfast in 1974 did not escape Watergate. It was precisely the kind of event that Nixon could not avoid. (The fact that the prayer breakfasts had become obligatory troubled Charles Colson, who suggested that if the nation was to be lifted out of the "doldrums of Watergate" the president should establish a smaller, more intimate breakfast with a bipartisan group that "unanimously wants to pray with and for you." Nixon dismissed this idea, averring that "Two breakfasts are too many.") Aware that Nixon had to attend, Graham proposed specific language that the president might use to indicate he was wrestling religiously with Watergate. His most pointed idea was to include a statement in his talk that people "are all in need of God's forgiveness, not only for mistakes in judgment, but our sins as well." Then he could add that he planned to rededicate himself to the God he had learned about at his mother's knee, giving some substance to that Quaker heritage he occasionally spoke of. Alexander Haig, who replaced H. R. Haldeman in the White House, labeled these ideas "unacceptable" because they amounted to a "Watergate mea culpa."[22] The closest Nixon got to adopting Graham's ideas was to quote his grandmother on silent prayer.

The breakfast was held in the ballroom of the Hilton Hotel on January 31, and twenty-five hundred people showed up to join Graham, Nixon and his wife, and their daughter Patricia and Edward Cox to listen to Democratic Senator Harold Hughes, a fervent evangelical, deliver what a reporter called a "sermon" that called for repentance, though not specifically naming Nixon. Hughes got a standing ovation, but Nixon, who had the last words, did not get off so easy. His remarks were certainly not controversial. He concentrated most of his fifteen minutes on the Abraham Lincoln who was not openly a believer, but, having read Elton Trueblood's recent study of Lincoln and his religion, the president made some comments about silent prayer. Using his grandmother's plain language, he cited her that explanation that Quakers prayed silently because the purpose of prayer was to listen to God rather than to plead for something.

When the breakfast broke up, John Huffman, pastor of Key Biscayne Presbyterian Church, which Nixon attended when he was in Florida, let it be known to a reporter that he was "upset." He wished the president had shown some of Senator Hughes's courage. To delve into the writings and prayer life of a former president rather than the Bible "is to make the history of the nation the authority, not God." "This would have been a great opportunity for him [Nixon] to state whether he was a Christian or not. For five years, by his silence, he has said he is not."[23] Here was the refreshing attitude of one supporter who saw through Nixon's pretense because he was grounded in his faith, as Henley suggested in White House Mystique.

Graham also weighed in again. Two days later, he wrote Nixon that he enjoyed the ride to the hotel with him, but in a mild rebuke he went on, "I had rather hoped that you would go from the wonderful expression about Lincoln's dependence on the Lord in time of crisis, to your own personal experience." And then Graham quoted an unnamed senator who told him the president "had gone to the brink and stepped back." In words that almost no one used to him directly, Graham wrote to his Quaker friend, "To be President is a great and thrilling attainment. However, there is one thing far greater than being President—that is being a committed child of God."[24]

When the presidential party returned to the White House, the two apparently did not discuss the president's remarks. Instead, Nixon and Graham talked for an hour and a half, their conversation ranging over Jewish control of the media to political strategy to China to religion and back. (This was the famous discussion that revealed an anti-Semitic cast to Graham that was so embarrassing when it was divulged after the tapes became available; the evangelist claimed he did not remember the conversation and disavowed the sentiments he expressed.) At one point Nixon commented that 90 percent of the nation's professors and associate professors were atheists, who did not believe in themselves or their country. He guessed that only 55 percent of the country would support "decent, strong virtues," with states like New York, Pennsylvania, and Ohio teetering toward the 45 percent. Then he demonstrated how religion fit nicely into his political thinking: "The South, that's the strongest. The South . . . is religious, it's the most patriotic, decent part of the country today. Really is. Without the South the country would be in a terrible shape." And he began to wander. California was overeducated, with too many "lousy" colleges, and Hollywood. "[We] gotta get in first." "But believe me," he told Graham, "once in it, then we got to *really* then start to, start to, to, to, re, reward the decent people, and, and, and frankly throw, throw out the, the, uh, 'Me, too'" types.[25]

Under intense pressure from the House Judiciary Committee, Nixon was forced to release printed and edited transcripts of the tape recordings relevant to its investigation of the break-in at the Watergate offices of the Democratic National Committee in June 1972 and the subsequent cover-up. He did so on April 30, 1974. The committee sought evidence of White House involvement in the break-in and cover-up—something that remained ambiguous, at best. Few members of the public, busy with their own affairs, plowed through the 1,252 pages of the papers, but enough eager buyers snapped up two paperback editions to make both immediate best-sellers. Most people preferred to rely on excerpts and guess what titillating gems were obscured by the phrase "expletive deleted" that the president inserted for profane words he wanted to hide. In fact, that phrase—even if not created by Nixon but one of his staff—was one of his lasting legacies, for it came into the language as a way to hide something incriminating. Even if the phrase only covered up "shit," the absence of a specific word allowed jokesters around numerous water coolers to imagine what tacky, coarse, or disgusting word had fallen before the editorial axe.[26]

The grossness of the supposed language in the transcripts smoked out Graham, who had remained publicly silent since his interview in his magazine at the turn of the year; perhaps he realized his behind-the-scene efforts had failed. It required nearly a month for him to comment publicly, and then he had to be badgered by the op-ed page editors of the *New York Times* and the Associated Press to issue a statement on May 28 after he went traveling and could not be reached for any clarification. Distancing himself from Nixon, he claimed the two were not as friendly as people believed—"I'm certainly not as close to him as Bebe Rebozo," the president's main religious advisor allowed. But his reading the transcripts was "a profoundly disappointing and discouraging experience." He focused on the "objectionable" language, admitting that the tapes "did not reveal the man I have known for many years." He pleaded for prayer and confession from the president to help save the country from situational ethics so it might return to the "righteousness" that God "demands at such a time as this." Though he had had "little contact" with Nixon for the past eighteen months, he said, "the President is my friend, and I have no intention of forsaking him now."[27]

What was so surprising during the period was that a man who postured as wedded to his faith, at least the outward practice of it, had fallen away from it completely, something Graham remarked on too. One might think that when he was beset on all sides by his enemies trying to bring him down, he would have turned toward his evangelical faith rather than away from it. If atheists did not thrive in foxholes, surely Nixon's trials should have driven him to seek divine grace. Eight months before he died more than twenty years in the future, he confessed that his faith wavered during his darkest days: "when it really felt like I had nothing left, it did [falter]. But it didn't last long before I realized that that was ridiculous. What happened was my fault."[28]

Just like that, Nixon fell back on his Peale-like mantra, which he had so carefully integrated into his Quaker faith: he had to rely on himself, he was self-reliant; there was nothing for any kind of God to do. His stance apparently bespoke the kind of compromises that evangelical, political Friends had made between their faith and their chosen professions. As the longtime conservative journalist Walter Trohan described the first Quaker president, so Nixon exemplified, "Herbert Hoover [was] a self-contained Quaker."[29]

Thus the minister he knew best and was closest to, Billy Graham, he would not invite to the White House. Graham wondered if the fact that he had written and spoken so candidly about Watergate's being sordid and symptomatic of a deep national moral crisis might have turned the president against him. Despite this rebuff, which few knew about at the time, Graham was still convinced that Nixon identified with the evangelical position on the Bible and the role of Christ,[30] but this identity did not drive him to any kind of introspection or public confession of wrong-doing.

Nor did it lead the president to pay much attention to other evangelicals he was close to. His East Whittier Friends pastor, T. Eugene Coffin, wrote him after taking a September 1973 trip to a Quaker conference in the south Pacific. Recounting the favorable popular opinion he had gleaned while he was there, he suggested that his parishioner might designate a week for "penitence and spiritual restoration" and ask all religious groups to participate. The president, he added, might then meet with officials whose views differed "sharply with your own," as a gesture of national reconciliation. Coffin concluded by suggesting one of their former neighbors might prepare a "well-written" article on his religious motivation behind his vision for world peace. There was no indication that Nixon deigned to respond and no article ever appeared.[31]

Graham was Nixon's kind of evangelical—socially and politically conservative, leery of any criticism of American power—so if the president's and the evangelist's relationship had cooled, imagine the iciness from the White House that overtook Oregon's evangelical Senator Mark Hatfield after he labeled the Vietnam war "a sin that has scarred the nation's soul" at the 1973 National Prayer Breakfast. When he was invited by a colleague to deliver the main address, Hatfield warned that he would speak his mind if he came and was reassured that he was free to say exactly what he believed. The presiding congressman had set the tone for the breakfast by noting that those present saw themselves "as a gathering of sinners," a comment that elicited scattered titters around the hall. Nixon and the early speakers limited themselves to lauding the recently signed peace agreement in Vietnam, ignoring any thoughts about sin. Hatfield, as outspoken as Graham—even more so when it came to questions of war and peace and poverty—exemplified a different tendency from Graham's notions.[32]

Raised in the Anabaptist tradition that distrusted political power, the Oregonian had an independent streak that tended to make him a rebel.[33] Hatfield asked Jim Wallis, an admirer and a young emerging evangelical, to prepare a draft speech for the annual gathering, expected to attract 2,000 people. He presented the speech pretty much as Wallis wrote it.[34]

Without mentioning the war by name, Hatfield referred to the conflict as "a national sin and disgrace" and attacked the "misplaced allegiance, if not outright idolatry" of failing "to distinguish between the god of an American civil religion and the God who reveals himself in the holy Scriptures and in Jesus Christ." He confessed that "we who sit here today are the wealthy and powerful" and reminded them that most of those who followed Christ would not find themselves hobnobbing with "comfortable majorities, but with miserable minorities." We need "a confessing church" "where lives [are] lived under the Lordship of Christ" and "put us at odds with [the] values of our society, abuses of political power [this could have been a reference to Watergate], and [the] cultural conformity of our church."[35] All in all, it was a devastating indictment of Nixon's brand of evangelicalism. Graham leaned on Hatfield "pretty hard" for an apology to the president, but the senator held that "all citizens had shared responsibility in this war I saw as so sinful."[36]

The 2,000 auditors, many congressional and military officials noted for their support for the war effort, greeted Hatfield's remarks with applause that a reporter described as "both sustained and energetic.[37] The speech led the networks' nightly television news with clips showing a clearly uncomfortable Graham and Nixon sitting on the dais listening to the kind of evangelical words never heard at previous prayer breakfasts.[38] Officials in the White House were so infuriated that they slapped Hatfield's name on the infamous "enemies list."[39]

Another evangelical minister apparently agreed with Hatfield. John A. Huffman Jr. was young—twenty-eight years old—when he became pastor of the Key Biscayne, Florida, Presbyterian Church, the church that Nixon's closest friend, Bebe Rebozo, regularly attended but never joined. Practically every time the president visited Key Biscayne to get away and pal around with Rebozo, he attended the Presbyterian Church. So well did Nixon get to know Huffman that the president invited the minister to preach at his own church in the East Room in April 1970. And at the end of January 1973, when the Paris Peace Accords finally and formally ended the Vietnam War, Nixon practically ordered Huffman to arrange a Saturday night service in Key Biscayne, to be televised live by all the major networks, and celebrate the end of the conflict. All in all, by Huffman's count, Nixon visited Key Biscayne Presbyterian Church eleven times before his resignation. It was heady fame for the young minister.

Huffman banked with Rebozo, and when he went in to conduct some business, he often dropped into the president's office. After Watergate broke, he sometimes used Rebozo as a conduit to the White House. Near Easter 1973, he saw Rebozo in his office at the bank and told him how he was concerned about the president and hoped that he would survive. Then he explained that the overwhelming majority of Americans, perhaps

75 percent, would forgive the president if he honestly admitted what he knew about the break-in and cover-up, but the people, he stressed, "will not accept being lied to." Rebozo responded that Nixon was protecting his brilliant attorney general, John Mitchell, who had been distracted during the campaign by his alcoholic wife and allowed his overzealous staff to engage in a lot of dirty tricks, including the break-in. They were all fearful that Senator Edward Kennedy would upstage and replace the weaker Democratic possibility, George McGovern, and thought they could get information confirming such maneuvering in the office of the Democratic National Committee.

Huffman was so sure of the correctness of his analysis of the public mood that on Thursday he called the White House to speak to Nixon, only to find that he was in a meeting; as chance would have it, however, Rebozo stood right beside the secretary's desk, so she handed the phone to the banker. He committed himself to raise Huffman's concern with their mutual friend. Pastor Huffman went back to preparing his Easter sermon. On Friday night he heard helicopters flying toward the presidential retreat not far from the manse, and the next morning he got a telephone call from Rebozo, who relayed the message that the first family would be attending church on Sunday. He made one request of the minister: "Please do not mention the word *Watergate* in your sermon." His sermon already finished, Huffman assured his caller that he had not, nor did he plan to, and he went to bed.

After the Easter service was over—the sermon was on the account in Acts 26 of Paul's description of Jesus' resurrection to King Agrippa—the president and preacher had a brief discussion outside the church during which Nixon told him, "Bebe has shared with me your concerns. I appreciate them very much." And he promised to get to the heart of the matter. When he went back inside the church, Huffman was set upon by the press, members of which were convinced that his talk of repentance was a veiled appeal to the president to come clean. The next day many newspapers ran pictures of Nixon and the preacher with their heads together in the parking lot. Huffman later made the pages of *Time* magazine when he was quoted as saying, after reading some of the White House transcripts of the notorious tape recordings, "If Nixon claims to be a Christian, he needs to repent of both the language used and the attitudes expressed toward people in those tapes."

These sentiments brought down an unexpected barrage of comments, both positive and negative, from friends and acquaintances from around the country. The most interesting came in a call from Billy Graham, who commended Huffman for speaking up "for what was right." He said that he had literally vomited when he read about half the transcripts. "To see this stream of profanity sickens me. I thought I knew him so well," the evangelist explained. "I'm convinced there is the demonic and that may have grabbed hold of him." Graham speculated that Nixon might have become "too dependent on sleeping pills to deal with jet lag. You know they say that drugs and the demonic so often go together."

The day of Nixon's resignation less than a year later on August 9, Huffman candidly told a former classmate from Princeton, now working for the *New York Times,* that Nixon had never told him anything about Watergate other than what he was saying to everyone. But then he added, "I question the moral qualifications for the presidency of a person who cannot be trusted to tell the truth." Hundreds of letters flooded into the Key Biscayne Church office—though Huffman had since moved to the First Presbyterian Church of Pittsburgh—attacking him for presuming to smear Nixon's moral qualifications. He flew to Miami on a family matter the next day only to find that the *Miami News* had a front-page headline, based on the *Times'* report, reading "'Nixon Lied to Me,' Former Minister Says." In his hotel lobby he encountered an older woman parishioner from Key Biscayne Church who hugged him, until her husband ordered firmly, "Stay away from that scum." Stunned, Huffman thought, "What could bring that kind of reaction?"[40]

In Congress only a handful of stubborn Republican congressman still felt the way that irate husband in Key Biscayne did. By the end of July 1974, Nixon had lost pretty much all of the political support there he had amassed after his landslide reelection victory less than two years before. The Supreme Court ruled unanimously that he had to turn over tapes that revealed he had known about the cover-up almost from the beginning and that he had personally ordered the Federal Bureau of Investigation to look the other way; once revealed, these tapes, popularly dubbed the "smoking gun," assured that even most Republican members on the House Judiciary Committee would vote for his impeachment. It was probably clear to everyone outside his immediate family and the most ardent Nixon supporters that the president would have to resign or be impeached and probably removed by a vote of the Senate.[41]

The weekend after the Court decision requiring Nixon to release the tapes (August 3 and 4), he decided that the entire family—Pat, Patricia and her husband Edward Cox, Julie and her spouse David Eisenhower—should accompany him to Camp David, the presidential retreat in the western Maryland mountains. They all tried to convince him to fight the mounting tide or at least delay announcing a resignation until after the tapes were released on Monday afternoon. But the president, always a loner and a man who made his own decisions on his own terms, "believed," as he recounted in his memoirs, "that my resignation had to be seen as something that I had decided upon completely on my own."[42] His family knew him and had watched him over the years, of course, something that made all these maneuverings seem even more poignant and touching, for it was clear that he was trying to find some way to avoid what could not be avoided. Despite his position as president he could not control this decision or its timeliness.

This entire Nixon episode was strikingly reminiscent of a story that Henry Kissinger remembered during what he referred to as the president's "final torment." It seemed that in the summer of 1970 Nixon asked Kissinger, then his national security advisor, and Bebe Rebozo to go with him and his Secret Service driver from San Clemente to his birthplace in Yorba Linda in an unmarked, unescorted Lincoln. As they walked around the modest Sears and Roebuck kit house, Nixon saw two cars, one filled with Secret Service agents, the other with the obligatory press pool, pull up. Instantly, Nixon lost his composure in a way Kissinger had never witnessed. At the top of his voice, he yelled to the newcomers that he wanted no company, that he was president, and that he would not move until the other cars returned to San Clemente. His guards were so shocked at this display that they obeyed and left him there with Kissinger, Rebozo, and the one agent, doubling as a chauffeur. Back in their car on the way to Whittier, the four listened and watched as an unusually laid-back Nixon showed them the gasoline station his family had run, though he apparently did not point out East Whittier Friends Church, just across the street. They drove by Whittier College, with Nixon recounting tales of the professors who had taught him there. Kissinger realized that Nixon, three years shy of sixty, was trying to understand himself by this excursion into his past. Kissinger pondered that Nixon "sought to move the world but he lacked a firm foothold" and seemed to be seeking one on this little tour. Not knowing himself—in Henley's terms, caught in the White House mystique of his own making— Nixon's gentleness on exhibit now trumped the exaggerated "tough guy" politician. The clearly amazed Kissinger understood something important about the enigmatic Nixon on that strange trip.[43]

And he learned something else on August 7, 1974, the night the president worked on his resignation speech for delivery the next day. Nixon called Kissinger about 9:00 p.m. and asked him to come by the Lincoln Sitting Room in the White House, one of his favorite spots in the mansion. Kissinger found him there, slouched in a brown leather chair, his feet on an ottoman, a yellow legal pad in his lap.[44] Nixon recalled that the meeting lasted about an hour, Kissinger said it went on until almost midnight.

Nixon was "deeply distraught" but fully in control of himself; to Kissinger, in fact, he no longer seemed so driven, so determined to overcome all the obstacles before him in a Peale-like fashion. It was as though he was fully satisfied once he had made his difficult decision to resign. These two men, who had planned the country's foreign policy so carefully during the past five years, ruminated about the place Nixon would occupy in American history, with Kissinger reassuring someone he really did not like that he would be treated well, and he mentioned specific achievements, such as the opening to China. In the kind of comment that he often made in private, one that indicated his learned distrust of scholars and outsiders, Nixon responded that his place all "depends on who writes the history." Their rambling conversation was fueled by more than one shot of brandy, something common to their previous late night conversations.

As Kissinger later related, he had been there about two hours, and he was growing tired of the tragedy of this man's inability to find solace for the plight that was being forced on him, and so as to excuse himself he got up to head for the elevator down the long hall. Nixon walked him out of the room, then surprised him by suggesting they step next door into Lincoln's bedroom to pray. In partial explanation, Nixon said that he knew that neither of them wore his religion on his sleeve—Kissinger was born a Jew—and they probably disagreed on the religious precepts they had. He then added the startling tidbit that most nights, after working in the Lincoln Sitting Room, he would kneel and pray, as his mother had, before he went on to bed. Unable to think of any better way to end such a strange evening, one of the last of Nixon's rapidly unwinding presidency, Kissinger assented to something he had obviously not considered before, or even thought possible. They actually got on their knees beside Lincoln's bed—Kissinger did not remember whether they knelt or not—for about half an hour. Neither apparently prayed aloud.[45] For Nixon, it was "a private, meaningful way during a dark moment."[46]

Kissinger went back to his White House Office, where two assistants were waiting. As they listened to, and no doubt marveled at, the secretary of state's account, the telephone rang. It was the president; he had gone back to work on his speech and now said that he hoped that Kissinger would not remember the events of the evening as signs of weakness, such a statement in itself an unusual concession coming from Nixon. That was last thing Kissinger had in mind, for he had seen an appealing side of the president he had never before witnessed—a man baring his soul, the epitome of "tenacity and resilience," and he reassured him that if he ever spoke of what had happened "it would be with respect." "And he had conducted himself humanly and worthily." He was much like the man who escorted him around Yorba Linda and Whittier back in 1970, though that tale would remain for his memoirs. Nixon, ever conscious of how others perceived him, must have fallen asleep with those words of high praise echoing in his mind, but of course he never gave any indication to others that he knew of his partner's assessment. The tight controls exercised by his religion had never permitted that.

The next evening, Thursday, August 8, the president announced his resignation to the nation on television. It was a somber affair, not because of any confession that Nixon made—he made none—but because it was the only time in the country's history that a president had resigned. The closest Nixon came to admitting errors was about halfway through his speech when he expressed regret for "any injuries" that may have been done "in the course of any events that has led to this decision." He added, "I would say only that if some of my judgments were wrong—and some were wrong—they were made in what I believed at the time to be the best interest of the Nation." Nixon could not bring himself to name any of his "mistakes." During his years in public life, he went on, he claimed to "have fought for what I have believed in," but he gave his beliefs no specific content, preferring to allow his audience to judge his beliefs from the things he had fought for. His central goal, emphasized so firmly in his first inaugural address, was peace, sentiments that could be taken as emerging from his Quaker background. Of course he did not forget to mention the "structure of peace" that still lurked, unattained, just over the horizon; he expressed hopes that this current generation would achieve that goal.[47]

Nixon's speech was typical of him; his former counsel John W. Dean, who was as responsible as anyone in bringing him down, thought he "was going out with a campaign speech."[48] Yet it was a striking anomaly in the context of his evangelical Quaker faith. He had always been a secretive, private person who could not open himself to public scrutiny, and especially at this personally wrenching event, he could not break this pattern. Those expecting him to lay out a catalog of his wrong-doings in what was the major crisis of personal presidential misconduct in the nation's history were grievously disappointed. For the rest of his life, Nixon would not go beyond what he had said in his television speech: admitting errors of judgment and unspecified mistakes. In his public statements he would never admit to committing a sin of any kind; to judge from these later comments, he did not consider that he owed another explanation to the people who had voted for him so often. Taking this course, he no doubt avoided unleashing a swarm of controversy, pro and con, about his sincerity. This would surely have pulled the Christian faith into the debate, but Christianity over the centuries had been able to survive much more than one man's desire to repent, even a president's.[49]

In his address, Nixon provided that his resignation would be final the next day, the ninth, at noon. A bit after 9:30 a.m., he appeared to give a farewell to members of the Cabinet and White House staff. More spontaneous than his formal speech the evening before, this one was personal, poignant, and watered with the sad tears of the participants. It was also self-serving for Nixon, understandable if not altogether forgivable. For example, he referred to his father—"my old man," Nixon termed him—repeating the Nixon family myth that Frank had sold his failed lemon ranch "before they found oil on it."[50] But he got it right when he reminded his audience that everyone there would say what he was about to say about his mother: "my mother was a saint," but no book would be written about her. And to laughter, he half-denigrated himself: "I am not educated, but I do read books."

Greatness comes, Nixon said as he drew near his conclusion, not when things go well, but when one is knocked about by events and faces disappointments and sadness, as he implied, he was just then. In the closest he came to religion and the Christian faith, he fell back on words, interestingly enough, not from his evangelical Quaker past, but from the broader Friends' tradition of his old professor Dean Hershel Coffin, who taught his senior-level course at Whittier College: "we come from many faiths," the president said, "we pray perhaps to different gods—but really the same God in a sense—but I want to say to each and every one of you . . . you will be in our hearts and you will be in our prayers." Echoing words he could well have practiced in East Whittier Friends church's Sunday school classes, he summed up with an aphorism that marked his specific case now: "always remember, others may hate you, but those who hate your don't win unless you hate them, and then you destroy yourselves." It also tellingly, if probably unconscious on his part, described the culture Nixon had brought to the White House, the one Wallace Henley had so aptly described, the one so distant from his Quaker faith. He then gave some substance to the words with which he began his talk, in the college French he also still remembered, *au revoir*, "We will see you again."

With that, the Nixons walked from the White House to board the helicopter on the lawn to take them to Air Force One, which in turn would fly them to California. A new and uncharted part of his life was beginning, but as "*au revoir*" suggested, Richard Nixon was not going completely into exile; at San Clemente he would prepare to be seen again.

12

Nixon in Retirement, 1974–1994

Richard Nixon was a full-time politician, and he never let us forget it. At home and abroad, every day of the week and whatever the occasion, he (and we) looked after politics.[1]

—John D. Ehrlichman

Nixon's resignation from the presidency in August 1974 initiated one of the longest periods in his life, twenty years, when he was out of the arena, in a formal sense, yet struggling to regain lost influence and reinsert himself and his expertise into the world of policy-making. He had spent nearly all of his professional life in the political world, and now he had to remain on its sidelines. By his own admission, as a "disgraced person," he experienced "a very dark time of despair"[2] when he confronted a reality he had rarely known—an absence from events that called for him to make decisions that would matter to millions of people. This Quaker had never experienced the kind of disgrace he now faced, much less an enforced absence from the only world that made much difference to him. And it was something that he had to face existentially each morning he got up and looked at himself in the bathroom mirror.[3]

Immediately after the Nixons arrived back at San Clemente, evangelist Billy Graham began calling in the hope of counseling his friend. Nixon did not take the calls, whether from illness, fatigue, busyness, or a lack of desire to talk with him; so Graham fell back on the mail to convey his continuing concern for Nixon's well-being. In one letter he recalled that after Nixon's disastrous 1960 loss of the presidency, the two of them had eaten peanuts and drunk coffee late into the night at the Nixon home as they reconciled themselves to the reality of failure. Graham had tried to cheer the battered Nixon by suggesting that he would rebound and prove victorious, but the vice president had dismissed that idea as unlikely. Graham suggested that "even now" in a more massive repudiation than 1960 he could make a great contribution to his country and closed by warmly repeating comments he had made before: "For nearly a quarter of a century, I have loved you as a friend and as a brother—and I have not changed!"[4]

The residual remains of his religious heritage helped him get through these early morning experiences, or that was what the former president told a former low-level staffer in his White House when Robert (Bud) McFarlane overdosed on 30 to 40 Valium pills on February 9, 1987. When McFarlane woke up, he had a telephone call from Nixon, and that after-noon Nixon appeared in his Bethesda hospital room where the two talked for over an hour; it was a turning point in the survivor's life, even close to a spiritual epiphany. Nixon described his depression after his resignation and "recounted how the Lord had lifted him up" and convinced him that his ideas had continuing merit. And then the former president got stern with McFarlane: "You are similarly blessed. . . . Get your butt out of bed, get back into mainstream life, and find a way to do something worthwhile." Nixon did not read from the Bible, but he insisted on praying with and for McFarlane.[5]

Nixon's comments, not necessarily Christian or Quaker in any formal sense, sounded like something he had absorbed from Norman Vincent Peale's self-help theology. They partook of a mixture of New Thought ther-apy, Emersonian self-reliance, and his own brand of Quaker determina-tion, the kind of amalgam he had molded to make his personal struggles bearable and enabled him to overcome them. What Nixon tried to convey to McFarlane was that he should not permit himself to succumb to per-sonal weaknesses. Instead he should be strong, determined, and sure of himself, qualities that would help him bounce back. Monica Crowley, a young woman who served as the former president's assistant the last four years of his life, affirmed that the thing Nixon most detested about those who criticized him was their assertions that he was insecure. "Politics," she heard Nixon say (in her words), "by its very nature, attracts the supremely secure." He knew he fit that description.[6]

There was a "two-ness" about Nixon and his religious convictions. His life had taught him that he had to rely on himself, draw on his own inner resources to overcome the trials and tribulations he faced. When he told McFarlane to get his butt out of bed and go out to find something useful to do, he drew on those fundamental experiences. That was one side of his life, probably the most important side. The other part appeared when he con-fided to Monica Crowley eight months before his death that everyone "goes about God in a different way. As you know, I'm a Quaker, and I believe in

God, and I believe in turning to Him." He admitted to praying and reading the Bible, "but I don't go out there preaching about what I know or think about it. That is mine to hold on to." Then he drew back and became even more reflective: when one becomes an elective official, "you start to think you know best. Not true." And when one becomes a leader, "you think that you can save a lot of people from themselves. You can try, but it's a tough, tough, thing. The bottom line is that the only one you are going to save is you." The only eternal question, he decided, is, "Do you believe?"[7] So Nixon believed, answering his own question, but he acted as though his belief—except in himself and his ability to overcome—made no difference at all. That was his "two-ness."

Very little of this duality came out as his relations warmed somewhat with old friend Billy Graham. Before and immediately after his resignation, Nixon had distanced himself from the evangelist, and they did not speak much of religion thereafter, usually making references to events that each thought might interest the other; they also saw each other less frequently than when Nixon was in the White House. One indication of this early renewal of their relationship came when two months after his resignation and a month after his pardon Nixon had to have an emergency operation for phlebitis, which had caused the veins in his legs to swell almost to the point of rupturing and produced a life-threatening blood clot. It was the most serious medical problem he had ever faced. Eighteen months after his surgery and fully recovered he was still praising Ruth Graham for her thoughtfulness in hiring an airplane to fly over the Long Beach, California, hospital where the operation had taken place. The plane pulled a banner that read, "We Love You and God Loves You"; he saw it through the window from his bed. "You gave me a big lift when I really needed it," he wrote her honestly.[8] It was a touching gesture indeed.

The two old buddies began to talk occasionally on the telephone, swapping stories about traveling and stroking each other—Nixon made some monetary contributions to Graham's crusades and Graham related to Nixon that in his travels he found that the former president was "held in high esteem around the world."[9] Graham was very conscious of the need to counter anti-Nixon views so that people could see the one he called "the real Nixon." Thus in March 1975, after their first face-to-face meeting in exile over a candlelight dinner in San Clemente he granted an interview to a reporter for the *Albuquerque* [New Mexico] *Tribune* and reported on the two and a half hours he had spent with Nixon. Without being specific, he judged that Watergate had "deepened [his host] religiously," though they had "studiously" not talked about Watergate, concentrating instead on religion. They prayed together in Nixon's private office, the former president showed him a biography of

Christ he was reading from his grandmother's library—Graham endorsed it as a "good" one—and they discussed the Bible. Nixon did not seem bitter about what he had gone through, Graham reported, only disappointed. It was all very upbeat, so much so that Nixon weighed in that the effort was "superb," and he filed away the clipping Graham had sent.[10]

In one personal letter about the visit, Graham demonstrated that he had not totally lost his critical evangelical edge, for he undertook what Quakers called "eldering," that is, he tried to suggest how Nixon could improve himself. He also modified at least part of the positive spin he placed on Nixon in his interview. Now it appeared that Nixon was not, in fact, reading his grandmother's study of Christ (which had to be more than fifty years old, for she had died in 1923), for Graham recommended that he take his grandmother's book and read it. While Graham hoped that the former president had "the inner moral and spiritual resources" to meet his future challenges, he prayed that the former president's experience in Watergate "will have brought you face to face with your own relationship with Christ." These suggestions were as specific, even as they seemed implicitly judgmental, as any he had ever permitted himself to broach with Nixon. And a bit later in another note, he wrote that he hoped "God will bring you into a closer walk with Himself."[11]

Graham must have sensed some lingering Nixon questions about the evangelist's public views of the scandal of Watergate because he took pains to reassure his old friend that he should not take too seriously public reports of Graham's comments. In July 1979, for example, a bit before Nixon was writing to Montreat that when he moved to New York City, he hoped to see more of Graham, the North Carolinian explained that some recently published biographical studies were filled with "inaccuracies" about his view of Watergate. Graham admitted that he had speculated that Nixon's problems leading up to Watergate might have represented a mixture of the demonic and sleeping pills; he certainly believed the entire Watergate affair reflected the demonic and that Nixon's slurred speech on some of the tapes may have resulted from his use of sleeping pills. Instead, he generalized his comments to make them less specific. He "certainly" did not want Nixon to think that he had ever thought he had been possessed by demons.[12]

The same approach, coupled with a surprising lack of clarity, marked what Nixon had to say about his religion during long taped conversations with a friend and former aide Frank Gannon, in 1983. These interviews were never edited nor telecast, depriving the public of revealing insights in some seldom-explored areas of Nixon's career. Religion, though, merited only two questions, which required not quite three minutes of the seven hours devoted to the interviews. Such scant attention to what some might regard as an important matter reflected the low priority given to religion by most people who examined political leaders. Yet three minutes may have been more than ample time for Nixon's faith.

Gannon initiated that part of the conversation by asking the former president to read a passage from his senior essay at Whittier College, written nearly fifty years before. Entitled "The Symbolic Importance of the Resurrection Story," Nixon had presented what in the 1930s was called a "modernist interpretation," one that asserted that the physical resurrection of Jesus might be a myth, but its significance was that Jesus had lived such a life of perfection that "He continued to live and grow after his death in the hearts of men." Orthodox scholars, Nixon expanded, had always insisted that the physical resurrection was the "cornerstone" of the Christian religion, yet he dismissed that position, "I believe that the modern world will find a real resurrection in the life and teachings of Jesus."

Nixon confided to Gannon that evangelicals, like his friend Billy Graham, would undoubtedly think his position inconsistent with a literal interpretation of the Bible, but Nixon went on, "not in a broader sense." Then in the same sentence he inexplicably brought in Charles Darwin and his theory of evolution. It was almost as though he was unknowingly harking back to the original reason Whittier College's administration and faculty had created the class in "The Philosophy of Christian Reconstruction," to move students away from a fundamentalist rejection of evolution and toward a more intelligent Christian faith. In any event he affirmed to Gannon that he did not believe "that everything Darwin wrote was correct. . . . It could have happened that way. My view is that it probably didn't happen that way, but I am certainly not going to fault those who believe otherwise. So, and as I see it," he wound up coming back to the original topic, "one can be a good Christian and not believe in the physical resurrection." Gannon instantly stepped to another question and inquired if Nixon believed in a God who watched over him. "Absolutely, absolutely. Oh, yes," he affirmed. And with that, they abruptly dropped all talk of religion and proceeded to explore the next item on Gannon's agenda.[13]

During the years of his retirement, Nixon was required to meet his old nemeses, press reporters, only on his own terms. He wrote books and a few articles and gave speeches on topics of his choice to keep his policy perspectives before the public. He especially liked to appear, speaking off the record, before the editorial boards of national newspapers and magazines so as to indirectly influence their editorial content.[14] He had no prayer breakfasts to attend where he was expected to conjure up inspiring little snippets of faith. He seldom went to church, or at least no reporters took note of any of his goings and comings at one. He half-joked that he went only for weddings and funerals.[15] He did make a number of foreign trips, to Russia, China, and Europe. Maybe he was too busy, for after moving to New York in late 1979, he left home to go downtown to his office every day, including Sundays. That frequency lessened when the Nixons moved further away, to Saddle River, New Jersey, two years later.[16] To rehabilitate himself he conferred (or tried to) with public officials, discovering that a Democrat like President Bill Clinton were more likely to listen to him than was Republican George Herbert Walker Bush, who resided in the White House from 1989 to 1993.

For most of what we know of Nixon's non-policy thoughts, then, observers have to rely on Monica Crowley's two volumes about her four years as the former president's assistant on foreign policy and his general private confidant. His choice of her for this role was rather curious. Still in college, Colgate University, and twenty years old when she read a loaned Nixon book (*1999: Victory without War*) in the summer before her senior year, Crowley wrote him a letter. He responded several weeks later, and they met at the beginning of her senior year, 1989, for a two-hour conversation. She joined his staff, a fresh college graduate, in June 1990. He was her mentor and, judging from her two books, a good conversationalist on a wide range of topics; she even accompanied him on foreign trips. William Safire, who got only one volume out of his time with Nixon, assured her after her boss's funeral, "Nixon knew that when he spoke to you, he was speaking to history." So having kept a diary of their conversations, unbeknownst to anyone but her, and claiming that his words were presented verbatim, she produced two books; she averred that while their discussions were confidential, each had "the implicit understanding that they would be recounted."[17] Her first volume, *Nixon off the Record* (1996), dealt with foreign policy and political leadership, topics that had always greatly interested the Quaker statesman; two years later, the second volume, *Nixon in Winter*, covered broader topics, ranging from philosophy to Watergate.

Crowley never said it in so many words, but it was clear that she had also become Nixon's almost fawning disciple, making sure that she presented his most favorable side. In one telling example, she began her chapter dealing with "philosophy, religion, and human nature" with her discovery of his Bible on his ottoman—not just any Bible but his "well-worn King James version," open to the verse in the Sermon on the Mount that blessed peacemakers as the sons of God. As she reported those details, the Quaker former president, always determined not to talk about religion or God, proclaimed presently after her arrival that day, "God, of course, is the greatest philosopher of all."[18] He had clearly planned what to talk about that morning and had set the stage accordingly, with his open and well-thumbed King James Bible readily at hand.

The policy problem that had dominated Nixon's public career and certainly required a philosopher of God's stature was the conflict between American capitalism and Soviet and Chinese communism. It continued to be the major focus in his retirement. Though he lived to see the collapse of the Soviet Union in 1991, and he opened the doors to American involvement with China with his visit in 1972, he never sensed that the Soviet Union was on the verge of imploding, nor did he reorient his anticommunist approach to world affairs, even as communism declined. The best example of this failure to recognize the changes going on around him probably appeared in his 1980 book, *The Real War*, characterized by a friendly biographer as "something of a pastiche of hortatory calls to stay the course in the Cold War."[19]

Written with the help of his old speechwriter Ray Price, *The Real War* highlighted Nixon's ambivalent attitude toward war, compounded of a Quaker's abhorrence to the barbarity of war and a policymaker's determination to retain it in the arsenal for a greater cause. Peace, merely the absence of conflict, was not so much the end of policy as something that always beckoned beyond the horizon and could never be reached, as Nixon saw it; keep it in mind, yes, but take care not to become so beguiled by it that one allowed it to subsume other, more achievable immediate goals. The very first sentence of the book's last section underlined this paradox: "Victory without war requires that we resolved to use our strength in ways short of war." The end was victory, not peace, the means "ways short of war." He then added that "we"—the United States—"need not duplicate [our enemy's] efforts, but we must counter them" even in "ways other than we would choose to in an ideal world." Once Nixon granted this potentially massive loophole there was no stopping where his approach would lead. "Some ends of transcendent moral value do justify some means that would not be justified in other circumstances." He undertook to name these "transcendent" moral goals: "Preserving liberty," "defeating aggression," "avoiding war," "establishing conditions that can maintain peace with freedom through our children's generation."

As he came to a close, he illustrated that he had changed little from those early strident anticommunist days back in the 1940s. "The United States," he posited, "represents hope, freedom, security, and peace. The Soviet Union stands for fear, tyranny, aggression, and war," those the two poles of "good and evil in human affairs." If one rejected this formulation, "then the concepts of good and evil have no meaning." The debate, as far as Nixon was concerned, was over.

In fact, however, he went one step further, expertly trying to tie his Quaker faith—without mentioning it explicitly; that would have been out of place in a manual like *The Real War*—to his policy prescriptions. Nixon's sword, honed with the spirit, would in turn defend the spirit, and victory, not peace, would come out on top: "If we determine to win, if we resolve to accept no substitute for victory, then victory becomes possible. Then the spirit gives edge to the sword, the sword preserves the spirit, and freedom will prevail."[20] It was a ringing conclusion that had every reason to gratify author Nixon. But generations of Quakers, including even perhaps his saintly mother and his acknowledged gruff Quaker father, would not have been able to comprehend that the Spirit they followed, the Christ, required a sword's services to prevail.

Nixon's thoughts on peace could be a mixed assortment, even contradictory at times. Three years after *The Real War* appeared, in a taped series that was never telecast, he replied to a question from his interviewer in a way that differed almost totally from the message of his book. Frank Gannon asked him on this occasion, before the collapse of the Soviet Union, if the Russians really desired peace. "Well, we, to our credit," he responded, "are for peace as an end in itself. They are for peace as a means to an end. They're for victory." He went on to stress that the Russians did not want war, having learned from World War II how horrible it was, but they wanted to dominate, while Americans saw peace as a worthy goal. "They want to win without [war]," but they did not want peace as an end in itself, he concluded.[21] Without apparently knowing it, perhaps even failing to realize it, he had ended up in the same place he said the Russians were.

Yet, to consider Nixon's thoughts on peace, the impression is clear that he was not sure that a people like Americans could be unified without having an enemy to bring them together. In 1993, a year before his death and as he planned his last book, *Beyond Peace*, he told Crowley that "peace as an end in itself was no longer enough to inspire policy." Even to get people to back war, he had long since decided, "it has to be cast in idealistic terms, or there is no way the people are going to support it." "War *is* a great enterprise, only because it brings people together in a common mission." The very title of his book indicated that he wanted to find something beyond peace that would gather people into a whole and galvanize them for a cause. People like Hillary Clinton, the president's wife, who prated on about something they called "the politics of meaning or whatever the hell it is . . . soggy, sentimental bullshit," such people, he decided, were on to something—"the end of the cold war left us without a mission to replace it." It was "a spiritual vacuum," and he rightly saw that critics would ask,

"'Who is this guy to talk about the crisis of the spirit when he contributed to it with Vietnam . . . and Watergate?'"[22]

Nixon's last book read as though it came from the pen of a man who knew "spiritual vacuum" only as a quasi-religious catchphrase he thought he was supposed to use when addressing the American public. The book echoed all the overarching themes that he had mouthed in his political speeches over the years—paeans to free enterprise, separation of church and state, progress, traditional values, and democratic procedure, to name only a few. They flowed through and out of the reader's mind like a fast-moving stream and then vanished down the river.[23] Nixon's Quaker heritage was rich with concepts to fill up the biggest vacuum, but he had long since lost the way to tap into them. So his hackneyed words were contained within the American political tradition. For only one example, he might have used a paraphrase of Friends' founder George Fox's 1656 advice to his followers, "be patterns, be examples in all countries, places, islands, nations, wherever your come; that your carriage and life may preach among all sorts of people, and to them. Then you will come to walk cheerfully over the world, answering that of God in every one."[24] Such sentiments might have seemed inappropriate for an essentially political volume, but they would certainly have presented a powerful substitute for the spiritual vacuum he wrote about, whether in himself or in the broader American public.

What Nixon wanted, but could not deliver outside the American political context, was something to make sure that peace after the end of the Cold War was not just a "holding pattern for the next war." That was why he concentrated his reading on classical political philosophy, even if he examined, as he did, Reformation thinkers like Martin Luther and John Calvin. Significantly, his list of philosophers omitted his fellow Quaker William Penn.[25] Nixon may have sensed the absence of goals beyond war, that "spiritual vacuum," but he simply had no way to describe any. The spiritual void he referred to had to be filled with spiritual realities, and he knew of none to recommend. To go down in history as a peacemaker, a calling he so longed for that he had it carved on his tombstone, Nixon had to win acceptance for his parochial notion that peace would usher in a world in which there was "no substitute for [American] victory." Certainly, the principles behind Penn's 1693 *An Essay toward the Present and Future Peace of Europe* would have offered a universally different, and Quaker, vision.[26]

Yet Nixon, a pessimist about human nature, could not agree with Penn that war could be abolished, because countries would always have differing interests they considered so vital that they would rush to go to war about. "There will always be some kind of strategic problem or ethnic explosion or religious hatred to start the ball rolling," he reasoned. "Conflict is, and always will be, a fact of life. Period. And there's nothing we can do to change that." Crowley, nearly always in agreement with her boss, did not challenge him by pointing out that nothing in human nature required nations to go to war over conflicts; what they could do was to find spiritual methods to avoid resorting to violent and destructive means to resolve the conflicts. Nixon himself was willing to concede that humans could "try to manage those differences, but," ever the pessimist about human beings' basic nature, he held that, "there's no way to prevent them."[27]

In their discussion on March 14, 1993, after he had reread Alex de Tocqueville's masterpiece, *Democracy in America*, Nixon made some observations to Crowley that lent clarity to why he distrusted modern Quakers—they sought to influence government rather than restricting themselves to what he and Tocqueville considered religion's rightful role, changing people "spiritually." Quoting the Frenchman, he explained that religion should not extend itself beyond its "proper sphere" lest it "run the risk of not being believed at all." A clergyman's job was to change people not to try to change governments; the latter was exclusively the job of politicians. "'Those on the religious right [he instanced the Christian Coalition, for a decade now an evangelical group attempting to flex its muscles in the political arena] and left have their place—*out of politics*,' he growled, curling his right hand into a fist."[28] Though he did not mention Friends specifically, the implication clearly was that those who risked involvement in politics were liable to soil their spiritual purity, which he wanted to preserve, even if they were too blind to see things as clearly as he did.

The final sections of *Beyond Peace* echoed these ruminations that Nixon had with Crowley, but they ring hollow. The penultimate section is entitled "God and Family: Rediscovering the True Heart of America." Nixon's words were empty because the thoughts he expressed were totally devoid of any personal examples or references to his own faith and family—he simply could not draw on his personal experiences to illustrate his call for a "spiritual revival" or show how his exemplary family life, to which almost all observers attested, had helped him.[29] Neither his family nor his faith prevented Watergate, nor lessened the import of the lies he told to cover it up; nor, as far as anyone can tell, did either inform his foreign policy involving Vietnam in a way that would lead toward peace.

"Governments," wrote Nixon, posing as a conservative, "cannot reach into people's hearts. Religion can." Religion, he insisted on the same page, "has inspired, strengthened and comforted millions." "Good ideas have consequences," he explained and then added: "So do bad ones."[30] But about the person that Richard Milhous Nixon presumably knew best, himself, he uttered nary a word. He never offered there nor anywhere else even one instance—in his entire life—of how his religion, either evangelical Christianity or evangelical Quakerism, had touched his innermost being, his heart, his bowels, to make him a better person. By his own admission, when he left office, it was something governmental that brought him to face the only course left to him, resignation, a loss of (Republican) political support in the Congress; nothing suggested his religion played a role. And his family—wife, two daughters, two sons-in-law—stood firmly together in its opposition to his chosen course of resignation.

It was not a good record, and it did not speak well for his religion, neither the one that represented his and his mother's heritage, nor the one he seldom spoke of, the one at the center of his being. The one at the cusp of his mother's faith put the utmost priority on speaking and living the Truth and the truth. Despite continued references to this heritage over his lifetime, he never demonstrated that he had known this central reality. And now, in the last words he wrote for publication, what Crowley related as a testament to his life and career, his dissembling—his failure to be honest and look squarely at his character—prevented his even approaching the standard his parents' faith had set.

I began this book by labeling Nixon a "ranter," a seventeenth-century sectarian term for religious radicals, sometimes including Quakers, no longer in wide use. These enthusiasts were antinomians who fashioned their own religion and were bound by none of the legal or religious rules and regulations that applied to ordinary people.[31] I seriously doubt that Richard Nixon knew the word, and, as the kind of conservative he tried to be in his last book, he would surely not have applied it to himself. Ranters resembled too much the kind of 1960s countercultural radicals who, he lamented, "created a moral and spiritual vacuum that weakens the foundations of American society."[32]

Yet it is hard to avoid the conclusion that, for all his posturing, Richard Nixon created his own private religion to serve his own ends with only an occasional public glance backward at his Quaker heritage. He successfully convinced some observers of the validity of his stances regarding Vietnam and Watergate—Monica Crowley devoted the last five pages of her final volume to a spirited defense of her boss's reputation, especially among "middle Americans." But when they did they had to overlook the total absence of any formal religion, especially evangelical Quakerism. Crowley's observations of Nixon do lend support to my ranter application, for she wrote, "Built into his character was a voice that uttered ambition at every turn: politics, higher offices, comebacks. He could not silence it."[33]

Quakers, too, spoke of an inward voice, but theirs did not begin and end in ambition—in fact, they wanted to suppress ambition. It was the voice of

Christ, with the power, they insisted, to inspire, strengthen, comfort, and lead. Like the one Crowley found so dominant in Nixon, it could not be silenced, but, as his life exemplified, it could be ignored and covered up.

Notes

Introduction

1. Jack M. Holl, "Dwight D. Eisenhower: Civil Religion and the Cold War," in Mark J. Rozell and Whitney Gleaves, eds., *Religion and the American Presidency*, 119.

2. On this topic, see Doug Underwood, *From Yahweh to Yahoo!: The Religious Roots of the Secular Press*.

3. Richard Nixon, *The Memoirs of Richard Nixon*, 13–14.

4. Garry Wills, "What Makes the New Nixon Run? The Old Nixon," *Esquire*, 69 (May 1968), 201.

5. William Safire, *Before the Fall: An Inside View of the Pre-Watergate White House*, 13.

6. Ibid., 97–106. To his credit, Stephen Ambrose, Nixon's most accomplished biographer, saw these layers too, in a little book he published toward the end of his life: *Comrades: Brothers, Fathers, Heroes, Sons, Pals*, 67–73.

7. James Reston, Jr., *The Conviction of Richard Nixon: The Untold Story of the Frost/Nixon Interviews*, 9.

8. Born after California Yearly Meeting abolished birthright membership in 1904 as a violation of its evangelical faith, Nixon was not technically a birthright member, but the phrase continued in popular use well into the future. The same sentence in the Discipline that rejected it affirmed its value. California Yearly Meeting of Friends Church, *Discipline of California Yearly Meeting of Friends*, 45.

9. A slight modification to this bald statement is the 1887 Declaration of Faith, adopted in Richmond, Indiana, by representatives of American Gurneyite and London yearly meetings. Staunchly evangelical and equally controversial, it was embraced by some yearly meetings, including California, but others rejected it time and again--most importantly London Yearly Meeting then and Friends United Meeting in 1987. See Mark Minear, *Richmond, 1887: A Quaker Drama Unfolds*. In some evangelical quarters, George Fox's 1671 "Letter to the Governor and Assembly at Barbados" had a similar status. See H. Larry Ingle, *First among Friends: George Fox and the Creation of Quakerism*, 234–35.

10. Milton Mayer, *The Nature of the Beast*, ed. W. Eric Gustafson, 310.

11. Ingle, *First among Friends*, 55–56; W. Penn, *A Brief Account of the Rise and Progress of the People Called Quakers*.

12. Safire, *Before the Fall*, 599–606, 702. Herbert Hoover, another Friend nurtured among west coast evangelical Quakers, referred to peace at the center as a Quaker "procedure." Martin L. Fausold, *The Presidency of Herbert C. Hoover*, 12. See also Richard N. Smith, *An Uncommon Man: The Triumph of Herbert Hoover*, 121.

The phrase does not go back to seventeenth-century Quakerism. References from Nixon and Hoover make me wonder if it may have been a west coast Quaker phrase among those who would become evangelicals. In his final memoir, Nixon attributed it to his Quaker grandmother, who, born in 1849 before the birth of evangelical Quakerism, may have heard it in the Midwest. See Richard Nixon, *In the Arena: A Memoir of Victory, Defeat, and Renewal*, 369. Thomas Kelly, a prominent Friend with roots among Ohio evangelicals, in the early 1940s noted its absence among "thin and anxious souls." Thomas R. Kelly, *Reality of the Spiritual World*, 43.

13. For a survey of the "new Nixon" phenomenon by one who rejected that characterization, see Herbert G. Klein, *Making it Perfectly Clear*, 232–41.

14. David Frost, *"I Gave Them a Sword": Behind the Scenes of the Nixon Interviews*, 99–100.

15. H. R. Haldeman, *The Haldeman Diaries: Inside the Nixon White House*, 283.

16. Tom Wicker, "Richard M. Nixon, 1969–1974," 127, in Robert A. Wilson, ed., *Character above All: Ten Presidents from FDR to Bush* (New York: Simon & Schuster, 1995).

17. Gerald S. Strober and Deborah H. Strober, *Nixon: An Oral History of His Presidency*, 34.

18. H. R. Haldeman, "High School Colloquium," *in Richard M. Nixon: Politician, President, Administrator,* eds. Leon Friedman and William F. Levantrosser, 49.

19. Maurice Stans, "A Balance Sheet," in *The Nixon Presidency: Twenty-Two Intimate Perspectives of Richard M. Nixon*, Kenneth W. Thompson, ed., 30.

20. John Ehrlichman, "The White House and Policy Making," in ibid., 140.

21. Garry Wills, *Confessions of a Conservative*, 81.

22. Henry Kissinger, *Years of Renewal*, 44–45.

23. Safire, *Before the Fall*, 599–600, 602–3.

24. Nixon, *In the Arena*, 369.

25. Frank van der Linden, *Nixon's Quest for Peace*, 22.

26. Baruch Korff, *The Personal Nixon: Staying on the Summit*, 46–47. See also, "I Did Not Want the Hot Words of TV," *Time*, 96 (5 Oct. 1970), 12.

27. http://www.presidence.ucsb.edu/ws/?pid=2945

28. Jonathan Aitken, *Nixon: A Life*, 572–76.

29. Nixon, *In the Arena*, 89.

30. He did refer to his avoidance of religious sentiments to a reporter in 1972. Van der Linden, *Quest for Peace*, 21.

31. Garry Wills, *Nixon Agonistes: The Crisis of the Self-Made Man*.

32. There have been volumes written about Jefferson and his religion, but a good brief survey is Garry Wills, *Head and Heart: American Christianities*, 159–65.

33. Richard J. Carwardine, *Evangelicals and Politics in Antebellum America*, 10.

34. Lou Cannon, "The Press and the Nixon Presidency," 194, in *The Nixon Presidency: Twenty-Two Intimate Perspectives of Richard M. Nixon*, ed. Kenneth W. Thompson.

Chapter 1

1. Strober and Strober, *An Oral History*, 527.

2. *New York Times*, 10 Mar. 1971, 14.

3. Stephen Ambrose, *Nixon: The Education of a Politician, 1913–1962*, 31.

4. On this general topic, see Chuck Fager, "Review Essay," *Quaker History*, 84 (Spring 1995), 65–76.

5. Richard Nixon Memorandum, "Answers to Questions, 8–8–1989," A, D, File 71, Richard Nixon Library, Yorba Linda, Cal. (hereinafter cited as Nixon Library). Nixon's quotation appears in Ambrose, *Nixon*, 31. Interestingly, Nixon did not comment on Ambrose's total misreading of his Quaker background on the same page. That error could stand.

6. Richard Nixon, *Memoirs of Richard Nixon*, 13–14.

7. The historiography of early Quakerism is rich and full. See Rosemary Moore, *Lights in Their Consciences: The Early Quakers in Britain, 1646–1666*, and Ingle, *First Among Friends*.

8. *Journal of George Fox*, ed. John L. Nickalls, 104, 445.

9. These developments can be followed in Thomas D. Hamm, *The Transformation of American Quakerism: Orthodox Friends, 1800–1907*, and H. Larry Ingle, *Quakers in Conflict: The Hicksite Reformation*.

10. Thomas D. Hamm, *The Road to ESR, Or, the Long, Tangled, and Often Confusing Story of How Friends Came to Embrace Theological Education*, 37.

11. The best account of these changes can be found in Hamm, *Transformation of American Quakerism*.

12. On these changes, see, Hugh Barbour and J. William Frost, *The Quakers*, 114, 197–200. Interestingly a generation before Nixon's mother's marriage, she would likely have been disowned had she wed a non-Quaker like Methodist Frank Nixon.

13. Blanche Burum to M. Haddad, 29 May 1970, Richard Nixon Oral History Project, California State University-Fullerton Library, hereinafter cited as Nixon OHP.

14. Walter C. Woodward, "The Exemplar of 'Western Quakerism,'" *American Friend*, 6 (N.S.) (19 Ninth Month, 1918), 775–76. I would like to thank Greg Hinshaw for referring me to this statement.

15. Transcript, Oral History Interview, Richard Arena with Jessamyn West, 30 June 1971, 49–50, Folder 18, Box 10, Dorn Coll., Nixon Library; Jessamyn West, *To See the Dream*, 131–32, 207. Hermon D. Williams, "The California Field," *American Friend*, 8 (23 Feb. 1911), 121.

16. Ed Nixon and Karen Olson, *The Nixons: A Family Portrait*, 22.

17. David Le Shana, *Quakers in California: The Effects of 19th Century Revivalism on Western Quakerism*, 120.

18. On the history of this tendency in California, see *ibid.* For the most startling example of the tendency to group the Quakers of East Whittier Church with the eastern version see Ambrose, *Nixon*, 31.

19. Elton Trueblood, quoted in James R. Newby, *Elton Trueblood: Believer, Teacher & Friend*, 148. The astute religion editor of the *New York Times* categorized Nixon's religious beliefs as landing somewhere between those of his traditional mother and the evangelical East Whittier Friends Church. New York *Times*, 6 June 1969. Even this characterization of Hannah Nixon is overstated, for, regardless of what she might tell questioners, her church was staunchly evangelical in faith and practice.

20. Le Shana, *California Quakers*, 119.

21. On this theme, see Darren Dochuk, *From Bible Belt to Sunbelt: Plain-Folk Religion, Grassroots Politics, and the Rise of Evangelical Conservatism*.

22. One of the best brief descriptions of Nixon's religious heritage is Doug Underwood, *From Yahweh to Yahoo!*, 193–97.

23. Charles W. Cooper, *Whittier: Independent College in California, Founded*

by Quakers, 1887, 16–17, 59, 97–105. See also Jessamyn West, *Hide and Seek: A Continuing Journey*, 188–89.

24. Virginia Mathony, *Whittier Revisited: The First 100 Years*, 63.

25. Mark A. Noll, *American Evangelical Christianity: An Introduction*, 245.

26. For only one example, see *Works of George Fox*, VII, 164–66, 170.

27. Arthur O. Roberts, *Through Flaming Sword: A Spiritual Autobiography of George Fox*, 94.

28. Richard M. Nixon, "A Nation's Faith in God," 4.

29. Harold Walker to M. Haddad, 29 Mar. 1970, 7–8, Nixon OHP. See also J. Douglas Brannon to Haddad, 14 Apr. 1970, 12, ibid. The Quaker church in Yorba Linda where Nixon spent the first nine years of his life enjoyed a similar reputation. Mrs. Cecil E. Pickering to Steven Guttman, 30 Jan. 1970, 10, ibid.

30. Mr. and Mrs. Robert Sullivan to M. Haddad, 3 Mar. 1970, 9–11, ibid.

31. Herman and Agnes Branson to M. Haddad, 15 Apr. 1970, 34–35, ibid. There were locals, however, who could not bring themselves to affiliate with a group that did not baptize and with a reputation for countenancing conscientious objection. Herb Warren to Greg Brolin, 1 Oct. 1970, 10, ibid.

32. Mrs. Pickering to Guttman, 30 June 1970, 17–18, ibid.; Hibbs, *Sermons*, vii; Edwin P. Hoyt, *The Nixons: An American Family*, 177–78. Marshburn was a half-brother of Oscar Marshburn, who married Olive Milhous, Hannah's sister. Mary Marshburn Perry to author, 9 July 2010, in author's possession. For Yorba Linda Friends Church as a community church, see Ralph C. Shook, Sr. to Richard Curtis, 10 Feb. 1970, 4, Nixon OHP. The church, now a megachurch with a sprawling "campus," still enjoys that broad status.

33. Cecil B. Currey, "The Devolution of Quaker Pacifism: A Kansas Case Study, 1860–1955, 129.

34. See interview with Hubert Perry, 25 Oct. 2007, Oral History Project, Nixon Library. Perry was a member of the First Church.

35. M. F. K. Fisher, *Among Friends*, 215.

36. Garry Wills, *Nixon Agonistes*, 160.

37. Perry interview, 25 Oct. 2007, Oral History Project, Nixon Library.

38. Herman and Agnes Bannon to Mitch Haddad, 15 Apr. 1970, 34–35, Nixon OHP. See also Ralph Palmer to Haddad, 20 May 1970, 4, ibid.

39. Fisher, *Among Friends*, 17, 109.

40. Richard Nixon, "What Can I Believe," 9 Oct. 1933, 1, Series V, Sub-series D, Box 12, folders 11, 12, Nixon Library.

41. Noll, *American Evangelical Christianity*, ch. 1.

Chapter 2

1. Hans J. Morgenthau and David Hein, *Essays on Lincoln's Faith and Politics*, ed. Kenneth W. Thompson, 6.

2. Bryce Harlow, "The Man and the Political Leader," in *The Nixon Presidency: Twenty-Two Intimate Perspectives of Richard M. Nixon*, 14.

3. Ed Nixon and Karen Olson, *The Nixons: A Family Portrait*, 22.

4. James Keogh wrote that Nixon's grandmother "followed" her mother into the ministry, which, while chronologically correct, should not be taken to mean that she chose to do so; the meeting made that decision. James Keogh, *This Is Nixon: The Man and His Work*, 18. For the family background of both the Nixons and the Milhouses, see Edwin P. Hoyt, *The Nixons: An American Family*.

5. Bela Kornitzer, *The Real Nixon: An Intimate Biography*, 29–31.

6. Myra Barton to Terri Burton, 3 June 1971, 4–5, Nixon OHP.

7. Fisher, *Among Friends*, 135.

8. E.P.M., *Christian Worker*, 24 (15 Feb. 1894), 107.

9. Richard Nixon to Frank Gannon, 9 Feb. 1983, http://www.libs.uga.edu/media/collections/nixon/nixonday1.html, accessed 5 July 2012.

10. Nixon and Olson, *Nixons*, 55–56.

11. Nixon memo to Earl Mazo, n.d., Wilderness Years, Series I: Correspondence, Box 26, Nixon Library. For the relevant passage, see Earl Mazo, *Richard Nixon: A Political and Personal Portrait*, 280.

12. William Safire, *Before the Fall*, 203.

13. Hoyt, *Nixons*, 144, 148; Thomas E. Drake, *Quaker and Slavery in Early America*, 165–66.

14. Ironically given Nixon's association with his party's staunch anti-communist wing, his family liked it, yet the movie's screenwriter Michael Wilson went unlisted in the film's credits because he was on the Hollywood blacklist. Nixon daughter Julie, who was seven when the movie appeared, was taken to see it at least four times. Richard Nixon to Jessamyn West, 15 Apr. 1957, Pre-Presidential Papers, Nixon papers, Box 809, National Archives, Laguna Nigel, Cal. Nixon had the movie screened twice while he lived at the White House, once there and then at Camp David, the last time five months before he resigned the presidency. Mark Feeney, *Nixon at the Movies: A Book about Belief*, 344, 354. For a full accounting of the book and movie, see Nicholas J. Cull, "Richard Nixon and the political appropriation of 'Friendly Persuasion' (1956)," *Historical Journal of Film, Radio and Television*, 19 (1999), 239+.

15. Richard Nixon, *Memoirs of Richard Nixon*, 8.

16. Merle West to Robert Davies, n.d., 6, Nixon OHP.

17. Nixon and Olson, *Nixons*, 64.

18. Kornitzer, *Real Nixon*, Dedication and Acknowledgments pages, 11, 239.

19. Nixon, Memo, "Answers to Questions," 8/8/1989, A, D, File 71, Nixon Library; Doris Faber, *The Presidents' Mothers*, 26–27.

20. Monica Crowley, *Nixon in Winter*, 362.

21. Nixon to Frank Gannon, 9 Feb. 1983, http://www.libs.uga.edu/media/collections/nixon/nixonday1.html, accessed 5 July 2012.

22. Nixon, Memo, "Answers to Questions," 8/8/1989, A, D, File 71 Nixon Library.

23. Carl F.H. Henry, *Confessions of a Theologian: An Autobiography*, 120.

24. Anthony Summers, *The Arrogance of Power: The Secret World of Richard Nixon*, 12.

25. Bela Kornitzer interview with Norman Chandler, Box 11, Folder 2, Evlyn Dorn Collection, Nixon Library.

26. On Frank Nixon's early life, see Hoyt, *Nixons*, 98–110. Son Richard would once, in public and inexplicably, miscast his father as born of Quaker parents. Ben Hibbs, ed., *White House Sermons*, 213.

27. Ambrose, *Nixon: Education*, 14.

28. Ibid., 172–73; Nixon, *Memoirs*, 6; Faber, *Mothers*, 29; Renée Schulte, ed., *The Young Nixon: An Oral Inquiry* (Fullerton, Cal.: Oral History Project, 1978), 10.

29. Mr. and Mrs. Richard Gaudlin to Milan Pavlovich, 8 May 1970, 10, Nixon OHP.

30. Nixon and Olson, *Nixons*, 60, 91.

31. Kay Marten, "Forward with Faith," *Christian Herald*, Jan. 1956, p. 6, Folder 5, Box 11, Dorn Collection, Nixon Library.

32. Kornitzer, *Real Nixon*, 236. Nixon became concerned that Kornitzer was taking too much of his mother's time and asked his secretary to monitor her calls and wire her phone with hers. Evlyn Dorn, undated memo, Folder 3, Box 1, Dorn Coll., Nixon Library.

33. Jessamyn West, *The Woman Said Yes: Encounters with Life and Death*, 55.

34. On Fox and early Friends, see Ingle, *First Among Friends*.

35. Charles Mylander, "What Future for Evangelical Friends?," in Paul Anderson and Howard R. Macy, eds., *Truth's Bright Embrace: Essays and Poems in Honor of Arthur O. Roberts*, 195.

36. Hannah Nixon, "Richard Nixon, A Mother's Story as told to Flora R. Schreiber," *Good Housekeeping*, 150 (June 1960), 212.

37. Nixon, *Memoirs*, 13–14.

38. Interview with Julia Nixon Eisenhower, 24 Jan. 1973, Folder 12, Box 10, Dorn Collection, Nixon Library.

39. Hannah Nixon, "A Mother's Story," *Good Housekeeping*, 214, 216.

40. Nixon, *Memoirs*, 13–14.

41. Raymond Burbank to Mitch Haddad, 16 Jan. 1970, 4–5, 9, 11–12, Mr. and Mrs. Robert Sullivan to Haddad, 3 Mar. 1970, 11, Nixon OHP.

42. *Minutes of California Yearly Meeting Friends Church*, insert.

43. West, *Hide and Seek*, 219, 233–34, 236.

44. Kornitzer, *Real Nixon*, 237, 238.

45. A brief description of modern Friends can be found in James E. Ryan, *Imaginary Friends: Representing Quakers in American Culture, 1650–1950*, 7–8.

46. See the most critical early biography, whose author highlighted the incongruity of Nixon's brand of Quakerism with his own preconceived ideas, William Costello, *The Facts about Nixon: An Unauthorized Biography*, 31–33, 201, 287.

47. Nixon, *Memoirs*, 13–14.

48. John A. Huffman, Jr., *A Most Amazing Call: One pastor's reflections on a ministry filled with surprises*, 190.

49. Richard Gardner, "Fighting Quaker (The Story of Richard Nixon)," unpublished mss., 1953, Whittier College Library, Whittier, Cal.

50. Nixon, *Memoirs*, 13–14. Nixon's youngest brother Edward emphasized that Frank evinced a renewed interest in revivalism after the death of son Arthur in August 1925. Nixon and Olson, *Nixons*, 34.

51. Richard Nixon, "A Nation's Faith in God," *Decision*, 3 (Nov. 1962), 4. Graham revealed in his autobiography that Hannah Nixon told him the Rader story and indicated that only the three brothers went down the aisle. Billy Graham, *Just As I Am: The Autobiography of Billy Graham*, 521. Actually, Nixon mentioned the incident on at least one other occasion, date unknown. Walking with Graham and his longtime friend, Grady Wilson, Nixon reminisced about his teen-age conversion and grabbed Wilson's arm tightly to say, "Pray for me. I'm a backslider." Marshall Frady, *Billy Graham: A Parable of American Righteousness*, 466. When he was running for president in 1960 and angling for an endorsement from *Christianity Today*, he had an hour-long conversation with its editor during which Nixon revealed that he had been converted at an Aimee Semple McPherson meeting. Henry, *Confessions*, 196. On Rader, see Joel A. Carpenter, *Revive Us Again: The Reawakening of American Fundamentalism*, 126–27.

52. Leonard Lurie, *The Running of Richard Nixon*, 30–31.

53. Gerhard Peters and John T. Woolley, The American Presidency Project. http://www.presidency.ucsb.edu/ws/?pid=2165.

54. Minutes of California Friends Church, 1930, 107.

55. Albert Upton interview with Bela Kornitzer, n.d., Folder 4, Box 11, Dorn Collection, Nixon Library.

56. Jessamyn West, *Double Discovery*, 5.

57. Cooper, *Whittier*, 196–98.

58. Cooper, *Whittier*, 155–56, 159–61, 166. Judging from what we know about him from this source and student Nixon's papers, Coffin could hardly be called one who "espoused a conservative brand of Protestantism," as one scholar claimed. Irwin E. Gellman, *The Contender: Richard Nixon, The Congress Years, 1946–1952*, 14.

59. Cooper, *Whittier*, 196–97.

60. See Class notes, Nixon Family Coll., Box 12, folders 4, 6, Lecture notes, Box 11, folder 18, Nixon Library.

61. Cooper, *Whittier*, 166.

62. Richard Nixon, "What Can I Believe?," 1–2, 19, 9 Oct. 1933, Series V, Sub-series D, Box 12, folders 11, 12, ibid.

63. Ibid., 4–6, 10–12.

64. Ibid., 19–23. For suggestions that Nixon used his notes of Coffin's lectures as at least a part of the basis for his essays, see his Lecture notes, Philosophy, in Nixon Family Collection, Boxes 11 (folder 18), 12 (folders 4, 6), Nixon Library.

65. Nixon, "What Can I Believe?," 25–26.

66. Ibid. 27.

67. West, *Hide and Seek*, 238–40; Jessamyn West, "Jessamyn West talks about her cousin President Nixon," *McCall's*, 96 (Feb. 1969), 70.

68. Nixon, "What Can I Believe?," 30–33, Nixon Library.

69. Transcript, Oral History Interview, Jessamyn West, 30 June 1971, p. 60–61, Folder 18, Box 10, Dorn Coll., Nixon Library.

70. Nixon, *Memoirs*, 16–17.

71. Nixon to Frank Gannon, 9 Feb. 1983, http://www.libs.uga.edu/media/collections/nixon/nixonday1.html, accessed 5 July 2012.

Chapter 3

1. But see Meredith B. Weddle, *Walking in the Way of Peace: Quaker Pacifism in the Way of Peace* (New York: Oxford Univ. Press, 2001) for the struggles meetings encountered over King Philip's War in the 1670s.

2. Milton Mayer, "Disownment: The Quakers and their President," *Christian Century*, 90 (10 Oct. 1973), 1000–1003. Douglas does not recount these details in his memoir, saying only that, despite his decision, he remained a Quaker by the meeting's "sufferance." Paul H. Douglas, *In the Fullness of Time*, 37.

3. Donald Jackson, "The Young Nixon," *Life*, 69 (6 Nov. 1970), 64.

4. Richard M. Nixon, *Six Crises*.

5. Jessamyn West, *To See the Dream*, 266–67.

6. Kay Martin, "Forward with Faith," *Christian Herald*, Jan. 1956, Folder 5, Box 11, Evlyn Dorn Collection, Nixon Library.

7. Patricia Nixon to folks, 29 [Sept. 1942?], Nixon Family Collection, Folder 18, Box 17, Nixon Library.

8. H. R. Haldeman, *Haldeman Diaries*, 397.

9. One especially astute observer, a journalist, suggested in the 1950s that Nixon would never have run for president of the student body at Whittier College had he not been interested in a political career. Stewart Alsop, "The Mystery of Richard Nixon," *Saturday Evening Post*, 231 (12 July 1958), 26–29.

10. Nixon to Gannon, 9 Feb. 1983, http://www.libs.uga.edu/media/collections/nixon/nixonday1.html.

11. Roger Morris, *Richard Milhous Nixon: The Rise of An American Politician*, 198–202.

12. Nixon to Gannon, 9 Feb. 1983, http://www.libs.uga.edu/media/collections/nixon/nixonday1.html.

13. *Vital Speeches of the Day*, 38 (15 Sept. 1972), 708.

14. Julie Nixon Eisenhower, *Pat Nixon: The Untold Story*, 85.

15. Statistical Report of Young Friends of Military Age during World War II, Board of Directors Minutes, 8 Jan. 1947, American Friends Service Committee Archives, Philadelphia.

16. *Discipline of California Yearly Meeting of Friends* (Whittier, Cal.: V.A. Kennedy, 1938), 40, 85.

17. Richard Nixon, "What Can I Believe?," n.d., 30, Series V, Sub-series D, Box 12 (folders 11, 12), ibid. On the general mood, see Lawrence S. Wittner, *Rebels Against War: The American Peace Movement, 1933–1983*, 2–3.

18. West, *Double Discovery*, 132, 138–9. Later, after he wrote his memoirs, Nixon sent his cousin an inscribed copy: "For Jessamyn, the most noted writer of the Milhous clan, from the most notorious, Richard." Ibid., 141.

19. Jessamyn West interview by Richard Arena, 30 June 1971, Folder 18, Box 10, Evlyn Dorn Collection, Nixon Library. On her grandfather specifically, see Jessamyn West, *Hide and Seek: A Continuing Journey* (New York: Harcourt Brace Jovanovich, 1973), ch. 12. West knew that Quakers did not risk chances. A God who produced such oddities as kangaroos, cannibals, and ostriches was hardly Quakerish: "Quakers were far too cautious to have ever taken a chance with such creations." See her novel, *Except for Me and Thee* (New York: Harcourt, Brace, & World, 1969), 7.

20. West interview by Arena, 30 June 1971, 60–61, Folder 18, Box 10, Dorn Collection, Nixon Library. Interestingly, former Nixon Attorney General Elliot Richardson took West's assessment one step farther: "You could easily say that, except by chance, no totally healthy human being is likely to become President of the United States under the present circumstances." Elliot Richardson, "The Paradox," in *The Nixon Presidency: Twenty-Two Intimate Perspectives* 63.

21. Charles Rhyne to Jonathan Aitken, Jonathan Aitken Collection, Box 11, Nixon Library.

22. Costello, *The Facts about Nixon*, 32.

23. Elbert Russell, *Elbert Russell, Quaker: An Autobiography* (Jackson, Tenn.: Friendly Press, 1956), 249, 275. An aunt in California who had heard Russell speak at a Peace Conference, asked the minister to greet Nixon when he returned to Durham. Aunt Edith (Timberlake) to Nixon, 12 July 1936, Nixon Family Collection, Box 16 (folder 1), Nixon Library.

24. Richard Nixon to folks, 1937[?], Nixon Family Collection, Folder 1, Box 16, Nixon Library. See Sermon Notes in ibid.

25. Nixon, *In the Arena*, 89. Nixon's friendliest biographer uncritically accepts his subject's assertions. Aitken, *Nixon: A Life*, 72.

26. Aitken, *Nixon*, 72. Aitken attributed Nixon's reaction to his Quaker heritage.

27. Second Oral History Interview, Thomas Bewley, 13 Aug. 1971, 2, 8, Folder 10, Box 10, ibid.

28. Richard Nixon to Armin Haeussler, 24 Feb. 1960, Series 320, Box 446, ibid.

29. *Pacific Friend*, 45 (Apr. 1938), 6.

30. Nixon Appointment books, 1938, 1940, Nixon Family Collection, Box 16 (folders 12, 13, 16), Nixon Library.

31. Nixon, Notes for speech, "The American Way," n.d., Nixon Family Collection, Box 17 (folder 18), ibid; *Pacific Friend*, 45 (Apr. 1938), 5.

32. *Pacific Friend*, 46 (Feb. 1939), 7.

33. Jonathan Aitken's biography of Nixon asserts that she was, to her husband-to-be's surprise, an agnostic. Aitken, *Nixon*, 93. His latest biographer added that she became a Friend before the wedding, a decision that pleased Hannah Nixon, who was not particularly close to her son's choice of a mate. Conrad Black, *Richard Nixon: A Life in Full*, 45. If this is true, and I know of no evidence that it is, then she did not join East Whittier Friends Church, because a staff member there checked their records in 2012 and told me that only Nixon was a member.

34. Lester David, *The Lonely Lady of San Clemente: The Story of Pat Nixon*, 27.

35. Wills, *Nixon Agonistes*, 173.

36. Eisenhower, *Pat Nixon*, 54, 69; Cooper, *Whittier:*, 227, 230. One source concluded that since they were wed in a Quaker ceremony, "Pat adopted Nixon's faith," a conclusion that I cannot substantiate. Paul F. Boller, Jr., *Presidential Wives*, 401.

37. Nixon and Olson, *The Nixons*, 117, 119.

38. Eisenhower, *Pat Nixon*, 71.

39. *Pacific Friend*, 47 (Aug. 1940), 2, (Oct. 1940), 5.

40. Richard Gardner, "Fighting Quaker (The Story of Richard Nixon)," unpublished [1953], 100, Whittier College Library.

41. *American Friend*, 49 (26 Feb. 1942), 98

42. Nixon, *Memoirs*, 25–27. A contemporary letter supports his recollection that he did not want to be deferred at the OPA. Nixon to folks (at law firm), n.d., Folder 1, Box 5, Dorn Collection, Nixon Library.

43. Nixon to folks, 29 Mar. [1942], Folder 1, Box 5, Dorn Collection, Nixon Library.

44. Kornitzer, *Real Nixon*, 149, 236. This early and generally overlooked biography, written by a journalist who became very close to Hannah Nixon, has a full chapter on the family's Quakerism and is strengthened by the interviews the author conducted with the then Vice President at a time when Nixon was willing to be more forthcoming about his religion than he would be later. Nixon considered the more popularly written Kornitzer work much better in appealing to the average voter than higher-class works about him. Richard Nixon, Memorandum, 11 Apr. 1960, Box 583, Pre-Presidential Papers, National Archives, Laguna Nigel, Cal.

45. Nixon, *Memoirs*, 27.

46. Norman B. Rohrer, "Quaker on Capitol Hill," *Youth for Christ*, 15 (June 1957), 19–21, Magazine Article File, Pre-Presidential Series 296, Box F, Nixon Library.

47. Nixon, *Memoirs*, 27. Oscar Marshburn brought back some shells and grenades, which the children, including Richard, played with over the years. Nixon to Frank Gannon, 9 Feb. 1983, http://www.libs.uga.edu/media/collections/nixon/nixonday1.html, accessed 5 July 2012.

48. Harold Walker to Mitchell Haddad, 29 Mar. 1970, 6; William A. Milhous to Haddad, 25 June 1970; Ralph Palmer to Haddad, 20 May 1970, 2–3; Herb Warren

to Greg Brolin, 1 Oct. 1970, 10; Nixon Oral History Project, California State University-Fullerton Library.

49. Korff, *Personal Nixon*, 47.

50. Kornitzer, *Real Nixon*, 238–39.

51. *New York Times*, 10 Mar. 1971, 14. For some inexplicable reason, Sulzberger dated this interview nearly two years later in C. L. Sulzberger, *The World and Richard Nixon*, 33–34.

52. On this topic, see Jack D. Marietta, *The Reformation of American Quakerism, 1748–1783*, Chap. 7.

53. Nixon to Herman L. Perry, 6 Oct. 1945, PE 146, Nixon Library.

54. Eisenhower, *Pat Nixon*, 76.

55. Korff, *Personal Nixon*, 48.

56. Gerhard Peters and John T. Woolley, The American Presidency Project. http://www.presidency.ucsb.edu/ws/?pid.25268.

57. Typescript, "Oral History Interview," Evlyn Dorn by Richard Arena, 4 May 1972, 12, Dorn Collection, Folder 11, Box 10, Nixon Library.

58. Hannah M. Nixon, "Richard Nixon, A Mother's Story as told to Flora R. Schreiber," 214.

59. Kornitzer, *Real Nixon*, 139.

60. Typescript, Bela Kornitzer interview with Tom Bewley, Apr. 1959, 4, Dorn Collection, Folder 2, Box 11, Dorn Collection, Nixon Library

61. John T. Woolley and Gerhard Peters, The American Presidency Project. Santa Barbara, Cal. www.presidency.ucsb.edu/ws/?pid.2698.

62. Hubert Perry interview, 25 Oct. 2007, Oral History Project, ibid.

63. Wills, *Lead Time: A Journalist's Education* (New York: Penguin Books, 1984), 74.

64. Garry Wills, "What Made the New Nixon Run? The Old Nixon," *Esquire*,69 (May 1968), 201.

65. Leonard Garment, *Crazy Rhythm: My Journey from Brooklyn, Jazz, and Wall Street to Nixon's White House, Watergate and Beyond . . .*, 85–86.

66. Ibid., 57.

67. Aitken, *Nixon*, 323. Aitken told one correspondent that Nixon "is very happy with my attempt to portray him in a more sensitive and revisionist light than any of his American biographers so far." Jonathan Aitken to Arnold A. Hutschnecker, 1 Mar. 1993, Aitken Coll., Folder 49, Nixon Library.

68. Aitken, *Nixon*, 323.

69. Hoyt, *Nixons: American Family*, 231–32.

70. Nixon, *Memoirs*, 29. Apparently Nixon did not play poker again after he left the navy. Wills, "New Nixon," 94.

71. Fawn M. Brodie, *Richard Nixon: The Shaping of His Character*, 167.

Chapter 4

1. Whittaker Chambers, *Witness*, 362.

2. Nixon, *Six Crises*, Chap. 1.

3. Herbert Perry to Errol Elliott, 4 Sept. 1946, PE 96, Nixon Library.

4. Perry to Elliott, 15 Nov. 1946, PE 213, ibid.

5. The campaign can be followed in Gellman, *The Contender*, chaps. 2, 3.

6. *American Friend*, 34 (31 Oct. 1946), 347.

7. David Hinshaw, *Herbert Hoover: American Quaker*, 39–40.

8. "Member in Good Standing," *Friends Journal*, 15 (1 Jan. 1969), 22.

9. A rumor has circulated among some Friends that Hannah Nixon had implicitly criticized her son after he went to Washington: "You know, he isn't living in the way in which we brought him up." See Larry McK. Miller, *Witness for Humanity: A Biography of Clarence Pickett* (Wallingford. Pa.: Pendle Hill Publications, 1999), 272.

10. Marjorie Hyer and Marianne Bernhard, "Churches of the Presidents," *Sunday World-Herald Magazine of the Midlands*, 116 (26 Apr. 1981), 17; *The Young Nixon: An Oral Inquiry*, ed. Renée K. Schulte (Fullerton, Cal.: California State University-Fullerton Oral History Project, 1978), 166.

11. East Whittier's pastor from 1958 to 1964 remembered that Nixon attended once when he was Vice President. Charles Ball to Mitchell Haddad, 22 Dec. 1969, 2, Richard Nixon Oral History Project (hereinafter cited as OHP), California State University-Fullerton Library.

12. *American Friend*, 36 (5 Feb. 1948), 35.

13. The standard history of the affair is Allen Weinstein, *Perjury: The Hiss-Chambers Case.*

14. Chambers, *Witness*, 193.

15. Whittaker Chambers, *Cold Friday* (New York: Random House, 1964), 236.

16. Sidney Hook, "The faiths of Whittaker Chambers," in *Alger Hiss, Whittaker Chambers, and the Schisms in the American Soul*, 69, 75, ed. Patrick A. Swan.

17. Chambers, *Witness*, 483–85. The standard biography of Chambers is Sam Tanenhaus, *Whittaker Chambers: A Biography* (New York: Random House, 1997), but it is overly skimpy on its subject's pilgrimage to Quakerism and its impact on his life.

18. Michael Kimmage, *The Conservative Turn: Lionel Trilling, Whittaker Chambers, and the Lessons of Anti-Communism* (Cambridge, Mass.: Harvard Univ. Press, 2009), 143. This historian, more interested in literary connections, mentions Chambers's Quakerism but excludes it swiftly, perhaps because it complicated his search for conservatism.

19. Whittaker Chambers to William F. Buckley, Jr., 29 Sept. 1954, in William F. Buckley, Jr., ed., *Odyssey to a Friend: Whittaker Chambers' Letters to William F. Buckley, Jr., 1954–1961*, 85.

20. "Whittaker Chambers and his 'Witness,'" *Saturday Review*, 35 (24 May 1952), 8–13. Nixon's thoughts are on pp. 12–13.

21. Chambers, *Witness*, 489.

22. John V. Fleming, *The Anti-Communist Manifestos: Four Books That Shaped the Cold War*, 12.

23. Nixon, *Six Crises*, 4. John F. Cronin, a Washington-based Catholic priest who specialized in ferreting Communists out of places of influence, explained to some of Nixon's early biographers that he told Nixon about Hiss as early as February 1947, but Nixon, apparently anxious to play up his own role in the affair, failed even to mention Cronin in *Six Crises*. Cronin did write speeches for Nixon in the 1950s. On this controversy, see John T. Donovan, *Crusader in the Cold War: A Biography of Fr. John F. Cronin, S.S. (1908–1994)*, 61–67.

24. Unfortunately, there is no biography of Hiss, although he wrote a short, unrevealing memoir, *Alger Hiss, Recollections of a Life* (New York: Henry Holt and Co., 1988). See also Tony Hiss, *Laughing Last: Alger Hiss by Tony Hiss*, and G. Edward White, *Alger Hiss's Looking Glass Wars: The Covert Life of a Soviet Spy*, whose subtitle accurately summarizes its thesis. My account of the Hisses here

comes from Larry Miller, "Clarence Pickett and the Alger Hiss Case," *Friends Journal*, 40 (Nov., Dec., 1995), 9–13, 12–15.

25. Nixon, *Six Crises*, 19–23. Weinstein does not date Nixon's visit to Westminster. Weinstein, *Perjury*, 26–27.

26. Clarence Pickett Journal, 16, 21, 23 Sept., 1948, Clarence Pickett papers, AFSC Archives, American Friends Service Committee, Philadelphia, Penn.

27. Weinstein, *Perjury*, 151.

28. Hiss, *Recollections*, 4, 55; Alger Hiss, *In the Court of Public Opinion*, 52.

29. White, *Looking Glass Wars*, 243.

30. On Fuchs, see Robert C. Williams, *Klaus Fuchs, Atom Spy*.

31. Susan Jacoby, *Alger Hiss and the Battle for History*, 151.

32. Stephen E. Ambrose, *Nixon: Ruin and Recovery, 1973–1990*, 554.

33. White, *Looking Glass Wars*, 249.

34. Nixon, *Six Crises*, 67.

Chapter 5

1. Nixon, *Memoirs*, 138–39.

2. Ibid., 138–39, and Oliver Pilat, *Drew Pearson: An Unauthorized Biography*, 26–27. For a full accounting of this episode, as well as the later relationship between Nixon and Pearson, see Mark Feldstein, "Fighting Quakers: The 1950s Battle between Richard Nixon and Drew Pearson," 76–90. Doug Underwood used this incident as bookends for chapter 13 of his valuable study, *From Yahweh to Yahoo!*.

3. Unfortunately there is no overall history of the AFSC, but see J. William Frost, "'Our Deeds Carry Our Message': The Early History of the American Friends Service Committee," *Quaker History*, 81 (Spring 1992) 1–51 and H. Larry Ingle, "The American Friends Service Committee, 1947–1949: The Cold War's Effect," *Peace & Change*, 23 (Jan. 1998), 27–48. Three popular accounts are Gerald Jonas, *On Doing Good* (New York: Charles Scribner's Sons, 1971), Mary H. Jones, *Swords into Plowshares: An Account of the American Friends Service Committee, 1917–1932* (New York: Macmillan, 1937), and Marvin R. Weisbord, *Some Form of Peace: True Stories of the American Friends Service Committee at Home and Abroad* (New York: Viking Press, 1968). See also Clarence Pickett, *For More than Bread: An Autobiographical Account of Twenty-two Years' Work with the American Friends Service Committee* (Boston: Little, Brown, 1953) by a participant.

4. Clarence Pickett to A.J. Muste, 13 May 1948, General Administration, 1948: Correspondence, AFSC Archives, Philadelphia, Pa. On this broad topic see Ingle, "American Friends Service Committee."

5. The only survey, brief as it is, on this topic is Lon Fendall, "Evangelical Quakers and Public Policy," in Paul M. Anderson and Howard R. Macy, eds., *Truth's Bright Embrace*, 323–33.

6. Nixon to Thomas Bewley, 20 July 1949, Box 80, Pre-Presidential Papers, NA.

7. Perry to Will Wickenshaw, 19 Jan. 1948, PE352, Nixon Library.

8. Herbert Perry to Nixon, 30 Jan. 1952, Pre-Presidential Papers, Box 589, NA.

9. Perry to Nixon, 27 Mar. 1948, PE 380; Perry to Walter S. Steele, n.d., PE 384; Steele to Perry, 1 Apr. 1948, PE387A-1, Nixon Library.

10. Nixon to Perry, 19 Apr. 1948, PE 293; Nixon to Perry, 5 Jan. 1949, PE 504;

Perry to Nixon, 23 Apr. 1948, PE 393; Anthony Olivari to John D. Lodge, 16 May 1949, PE 515, ibid.

11. Thomas E. Jones to Nixon, 18 May 1949, PE 516; H.J. Bourne to Nixon, 14 Feb. 1950, PE 662, ibid.

12. Perry to Bourne, 1 Mar. 1950, PE 677; Nixon to Perry, 6 Mar. 50, PE 684, ibid.

13. J. B. Blue to Nixon, 9 Nov. 1950, PE 895; Nixon to Blue, 4 Dec. 1950, PE 906; Perry to Nixon, 30 Nov. 1948, PE 287 B.1, ibid.

14. Clipping from [Whittier] *Daily News*, 22 May 1950, in Ruth Arnold to Perry, 22 May 1950, Folder 13, Box 2, Herman L. and Hubert C. Perry Coll., Nixon Library.

15. Perry to Murray Chortiner, 20 Oct. 1950, Folder 4, Box, 2; News Release from Congressman Richard Nixon for United States Senate Campaign Committee, n.d. Perry Coll. ibid.

16. My source, unless otherwise noted, for this affair is Kevin Mattson, *Just Plain Dick: Richard Nixon's Checkers Speech and the "Rocking, Socking" Election of 1952*, 98–123.

17. Kornitzer, *Real Nixon*, 192; Nixon, *Six Crises*, 92–97

18. Kornitzer, *Real Nixon*, 193; Nixon, *Six Crises*, 97; *Northwest Friend*, 31 (Oct. 1952), 18; *New York Times*, 22 Sept. 1952, 1.

19. Kornitzer, *Real Nixon*, 193–94.

20. Nixon, *Six Crises*, 98–118.

21. James C. Worthy, *Brushes with History: Recollections of a Many-Favored Life*, 260.

22. I do not like labeling Peale an evangelical because he was not noted for championing traditional Christian orthodoxy but a kind of self-help gospel that differed rather sharply from it. Yet evangelicals, such as Graham, did not make such fine distinctions. On Peale, see Carol V. R. George: *God's Salesman: Norman Vincent Peale and the Power of Positive Thinking.*

23. Herbert M. Hadley to Richard Nixon, 7 Apr. 1949, Series 320, Box 830, Nixon Library.

24. Westmoreland Congregational Church bulletin, 24 Jan. 1954, Folder 4, Box 6, Evlyn Dorn Collection, ibid.

25. See Richmond P. Miller to Rose Mary Woods, 1 Sept. 1960, Box 518, Nixon Pre-Presidential Papers, National Archives, Laguna Nigel, Cal. (hereinafter cited as NA); Eisenhower, *Pat Nixon*, 151, 168.

26. Kornitzer, *Real Nixon*, 241.

27. Ben Hibbs, ed., *White House Sermons*, 31.

28. Edward L. R. Elson to Mr. and Mrs. Richard Nixon, 13 Nov. 1968, White House Special Files, Folder 14, Box 22, Nixon Library.

29. Summers, *Arrogance of Power*, 12.

30. Herbert Petty to Nixon, 23 Jan. 1952, Folder 3, Box 5, Dorn Coll., Nixon Library.

31. T. Jeremy Gunn, *Spiritual Weapons: The Cold War and the Forging of an American National Religion*, 58–59, *New York Times*, 2 Feb. 1953.

32. See Gunn, *Spiritual Weapons*, 197–208. While Gunn mentions sociologist Robert Bellah, who popularized the phrase "civil religion," only on p. 9, he does not discuss civil religion as a concept, so see the article on American Civil Religion in Wikipedia.

33. Gunn, *Spiritual Weapons*, 9.

34. Jerry Bergman, "Religion and the Presidency of Dwight D. Eisenhower," in *Religion and the American Presidency: George Washington to George Bush with Commentary and Primary Sources*, ed. Gaston Espinosa, 263.

35. See Nixon, Memo, 15 Sept. 1958, PPS Series 320, Box 617, ibid. The major reason for sending Patricia and Julie to Sidwell was the ease of transportation, not that it gave them a taste of Quakerism, although the younger Julie long regarded herself as a Friend. Jeffrey Frank, *Ike and Dick: A Portrait of a Strange Political Marriage*, 321.

36. Nixon to Frank Gannon, 27 May 1983, http://www.libs.uga.edu/media/collections/nixon/nixonday6, accessed 11 July 2012.

37. Richmond P. Miller to Richard Nixon, 13 Oct., 25 Nov. 1955, 31 Mar., 9 May, 24 July, 1956, Memo, Lil to Bob [Finch], 31 Apr. 1956, Nixon to Miller, 15 May 1956, 8, 27 Oct., 6 Nov. 1956, 25 Mar. 1957, Miller to Rose Mary Woods, 4 Mar. 1957, Mary A. Fenton to Miller, 6 Mar. 1957, Nixon to Herbert Hoover, 6 May 1957, Miller to Nixon, 9 July 1957, Nixon to Miller, 30 July 1957, Pre-Presidential Papers, Series 518, NA.

38. Elizabeth Gray Vining, memorandum, 25 Apr. 1957, appendix to Lydia Murray Huneke interview, Oral History Collection, Herbert Hoover Library, West Branch, Iowa.

39. Clarence Pickett to Nixon, 24 Aug. 1959; Nixon to Pickett, 4 Sept. 1959, Series 320, Box 248, Nixon Library.

40. Lewis Hoskins to Nixon, 13 Sept. 1957, 7 Mar. 1958; Hoskins to James D. Hughes, 14 Jan. 1958; Nixon to Hoskins, 24 Sept., 31 Dec. 1957; Unsigned Memo, 4 Sept. 1958, Pre-Presidential Papers, Box 355, NA.

41. Washington Diary #1, 1–30–52 [probably 1953]–2–11–53, Community Relations, AFSC Archives, Philadelphia, Penn.

42. *American Friend*, 43 (24 Mar. 1955), 96.

43. Nancy Gibbs and Michael Duffy, *The Preacher and the Presidents: Billy Graham in the White House*, 97. In 1962, restrictive covenants became an issue in Nixon's race for the governorship of California because the Nixons had signed a covenant when they purchased a home in Beverly Hills. John Ehrlichman, *Witness to Power: The Nixon Years*, 31.

44. Ehrlichman, *Witness to Power*, 223.

45. Roger Mudd, *The Place to Be: Washington, CBS, and the Glory Days of Television*, 241–42.

46. H. L. Perry to Helen Steere, 24 Mar. 1954, Box 598; Perry to Steere, 29 Mar. 1954; Rose M. Woods to Perry, 26 Mar. 1954, Box 616, Pre-Presidential Papers, N.A. After graduation, Steere did work for AFSC. F. Glenn Hinson, *Love at the Heart of Things: A Biography of Douglas V. Steere* (Wallingford, Penn.: Pendle Hill, 1998), 85.

47. Hoskins to John W. Hughes, 14 Jan. 1958, Series 320, Box 248, Nixon Library.

48. Edgar C. Bundy to Nixon, 14 June 1959, Nixon to Mildred Dunn, 28 Apr. 1960, ibid.

49. *Speak Truth to Power: A Quaker Search for an Alternative to Violence* (Np: American Friends Service Committee, [1955]).

50. Nixon to Mrs. R. S. Hayes, 10 Dec. 1959, Box 34, Pre-Presidential papers, NA.

51. *American Friend*, 45 (22 Aug. 1957), 269.

52. For a different take on Eisenhower's religion, see Jack M. Holl, "Dwight D. Eisenhower: Religion, Politics, and the Evils of Communism," in Steven Mintz and

John Stauffer, *The Problem of Evil: Slavery, Freedom, and the Ambiguities of American Reform*, 382–96.

53. On this topic, see Ryan, *Imaginary Friends*.

54. Thomas D. Hamm, Margaret Marconi, Gretchen Kleinhen Salinas, and Benjamin Whitman, "The Decline of Quaker Pacifism in the Twentieth Century: Indiana Yearly Meeting of Friends as a Case Study," 45–72.

55. Richard Nixon, "The Deeper Contest Before Us," *American Friend*, 44 (9 Aug. 1956), 248–50. Interestingly, D. Elton Trueblood, an Editorial Contributor to the magazine, secured its place in the periodical.

56. Stewart Alsop, "Nixon on Nixon," *Saturday Evening Post*, 231 (12 July 1958), 26.

57. "Notes written by Evlyn Dorn regarding her impressions of RN's personality, convictions, etc.," n.d. (probably about 1950), Folder 3, Box 1, Dorn Collection, Nixon Library.

58. Martin Luther King, Jr., to Earl Mazo, 2 Sept. 1958 in *Papers of Martin Luther King, Jr.*, ed. Clayborne Carson, IV, 482.

59. Nixon, *Six Crises*, 366.

60. Haldeman, *Diaries*, 101.

61. Crowley, *Nixon in Winter*, 358.

62. Henry Kissinger, *White House Years*, 1480.

63. Robert Dallek, *Nixon and Kissinger: Partners in Power*, 91.

64. *Rules of Discipline of the Religious Society of Friends*, 151.

65. "My Quaker Friend" was the title of Graham's chapter on Nixon, the longest in his book. Graham, *Just As I Am*, 522–23.

66. Graham to Nixon, 11 Nov. 1962, Box 299, Pre-Presidential Papers, NA.

67. Billy Graham to Nixon, 13 Sept.; Nixon to Graham, 28 Sept. 1955, ibid.

68. Graham to Nixon, 4 June, 14 July, 24 Aug.; Nixon to Graham, 16 Aug. 1956, ibid. "Assembly Daily," 6 Aug. 1956, in Southeastern Jurisdictional Heritage Center of the United Methodist Church, Lake Junaluska, N.C.

69. Graham to Nixon, 8 May, 25 July 1957, N.A.; Steven P. Miller, *Billy Graham and the Rise of the Republican South*, 76.

70. Graham to Nixon, 11 Nov. 1962, N.A.

71. Graham to Nixon, n.d. [1957], 22 Sept.; Nixon to Graham, 25 Sept. 1958, ibid.

Chapter 6

1. West, *Double Discovery*, 125–26.

2. Nixon, *Six Crises*, 366, 368.

3. *New York Times*, 8 Sept. 1960, 1.

4. Bela Kornitzer interviews with Bill Henry, 22 Dec. 1958, 11, and Bob King, 22 Sept. 1959, [2], Folder 3, Box 11, Evlyn Dorn Collection, Nixon Library.

5. L. Nelson Bell to Richard Nixon, 11 Nov. 1960, L. Nelson Bell Papers, Billy Graham Collection-A, Wheaton College Library, Wheaton, Ill.

6. Henry, *Confessions of a Theologian*, 195.

7. Shaun A. Casey, *The Making of a Catholic President: Kennedy vs. Nixon in 1960*, 8.

8. Kornitzer, *Real Nixon*, 239. Though neither author explored Quakerism's impact on Nixon, two major revisionist studies certainly reflected the candidate's personal assessment above: Tom Wicker, *One of Us: Richard Nixon and the American Dream*, and Joan Hoff, *Nixon Reconsidered*.

9. Billy Graham to Richard Nixon, 8 Oct. 1955; Nixon to Graham, 7 Nov. 1955, Box 299, Pre-Presidential Papers, NA.

10. John C. Pollock, *Billy Graham: The Authorized Biography*, 218.

11. George, *God's Salesman*, 175–83.

12. Ben Hibbs, ed., *White House Sermons*, 55. George is incorrect in dating their first encounter during the war. George, *God's Salesman*, 198–99.

13. George, *God's Salesman*, 131.

14. Norman Vincent Peale to Nixon, 1 Aug. 1960, Box 583, Nixon Pre-Presidential Papers, N.A.

15. Billy Graham to Richard Nixon, 17 Nov. 1959, Box 299, Nixon Pre-Presidential Papers, N.A.

16. Graham, *Just As I Am*, 546.

17. Nixon to Graham, 29 Aug. 1960, Pre-Presidential Papers, N.A.

18. Frady, *Billy Graham*, 438.

19. Bell to Nixon, 6 July 1959, Graham Collection.

20. Graham to Nixon, 2 June 1960, Pre-Presidential Papers, N.A.

21. Graham to Nixon, 22 Aug. 1960, ibid.

22. Graham, *Just As I Am*, 464.

23. My account of these events, unless otherwise noted, is based on the excellent account in George, *Salesman*, chapter 7, and Graham to Nixon, 22 Aug. 1960, Pre-Presidential papers, N.A. Graham apparently prepared a fuller account of the meeting that has not been found. Graham of Nixon, 17 July 1961, Pre-Presidential Papers, N.A.

24. Graham, *Just As I Am*, 463.

25. *New York Times*, 3 Aug. 1973; George Marsden, *Reforming Fundamentalism: Fuller Seminary and the New Evangelicalism*, 156.

26. On Ockenga, see Garth M. Rosell, *The Surprising Work of God: Harold John Ockenga, Billy Graham, and the Rebirth of Evangelicalism*, quotation 17.

27. Marsden, *Reforming Fundamentalism*, 10–11; on Friends, see Arthur O. Roberts, *The Association of Evangelical Friends: A story of Quaker renewal in the twentieth-century.*

28. *New York Times*, 3 Apr. 1957, 29, 17 Sept. 1960. Casey, *Catholic President*, 132–35, builds on little evidence trying to tie these two's anti-Catholic efforts with Graham and, through him, to Nixon's campaign.

29. *New York Times*, 8 Feb. 1968, 1.

30. Ibid., 2 Nov. 1963, 19. The most complete listing is in Casey, *Catholic President*, 123.

31. Graham to Nixon, 23 Aug. 1960, ibid.

32. This interpretation stands between those of Casey (*Catholic President*, chap. 6), who posits but does not adequately document a joint Nixon-evangelical plot to use the religious issue as a way to win votes, and Edmund F. Kallina, Jr., (*Kennedy v. Nixon: The Presidential Election of 1960*, 171), who accepts Nixon's claim (*Six Crises*, 368) that he kept the lid on the caldron of anti-Catholic bigotry and averred that "Nixon's refusal to play the religion card was his finest moment in the fall campaign." Nixon refrained from using the religion card himself, true enough, but he kibitzed while evangelical supporters dealt and dealt again and again among their constituents.

33. Graham, *Just As I Am*, 464.

34. Nixon, *Six Crises*, 325–26.

35. Unless otherwise noted, my account of this meeting comes from George,

Salesman, chap. 7, and Casey, *Catholic President,* chap. 6. Though uncovering valuable new information, Casey must be used with care, for he is convinced that Nixon was behind (and seeking to hide) this effort to raise the religious issue.

36. Graham, *Just As I Am,* 64.

37. On this point, see "A Statement of Concern" approved by NAE's Board in United Evangelical Action, 19 (Nov. 1960), 17.

38. "Power of Negative Thinking," *Time,* 22.

39. Douglas Cater, "The Protestant Issue," *Reporter,* 30.

40. Graham to Nixon, 12 June 1961, N.A.

41. Nixon, *Six Crises,* 328–29; Meet the Press transcript, 11 Sept. 1960, 8, Pre-Presidential Papers, 1960 Campaign, Box 16, Nixon Library.

42. "Remarks of THE VICE PRESIDENT OF THE UNITED STATES before the AMERICAN SOCIETY OF NEWSPAPER EDITORS, Washington, D.C., Apr. 23, 1960," Pre-Presidential Papers, 1960 Campaign, Box 4, Nixon Library.

43. The classic statement of this "civil religion" is Robert N. Bellah, "Civil Religion in America," *Daedalus,* 96 (Winter 1967), 1–21.

44. "A Statement of Concern," *United Evangelical Action,* 19 (Nov. 1960), 17.

45. "A Protestant Strategy for the Sixties," ibid., 19 (Dec. 1960), 5–7.

46. J. Elwin Wright, "Free Speech Has a Price," ibid., 19 (Nov. 1960), 16.

47. Graham to Nixon, 1 Sept. 1960, N.A.

48. W.J. Rorabaugh, *The Real Making of the President: Kennedy, Nixon, and the 1960 Election* (Lawrence: Univ. Press of Kansas, 2009), 144–45.

49. Gerhard Peters and John T. Woolley, The American Presidency Project. http://www.presidency.ucsb.edu/ws/?pid=25387.

50. Gerhard Peters and John T. Woolley, The American Presidency Project. http://www.presidency.ucsb.edu/ws/?pid=2541.

51. *Ibid.,* 25367.

52. Casey, *Catholic President,* 133–35, 181, is especially good on tracts.

53. George L. Ford, "A Catholic President: How Free from Church Control?," *United Evangelical Action,* 19 (May 1960), 5–7. See also L. Nelson Bell to J. Howard Pew, 1 Sept. 1960, L. Nelson Bell papers, Billy Graham Center, Col. 318, Folder 41–47, Wheaton College, Wheaton, Illinois.

54. Anonymous to Hannah Nixon, 8 Mar. 1960, Folder 1, Box 3; R. Maxwell William to Nixon, 6 Oct. 1906, Folder 3, Box 3; Bob and Bridget Morris to Nixon, n.d., Folder 1, Box 4, Dorn Collection, Nixon Library.

55. Nixon memo to Len Hall and Bob Finch, 5 Oct. 1960; Graham to Nixon, 24 Sept. 1960, N.A.

56. Stan McCaffrey memo to Len Hall and Bob Finch, 10 Sept. 1960, Box 616, Pre-Presidential Papers, NA. Nothing remains to indicate that Nixon was directly involved in this matter, but it's hard to believe that McCaffrey did not telephone him at Walter Reed.

57. *Washington Post,* 14, 15 Nov. 1960.

58. The draft, undated and in a different typeface from the one normally used for Graham's letters, is headed, "Billy Graham's story LIFE magazine did not use," N.A.

59. On this theme, see Jonathan P. Herzog, *The Spiritual-Industrial Complex: America's Religious Battle against Communism in the Early Cold War* (New York: Oxford Univ. Press, 2011), 181–83. Nixon's account can be found in Nixon, *Six Crises,* 235–91.

60. Pollock, *Billy Graham,* 219.

61. Graham to Nixon, 12 June 1961, Pre-Presidential Papers, N.A.; for the second article, see Billy Graham, ""We Are Electing a President of the World," *Life*, 49 (7 Nov. 1960), 109–10.

62. Graham to Nixon, 17 July 1961, N.A.

63. Nixon to Graham, 17 Aug. 1961, Box 299, ibid.

64. Nixon, *Six Crises*, 365.

65. Casey, *Catholic President*, 196–99, 201.

66. John Pollock, *Billy Graham: Evangelist to the World, An Authorized Biography of the Decisive Years*, 173.

67. Ibid., 197.

68. On this point, see also Charles P. Henderson, Jr., *The Nixon Theology*, 138.

69. Nixon, *In The Arena*, 88–89.

70. Walter Trohan, *Political Animals: Memoirs of a Sentimental Cynic*, 331, 369.

71. Rorabaugh, *Making of the President*, 111–12.

72. John Phillips to Nixon, 9 April; Memo, Rose Mary Woods to RLK, 2 June 1956; Boxes 595, 393, Pre-Presidential Papers, N.A.

73. Nixon spent 132 pages on the campaign, 69 on the Hiss case. Nixon, *Six Crises*.

74. Ibid. 295.

75. Nixon, *In the Arena*, 369.

76. Interestingly, Nixon agreed that religion was, on balance, a benefit to the Kennedy campaign. Nixon, *Crises*, 307–8.

77. Garry Wills, "'Born Again' Politics," *New York Times Magazine*, 1 Aug. 1976, 8.

Chapter 7

1. Richard Nixon to Norman Vincent Peale, 18 Jan. 1961, Box 853; Nixon to Billy Graham, 17 Aug. 1961, Box 299; Pre-Presidential Papers, N.A.; Nixon, *Six Crises*, 293–426. It may say something about Nixon's wish to distance himself from Quakerism—it is impossible to know for sure--but this was his last time to use "M" in his name. The "M" stood for Milhous, his Quaker forbears' name.

2. Rose Mary Woods memo to Earl Mazo [?], 17 June 1961, Wilderness Years, Series I: Correspondence, Nixon Library.

3. Richard Nixon, "Lessons of the Hiss Case," Address at meeting of Pumpkin Papers Irregulars, 31 Oct. 1985, Folder 1, Box 9, Evlyn Dorn Coll., ibid.

4. J. A. Williams to Nixon for Governor Committee, 30 Mar. 1962, Wilderness Years, Series I, Correspondence, Box 2, ibid.

5. Ambrose, *Nixon: The Education*, 668–71.

6. Richard J. Whalen, *Catch the Falling Flag: A Republican's Challenge to His Party*, 14.

7. Graham to Nixon, 11 Nov. 1962, Box 290, Pre-Presidential Papers, N.A.

8. Costello, *The Facts about Nixon*, 51–55.

9. Greg Mitchell, *Tricky Dick and the Pink Lady: Richard Nixon vs. Helen Gahagan Douglas--Sexual Politics and the Red Scare, 1950* (New York: Random House, 1998), 170.

10. Strober and Strober, *An Oral History*, 12.

11. John Osborne, *The Third Year of the Nixon Watch*, 167.

12. Whalen, *Catch the Flag*, 15.

13. Joan Hoff, *Nixon Reconsidered*, 154.

14. Whalen, *Catch the Flag*, 24.

15. Aitken, *Nixon: A Life*, 207–27; Hibbs, *White House Sermons*, 55.

16. Aitken, *Nixon*, 338.

17. Nixon to Graham, 7 Nov. 1963, Wilderness Years, Series I: Correspondence, Nixon Library.

18. Peale to Nixon, 23 Dec. 1963, 13 Jan., 18 March, 11 May 1964, 8 Jan. 1965; Nixon to Peale, 29 Nov. 1963, Wilderness Years, Series I: Correspondence, Box 29, ibid.

19. Lewis Chester, Godfrey Hodgson, and Bruce Page, *An American Melodrama: The Presidential Campaign of 1968* (New York: Dell Publishing, 1969), 265–66.

20. Nixon, *Memoirs*, 287–88. Nearly twenty years later, Nixon was still "deeply moved when I read the sermon that you delivered at my mother's funeral." Nixon to Graham, 2 Sept. 1986, Post-Presidential Correspondence, Special People, A-K, Billy Graham and Ruth Graham, 1990– , Nixon Library.

21. Nixon to Aunt Olive and Uncle Oscar Marshburn, 17 Aug. 1965, Wilderness Years, Correspondence, Nixon Library.

22. Henderson, *Nixon Theology*, 187. Unfortunately this book includes neither notes nor bibliography, so it is impossible to determine when, where, and under what circumstances Nixon made this comment.

23. Haldeman, *Haldeman Diaries*, 325–26.

24. Richard Nixon, *Leaders*, 328–29. William Bundy, a high level foreign policy analyst in the Johnson administration, picked up on this fascinating side of Nixon but did not, of course, mention its religion side. William Bundy, *A Tangled Web: The Making of the Foreign Policy of the Nixon Presidency*, 55.

25. *Faith and Practice of the Five Years Meeting of Friends*, 109.

26. *Journal of George Fox*, ed. John L. Nickalls, 194.

27. Quoted in Elton Trueblood, *Abraham Lincoln: Theologian of American Anguish*, 128.

28. *Speak Truth to Power: A Quaker Search for an Alternative to Violence*. The title's individual author remains unclear. See Ralph Keyes, *The Quote Verifier: Who Said What, Where, and When*, 205–6.

29. Elizabeth Walker Mechling and Jay Mechling, "Hot Pacifism and Cold War: The American Friends Service Committee's Witness for Peace in 1950s America," *Quarterly Journal of Speech*, 173–96.

30. Elton Trueblood to Nixon, 15 Jan. 1964, Wilderness Years: Series I, Correspondence, Box 35, Nixon Library.

31. Trohan, *Political Animals*, 374–75.

32. Flora R. Schreiber, "Pat Nixon Reveals for the First Time, 'I Didn't Want Dick to Run,'" *Good Housekeeping*, 64.

33. Graham to Nixon, 21 Oct. 1963; Nixon to Graham, 30 Dec. 1963; Rose Mary Woods memo to Nixon, 7 Feb. 1964; Graham to Nixon, 9 June 1965; Box 42, Wilderness Years, Series I: Correspondence, Nixon Library.

34. Nixon to Graham, 12 Sept. 1966, ibid.

35. Whalen, *Catch the Flag*, 94.

36. Trueblood to Nixon, 19 Sept. 1967, Box 35, Wilderness Years, Series I: Correspondence, Nixon Library.

37. Whalen, *Catch the Flag*, 137.

38. *New York Times*, 2 Aug. 1968, 16. Richard Whalen wrote the first draft of this statement. Whalen, *Catch the Flag*, 184–91.

39. Tom Wicker, "In the Nation," *New York Times*, 6 Aug. 1968, 1, 36.

40. Graham, *Just As I Am*, 528–29.

41. Mark Hatfield, *Against the Grain: Reflections of A Rebel Republican*, 122, 128–32.

42. Barry Ferrell, "Billy in the Garden," *Life*, 67 (4 July 1969), 2B; *Time*, "The Politicians' Preacher," 92 (4 Oct. 1968), 58.

43. Frady, *Billy Graham*, 447. Frady is my questionable source for this quotation, whose provenance is doubtful, given Frady's erratic citations.

44. Hatfield, *Grain*, 134.

45. My overall source for information about Nixon's maneuvering in this section comes from the fine work of Dallek, *Nixon and Kissinger*, 72–78. See also Bundy, *A Tangled Web*, 28–48.

46. Nixon, *Memoirs*, 323–24.

47. Anna Chennault, *The Education of Anna*, 176.

48. H. R. Haldeman interview with Herbert S. Parmet, Herbert S. Parmet, *Richard Nixon and his America* (Boston: Little, Brown, 1990), 522–23.

49. Elton Trueblood, "Plain Speech: Hoover and Nixon," *Quaker Life*, Series 8, No. 10 (Oct. 1968), 326.

50. Nixon, *Memoirs*, 269, 289, 298.

51. Memo, Glen Olds to Richard Nixon, 4 Oct. 1968, White House Special Files, Box 36, Folder 8, Nixon Library.

52. See Chester, et al, *American Melodrama*.

53. Whalen, *Catch the Flag*, 12.

54. Nixon memo to Earl Mazo, n.d., Wilderness Years, Series I: Correspondence, Box 26, Nixon Library.

55. See Ralph de Toledano, *Nixon*, 200–1, on how his stance put Nixon in the best light. For a contrary view, see Douglas, *In the Fullness of Time*, 285.

56. "The Nixon Record," *U.S. News and World Report*, 65 (16 July 1968), 48.

57. Frady, *Graham*, 447, 450.

58. "The Preaching and the Power," *Newsweek*, 70 (20 July 1970), 54.

Chapter 8

1. Nixon, *Leaders*, 321.

2. Haldeman, *Diaries*, 24. John Ehrlichman said that Nixon found the White House "liberating" because he no longer had to do things that he did not want to; he could now indulge his personal likes and dislikes without fears of electoral retribution. Tom Wicker, Memo of interview with John Ehrlichman, 1 Feb. 1989, Tom Wicker papers, Series 1.1, Folder 40, Southern Historical Collection, University of North Carolina Library, Chapel Hill, N.C.

3. Henderson, *Nixon Theology*, 179–80.

4. For example, note Billy Graham's comment in "Watergate," *Christianity Today*, 18 (4 Jan. 1974), 13.

5. Stewart Alsop, "Nixon on Nixon," *Saturday Evening Post*, 231 (12 July 1958), 26.

6. Tom Wicker, Memo of interview with Arnold Hutschnecker, 2 July 1986, Tom Wicker papers, Series 1.1, Folder 39, University of North Carolina, Southern Historical Collection, Chapel Hill, N.C. Wicker kept his promise, not mentioning

Hutschnecker in the index to *One of Us.* Hutschnecker is identified as a pacifist in Aitken, *Nixon: A Life*, 196, a position Nixon was aware of because he read a draft of Aitken's book.

7. *Whittier Daily News*, 3 Jan. 1969, Folder 7, Box 7, Evlyn Dorn Collection, Nixon Library.

8. Henderson, *Nixon Theology*, 179–80.

9. Whalen, *Catch the Falling Flag*, 15, 18.

10. *New York Times*, 15 Jan. 1969.

11. *Vital Speeches of the Day,* 35 (1 Feb. 1969), 227. Others later remarked on the phrase. See Raymond K. Price, Jr., in *The Nixon Presidency: Twenty-Two Intimate Perspectives of Richard Nixon*, Kenneth W. Thompson, ed., 385, and David Gergen, *Eyewitness to Power: The Essence of Leadership, Nixon to Clinton*, 30, 62.

12. Stanley I. Kutler, ed., *Abuse of Power: The New Nixon Tapes*, 453.

13. *Vital Speeches of the Day*, 40 (15 Aug. 1974), 644.

14. Richard Nixon, *The Real War*, 1.

15. Ibid., 35 (1 Feb. 1969), 226–27. For the "open door" theme, see William A. Williams, *The Contours of American History* (New York: World Publishing Co., 1961), 368–69.

16. *New York Times*, 9 June 2013, 17, 19.

17. Gerhard Peters and John T. Woolley, The American Presidency Project. http://www.presidency.ucsb.edu/ws/?pid=9266.

18. Tom Wicker, Memo of interview with Arnold Hutschnecker, 2 July 1986, Tom Wicker Papers, Series 1.1, Folder 39, Southern Historical Collection, University of North Carolina Library, Chapel Hill, N.C.

19. *Friends Journal*, 15 (1 Jan. 1969), 21.

20. Robert G. Gronewald to Richard Nixon, 20 Jan. 1969, *Religious Matters*, 3/1/69–4/9/69, Box 1, Nixon Library.

21. Dwight Chapin to Gronewald, 25 Jan.; Chapin to Bud Wilkinson, 27 Jan. 1969, ibid.

22. Edward L.R. Elson to Mr. and Mrs. Richard Nixon, 13 Nov. 1968, White House Special Files, Folder 14, Box 22, ibid. Elson may have used "Community Church" here to refer to the Wilshire Avenue-Westwood Community church that the Nixons attended when they lived in Los Angeles after 1960. Another report circulated that Mrs. Nixon was a Presbyterian. *Friends Journal*, 15 (1 Jan. 1969), 22. The following year, a report circulated that the entire Nixon family was listed as members of East Whittier Friends Church. *Christianity Today*, 13 (18 July 1969), 39.

23. Aitken, *Nixon: A Life*, 338.

24. David R. Stokes, "The Little Church in the East Room," The New Nixon (blog), 8 Dec. 2009, http://blog.nixonfoundation.org/2009/12/the-little-church-in-the-east-room, accessed 10 Dec. 2012.

25. Haldeman, *Diaries*, 270.

26. Memo, Dwight Chapin to Lucy Winchester, 8 Jan. 1971, Religious Matters, Folder 1–1–71/2–28–71, Box 14, Nixon Library.

27. Memo, David Parker to Chapin, 2 Sept. 1971, Religious Matters, Folder 9–1–71/9–30–71, Box 15, .

28. Strober and Strober, *An Oral History*, 32–33.

29. Richard Nixon, *Grand Jury Testimony*, 23 June 1975, 119, Nixon Library.

30. Billy Graham, "Watergate," *Christianity Today*, 18 (4 Jan. 1974), 10.

31. *New York Times*, 16 May 1970.

32. Joseph R. Wood to Nixon, 17 Feb. 1970, Religious Matters, Box 13, 3-1-70/3-31-70 Folder, Nixon Library.

33. Hibbs, *White House Sermons*, v–ix.

34. K. R. Cole, Jr., memo to Charles Colson, 4 Mar. 1970, *Religious Matters*, Box 12, Nixon Library.

35. *New York Times*, 26 Jan. 1969, 54.

36. Graham, *Just As I Am*, 534.

37. *New York Times*, 27 Jan. 1969, 1.

38. Ron Graybill, "Going to Church at the White House," *Liberty*, 68 (May-June 1973), 3–4.

39. H. R. Haldeman memo to Rose Mary Woods, 15 Dec. 1969, President's Personal Files, Rose Mary Woods Files: Name/Subject, 1969–74, Folder 1, Box 28, Nixon Library.

40. Haldeman memo to Woods, 15 Mar. 1972, Ibid.

41. Plans for Services, 20 July 1969, President's Personal Files, President's Speech Files, 1969–74, Folder 2, Box 50, ibid.

42. Haldeman, *Diaries*, 67–68

43. White House Worship Services, Box 10, White House Central Files, ibid. Trueblood, who was considered theologically conservative but dovish in sentiment but independent in character, preached but received two handwritten notes instructing him not to include any political issues in his sermon. William Miller, *A Prophet With Honor: The Billy Graham Story*, 357.

44. Harry Dent to Woods, 20 May 1971, Rose Mary Woods Name File, Folder 8, Box 19, President Personal File, ibid. Dent promised to find another Catholic from "good ole Dixie" who might fit the bill.

45. Tom Wells, *The War Within: America's Battle over Vietnam*, 428.

46. Reinhold Niebuhr, "The King's Chapel and the King's Court," *Christianity and Crisis*, 29 (4 Aug. 1969), 211–12.

47. Maurice H. Stans, *The Terrors of Justice: The Untold Story of Watergate*, 445. Of course Stans also thought that Nixon's association with such "top churchman" as Graham and Peale also were indications of his religious bent. ibid.

48. Edward B. Fiske, "Praying with the President in the White House," 27.

49. Chennault, *Education*, 180.

50. William Miller, *With God on Our Side: The Rise of the Religious Right in America*, 99.

51. Richard M. Nixon, "A Nation's Faith in God," *Decision*, 3 (Nov. 1962), 4.

52. Rose Mary Woods memo to Ron Ziegler, 17 Oct. 1972, Rose Mary Woods Name File, Folder 2, President's Personal Files, Box 18, Nixon Library.

53. Jeff Sharlett, *The Family: The Secret Fundamentalism at the Heart of American Power*, 195–98.

54. John T. Woolley and Gerhard Peters, The American Presidency Project. Santa Barbara, CA. www.presidency.ucsb.edu/ws/?pid=1986.

55. Bethlehem Assembly of God to Richard Nixon, 10 Mar. 1969, *Religious Matters*, 3/1/69–4/9/69, Box 1, ibid.

56. John T. Woolley and Gerhard Peters, The American Presidency Project. www.presidency.ucsb.edu/ws/?pid=2278.

57. Haldeman, *Diaries*, 101.

58. *Christianity Today*, 13 (6 Dec. 1968), 38.

59. *Works of George Fox*, 8: 178.

Chapter 9

1. H. R. Haldeman, "The Evolution of the Nixon Legacy," in Leon Friedman and William T. Levantrosser, eds., *Watergate and After: The Legacy of Richard M. Nixon*, 320.

2. Nixon Presidential Materials Staff, Conversation 489–21#2, 26 Apr. 1971, 3–4, Nixonmaterials.org. Nixon made a similar comment about his Quaker background at a press conference on June 1. See www.presidency.ucsb.edu/ws/?pid=3031.

3. Nixon, *Memoirs*, 123.

4. Ibid., 151–55.

5. Andrew L. Johns, *Vietnam's Second Front: Domestic Politics, the Republican Party, and the War*, 339.

6. Stephen E. Ambrose, *Nixon: The Triumph of a Politician, 1962–1972*, 64.

7. Wicker, *One of Us*, 31–32. Nixon apparently did not read this book, but he reported that daughter "Julie liked it." Jonathan Aitken interview with Nixon, 7 Jan. 1991, Author Collection, Box 11, Nixon Library.

8. http://www.libs.uga.edu/media/collections/nixon/nixonday5.html, 13 May 1983, accessed 11 July 2012

9. http://www.presidency.ucsb.edu/ws/?pid=3031, accessed 21 May 2012.

10. On this theme, see Chris Hedges, *War Is a Force that Gives Us Meaning*, 20–26. On Vietnamese nationalism, see Frances FitzGerald, *Fire in the Lake: The Vietnamese and the Americans in Vietnam*.

11. Kissinger, *White House Years*, 242–43.

12. http://www.presidency.ucsb.edu/ws/?pid=2303, accessed 7 Feb. 2012.

13. Nixon Notes, 18 Jan. 1970, President's Personal Files, Box 185, Nixon Library.

14. Hatfield, *Against the Grain*, 147.

15. Kornitzer, *Real Nixon*, 106–7.

16. Whalen, *Catch the Falling Flag*, 98.

17. Nixon Notes, 14 Jan. 1970, PPF, Box 185, Nixon Library.

18. Nixon Notes, 18 Jan. 1970, ibid.

19. Allen Drury, *Courage and Hesitation: Notes and Photographs of the Nixon Administration*, 223.

20. http://www.presidency.ucsb.edu/ws/?pid=2496, accessed 7 Feb. 2012.

21. Arthur O. Roberts, "The Vietnam Era and the Evangelical Quaker Community," 284–85, in Chuck Fager, ed., *Friends and the Vietnam War: Papers and Presentations from a Pendle Hill Conference*. Roberts made no comments about Nixon in his remarks.

22. Johan Maurer, "Was There a War Going On?," 319 in Fager, *Friends and the Vietnam War*.

23. Milton Mayer, "Disownment: The Quakers and Their President," *Christian Century*, 90 (10 Oct. 73), 1000–1003.

24. T. Eugene Coffin, "Speaking Out: Richard Nixon and the Quaker Fellowship," *Christian Century*, 91 (2–19 Jan. 74), 5–6; letters, ibid. (13 Feb. 74), 187.

25. Bill Gulley with Mary E. Reese, *Breaking Cover*, 167.

26. Nixon memo to Bob Haldeman, 13 May 1970, PPF, Box 2, Nixon Library. Unless otherwise mentioned, my account of this episode comes from this memo.

27. Christopher Lehmann-Haupt, "What Only History Can Tell," *New York Times*, 18 Feb. 1975, 27.

28. Safire, *Before the Fall*, 202.

29. Gergen, *Eyewitness to Power*, 77.

30. Parmet, *Nixon and His America*, 3–13.

31. Egil Krogh, *Integrity: Good People, Bad Choices, and Life Lessons from the White House*, 116, 118.

32. http://www.presidency.ucsb.edu/ws/?pid=2496, accessed 7 Feb. 2012.

33. Gulley with Reese, *Breaking Cover*, 167–68.

34. There is a discrepancy here, as the White House telephone logs, reprinted in Safire, *Before the Fall*, 204, show that longest gap was between 1:55 and 3:24.

35. Krogh, *Integrity*, 110.

36. Nixon, *Memoirs*, 460.

37. Michael Raoul-Duval, "Foreign Policy and the Bureaucracy," 292, in *The Nixon Presidency: Twenty-Two Intimate Perspectives of Richard M. Nixon*, Kenneth W. Thompson, ed..

38. Krogh, *Integrity*, 114–15.

39. Nixon memo to Haldeman, 13 May 1970, PPF, Box 2, Nixon Library.

40. Nixon Notes, 19 July 1970, PPF, Box 185, Nixon Library.

41. Charles Colson, *Born Again*, 64

42. Drury, *Courage*, 400.

43. See, for two examples, I John 3:17, Colossians 2:12.

Chapter 10

1. Richard Nixon to Frank Gannon, Day 5, 13 May 1983, http://www.libs.uga.edu/media/collections/nixon/nixonday3.html, accessed 11 July 2012.

2. See "Introduction" above, and Nixon, *In the Arena*, 369.

3. Nixon, *Memoirs*, 457. A fine account of this period is Wells, *The War Within*, chapter 8.

4. Nixon, *Six Crises*, xv.

5. Kissinger, *White House Years*, 514.

6. A full account of the visit is in Randall E. King, "When Worlds Collide: Politics, Religion, and Media at the 1970 East Tennessee Billy Graham Crusade," *Journal of Church and State*, 273–95. Unless otherwise noted my account comes from that source.

7. Pollack, *Evangelist to the World*, 106.

8. Ibid., 106–7.

9. *Knoxville News-Sentinel*, 29 May 1970, 1.

10. *Knoxville Journal*, 30 May 1970, 1, 4.

11. *Knoxville News-Sentinel*, 29 May 1970, 1.

12. Gerhard Peters and John T. Woolley, The American Presidency Project, http://www.presidency.ucsb.edu/ws/?pid=2523, accessed, 26 Dec. 2012.

13. Pollard, *Graham*, 108.

14. Graham, *Just As I Am*, 544.

15. Colson, *Born Again*, 174–80. For the description of Colson as "Hatchet Man," see this book's dust jacket.

16. Colson, *Born Again*, 64.

17. Summers, *Arrogance of Power*, 12. I am not sure of the accuracy of Summers, given his murky documentation and unclear attribution. If I did not also have Colson's recollection, I would not rely on Summers here.

18. Kissinger, *Years of Renewal*, 90.

19. Crowley, *Nixon in Winter*, 350.

20. Ibid. 357.

21. Trohan, *Political Animals*, 372.

22. Kissinger, *Renewal*, 71.

23. Safire, *Before the Fall*, 599.

24. Wills, *Nixon Agonistes*, 372. Billy Graham's remembrance of Nixon contained the only other reference to Quakers at the funeral.

25. Kissinger, *Renewal*, 91.

26. *Journal of George Fox*, Norman Penney, ed., 399–400.

27. http://www.presidency.ucsb.edu/ws/?pid=3031

28. Nixon to Haldeman, 12 June 71, rmn_e518a, Miller Center, University of Virginia.

29. Day 5, 8 Apr. 1983, http://www.libs.uga.edu/media/collections/nixon/nixonday3.html

30. Richard Nixon to Billy Graham, 28 Feb. 1991, Post-Presidential Correspondence, Special People, A-K, Billy Graham and Ruth Graham, 1990– , Nixon Library.

31. Nixon Presidential Material Staff, Conversation, 484–13#1, 20 Apr. 1971, 22, Nixonmaterials.org.

32. Graham, *Just As I Am*, 545–46.

33. *New York Times*, 17 Oct. 1971, p. 27.

34. Gerhard Peters and John T. Woolley, The American Presidency Project, http://www.presidency.ucsb.edu/ws/?pid=3192, accessed 17 Jan. 2013.

35. Gibbs and Duffy, *Preacher and Presidents*, 198.

36. Memorandum, Ronald Walker to H.R. Haldeman, 14 Oct. 1971*, Hearings before the Senate Select Committee on Presidential Campaign Activities*, VIII, 3322–23; *Final Report of the Senate Select Committee on Presidential Campaign Activities*, VIII, 201.

37. Gibbs and Duffy, *Preacher and Presidents*, 199–200.

38. *New York Times*, 29 Oct. 1971, 35.

39. Memos, President to Haldeman, 8 Feb. 1971, 14 Mar. 1972, Bruce Oudes, ed., *From the President: Richard Nixon's Secret Files*, 213, 388.

Chapter 11

1. William F. Buckley, Jr., *A Hymnal: The Controversial Arts*, 122, 103.

2. Bill Gulley with Mary E. Reese, *Breaking Cover*, 21.

3. Wallace Henley, *The White House Mystique*. For a description and analysis of Lyndon Johnson's White House and the artificial world created there by an equally astute journalist, see George E. Reedy, *The Twilight of the Presidency*. Henley referred to Reedy's work a number of times, as did Richard Whalen, recommending it to the President in his imagined memorandum to Nixon. See Whalen, *Catch the Falling Flag*, 275. Though he did not refer to the book by name, even Billy Graham recognized the problem of an isolated President. See "Watergate: Questions and Answers," *Christianity Today*, 18 (4 Jan. 1974), 12.

4. Whalen, *Catch the Flag*, 253–58, 275–80.

5. Kutler, *Abuse of Power*, 10–12.

6. Henley, *Mystique*, 20–21, 27, 28–29, 33–44, 55–56.

7. Niebuhr, "The King's Chapel and the King's Court,", 211–12.

8. Henley, *Mystique*, 66–67, 72–73, 89.

9. Ibid., 94, 96.

10. Gergen, *Eyewitness*, 46, 97.

11. *New York Times*, 29 May 1972, 16.

12. Wells, *The War Within*, 295.

13. *Hearings before the Senate Select Committee on Presidential Campaign Activities*, XI, 4641.

14. H. R. Haldeman, *The Ends of Power*, 13.

15. Jeb S. Magruder, *An American Life: One Man's Road to Watergate*, 260. For a fine rendering of Watergate, see Fred Emery, *Watergate: The Corruption of American Politics and the Fall of Richard Nixon*, esp. 36, 118, 153 for this paragraph.

16. White House Worship Services, Box 10, White House Central Files, Nixon Library.

17. http://www.presidency.ucsb.edu/ws/?pid=3824, accessed 12 Mar. 2013.

18. Graham, *Just As I Am*, 541–43.

19. "Watergate: Questions and Answers," *Christianity Today*, 18 (4 Jan. 1974), 8–10ff; *New York Times*, 23 Dec. 1973.

20. "Watergate," *Christianity Today*, 8–10ff.

21. Martin, *A Prophet with Honor: The Billy Graham Story*, 429–30.

22. *New York Times*, 1 Feb. 1974, 10; http://www.presidency.ucsb.edu/ws/?pid=4329.

23. Oudes, ed., *From the President*, 609.

24. John Prados, *The White House Tapes: Eavesdropping on the President*, 238–55, quotation, 249.

25. Emery, *Watergate*, 429–30.

26. *New York Times*, 29 May 74, 1.

27. Crowley, *Nixon in Winter*, 358.

28. Trohan, *Political Animals*, 133.

29. Graham, *Just As I Am*, 542, 544.

30. T. Eugene Coffin to Richard Nixon, 7 Sept. 1973, President's Personal Files, Rose Mary Wood File, Folder 9, Box 25, Nixon Library.

31. On this side of evangelicalism, see David R. Swartz, *Moral Minority: The Evangelical Left in an Age of Conservatism*.

32. Hatfield, *Against the Grain*, 238.

33. See Wallis's recollections in the "Foreword" of Lon Fendall, *Stand Alone or Come Home: Mark Hatfield as an Evangelical and a Progressive*, xii–xv.

34. The text of the speech is in *Christian Century*, 90 (21 Feb. 1973), 221. On the occasion, see *New York Times*, 3 Feb. 1973, 12.

35. Hatfield, *Grain*, 165.

36. *New York Times*, 2 Feb. 1973, 12.

37. Wallis, "Foreword," in Fendall, *Stand Alone*, xiv.

38. Swartz, *Moral Minority*, 78.

39. John A. Huffman, Jr., *A Most Amazing Call: One pastor's reflections on a ministry full of surprises*, chs 18, 19.

40. Some Evangelical Friends, who continued to champion Nixon as a Christian, were willing to discount his conduct as President. See Isaac May, "The President's Friends and Foes: The Effect of the Nixon Presidency on the Divisions of American Quakerism," *Quaker History*, 102 (Spring 2013), 30.

41. Nixon, *Memoirs*, 1061–62.

42. Henry Kissinger, *Years of Upheaval*, 1185–86.

43. There are three accounts of their time together, one each by each participant and the earliest by journalists Bob Woodward and Carl Bernstein, who did not interview Nixon but claim their book's accounts are based on at least two sources

(Bob Woodard and Carl Bernstein, *The Final Days*, 12, 422–24). I have thus relied on the memoirs of Nixon and Kissinger for most details: Nixon, *Memoirs*, 1076–77; Kissinger, *Years*, 1207–10.

44. Woodward and Bernstein have the President praying out loud, "asking for help, rest, peace and love" and then sobbing and beating his fist on the carpeted floor, crying out by way of confession, "What have I done? What has happened?" Woodward and Bernstein, *Final Days*, 423. Neither participant remembered any such scene.

45. Crowley, *Nixon*, 358.

46. http://www.presidency.ucsb.edu/ws/?pid=4324.

47. John W. Dean III, *Blind Ambition: The White House Years*, 357.

48. On the course chosen by William Clinton following his adultery with a young female aide, see Espinosa, "Religion and the Presidency of William Jefferson Clinton," 461–65, in *Religion and the American Presidency: George Washington to George W. Bush with Commentary and Primary Sources*.

49. On this story, see Morris, *Richard Milhous Nixon*, 67.

50. http://www.presidency.ucsb.edu/ws/?pid=4325.

Chapter 12

1. Ehrlichman, *Witness to Power*, 317.

2. D. Michael Lindsay, *Faith in the Halls of Power: How Evangelicals Joined the American Elite*, 34.

3. The only biography covering the retirement years is unfortunately marred by its excessively pro-Nixon stance and few and skimpy citations. Black, *Richard Nixon*, ch. 16.

4. Billy Graham to Richard Nixon, 17 Aug. 1974, Post-Presidential Correspondence, 1974–1979, Rev. Billy Graham, Folder 2, Nixon Library.

5. Lindsay, *Faith*, 34; *New York Times*, 10 Feb. 1987. Lindsay interviewed Macfarlane on 8 Dec. 2004. Lindsay, *Faith*, 242.

6. Monica Crowley, *Nixon Off the Record*, 5, 37.

7. Crowley, *Nixon in Winter*, 358–59.

8. Aitken, *Nixon: A Life*, 532–3; Nixon to Ruth Graham, 10 Mar. 1975, Folder 2, Nixon Library.

9. Billy Graham to Nixon, 22 Dec., 10 Sept. 1975, ibid.

10. *Albuquerque Tribune*, 18 Mar. 1975, Nixon to Graham, 28 Mar. 1975, 1 Apr. 1975; Graham to Nixon, 15 Mar. 1975, ibid.

11. Graham to Nixon, 15 March, 1 Apr. 1975, ibid.

12. Nixon to Graham, 31 July 1979; Graham to Nixon, 3 July 1979, ibid.

13. http://www.libs.uga.edu/media/collections/nixon/nixonday1.html, 9 Feb. 1983, Day 1, Tape 2, 01:24:15–1:26:54.

14. Nixon, *In the Arena*, 73–74.

15. Crowley, *Winter*, 401.

16. Black, *Nixon*, 1030, 1032.

17. Crowley, *Off the Record*, xii–iv.

18. Crowley, *Winter*, 339.

19. Black, *Nixon*, 1022.

20. Crowley, *Winter*, 139; Nixon, *The Real War*, 313–15.

21. http://www.libs.uga.edu/media/collections/nixon/nixonday3.html.

22. Crowley, *Winter*, 141–42.

23. Richard Nixon, *Beyond Peace*.

24. *Journal of George Fox*, ed. Norman Penney , 263.

25. Crowley, *Winter*, 340–41.

26. [William Penn,] *An Essay toward the Present and Future Peace of Europe* (London: no publ., 1693). On Penn and his essay, see Melvin B. Endy, Jr., "William Penn's Political Pacifism as Seen in Pennsylvania and in his Essay On the Present and Future Peace of Europe," 100–32 in Chuck Fager and Becky Ingle, eds., *Keeping Us Honest, Stirring the Pot: A Book for H. Larry Ingle*. The statement on Nixon's tombstone read, "The greatest honor history can bestow is the title of peacemaker." He did not claim, interestingly enough, that history had bestowed it on him.

27. Crowley, *Winter*, 345.

28. Ibid., 350–51. In 1989 Nixon issued a statement commending Billy Graham for his refusal to mix religion and politics, a stance that would have made him "a great president." Statement by Nixon, 24 Apr. 1989, Post-Presidential Correspondence, "Special People" A-K, Graham, Billy and Ruth Graham, Nixon Library.

29. Nixon, *Peace*, 233–42.

30. Ibid., 236, 238–39.

31. See the definition in *Oxford Dictionary of the Christian Church*, F. L. Cross and E. A. Livingstone, eds. (Oxford, Eng.: Oxford Univ. Press, 1997; 3rd ed.), 1365.

32. Nixon, *Peace,* 235.

33. Crowley, *Winter*, 405–10, quotation 408.

A Note on Sources

As Richard Nixon so well knew, a person's religion is personal, private, and subjective and its contours often easily obscured. Historians have, accordingly, left presidents' religion to God, generally content to recount White House occupants' actions rather than trying to determine how their faith affected them. It is my belief that this failure to delve deeply into a person's religious convictions is to ignore one of the main forces that has produced who that president is as a person and a human being, both vital to a full understanding.

I have made such a judgment, and in so doing, I have relied on what historians call "primary sources," letters and memoranda that are a major part of the subject's collection of private papers. Nixon's are housed at the library that bears his name in Yorba Linda, California, and they are a treasure trove, ably and expertly administrated now by the National Archives and Record Service. (Stories abound of what it was like before the archives took it over; I could tell a few myself.) Of course, the collection contains only those materials that Nixon or his staff wanted to save, and it is impossible to tell if he destroyed any. Except in a very few instances, I was surprised to find the acclaimed Nixon tapes to be less than useful, because of both their poor quality and also because religion was so peripheral to discussion in the White House that it was seldom mentioned where the taping machines were positioned to work.

Other major primary sources for this study are published memoirs, those of the president himself as well as those of members of his staff such as William Safire, H. R. (Bob) Haldeman, Henry Kissinger, Charles Colson, people like journalists who knew him in their professional capacities, and close friends, the most important being Billy Graham. I have quoted these memoirs extensively when it comes to their assessment of my subject and any light they can shed on his motivations, but I have seldom relied alone on their recounting of events because my interest had not been what happened so much as why something happened and the role religion played. One I stumbled onto late was that of Nixon's brother Ed, *The Nixons: A Family Portrait,* replete with interesting stories but not well known, having received little attention up till now. Another family member often overlooked is Nixon's second cousin, the novelist Jessamyn West, whose corpus abounds with memoirs—at least four—none of them indexed but all sure to richly reward the page-turner. Monica Crowley's two volumes on Nixon in retirement also offer many useful insights.

Biographies of Nixon are also important and vary in quality. The best nearly full one is probably Stephen Ambrose's three-volume work, but Ambrose gives little attention to religion and is patently wrong in his conclusions when he comes to Quakers. My personal favorite, monumental in its extensive research but going only to 1960, is Roger Morris's *Nixon: The Rise of an American Politician*; it is especially strong on its subject's Quaker background. Jonathan Aitken's *Nixon: A Life* has the advantages and disadvantages of its author's closeness to its subject. Herbert Parmet and Conrad Black should be mentioned, the former because he bent a bit too far to be fair, the latter because he published the only biography after Nixon's death. Joan Hoff and Tom Wicker produced revisionist studies that make valid points but fail to convince me. The partisan anti-Nixon briefs go back to 1960, to William Costello's *The Facts about Nixon: An Unauthorized Biography*. If Morris's projected multi-volume study is never completed, a gap remains in the biographical literature.

My more extensive listing of sources, as well as the titles of the works mentioned above, follows.

Bibliography

Unpublished Material

Gary S. Smith. "A Private and Enigmatic Faith," in my possession.

Manuscripts

American Friends Service Committee Archives, Philadelphia: Clarence Pickett Papers. Community Relations Division Files.

Herbert Hoover Library, West Branch, Iowa: Herbert Hoover Papers

National Archives, Laguna Nigel, California: Richard Nixon Pre-presidential Papers

Richard Nixon Library, Yorba Linda, California: Richard Milhous Nixon papers

Southeastern Jurisdictional Center of the United Methodist Church, Lake Junaluska, N.C.: "Assembly Daily," 1956

Swarthmore College, Swarthmore, Pennsylvania: Friends Historical Collection, Richmond P. Miller Papers

——, Peace Collection: E. Raymond Wilson Papers

University of North Carolina Wilson Library, Chapel Hill: Tom Wicker Papers

Wheaton College Library, Wheaton, Illinois: Billy Graham Evangelistic Association: Media Office, Grady B. Wilson Papers

——, Billy Graham Collection: L. Nelson Bell, Eugene R. Bertermann, Charles Colson, *Christianity Today,* Billy Graham Evangelistic Association Media Office, Harold Lindsell, Papers

Whittier College Library, Whittier, California, Richard Gardner, "Fighting Quaker (The Story of Richard Nixon)," unpublished mss., 1953

Government Documents

Grand Jury Testimony, 23, 24 June 1975, Richard Nixon Library, Yorba Linda, California.

Final Report of the Senate Select Committee on Presidential Campaign Activities. Washington: Government Printing Office, 1973, vol. 8.

Hearings before the Senate Select Committee on Presidential Campaign Activities. Washington: Government Printing Office, 1973.

Dissertations

Strachan, Jill P. "Richard Nixon: Representative Religious American." Ph.D. Syracuse University, 1981.

Printed Primary Sources (Articles)

Alsop, Stewart. "Nixon on Nixon," *Saturday Evening Post*, 231 (12 July 1958), 26.

Graham, Billy. "We are Electing a President of the World," *Life*, 49 (7 Nov. 1960), 109–10.

Graybill, Ron. "Going to Church at the White House," *Liberty*, 68 (May-June 1973), 2–5.

Niebuhr, Reinhold. "The King's Chapel and the King's Court," *Christianity and Crisis*, 29 (4 Aug. 1969), 211–12.

Nixon, Hannah M. "Richard Nixon, A Mother's Story as told to Flora R. Schreiber," *Good Housekeeping*, 150 (June 1960), 212–16.

Nixon, Richard. "A Nation's Faith in God," Decision, 3 (Nov. 1962), 4.

———. "Needed in Vietnam: The Will to Win," *Reader's Digest*, 85 (Aug. 1964), 37–43.

Wallis, Jim. "The Courage of Conviction: An Interview with Sen. Mark Hatfield," *Sojourners*, (Sept.-Oct. 1996), 26–29.

Printed Primary Sources (Books)

Arnold, William A. *Back When It All Began: The Early Nixon Years*. New York: Vantage Press, 1975.

Barclay, Robert. *An Apology for the True Christian Divinity*. Philadelphia: Friends Book Store, n.d.

Brinkley, Douglas, and Luke A. Nichter, eds. *The Nixon Tapes, 1971-1972*. Boston: Houghton Mifflin Harcourt, 2014.

Brookes, George S. *Friend Anthony Benezet*. Philadelphia: Univ. of Pennsylvania Press, 1937.

Buckley, William F., Jr., ed. *Odyssey of a Friend: Whittaker Chambers' Letters to William F. Buckley, Jr., 1954–1961*. New York: G.P. Putnam's Sons, 1969.

California Yearly Meeting of Friends Church. *Discipline of California Yearly Meeting of Friends*. Philadelphia: American Friend Publishing Co., 1904.

Chambers, Whittaker. *Cold Friday*. New York: Random House, 1964.
———. *Witness*. New York: Random House, 1952.
Chennault, Anna. *The Education of Anna*. New York: Times Books, 1980.
Colson, Charles W. *Born Again*. Old Tappan, N.J.: Chosen Books, 1976.
Crowley, Monica. *Nixon in Winter*. New York: Random House, 1998.
———. *Nixon Off the Record*. New York: Random House, 1996.
Discipline of California Yearly Meeting of Friends. Whittier, Cal.: V.A. Kennedy, 1938.
Dean, John W., III. *Blind Ambition: The White House Years*. New York: Simon & Schuster, 1976.
Douglas, Helen G. *A Full Life*. Garden City, N.Y.: Doubleday & Co., 1982.
Douglas, Paul H. *In the Fullness of Time*. New York: Harcourt Brace Jovanovich, 1972.
Ehrlichman, John. *Witness to Power: The Nixon Years*. New York: Simon & Schuster, 1982.
Evangelical Action!: A Report of the Organization of the National Association of Evangelicals for United Action. Boston: United Action Press, 1942.
Faith and Practice of the Five Years Meetings of Friends. Richmond, Ind.: Friends Book and Supply House, 1949.
Fisher, M. F. K. *Among Friends*. New York: Alfred A. Knopf, 1971.
Friends & the Vietnam War: Papers and Presentations from a Pendle Hill Conference. Ed. Chuck Fager. Wallingford, Penn.: Pendle Hill, 1998.
From the President: Richard Nixon's Secret Files. Ed. Bruce Oudes. New York: Harper & Row, 1989.
Frost, David. *"I Gave Them a Sword": Behind the Scenes of the Nixon Interviews*. New York: William Morrow, 1978.
Garment, Leonard. *Crazy Rhythm: My Journey from Brooklyn, Jazz, and Wall Street to Nixon's White House, Watergate, and Beyond . . . .* New York: Random House, 1997.
Gergen, David. *Eyewitness to Power: The Essence of Leadership, Nixon to Clinton*. New York: Simon & Schuster, 2000.
Gold, Gerald. *The White House Transcripts*. New York: Viking Press, 1974.
Graham, Billy. *Just As I Am: The Autobiography of Billy Graham*. New York: Harper Paperbacks, 1998.
Gulley, Bill with Mary Ellen Reese. *Breaking Cover*. New York: Simon & Schuster, 1980.
Haldeman, H.R. *The Haldeman Diaries: Inside the Nixon White House*. New York: G.P. Putnam's Sons, 1994.
———. *The Ends of Power*. New York: Times Books, 1978.
Hartmann, Robert T. *Palace Politics: An Inside Account of the Ford Years*. New York: McGraw-Hill, 1980.

Hatfield, Mark O. *Not Quite So Simple*. New York: Harper & Row, 1968.

——. *Against the Grain: Reflections of A Rebel Republican*. Ashland, Ore.: White Cloud Press, 2001.

Henley, Wallace. *The White House Mystique*. Old Tapham, N.J.: Fleming H. Revel Co., 1976.

Henry, Carl F. H. *Confessions of a Theologian: An Autobiography*. Waco, Texas: Word Books, 1986.

Hibbs, Ben, ed. *White House Sermons*. New York: Harper & Row, 1972.

Hiss, Alger. *In the Court of Public Opinion*. New York: Alfred A. Knopf, 1957.

——. *Recollections of a Life*. New York: Henry Holt & Co., 1988.

Huffman, John A., Jr. *A Most Amazing Call: One pastor's reflections on a ministry full of surprises*. N.p.: No publ, [2011].

Journal of George Fox, John L. Nickalls, ed. Cambridge: Cambridge Univ. Press, 1952.

Kissinger, Henry. *White House Years*. Boston: Little, Brown, 1979.

——. *Years of Renewal*. New York: Simon & Schuster, 1999.

——. *Years of Upheaval*. Boston: Little, Brown, 1982.

Klein, Herbert G. *Making It Perfectly Clear*. Garden City, N.Y.: Doubleday, 1980.

Korff, Baruch. *The Personal Nixon: Staying on the Summit*. Washington, D.C.: Fairness Publishers, 1974.

Kutler, Stanley I., ed. *Abuse of Power: The New Nixon Tapes*. New York: Free Press, 1997.

Magruder, Jeb Stuart. *An American Life: One Man's Road to Watergate*. New York: Atheneum Books, 1974.

Mayer, Milton. *The Nature of the Beast*. Ed. W. Eric Gustafson. Amherst: Univ. of Massachusetts Press, 1975.

Minutes of California Yearly Meetings, Friends Church. Whittier, Cal.: Western Printing Co., 1929–30.

Ed Nixon and Karen Olson. *The Nixons: A Family Portrait*. Bothell, Wash.: Book Publishers Network, 2009.

Nixon, Richard. *Beyond Peace*. New York: Random House, 1994.

——. *Leaders*. New York: Warner Books, 1982.

——. *In the Arena: A Memoir of Victory, Defeat, and Renewal*. New York: Simon & Schuster, 1990.

——. *The Memoirs of Richard Nixon*. New York: Grosset & Dunlap, 1978.

——. *Nixon Speaks Out*. New York: Nixon-Agnew Campaign Committee, 1968.

——. *No More Vietnams*. New York: Arbor House, 1985.

——. *Real Peace: A Strategy for the West*. New York: n.publ, 1983.

——. *The Real War*. New York: Warner Books, 1980.

——. *Seize the Moment: America's Challenge in a One-Superpower World*. New York: Simon & Schuster, 1992.

——. *Six Crises*. Garden City, N.Y.: Doubleday, 1962.

Papers of Martin Luther King, Jr. Clayborne Carson, ed. Berkeley: Univ. of California Press, 1994–2005. 5 vols.

Penn, William. *A Brief Account of the Rise and Progress of the People Called Quakers*. London: T. Sowle, 1694.

Prados, John, ed. *The White House Tapes: Eavesdropping on the President*. New York: New Press, 2003.

Rather, Dan. *The Camera Never Blinks: Adventures of a TV Journalist*. New York: William Morrow & Co., 1977.

Reston, James, Jr. *The Conviction of Richard Nixon: The Untold Story of the Frost/Nixon/ Interviews*. New York: Random House, 2007.

Rules of Discipline of the Religious Society of Friends. London: Darton and Harvey, 1834.

Safire, William. *Before the Fall: An Inside View of the Pre-Watergate Nixon White House*. Garden City, N.Y.: Doubleday, 1975.

Schulte, Renée K., ed. *The Young Nixon: An Oral Inquiry*. Fullerton: California State University, Fullerton, Oral History Project, 1978.

Speak Truth to Power: A Quaker Search for an Alternative to Violence. Np.: No pub., 1955.

Stans, Maurice H. *The Terrors of Justice: The Untold Side of Watergate*. New York: Everest House, 1978.

Strober, Gerald S., and Deborah H. Strober. *Nixon: An Oral History of His Presidency*. New York: Harper Collins, 1994.

Thompson, Kenneth W., ed. *The Nixon Presidency: Twenty-Two Intimate Perspectives of Richard M. Nixon*. Lanham, Mary.: Univ. Press of America, 1987.

Trohan, Walter. *Political Animals: Memoirs of a Sentimental Cynic*. Garden City, N.Y.: Doubleday, 1975.

West, Jessamyn. *Double Discovery*. New York: Harcourt Brace Jovanovich, 1980.

——. *Except for Me and Thee*. New York: Harcourt, Brace, & World, 1969.

——. *Hide and Seek: A Continuing Journey*. New York: Harcourt Brace Jovanovich, 1973.

——. *To See the Dream*. New York: Harcourt, Brace, 1957.

——. *The Woman Said Yes: Encounters with Life and Death*. New York: Harcourt Brace Jovanovich, 1976.

Whalen, Richard J. *Catch the Falling Flag: A Republican's Challenge to His Party*. Boston: Houghton Mifflin Co. 1972.

Wills, Garry. *Outside Looking In: Adventures of an Observer*. New York: Viking, 2010.

Works of George Fox, vols. VII, VIII. Philadelphia: Marcus T. C. Gould, 1831.

Worthy, James C. *Brushes with History: Recollections of a Many-Favored Life*. N.p.: James C. Worthy, 1998.

Newspapers and Magazines

American Friend
California Friend
Christian Century
Christian Worker
Christianity Today
Decision
Esquire
Good Housekeeping
Harper's
Knoxville Journal
Knoxville News-Sentinel
Liberty
Life
New York Times
Newsweek
Northwest Friend
Pacific Friend
Reporter
Time
United Evangelical Action
U.S. News and World Report

Secondary Sources: Articles

Aitken, Jonathan. "The Nixon Character," *Presidential Studies Quarterly*, 26 (Winter 1996), 239–47.

Cater, Douglas. "The Protestant Issue," *Reporter*, 23 (13 Oct. 1960), 30–32.

Christian Century. "Religious Smoke Screen," 77 (21 Sept. 1960), 1075–77.

Cull, Nicholas J. "Richard Nixon and the political appropriation of 'Friendly Persuasion' (1956)." *Historical Journal of Film, Radio and Television* 19 (1999), 239+.

Currey, Cecil B. "The Devolution of Quaker Pacifism: A Kansas Case Study, 1860–1955," *Kansas History*, 6 (Summer 1983), 120–33.

Dmohowski, Joseph, "From a Common Ground: The Quaker Heritage of Jessamyn West and Richard Nixon," *California History*, 73 (Fall 1994).

Feldstein, Mark. "Fighting Quakers: The 1950s Battle between Richard Nixon and Drew Pearson," *Journalism History*, 30 (Summer 2004), 76–90.

Fiske, Edward B. "Praying with the President in the White House," *New York Times Magazine*, 8 Aug. 1971, 14–15.

Hamm, Thomas D. Margaret Marconi, Gretchen Kleinhen Salinas, and Benjamin Whitman, "The Decline of Quaker Pacifism in the Twentieth Century: Indiana Yearly Meeting of Friends as a Case Study," *Indiana Magazine of History*, 96 (March 2000), 45–72.

Holl, Jack M. "Dwight D. Eisenhower: Religion, Politics, and the Evils of Communism," in Steven Mintz and John Stauffer, *The Problem of Evil: Slavery, Freedom, and the Ambiguities of American Reform* (Amherst: Univ. of Massachusetts Press, 2007), 382–96.

Kimmage, Michael. "Whittaker Chambers's *Witness* and the Dilemmas of Modern Conservatism," *Literature Compass*, 3 (Sept. 2006), 940–66.

King, Randall E. "When Worlds Collide: Politics, Religion, and Media at the 1970 East Tennessee Billy Graham Crusade," *Journal of Church and State*, 39 (Spring 1997), 273–95.

Lindley, E. K. "Clergy. Catholics. Clarity.," *Newsweek*, 56 (19 Sept. 1960), 43.

May, Isaac. "The President's Friends and Foes: The Effect of the Nixon Presidency on the Divisions of American Quakerism," *Quaker History*, 102 (Spring 2013), 15–38.

Mechling, Elizabeth Walker and Jay Mechling. "Hot Pacifism and Cold War: The American Friends Service Committee's Witness for Peace in 1950s America," *Quarterly Journal of Speech*, 78 (May 1992), 173–96.

Moellering, Ralph L. "Civil Religion, the Nixon Theology and the Watergate Scandal," *Christian Century*, 90 (26 Sept. 1973), 947–51.

Pierard, Richard V. "Billy Graham and the U.S. Presidency," *Journal of Church and State*, 22 (Spring 1980), 107–27.

Schreiber, Flora R., "Pat Nixon Reveals for the First Time, 'I Didn't Want Dick to Run,'" *Good Housekeeping*, 167 (July 1968), 64.

Small, Melvin. "Evaluating Nixon--Without Watergate," *New England Journal of History*, 56 (Winter 1999–Spring 2000), 1–13.

Swartz, David R. "Identity Politics and the Fragmenting of the 1970s Evangelical Left," *Religion and American Culture*, 21 (Winter 2011), 81–120.

Time. "I Did Not Want the Hot Words of TV," 96 (5 Oct. 1970), 12–13.

Time. "Power of Negative Thinking," 76 (19 Sept. 1960), 21–22.

U.S. News and World Report. "The Nixon Record," 65 (15 July 1968), 48–52.

West, Jessamyn. "Jessamyn West talks about her cousin President Nixon," *McCall's,* 96 (Feb. 1969), 69–70.

———. "The Real Pat Nixon: An Intimate View," *Good Housekeeping,* 172 (Feb. 1971), 69–71.

Wicker, Tom. "Richard M. Nixon, 1969–1974," *Presidential Studies Quarterly,* 26 (Winter 1996), 249–57.

Wills, Garry. "What Makes the New Nixon Run? The Old Nixon," *Esquire,* 69 (July 1968), 89–96.

Worsthorne, Peregrine. "Nixon Speaks for Himself," *Sunday Telegraph* (London), 14 Feb. 1971, 6.

Secondary Sources: Books

Abbott, Philip. *Bad Presidents: Failure in the White House.* New York: Palgrave Macmillan, 2013.

Aitken, Jonathan. *Nixon: A Life.* Washington, D.C.: Regnery Publishing, 1993.

Alley, Robert S. *So Help Me God: Religion and the Presidency, Wilson to Nixon.* Richmond, Vir.: John Knox Press, 1972.

Ambrose, Stephen E. *Comrades: Brothers, Fathers, Heroes, Sons, Pals.* New York: Simon & Schuster, 1999.

———. *Nixon: The Education of a Politician, 1913–1962.* New York: Simon & Schuster, 1987.

———. *Nixon: Ruin and Recovery, 1973–1990.* New York: Simon & Schuster, 1991.

———. *Nixon: The Triumph of a Politician, 1962–1972.* New York: Simon & Schuster, 1989.

Anderson, Paul M., and Howard R. Macy. *Truth's Bright Embrace: Essays and Poems in Honor of Arthur O. Roberts.* Newberg, Ore.: George Fox University Press, 1996.

Andrews, Lawrence J. *What They Wished For: American Catholics and American Presidents, 1960–2004.* Athens, Ga.: Univ. of Georgia Press, 2014.

Angelo, Bonnie. *First Mothers: The Women Who Shaped the Presidents.* New York: Harper Collins, 2000.

Anson, Robert Sam. *Exile: the Unquiet Oblivion of Richard M. Nixon.* New York: Simon and Schuster, 1984.

Arnold, William A. *Back Where It All Began: The Early Nixon Years.* New York: Vantage Press, 1975.

Austin, Allan W. *Quaker Brotherhood: Interracial Activism and the Amer-*

ican Friends Service Committee, 1917–1950 (Urbana: Univ. of Illinois Press, 2012.

Balmer, Randall. *God in the White House: How Faith Shaped the Presidency from John F. Kennedy to George W. Bush*. New York: Harper One, 2008.

———. *Redeemer: The Life of Jimmy Carter*. New York: Basic Books, 2014.

Beattie, Ann. *Mrs. Nixon: A Novelist Imagines a Life*. New York: Scribner, 2011.

Beebe, Ralph K. *A Garden of the Lord: A History of Oregon Yearly Meeting of Friends Church*. Newberg, Ore.: Barclay Press, 1968.

Black, Conrad. *Richard M. Nixon: A Life in Full*. New York: Public Affairs, 2007.

Boller, Paul F. *Presidential Wives*. New York: Oxford Univ. Press, 1998.

Bonnell, John S. *Presidential Profiles: Religion in the Life of American Presidents*. Philadelphia, Penn.: Westminster Press, 1971.

Bothwell, Cecil. *The Prince of War: Billy Graham's Crusade for a Wholly Christian Empire*. Asheville, N.C.: Brave Ulysses Books, 2007.

Brennan, Macy C. *Pat Nixon: Embattled First Lady*. Lawrence: Univ. Press of Kansas, 2011.

Brodie, Fawn M. *Richard Nixon: The Shaping of his Character*. New York: W. W. Norton, 1981.

Buckley, William F., Jr. *A Hymnal: The Controversial Arts*. New York: G. P. Putnam's Sons, 1978)

Burkeimer, Michael. *Lincoln's Christianity*. Yardley, Penn.: Westholme, 2007.

Bundy, William. *A Tangled Web: The Making of the Foreign Policy in the Nixon Presidency*. New York: Hill & Wang, 1998.

Burke, Vincent J. and Vee Burke. *Nixon's Good Deed: Welfare Reform*. New York: Columbia Univ. Press, 1974.

Butler, Jon. *Awash in a Sea of Faith: Christianizing the American People*. Cambridge, Mass.: Harvard Univ. Press. 1990.

Carpenter, Joel A. *Revive Us Again: The Reawakening of American Fundamentalism*. New York: Oxford Univ. Press, 1997.

Carty, Thomas J. *A Catholic in the White House?: Religion, Politics, and John F. Kennedy's Presidential Campaign*. New York: Palgrave Macmillan, 2004.

Carwardine, Richard J. *Evangelicals and Politics in Antebellum America*. New Haven, Conn.: Yale Univ. Press, 1993.

Casey, Shaun A. *The Making of a Catholic President: Kennedy vs. Nixon, 1960*. New York: Oxford University Press, 2009.

Cavan, Sherri. *20th Century Gothic: America's Nixon*. San Francisco: Wigan Pier Press, 1979.

Chester, Lewis, Godfrey Hodgson, and Bruce Page, *An American Melodrama: The Presidential Campaign of 1968*. New York: Dell Books, 1969.

Costello, William. *The Facts about Nixon: An Unauthorized Biography.* New York: Viking Press, 1960.

Cooper, Charles W. *Whittier: Independent College in California, Founded by Quakers, 1887.* Los Angeles, Cal.: Ward Ritchie Press, 1967.

Cross, F. L. and E. A. Livingstone, eds. *The Oxford Dictionary of the Christian Church.* Oxford: Oxford Univ. Press, 1997, 3rd ed.

Dallek, Robert. *Nixon and Kissinger: Partners in Power.* New York: Harper Collins, 2007.

——. *An Unfinished Life: John F. Kennedy, 1917–1963.* Boston: Little, Brown, 2003.

David, Lester. *The Lonely Lady of San Clemente: The Story of Pat Nixon.* New York: Thomas Y. Crowell, 1978.

Dochuk, Darren. *From Bible Belt to Sunbelt: Plain-Folk Religion, Grassroots Politics, and the Rise of Evangelical Conservatism.* New York: W.W. Norton, 2011.

Donovan, John T. *Crusader in the Cold War: A Biography of Fr. John F. Cronin, S.S. (1908–1994).* New York: Peter Lang, 2005.

Drake, Thomas E. *Quakers and Slavery in America.* Gloucester, Mass.: Peter Smith, 1965.

Drury, Allen. *Courage and Hesitation: Notes and Photographs of the Nixon Administration.* Garden City, N.Y.: Doubleday, 1971

Eisenhower, Julie Nixon. *Pat Nixon: The Untold Story.* New York: Simon & Schuster, 1986.

Emery, Fred. *Watergate: The Corruption of American Politics and the Fall of Richard Nixon.* New York: Times Books, 1994.

Espinosa, Gaston, ed. *Religion and the American Presidency: George Washington to George Bush with Commentary and Primary Sources.* New York: Columbia Univ. Press. 2009.

Faber, Doris. *The Presidents' Mothers.* New York: St. Martin's Press, 1973.

Fager, Chuck, and Becky Ingle, eds. *Keeping Us Honest, Stirring the Pot: A Book for H. Larry Ingle.* Fayetteville, N.C.: Kimo Press, 2011.

Fausold, Martin L. *The Presidency of Herbert C. Hoover.* Lawrence: Univ. Press of Kansas, 1985.

Feeney, Mark. *Nixon at the Movies: A Book about Belief.* Chicago: University of Chicago Press, 2004.

Fendall, Lon. *Stand Alone or Come Home: Mark Hatfield as an Evangelical and a Progressive.* Newberg, Ore.: Barclay Press, 2008.

FitzGerald, Frances. *Fire in the Lake: The Vietnamese and Americans in Vietnam.* Boston: Little, Brown, 1972.

Fleming, John V. *The Anti-Communist Manifestos: Four Books that Shaped the Cold War.* New York: W.W. Norton, 2009.

Fowler, Robert B. *A New Engagement: Evangelical Political Thought, 1966–1976.* Grand Rapids, Mich.: William B. Eerdmans Publishing Co., 1982.

Fox, Richard W. *Reinhold Niebuhr. A Biography.* New York: Pantheon, 1985.

Frady, Marshall. *Billy Graham: A Parable of American Righteousness.* Boston: Little, Brown, 1979.

Frank, Jeffrey. *Ike and Dick: Portrait of a Strange Political Marriage.* New York: Simon & Schuster, 2013.

Frick, Daniel. *Reinventing Richard Nixon: A Cultural History of an American Obsession.* Lawrence,: Univ. Press of Kansas, 1987.

Friedman, Leon and William F. Levantrosser, eds. *Cold War Patriot and Statesman: Richard M. Nixon.* Westport, Conn.: Greenwood Press, 1993.

——. *Richard M. Nixon: Politician, President, Administrator.* New York: Greenwood Press, 1991.

——. *Watergate and Afterward: The Legacy of Richard M. Nixon.* Westport, Conn.: Greenwood Press, 1992.

Gaustad, Edwin S. *Sworn on the Altar of God: A Religious Biography of Thomas Jefferson.* Grand Rapids, Mich.: William B. Eerdmans Publishing, 1996.

Gellman, Irwin E. *The Contender: Richard Nixon, The Congress Years, 1946–1952.* New York: Free Press, 1999.

George, Carol V. R. *God's Salesman: Norman Vincent Peale and the Power of Positive Thinking.* New York: Oxford University Press, 1993.

Gibbs, Nancy, and Michael Duffy. *The Preacher and the Presidents: Billy Graham in the White House.* New York: Center Street, 2007.

Greenberg, David. *Nixon's Shadow: The History of an Image.* New York: W. W. Norton & Co., 2003.

Greene, Bob. *Cheeseburgers: The Best of Bob Greene.* New York: Atheneum, 1985.

Guelzo, Allen C. *Abraham Lincoln: Redeemer President.* Grand Rapids, Mich.: William B. Eerdmans Publishing Co., 1999.

Gunn, T. Jeremy. *Spiritual Weapons: The Cold War and the Forging of an American National Religion.* Westport, Conn.: Praeger, 2009.

Hall, Simon. *Rethinking the American Anti-War Movement.* New York: Routledge, 2012.

Hatch, Nathan O. *The Democratization of American Christianity.* New Haven, Conn.: Yale Univ. Press, 1989.

Hedges, Chris. *War Is a Force that Gives Us Meaning.* New York: Public Affairs, 2002.

Henderson, Charles P. *The Nixon Theology.* New York: Harper & Row, 1972.

Hinshaw, David. *Herbert Hoover: American Quaker*. New York: Farrar, Straus and Co., 1950.

Hinson, F. Glenn. *Love at the Heart of Things: A Biography of Douglas V. Steere*. Wallingford, Penn.: Pendle Hill, 1998.

Hiss, Tony. *Laughing Last: Alger Hiss by Tony Hiss*. Boston: Houghton Mifflin, 1977.

Hoff, Joan. *Nixon Reconsidered*. New York: Basic Books, 1994.

Holmes, David L. *The Faiths of the Postwar Presidents*. Athens: Univ. of Georgia Press, 2012.

Hoyt, Edwin P. *The Nixons: An American Family*. New York: Random House, 1972.

Hughes, Ken. *Chasing Shadows: The Nixon Tapes, the Chennault Affair, and the Origins of Watergate*. Charlottesville, Va.: Univ. of Virginia Press, 2014.

Hutcheson, Richard G., Jr. *God in the White House: How Religion Has Changed the Modern Presidency*. New York: Macmillan, 1988.

Ingle, H. Larry. *First Among Friends: George Fox and the Creation of Quakerism*. New York: Oxford Univ. Press, 1994.

———. *Quakers in Conflict: The Hicksite Reformation*. Knoxville: Univ. of Tennessee Press, 1984.

Isaacson, Walter. *Kissinger: A Biography*. New York: Simon & Schuster, 1992.

Jacoby, Susan. *Alger Hiss and the Battle for History*. New Haven, Conn.: Yale Univ. Press, 2009.

Jones, Andrew L. *Vietnam's Second Front: Domestic Politics, the Republican Party, and the War*. Lexington: Univ. Press of Kentucky, 2010.

Kallina, Edmund F., Jr. *Kennedy v. Nixon: The Presidential Election of 1960*. Gainseville: Univ. Press of Florida, 2010.

Kelly, Thomas R. *Reality of the Spiritual World*. Wallingford, Penn.: Pendle Hill, 1976.

Keyes, Ralph. *The Quote Verifier: Who Said What, Where, and When*. New York: St. Martin's Griffin, 2006.

Keogh, James. *This Is Nixon: The Man and His Work*. New York: G.P. Putnam's Sons, 1956.

Kimball, Jeffrey. *Nixon's Vietnam War*. Lawrence: University Press of Kansas, 1998.

Kornitzer, Bela. *The Real Nixon: An Intimate Biography*. New York: Rand McNally, 1960.

Krogh, Egil. *Integrity: Good People, Bad Choices, and Life Lessons from the White House*. New York: Public Affairs, 2007.

Le Shana, David C. *Quakers in California: The Effects of 19th Century Revivalism on Western Quakerism*. Newberg, Ore.: Barclay Press, 1969.

Levitt, Morton and Michael Levitt. *A Tissue of Lies: Nixon vs. Hiss.* New York: McGraw-Hill Book Co., 1979.

van der Linden, Frank. *Nixon's Quest for Peace.* Washington: Robert B. Luce, 1972.

Lindsay, D. Michael. *Faith in the Halls of Power: How Evangelicals Joined the American Elite.* New York: Oxford Univ. Press, 2007.

Linker, Damon. *The Theocons: Secular America under Siege.* New York: Doubleday, 2006.

Longford, Lord. *Nixon: A Study in Extremes of Fortune.* London: Weidenfeld and Nicolson, 1980.

Lungren, John C., and John C. Lungren, Jr. *Healing Richard Nixon: A Doctor's Memoir.* Lexington: Univ. of Kentucky, 2003.

Lurie, Leonard. *The Running of Richard Nixon.* New York: Coward, McCann & Geoghegan, 1972.

Marietta, Jack D. *The Reformation of American Quakerism, 1748–1738.* Philadelphia: Univ. of Pennsylvania Press, 1984.

Marsden, George. *Reforming Fundamentalism: Fuller Seminary and the New Evangelicalism.* Grand Rapids, Mich.: William B. Eerdmans Publishing Co., 1987.

Martin, William C. *A Prophet with Honor: The Billy Graham Story.* New York: William Morrow, 1991.

———. *With God on Our Side: The Rise of the Religious Right in America.* New York: Broadway Books, 1996.

Mason, Robert. *Richard Nixon and the Quest for a New Majority.* Chapel Hill: Univ. of North Carolina Press, 2004.

Mathony, Virginia. *Whittier Revisited: The First 100 Years.* N.p.: Virginia Mathony, 1991.

Matthews, Arthur H. *Standing Up, Sanding Tall!: The Emergence of the National Association of Evangelicals.* Carol Spring, Ill.: National Association of Evangelicals, 1992.

Mattson, Kevin. *Just Plain Dick: Richard Nixon's Checkers Speech and the "Rocking, Socking" Election of 1952.* New York: Bloomsbury, 2012.

Mazo, Earl. *Richard Nixon: A Political and Personal Portrait.* New York: Harper & Row, 1959.

Miller, Steven P. *Billy Graham and the Rise of the Republican South.* Philadelphia: University of Pennsylvania Press, 2009.

Minear, Mark. *Richmond, 1887: A Quaker Drama Unfolds.* Richmond, Ind.: Friends United Press, 1987.

Morgenthau, Hans J. and David Hein. *Essays on Lincoln's Faith and Politics.* Kenneth W. Thompson, ed. Lanham, Mary.: Univ. Press of America. 1983.

Morris, Roger. *Richard Milhous Nixon: The Rise of an American Politician.* New York: Henry Holt, 1990.

Nash, George H. *The Conservative Intellectual Movement in America: Since 1945.* New York: Basic Books, 1976.

Nelson, Carl H. *Eighty-Eight Years of Service: Whittier Friends Church, 1887–1975* [Whittier, Cal.: no publ], 1975.

Newby, James R. *Elton Trueblood: Believer, Teacher & Friend.* San Francisco, Calif.: Harper & Row, 1990.

Noll, Mark A. *American Evangelical Christianity: An Introduction.* Oxford: Blackwell Publishers, 2001.

Noll, Mark A., and Luke E. Harlow, eds. *Religion and American Politics: From the Colonial Period to the Present.* New York: Oxford Univ. Press, 2007, 2nd ed.

Osborne, John. *The Third Year of the Nixon Watch.* New York: Liveright, 1972.

Pearce, Phyllis M., Claire G. Radford, and Mary A. Rummel, *Founders and Friends.* Whittier, Cal.: Rio Hondo College Community Services, 1977.

Pilat, Oliver. *Drew Pearson: An Unauthorized Biography.* New York: Harper's Magazine Press, 1973.

Pollock, John C. *Billy Graham: The Authorized Biography.* New York: McGraw-Hill Book Co., 1966.

———. *Billy Graham: Evangelist to the World, An Authorized Biography of the Decisive Years.* New York: Harper & Row, 1979.

Punshon, John. *Reasons for Hope: The Faith and Future of the Friends Church.* Richmond, Ind.: Friends United Press, 2001.

Reedy, George E. *The Twilight of the Presidency.* New York: World Publishing Co., 1970.

Reeves, Richard. *President Nixon: Alone in the White House.* New York: Simon & Schuster, 2001.

Roberts, Arthur O. *The Association of Evangelical Friends: A Story of Quaker Renewal in the Twentieth Century.* Newberg, Ore.: Barclay Press, 1975.

———. *Through Flaming Sword: A Spiritual Autobiography of George Fox.* Newberg, Ore.: Barclay Press, 2008.

Rosell, Garth M. *The Surprising Work of God: Harold John Ockenga, Billy Graham, and the Rebirth of Evangelicalism.* Grand Rapids, Mich.: Baker Academic, 2008.

Rozell, Mark J. and Gleaves Whitney, eds. *Religion and the American Presidency.* New York: Palgrave Macmillan, 2007.

Rust, William J. *Before the Quagmire: American Intervention in Laos, 1954–1961.* Lexington: Univ. of Kentucky Press, 2012.

Ryan, James E. *Imaginary Friends: Representing Quakers in American Culture, 1650–1950*. Madison: Univ. of Wisconsin Press, 2009.

Sanford, Charles B. *The Religious Life of Thomas Jefferson.* Charlottesville: Univ. Press of Virginia, 1984.

Schulman, Bruce J., and Julian E. Zelizer. *Rightward: Making America Conservative in the 1970s*. Cambridge, Mass.: Harvard Univ. Press, 2008.

Sehat, David. *The Myth of American Religious Freedom*. New York: Oxford Univ. Press, 2011.

Shah, Timothy S., Alfred Stephan, Monica D. Toft, eds. *Rethinking Religion and World Affairs*. New York: Oxford Univ. Press, 2012.

Sharlet, Jeff. *The Family: The Secret Fundamentalism at the Heart of American Power*. New York: Harper Collins, 2008.

Smith, Gary S. *Faith and the Presidency: From George Washington to George W. Bush*. New York: Oxford Univ. Press, 2006.

Smith, Richard N. *An Uncommon Man: The Triumph of Herbert Hoover*. New York: Simon & Schuster, 1984.

Spalding, Henry D. *The Nixon Nobody Knows*. Middle Village, N.Y.: Jonathan David, Publishers, 1972.

Stevens, Jason. *God-fearing and Free: A Spiritual History of America's Cold War*. Cambridge, Mass.: Harvard Univ. Press, 2010.

Streiker, Lowell D., and Gerald S. Strober. *Religion and the New Majority: Billy Graham, Middle America, and the Politics of the 70s*. New York: Association Press, 1972.

Sulzberger, C. L. *The World and Richard Nixon*. New York: Prentice Hall Press, 1987.

Summers, Anthony. *The Arrogance of Power: The Secret World of Richard Nixon*. New York: Viking, 2000.

Swaim, John G., ed. *Historical Volume and Reference Notes Covering Bassett, . . . Whittier*, II: Los Angeles County. Whittier, Cal.: Historical Publishers, 1963.

Swan, Patrick A., ed. *Alger Hiss, Whittaker Chambers, and the Schism in the American Soul*. Wilmington, Del.: ISI Books, 2003.

Swartz, David R. *Moral Minority: The Evangelical Left in an Age of Conservatism*. Philadelphia: Univ. of Pennsylvania Press, 2012.

Swift, Will. *Pat and Dick: The Nixons: An Intimate Portrait of a Marriage*. New York: Threshold Edition, 2014.

Toledano, Ralph de. *Nixon: Revised and Expanded Edition*. New York: Duell, Sloan, and Pierce, 1960.

Tolles, Frederick B. *Quakerism and Politics*. [Greensboro, N.C.:] Guilford College, 1956.

Trueblood, Elton. *Abraham Lincoln: Theologian of American Anguish*. New York: Harper & Row, 1973.

Underwood, Doug. *From Yahweh to Yahoo!, The Religious Roots of the Secular Press*. Urbana: Univ. of Illinois Press, 2002.

Volkan, Vamik D., Norman Itzkowitz, Andrew W. Dod. *Richard Nixon: A Psychobiography*. New York: Columbia University Press, 1997.

Weddle, Meredith B. *Walking in the Way of Peace: Quaker Pacifism in the Seventeenth Century*. New York: Oxford Univ. Press, 2001.

Wells, Tom. *The War Within: America's Battle over Vietnam*. Berkeley: Univ. of California Press, 1994

Weinstein, Allen. *Perjury: The Hiss-Chambers Case*. New York: Alfred A. Knopf, 1978.

White, G. Edward. *Alger Hiss's Looking-Glass Wars: The Covert Life of a Soviet Spy*. New York: Oxford Univ. Press, 2004.

White, Theodore H. *In Search of History: A Personal Adventure*. New York: Harper & Row, 1978.

Wicker, Tom. *One of Us: Richard Nixon and the American Dream*. New York: Random House, 1991.

William, Robert C. *Klaus Fuchs, Atom Spy*. Cambridge, Mass.: Harvard University Press, 1987.

Williams, Daniel K. *God's Own Party: The Making of the Christian Right*. New York: Oxford Univ. Press, 2010

Wills, Garry. *Confessions of a Conservative*. Garden City, N.Y.: Doubleday, 1979.

———. *Head and Heart: American Christianities*. New York: Penguin Press, 2007.

———. *Nixon Agonistes: The Crisis of the Self-Made Man*. New York: Signet, 1970.

Wilson, Robert A. ed. *Character above All: Ten Presidents from FDR to George Bush*. New York: Simon & Schuster, 1995.

Witcover, Jules. *The Resurrection of Richard Nixon*. New York: G.P. Putnam's Sons, 1970.

Wittner, Lawrence S. *Rebels against War: The American Peace Movement, 1933–1983*. Philadelphia: Temple Univ. Press, 1984.

Wolf, William J. *Lincoln's Religion*. Philadelphia: Pilgrim Press, 1970.

Woodward, Bob, and Carl Bernstein. *The Final Days*. New York: Simon & Schuster, 1976.

Yuill, Kevin L. *Richard Nixon and the Rise of Affirmative Action: The Pursuit of Racial Equality in an Era of Limits*. Lanham, Mary.: Rowman & Littlefield, 2006.

Zeligs, Meyer A. *Friendship & Fratricide: An Analysis of Whittaker Chambers and Alger Hiss*. New York: Viking Press, 1967.

Index